# New Area-Based Anti-Aliasing for CGI

**Michel A Rohner**

**Gotham Books**

30 N Gould St.
Ste. 20820, Sheridan, WY 82801
https://gothambooksinc.com/

Phone: 1 (307) 464-7800

© 2024 *Michel A Rohner*. All rights reserved.

No part of this book may be reproduced, stored in a retrieval system, or transmitted by any means without the written permission of the author.

Published by Gotham Books (March 15, 2024)

ISBN: 979-8-88775-593-9 (P)
ISBN: 979-8-88775-594-6 (E)

Because of the dynamic nature of the Internet, any web addresses or links contained in this book may have changed since publication and may no longer be valid.

The views expressed in this work are solely those of the author and do not necessarily reflect the views of the publisher, and the publisher hereby disclaims any responsibility for them.

# Contents

Chapter 1 Introduction ................................................................................................. 1
  1.1 From TV to CGI ................................................................................................. 1
    1.1.1    TV Images and Displays ................................................................................. 1
    1.1.2    TV Images and Movies .................................................................................. 1
    1.1.3    Interlaced Display .......................................................................................... 3
    1.1.4    Progressive Displays ..................................................................................... 4
    1.1.5    Color Display Standards ................................................................................ 4
    1.1.6    TV Images vs CGI ......................................................................................... 6
  1.2 CGI ..................................................................................................................... 6
    1.2.1    Early CGI Contributors .................................................................................. 7
    1.2.2    Non-Real-Time CGI ...................................................................................... 7
    1.2.3    Real-Time CGI Systems ................................................................................ 7
    1.2.4    Evolution of AA in RT CGI Systems .......................................................... 10
    1.2.5    Data Base Models ........................................................................................ 11
    1.2.6    2D Coordinate Systems ............................................................................... 11
    1.2.7    Database Coordinate systems ...................................................................... 12
  1.3 Geometry Transformations in 3D and 2D Spaces ............................................ 15
    1.3.1    Objects in 3D Space .................................................................................... 15
    1.3.2    Object Transformations of from 3D to 2D ................................................. 15
    1.3.3    2D Geometric Processor .............................................................................. 19
  1.4 Image Rendering ............................................................................................... 20
    1.4.1    Image Plane and Image Size ....................................................................... 20
    1.4.2    Image Coordinates ....................................................................................... 22
    1.4.3    Rendering Triangles .................................................................................... 24
    1.4.4    Selecting the Pixel Sample Point ................................................................ 25
    1.4.5    Pixel Sampling with Jaggies ....................................................................... 28
  1.5 Color Space ....................................................................................................... 31
    1.5.1    RGB in Color Space .................................................................................... 31
    1.5.2    *YCbCr* in Color Space ................................................................................ 32
    1.5.3    Color Space and Conversion ....................................................................... 33

| Chapter 2 Aliasing | 35 |
|---|---|
| 2.1 Aliasing and Anti-Aliasing | 35 |
|     2.1.1 Aliasing | 35 |
|     2.1.2 Anti-Aliasing and Edge Smoothing | 35 |
|     2.1.3 Digital Signal Processing | 36 |
| 2.2 Simple Example of Signal Sampling | 36 |
| 2.3 Anti-Aliasing in Real Time CGI Systems | 38 |
|     2.3.1 Definitions of AA for RT CGI with the 5 A's | 38 |
|     2.3.2 Spatial and Temporal Image Artifacts | 39 |
|     2.3.3 Double Imaging | 48 |
| 2.4 Aliasing Examples with Analog Signals | 51 |
|     2.4.1 Definition of Aliasing in Broadcast TV | 51 |
|     2.4.2 Sine Function and Frequency | 52 |
|     2.4.3 Aliasing when Sampling a Sine Function | 53 |
|     2.4.4 Sampling Frequency and Nyquist Frequency | 53 |
|     2.4.5 Sampling of a Sine Function as Aliasing Example | 55 |
|     2.4.6 Aliasing when Sampling a Sine or Cosine Function | 59 |
|     2.4.7 Sine and Cosine Functions after Sampling | 62 |
| 2.5 Sampling of TV Signals | 64 |
|     2.5.1 Standard TV | 64 |
|     2.5.2 High-Definition TV (HDTV) | 67 |
| 2.6 Aliasing with Digital Signals | 69 |
|     2.6.1 Point Sampling and Z-Buffer | 69 |
|     2.6.2 Sampling Frequency and Nyquist Frequency | 70 |
|     2.6.3 Checkerboard Pattern with 1 Sample per Pixel | 71 |
|     2.6.4 Box Filter and Frequency Response | 78 |
| Chapter 3 Anti-Aliasing with Super-Sampling | 81 |
| 3.1 Super Sampling AA (SSAA) | 81 |
|     3.1.1 SSAA Examples | 81 |
|     3.1.2 SSAA with Filtering | 82 |
| 3.2 One-Dimensional Super-Sampling | 82 |
|     3.2.1 Sampling Image with One Sample per Pixel | 83 |

|     |     |     |
| --- | --- | --- |
| 3.2.2 | One-Dimensional Super-Sampling with *2x1* | 83 |
| 3.2.3 | Checkerboard Pattern with 3 Samples per Pixel | 86 |
| 3.2.4 | Checkerboard Sampling from ½ to 1 Pixel. | 88 |
| 3.2.5 | Box Filter and Tent Filter | 93 |
| 3.2.6 | Frequency Response for 1 to 3 Sample Points | 96 |
| 3.2.7 | Selecting an AA Filter with Subpixels | 99 |
| 3.2.8 | AA Filter Comparison | 101 |

3.3 Two-Dimensional Super-Sampling ............................................................. 103

|     |     |     |
| --- | --- | --- |
| 3.3.1 | Two-Dimensional Box Window | 103 |
| 3.3.2 | Two-Dimensional Bartlett Window | 106 |

3.4 Selecting AA Filters ................................................................................... 107

|     |     |     |
| --- | --- | --- |
| 3.4.1 | Non-RT AA Solutions with Super-Sampling | 107 |
| 3.4.2 | Pixel Averaging with Box and Bartlett Windows | 107 |

# Chapter 4 Multi-Sample AA (MSAA) .............................................................. 113

4.1 From SSAA to MSAA ................................................................................ 113

4.2 Selecting Subpixels for Sampling .............................................................. 113

4.3 Processing Subpixels as Bed of Nails ........................................................ 116

4.4 MSAA and the 8 Queens Puzzle ................................................................ 118

# Chapter 5 RT CGI with Anti-Aliasing ............................................................... 125

5.1 ABAA vs MSAA ......................................................................................... 125

5.2 AA in Early RT CGI Systems ...................................................................... 127

|     |     |     |
| --- | --- | --- |
| 5.2.1 | Link DIG AA Implementation with 4x4 Subpixels | 127 |
| 5.2.2 | RT CGI AA Implementation with Bed of Nails (BON) | 129 |
| 5.2.3 | Accuracy of Pixel Entry and Exit Points | 129 |
| 5.2.4 | Use Edge Distance to Detect Covered Subpixels. | 132 |

5.3 Comparison of MSAA with ABAA ............................................................. 134

|     |     |     |
| --- | --- | --- |
| 5.3.1 | My Experience with MSAA and ABAA | 134 |
| 5.3.2 | MSAA and ABAA with 4 or 8 Subpixels | 134 |
| 5.3.3 | Advantages and Limitations | 135 |

5.4 Selecting Subpixels for AA ........................................................................ 136

|     |     |     |
| --- | --- | --- |
| 5.4.1 | Advantages of ABAA over MSAA | 140 |

5.5 From SSAA to ABAA ................................................................................. 143

|       | 5.5.1 | Convert SSAA Sample Points into ABAA Areas ................................................. 143 |
|-------|-------|---|
|       | 5.5.2 | Identify Shortcomings of MSAA ........................................................................ 145 |

## Chapter 6 Evolution of ABAA ............................................................................................ 147

6.1 First 3D RT CGI Systems Had AA ................................................................................ 147

6.2 Edge Smoothing in the Link DIG Systems .................................................................... 149

    6.2.1 DIG-1 with Analog Edge Smoothing (4x4 ABAA) ........................................... 150

    6.2.2 DIG-2 with Digital Edge Smoothing (4x4 ABAA) ............................................ 152

6.3 Edge Smoothing with Bed of Nail .................................................................................. 154

6.4 Optimized Edge Definition for Area Based Anti-Aliasing ............................................. 155

    6.4.1 Area of Trapezoid ................................................................................................ 156

    6.4.2 Converting Trapezoidal Area into Subpixel Areas .............................................. 160

    6.4.3 Implementation of ABAA with 4 Subpixel Areas ............................................... 160

    6.4.4 Early Implementation of ABAA with 8 Subpixel Areas ..................................... 162

    6.4.5 Improved Implementation of ABAA with 8 Subpixel Areas .............................. 164

6.5 ABAA with N Subpixel Areas ........................................................................................ 167

6.6 Delayed Implementation ................................................................................................. 168

6.7 ABAA Implementation with 16 and 32 Subpixels ......................................................... 169

## Chapter 7 Rendering Polygons and Triangles ..................................................................... 175

7.1 Image Coordinates .......................................................................................................... 175

    7.1.1 Fixed-Point and Floating-Point Image Coordinates ............................................ 176

7.2 Projected Triangles into Image Coordinates .................................................................. 178

    7.2.1 Basic Triangle Edge Definition ........................................................................... 178

    7.2.2 Edge Parameters Computation ............................................................................ 179

    7.2.3 Edge Definition for Triangle Rendering ............................................................. 181

    7.2.4 Definition of Edge Directions and Types ........................................................... 182

    7.2.5 Rendering a Triangle Inside of Spans ................................................................. 185

    7.2.6 Edges Traversing Spans for Triangle Rendering ................................................ 187

    7.2.7 Span-to-Span Traversing with ABAA ................................................................ 189

    7.2.8 Span-to-Span and Pixel-to-Pixel Traversing with ABAA .................................. 190

    7.2.9 Span-to-Span Traversing with MSAA ................................................................ 190

    7.2.10 Pixel-to-Pixel Traversing with MSAA .............................................................. 190

7.3 ABAA Example of Triangle Processed with 4 Subpixels .............................................. 191

|         | 7.3.1 Definition of Data Structures in C for Simulation ................................................... 192 |

## Chapter 8 ABAA with 4 Subpixel Areas ............................................................... 197

### 8.1 Solution with 4 Square Subpixel Areas .......................................................... 197
8.1.1 ABAA vs MSAA Examples with 4 Subpixels ................................................. 200

### 8.2 Example of ABAA4-X with Fans of Thin Triangles ........................................... 202
8.2.1 Comparison of ABAA vs MSAA with 4 Subpixels ........................................... 202
8.2.2 Comparison of ABAA vs MSAA with 4 Subpixels ........................................... 205

### 8.3 Combined Examples of ABAA4 vs MSAA4 ....................................................... 213

## Chapter 9 ABAA with 8 Subpixel Areas ............................................................... 215

### 9.1 ABAA8-X Solution with 8 Half-Square Subpixel Areas ..................................... 215

### 9.2 Comparison of ABAA8 vs MSAA8 .................................................................... 225
9.2.1 Thin Triangles Processed with 8 Subpixels ...................................................... 225
9.2.2 Four Examples of ABAA8 vs MSAA8 with Tri-Fans ........................................ 225

### 9.3 Combined Examples of ABAA8 vs MSAA8 ....................................................... 232
9.3.1 Other Example of Thin Faces ........................................................................ 236

## Chapter 10 Flight Simulation and RT CGI ............................................................ 239

### 10.1 Visualization for Flight simulation ................................................................. 239
10.1.1 Flight Simulation Takes off ......................................................................... 239
10.1.2 "Image Generators", 1970s to Present ......................................................... 240
10.1.3 Flight Simulation vs. Gaming ...................................................................... 241
10.1.4 Throw Hardware at It! ................................................................................ 241
10.1.5 More powerful CGI systems with GPU ......................................................... 242

### 10.2 Big Irons as 3D RT CGI Systems ................................................................... 242
10.2.1 The Purpose of Flight simulators is to "Save Lives" .................................... 242
10.2.2 Early RT CGI Systems ................................................................................ 243
10.2.3 Big Iron RT CGI Systems had AA ............................................................... 243
10.2.4 The Link DIG and the E&S CT-5 ................................................................. 246
10.2.5 First 3D RT CGI with Edge Smoothing ....................................................... 248
10.2.6 Shading, Fog and Texture with Multi-Sample ............................................. 249

### 10.3 Memories and Memories of Memories ............................................................ 252
10.3.1 Increase in Chip and Memory Density ........................................................ 253
10.3.2 Memory Requirement for Frame Buffers .................................................... 253

|        | 10.3.3 | RT CGI and the Personal Computer | 254 |
|--|--|--|--|

    10.3.3 RT CGI and the Personal Computer ............................................................. 254
    10.3.4 The Warp5 from Oak Technology .............................................................. 256
    10.3.5 RT CGI and the PC after 2000 ..................................................................... 257

## Chapter 11 Inside the Binary World .............................................................................. 259

  11.1 Programmer and Computer Interaction ................................................................ 259
    11.1.1 Fixed Point vs Floating Point ....................................................................... 259
    11.1.2 Inside each Computer there is a Binary World .......................................... 260
    11.1.3 Pixel Colors and ARGB Color Components .............................................. 261
  11.2 Decimal vs Binary Number ................................................................................... 261
    11.2.1 What's Funny about HW Designers? ......................................................... 262
    11.2.2 Decimal Digit vs Binary Digit ..................................................................... 264
  11.3 Binary Numbers .................................................................................................... 267
    11.3.1 Operations with Binary numbers ................................................................. 267
    11.3.2 Boolean Single-Bit Operator ....................................................................... 269
    11.3.3 Integer Multiple-Bits Bitwise Operator ...................................................... 272
    11.3.4 Binary Coded Decimal Integers ................................................................... 272
  11.4 Comparison of Different Integer Types ................................................................. 273
    11.4.1 Integer Tables ............................................................................................... 273
  11.5 Examples: Detecting Bits within a Word .............................................................. 276
    11.5.1 General Solution ........................................................................................... 276
    11.5.2 Specific Good Solutions .............................................................................. 276
    11.5.3 Another Divide and Conquer approach ...................................................... 278
    11.5.4 Integer, Fixed-Point and Floating-Point Numbers .................................... 280

*References* ........................................................................................................................ 281

*About the Author* .............................................................................................................. 291

# List of Figures

Figure 1-1 TV Image ............................................................................................................. 2
Figure 1-2 TV Image with Interlaced Scanlines in Field0 and Field1 ............................... 3
Figure 1-3 Progressive Display Image (Non-Interlaced SLs) ............................................. 4
Figure 1-4 Triangle In 2D Coordinate System .................................................................. 12
Figure 1-5 Gaming Area and Coordinate Systems ............................................................ 14
Figure 1-6 Triangle, Strip and Fan .................................................................................... 15
Figure 1-7 Vertex Translation ............................................................................................ 16
Figure 1-8 Vertex Vt Rotated into Window Coordinate .................................................... 17
Figure 1-9 Window Clipping .............................................................................................. 18
Figure 1-10 Projection from 3D to 2D ............................................................................... 19
Figure 1-11 Triangle In 2D Image Coordinates *(Xi, Yi)* ................................................... 20
Figure 1-12 Image Size of *PixMax* Pixels by *SLMax* Scanlines ...................................... 21
Figure 1-13 *(Pix, SL)* and *(xi, yi)* Image Coordinates ..................................................... 22
Figure 1-14 Single Sample Point Selection ....................................................................... 24
Figure 1-15 Sample Point Selection ................................................................................... 25
Figure 1-16 Pixels Located Inside of *SL* and *Pix* Grid .................................................... 28
Figure 1-17 Assign Color Using 1 Sample Point per Pixel ............................................... 29
Figure 1-18 Mix Color of Half-Covered Pixels ................................................................. 30
Figure 1-19 Pixels along SL with *ARGB* or *RGB* Color Components ............................ 32
Figure 1-20 Pixels along SL with *YCbCr* Color Format for Television .......................... 33
Figure 1-21 *RGB* and *YCbCr* in Color Space ................................................................. 34
Figure 2-1 Sampling Example of Sprinter Running *100 meters* in *10 seconds* ............. 37
Figure 2-2 Edge Stairstep and Edge Crawling .................................................................. 40
Figure 2-3 Examples of Narrow Face Breakup ................................................................. 41
Figure 2-4 Examples of Face Popping ............................................................................... 42
Figure 2-5 Example of Moiré Pattern ................................................................................ 43
Figure 2-6 Checkerboard with Squares Equal to Pixel Size ............................................. 44
Figure 2-7 Checkerboard with Squares Greater than Pixel Size ...................................... 45
Figure 2-8 Small Checkerboard Moving 1/4 Pixel to the Right ....................................... 46
Figure 2-9 Displayed Squares from Shrinking Checkerboard. ......................................... 47
Figure 2-10 Example of Double Image .............................................................................. 49
Figure 2-11 Double Imaging During Plane Roll ............................................................... 50
Figure 2-12 Sine and Cosine Functions ............................................................................ 53
Figure 2-13 Signal to Sample and Signal after Sampling ................................................. 55
Figure 2-14 Function with Aliasing: *Sine((x+1) * Pi/6)* ................................................... 58
Figure 2-15 Function with Aliasing: *Sine((x+3) * Pi/6)* ................................................... 58
Figure 2-16 Function with Aliasing: *Sine((x+5) * Pi/6)* ................................................... 58
Figure 2-17 Aliasing when Sampling Sine Function ........................................................ 60
Figure 2-18 Aliasing when Sampling Cos Function ......................................................... 61
Figure 2-19 Signal to Sample and Signal after Sampling ................................................. 62

Figure 2-20 Cosine Function Sampled at Nyquist Frequency (*fN=2\*fS*) .................. 63
Figure 2-21 Sin and Cos Func Sampled at Twice the Nyquist Freq (*2fN=4\*fS*) ........ 64
Figure 2-22 Pixel Data Sampling and Transfer .................................................... 67
Figure 2-23 Sampled Signal with 1 Sample per Pixel ........................................... 72
Figure 2-24 Checkerboard with Squares Close to the Pixel Size ........................... 73
Figure 2-25 Sampling when Sample Freq > Nyquist Freq .................................... 74
Figure 2-26 Checkerboard with Squares near the Pixel Size ................................. 76
Figure 2-27 Pixel Frequency Equal to 1/2 Nyquist Frequency ............................... 77
Figure 2-28 Two-Dimensional Box Filter in Spatial Domain ................................. 78
Figure 2-29 Box Filter in Spatial Domain and Frequency Domain ........................ 79
Figure 2-30 Box Frequency Response with sinc() Function .................................. 80
Figure 2-31 Signal to Sample and Signal after Sampling ...................................... 80
Figure 3-1 One-Dimensional 2x Super Sampling and 2x Subpixel Sampling ........ 84
Figure 3-2 Squares of Width=1, with 1 and 2 Samples per Pixel ........................... 85
Figure 3-3 One-Dimensional 2x Super Sampling .................................................. 86
Figure 3-4 Squares of Width=1, with 3 Samples per Pixel .................................... 87
Figure 3-5 Checkerboard with *f = 1.14 fP/2* ........................................................ 89
Figure 3-6 Checkerboard with *f = 1.33 fP/2* ........................................................ 90
Figure 3-7 Checkerboard with *f = 1.60 fP/2* ........................................................ 91
Figure 3-8 Checkerboard with *f = 2.0 fP/2* .......................................................... 92
Figure 3-9 Convolution of 2 Pairs of Pixels '0, 1, 1, 0' and '0, 1, 1, 0' .................. 94
Figure 3-10 Frequency Response of Box and Bartlett Filters ................................ 95
Figure 3-11 Freq Response for 1 Sample per Pixel ............................................... 96
Figure 3-12 Freq Response for 2 Samples per Pixel .............................................. 97
Figure 3-13 Freq Response for 3 Samples per Pixel .............................................. 98
Figure 3-14 Box Filter and Nice Filter ................................................................ 100
Figure 3-15 Filters in Spatial Domain Frequency Domain .................................. 102
Figure 3-16 One- and Two-Dimensional Super-Sampling ................................... 104
Figure 3-17 Two-Dimensional Super Sampling .................................................. 105
Figure 3-18 Selection of 2x2 Sample Points ....................................................... 105
Figure 3-19 Comparison between Box and Bartlett Windows ............................. 110
Figure 3-20 H or V Slices for Tent Windows 3x3, 5x5 and 7x7 to 1x1 ................ 111
Figure 4-1 Examples of Pixel divided into Subpixels or Bed of Nails .................. 115
Figure 4-2 Edge to Subpixel Distance in *(xi, yi)* Image Coordinate System ........ 117
Figure 4-3 Edges vs 4 Subpixels in *(xi, yi)* Image Coordinate System ................ 118
Figure 4-4 Knights and Queens ........................................................................... 120
Figure 4-5 Non-8-Queens Solutions .................................................................... 122
Figure 4-6 Four Examples of 8 Queens Solutions ............................................... 123
Figure 4-7 Identified ¼ Pixel Gaps in 8 Queens Solutions ................................... 124
Figure 5-1 Comparison of Subpixels with ABAA and MSAA ............................. 126
Figure 5-2 Triangle with 2 *VEs* and 1 *HE* Rendered with Subpixels ................. 128
Figure 5-3 Edge Accuracy at Pixel Boundaries ................................................... 130
Figure 5-4 Comparison between BON and ABAA Accuracy ............................... 131

Figure 5-5 Edge to Subpixel Distance in *(xp, yp)* Pixel Coordinate System .............................. 133
Figure 5-6 SSAA Examples of Triangles and 4x4 Subpixels...................................................... 137
Figure 5-7 SSAA Examples of Triangles and 8x8 Subpixels...................................................... 138
Figure 5-8 SSAA Examples of Triangles and 4x8 Subpixels...................................................... 138
Figure 5-9 MSAA or BON: Examples of Triangles and 8 Sparse Subpixels ............................. 139
Figure 5-10 ABAA4 Examples of Triangles and 4 Subpixel Areas ........................................... 139
Figure 5-11 ABAA8 Examples of Triangles and 8 Subpixel Areas ........................................... 140
Figure 5-12 Number of Intensity steps for ABAA8 and MSAA8 ............................................... 142
Figure 5-13 From SSAA to ABAA4 ........................................................................................... 144
Figure 5-14 Old Fashioned Weight Scale .................................................................................... 145
Figure 6-1 Triangle with 1 *VE* and 2 *HEs* Rendered with 4 Subpixel Areas............................ 149
Figure 6-2 DIG-1 with Analog Edge Smoothing......................................................................... 150
Figure 6-3 Analog VE Edge Smoothing with 4 Subpixel Areas ................................................. 151
Figure 6-4 Exponential Function from RC Circuit ..................................................................... 152
Figure 6-5 DIG-2 with Digital Edge Smoothing ......................................................................... 152
Figure 6-6 VE and HE Subpixel Areas........................................................................................ 153
Figure 6-7 *HE* with 4 Steps Area Increment: Mix Faces with Top 2 Priorities........................ 153
Figure 6-8 Pixel with 4 or 8 Subpixel BON ................................................................................ 154
Figure 6-9 Area Measurements when Intersection within *0.0* and *1.0* ................................. 157
Figure 6-10 Pixel Covered Area Computation for *VE*.............................................................. 158
Figure 6-11 Pixel Covered Area Computation for *HE* ............................................................. 159
Figure 6-12 Four Subpixel Areas Intersected by *VE(BE)* and *HE(BE)* ................................ 161
Figure 6-13 Four Cases of ABAA4 with Edge Crossing 4 Subpixel Areas ................................ 162
Figure 6-14 Eight Subpixel Areas Intersected by *VE* and *HE* .............................................. 163
Figure 6-15 Convert Rectangular Subpixels to Triangular Subpixels ......................................... 164
Figure 6-16 Expanding from 4 Subpixels to 8 Subpixels............................................................. 165
Figure 6-17 ABAA8: 4 Cases with 4 *BE* Edges Moving Across Pixels (|*Slp*|<0.5) .............. 166
Figure 6-18 Subpixel Coverage Decoder According *EFlg* and *Dist* ..................................... 167
Figure 6-19 Four Pixel Quadrants and *VE* and *HE* Symmetry .............................................. 170
Figure 6-20 Pixel Divided into 4 Quadrants of 4 or 8 Subpixels Each........................................ 171
Figure 6-21 Vertical Edge Intersection with Pixel Midlines in a Span ....................................... 172
Figure 7-1 2D Orthogonal Coordinate Systems........................................................................... 175
Figure 7-2 (*Pix, SL*) and (*xi, yi*) Coordinates Inside Square Canvas .................................... 177
Figure 7-3 Triangle Consisting of 3 Vertices or 3 Edges ............................................................ 179
Figure 7-4 Triangle in 2D Image Coordinates ............................................................................. 180
Figure 7-5 Beginning and Ending Edge Types ............................................................................ 182
Figure 7-6 Edge Parameter Decoding.......................................................................................... 183
Figure 7-7 Eight Edge Types ....................................................................................................... 184
Figure 7-8 Triangle Rendering According to Edge Info.............................................................. 186
Figure 7-9 Span Traversing with 3 Triangle Edges..................................................................... 188
Figure 7-10 Edge Intersection with Pixel Midlines ..................................................................... 189
Figure 7-11 Edge Intersection with Subpixel Midlines of the Queens ....................................... 191
Figure 7-12 Processing of Edges *E0* and *E1*......................................................................... 195

Figure 7-13 Processing of Edge *E2* and Final Triangle ............................................................... 196
Figure 8-1 Pixel Covered Area Computation for Negative VE .................................................... 197
Figure 8-2 Pixel Map Showing 4 Cases of Subpixel Mapping for ABAA4-X ......................... 198
Figure 8-3 Flowchart to Decode Subpixel Mapping for ABAA4-X ............................................ 199
Figure 8-4 ABAA4-X: Four Cases of Edge Crossing 4 Subpixel Areas .................................... 200
Figure 8-5 ABAA vs MSAA: Moving edge across 4 Subpixels ................................................. 201
Figure 8-6 ABAA 4 vs MSAA 4 for Pos Edges A ........................................................................ 206
Figure 8-7 ABAA 4 vs MSAA 4 for Pos Edges B ........................................................................ 207
Figure 8-8 ABAA 4 vs MSAA 4 for Neg Edges A ....................................................................... 208
Figure 8-9 ABAA 4 vs MSAA 4 for Neg Edges B ....................................................................... 209
Figure 8-10 Description of the Summary Tables .......................................................................... 211
Figure 8-11 Summary of Results for 4 Examples with 4 Subpixels ............................................ 212
Figure 8-12 Fan of 16 Triangles with Pos Edge Slopes and 4 Subpixels ................................... 213
Figure 8-13 Fan of 16 Triangles with Neg Edge Slopes and 4 Subpixels .................................. 214
Figure 9-1 Example of Pixel Covered Area Computation for Negative *VE* ............................ 215
Figure 9-2 Pixel Map Showing 8 Cases of Subpixel Mapping for ABAA8-X ......................... 216
Figure 9-3 Flowchart to Decode Subpixel Mapping for ABAA8-X ............................................ 217
Figure 9-4 Example of Slope Transition from *S0* to *S1* for *dist=0.0*................................. 219
Figure 9-5 ABAA8-X: 4 Cases of Edge Moving Across 8 Subpixels (*S0: |Slp|<0.5*) ............ 220
Figure 9-6 ABAA8-X: 4 Cases of Edge Moving Across 8 Subpixels (*S1: |Slp|>0.5*) ............ 221
Figure 9-7 Tile Intersected by Vertical Edge (*VE*) .................................................................... 222
Figure 9-8 Tile Intersected by Horizontal Edge (*HE*) ............................................................... 223
Figure 9-9 ABAA vs MSAA: Edge Moving Across 8 Subpixels ............................................... 224
Figure 9-10 ABAA8 vs MSAA8 for Pos Edges A ........................................................................ 226
Figure 9-11 ABAA8 vs MSAA8 for Pos Edges B ........................................................................ 227
Figure 9-12 ABAA8 vs MSAA8 for Neg Edges A ....................................................................... 228
Figure 9-13 ABAA8 vs MSAA8 for Neg Edges B ....................................................................... 229
Figure 9-14 Four Cases of Thin Triangles with ABAA8 vs MSAA8 ......................................... 231
Figure 9-15 Fan of 16 Triangles with Pos Edge Slopes and 8 Subpixels ................................... 232
Figure 9-16 Fan of 16 Triangles with Neg Edge Slopes and 8 Subpixels .................................. 233
Figure 9-17 Four Stages when Rendering Triangle Fan ............................................................... 234
Figure 9-18 Rendering of Not Equally Spaced Triangle Fan ....................................................... 235
Figure 9-19 ABAA8 vs MSAA8: Two Thin Rectangles at +/- 45-Degrees ............................... 237
Figure 10-1 Color at Pixel Center and Z-Dist at Subpixel Center of Gravity ........................... 250
Figure 10-2 Estimated Density of Memory Chip .......................................................................... 253
Figure 11-1 Interaction between Programmer and Computer ...................................................... 260
Figure 11-2 AND, NAND, OR and NOR Truth Tables and Gate Symbols .............................. 270
Figure 11-3 Exclusive OR and NOR Truth Tables and Gate Symbols ....................................... 271

# List of Tables

Table 1-1 TV Standards ............................................................................................... 5
Table 1-2 Graphics Display Resolution ....................................................................... 5
Table 2-1 Sampling of a Sine Function ...................................................................... 57
Table 2-2 TV Digital Encoding ................................................................................... 65
Table 3-1 Sample Frequency vs Nyquist Frequency ................................................. 93
Table 3-2 Comparison of Filtering with Box and Bartlett Windows ....................... 109
Table 3-3 Super-Sampling with Box and Bartlett Window ..................................... 112
Table 4-1 Intensity Jumps for Knight and Queens ................................................... 120
Table 5-1 Comparison of Intensity Steps vs Edge Slopes ....................................... 142
Table 6-1 Bits Selection for *MidLn* Measurements ............................................... 173
Table 9-1 Four Rendering Stages with Triangle Fan ............................................... 234
Table 9-2 Three Rendering Stages with Not Equally Spaced Triangle Fan ............. 235
Table 10-1 Size of Memory Chips During a 20 Years Period ................................. 254
Table 10-2 Evolution of Real-Time 3D Graphics Processing .................................. 255
Table 11-1 Example of Number Bases ..................................................................... 262
Table 11-2 Comparison between Decimal and Binary Numbers ............................. 265
Table 11-3 Numbers and Bases ................................................................................ 266
Table 11-4 Decimal 1k vs Binary 1k ........................................................................ 267
Table 11-5 Operations with Decimal and Binary Numbers5 ................................... 268
Table 11-6 Examples of Bitwise AND, OR, EX-OR and Invert .............................. 272
Table 11-7 Decimal Numbers vs EBCDIC ............................................................... 272
Table 11-8 Examples of Binary, Binary Hex and BCD Integers ............................. 273
Table 11-9 Decimal vs Binary Positive Integer Numbers ........................................ 274
Table 11-10 Decimal vs Binary Negative Integer Numbers .................................... 275
Table 11-11 Example of Integer, Fixed-Point and Floating-Point Number ............. 280

## Code Listings

Listing 7-1 C-Structure for Edge Type .................................................................................. 192
Listing 7-2 Edge Conversion from ASCII to Binary .............................................................. 193
Listing 7-3 Definition of Three Triangle Edges ..................................................................... 194
Listing 7-4 ABAA4 Subpixel Char Array for Printing............................................................ 194
Listing 8-1 ABAA 4 Subpixel Character Array for Printing.................................................. 203
Listing 8-2 MSAA 4 Subpixel Character Array for Printing.................................................. 203
Listing 8-3 Triangle Edges in Octal Format for 8 Triangle-Fans .......................................... 204
Listing 9-1 Two Thin Faces at +/- 45-degrees (Pi/4)............................................................. 236
Listing 11-1 Ugly General Solution for Counting Set-Bits ................................................... 276
Listing 11-2 Good 'Divide and Conquer' Solution for Counting Set-Bits.............................. 278
Listing 11-3 Good Solutions for Clearing the LSB Set ........................................................ 278
Listing 11-4 Good Solutions for Detecting 1Bit Set.............................................................. 279
Listing 11-5 Examples with w=8 .......................................................................................... 279
Listing 11-6 Other Good Solutions for Counting Set Bits..................................................... 279

# Preface

Anti-Aliasing (AA) is an important topic in Computer Generated Imagery (CGI). Several AA techniques have been developed for non-real time CGI applications. For real-time (RT) CGI applications, algorithms are limited to methods that can produce new images at rate of at least 50 images per second.

*Multi-Sample or Multisampling AA (MSAA)*

For RT CGI applications like computer games and flight simulators, the most widely used approach is Multi-Sample AA (MSAA). It consists of taking several samples within a Pixel and averaging the results. Also, see references [60] to [69].

*Area-Based AA (ABAA)*

In this book a new approach to AA is introduced, the Subpixel Area-Based AA (ABAA). Instead of sampling Subpixel points inside of a Pixel, ABAA computes the area that is partially covered by polygons within a Pixel. Then, it assigns this area to Subpixel Areas. Unlike MSAA, ABAA does not require multiple image computations.

My implementation of ABAA has evolved over the years. I have implemented and simulated several solutions to AA. In this book, I describe my latest ABAA implementations with 4 and 8 Subpixels. ABAA and MSAA approaches are compared, using many examples with analytic approaches as well as computer simulations. With half the number of Subpixels, ABAA can achieve an image quality comparable to MSAA, and at a significant lower cost.

The ABAA implementation described in this book is patent pending.

*Two versions of the book*

I have written 2 versions of this book about "Anti-Aliasing". The information provided in these books is similar, but directed at different audiences.

The 'New Area-Based Anti-Aliasing for CGI' version contains more detailed analysis and descriptions of AA, for those interested in more technical depth. It also shows how the ABAA algorithm can be expanded from 4 and 8 Subpixels to 16 and 32 Subpixels.

The 'Anti-Aliasing with MSAA vs ABAA' version contains the same subjects but with less analysis details. This should make it more accessible for most readers.

*Computer Generated Imagery (CGI)*

Computer Generated Imagery [50] consists of computer applications for creating images in art, printed media, video games, simulators and computer animation. For CGI, the most generally used approach is to process models made of polygons (mostly triangles) in 3D coordinates, then project them onto a 2D image plane. The rendering consists of assigning the contribution of one or more triangles to each Pixel (abbreviation for Picture Element) of the computer-generated images.

There are other approaches like 'ray tracing' and 'voxel processing', that are even more computation intensive. But these implementations are not part of this book.

*Non-RT CGI*

At first, CGI consisted of static pictures, then movies that were produced in non-real-time.by general purpose computers. Because of the amounts of computations, most of the new algorithms for CGI were executed in non-real-time using the fastest computer systems. It took many hours (or even days) and many high-speed computers to produce beautiful 3D graphics static images and animated scenes for TV commercials and movies.

*Triangles Forever*

Because of my experience and emphasis on fast processing for 3D RT CGI systems, I am mostly interested in algorithms that use triangle processing. The algorithms described in this book assume triangle processing, at least, in the last step of rendering.

For curved surfaces, there are algorithms for creating models with curved surfaces using bicubic patches. They can produce more realistic images. But these models still have to be converted into triangle meshes [13][14][15] in 3D space before the projection onto the 2D image plane. Then the projected triangles can be rendered by the computer hardware.

As the RT CGI processing hardware has evolved with curved surfaces and 3D texture, the computer-generated images are becoming more realistic. But one thing has not changed: the last step in rendering still consists of mapping small triangles onto image Pixels. During rendering, the Pixels covered by the projected triangles are assigned colors samples derived from these triangles. When taking only one single sample per Pixel from the triangles, the sample color is assigned to the whole Pixel. The resulting image shows distracting effects, or artifacts. One approach is to take several samples per pixel, at the cost of increased processing time or more expensive hardware.

This book presents an efficient method for rendering triangles with minimum artifacts. Instead of taking sample points, the area that the triangle covers a Pixel is assigned to a set of Subpixel with equivalent area.

*Aliasing in CGI*

For CGI, each image consists of 2-dimensional arrays of Pixels (picture elements), each having a single color. These arrays consist of *PixMax* Pixels horizontally by *SLMax* Scanlines vertically. VGA (Video Graphics Array) was an early standard from IBM for color display adapters in Personal Computers (PC). It has an image resolution of 640x480 Pixels. For HDTV, the image resolution can be 1920x1080, or even UHD at 3480x2160, which is common today.

When each Pixel is computed using a single sample, the resulting images show 'aliasing artifacts' such as stairsteps on feature edges, also referred to as jaggies. In dynamic scenes, 'aliasing artifacts' are more noticeable, resulting in edge crawling, line breaking and small features popping in-and out of the scenes.

Aliasing artifacts can be minimized, if not eliminated by applying anti-aliasing (AA) techniques. There are several early articles from *Ed Catmull*, *F.C Crow* and *Jim Blinn* about AA for non-real-time solutions, such as Super-Sampling (SSAA). With SSAA, static images using one sample point per Pixel are computed at higher resolutions, then downscaled with filtering (2048x2048 to 512x512 for example). Because of the large amounts of computations, SSAA is not suitable for RT CGI applications. For RT CGI applications like computer games and flight simulators, a similar approach consists of Multi-Sample AA (MSAA). With MSAA, several images are generated by selecting a selection of sample points, or Subpixels, within Pixels. The anti-aliased image is produced by averaging these images. Because of the burden of generating several images, MSAA methods can be computation intensive and costly.

## *Designing Hardware for RT CGI*

I have many years of experience designing several 3D RT CGI systems with innovative approaches to Subpixel Anti-Aliasing. I got involved into 3D computer graphics when there was a rapid development in 3D computer graphics algorithms. I was fortunate to get my first US job at the Advanced Product Operation (APO) of Link Flight Simulation in Sunnyvale, CA. The Link Company had a long history designing simulators and trainers for the Army, Navy, Air Force and NASA [90]. It has been the leader in Flight Simulators [81] since WWII, after Ed Link invented the Blue Box [98], the first Flight Simulator that was used to train around half a million pilots in WWII. Since then, the Link Company had delivered many Flight Simulator systems for the US Military and NASA. For airlines, there were flight simulators from other companies that produced lower cost systems.

Soon after joining Link Flight Simulation, I became one of the key designers and architects for the company's first Digital Image Generator (DIG). The Link DIG was a high-speed computer for producing RT CGI. Because of their cost (above $1M), only 4 companies could design and deliver such RT CGI systems at that time. Most of these RT CGI systems were used in flight simulators to train pilots for the US Military and NASA.

The DIG was a specialized computer generating 3D scenes in real-time to be used in aircraft simulators. The first DIG was delivered to NASA at the Houston Space Center, TX, for training astronauts in the Shuttle Mission Simulator (SMS) [96]. At the time of delivery, the Link DIG was the fastest RT CGI system in the world. It had edge smoothing and could produce out of the windows images made of 4000 projected triangles (12,000 edges) at a rate of 60 times per sec. With a price tag of $2M dollars, the DIG systems were not available to the general public. A total of four Link DIG systems were delivered to NASA in Houston for the SMS.

I continued working at Link for several years, making many improvements to the DIG. During a period of 10 years, Link sold around 70 flight simulators with 3 or 4 window displays driven by DIG systems, for use in helicopter and military aircrafts.

## *Anti-Aliasing in RT CGI*

Besides the need for high-speed computations, edge smoothing was an important requirement for RT CGI systems to be delivered to the US Military and NASA. Distracting artifacts like jaggies, edge crawling and faces popping in-and-out of scenes were not allowed. So, I was involved with AA early on in my engineering career.

In the 1990s 3D RT CGI became feasible for implementation in the PC market. In 1996, while working at Oak Technology in Sunnyvale, I was one of the main designers of the Warp5, one of the first 3D graphics adapter/accelerator for the PC Market. Several members of the Warp 5 design team had experience designing RT CGI with AA for the Military and NASA. The Warp5 was the only PC graphics adapter with AA. There were many other 3D graphics adapters in the industry that were producing images using a Z-buffer with only one sample point per Pixel. Some were fast, but had jaggies. The Warp5 was the only adapter that could process anti-aliased images with 8 Subpixel samples, referred to as Bed of Nails (BON). A few years later, some manufacturers started to produce adapters with MSAA, but at the cost of reduced performances.

The AA solution adopted by most PC card manufacturer was Super-Sampling (SSAA) or Multi-Sample AA (MSAA) with reduced system performances. In the mean-time, I have experimented with various AA methods, including my own Area-Based AA (ABAA) algorithms. After several improvements, I have come up with the ultimate and best ABAA solution.

### *MSAA vs ABAA*

There are several advantages of Subpixel processing with ABAA over MSAA. It will be shown with examples and simulation that ABAA is widely superior to MSAA.

For example, assume that each Pixel contains N Subpixels. Then consider a triangle edge moving over time from one end to the other end across a Pixel. For a good AA solution, is should be expected that when an edge moves across a Pixel, it should result in N equal color transitions, or increments. This is not true for MSAA

In the **MSAA** Implementation, the number of covered Subpixel is detected with point sampling.

1) Since MSAA uses Subpixel point samples, there are always pairs of Subpixels that are aligned with some edge orientations. For example, with 8 Subpixels there are at least 7+6+5+4+3+2+1=28 such pairs. Each time an edge moves across a Subpixel pair, it results in one double increment instead of 2 distinct increments.
2) The increments are not evenly spaced.
3) The quality of MSAA depends on edge orientation. It works fine for triangle edges that are near horizontal or near vertical. It produces the worst results for edges that are near 30 degrees.
4) The detection of covered Subpixels points is more computation intensive.

In the **ABAA** implementation, Pixels are subdivided into N Subpixel Areas of equal size. As an edge moves in any direction across the Pixel, the covered Subpixel Area corresponds to the Pixel covered area.

1) As an edge moves across a Pixel, the covered area gradually increases from 0.0 to 1.0, in N increments evenly spaced.
2) The quality with ABAA is independent of edge orientation.
3) There is no need for Multi Samples. For each edge position, the sampled area is detected in only one sampling, or measurement.

*ABAA is the Green Solution to AA*

When compared to ABAA, because of the duplication of circuitry, MSAA implementations require more HW and thus produce more heat.

Although the derivation of the ABAA algorithm may be harder to understand, its implementation with logic circuits is simpler than MSAA. There are many advantages of ABAA.

- Better Image Quality, with less Subpixel samples when compared to MSAA.
- Proposed implementations are more accurate and can be scaled to 4 and 8 Subpixels.
- Simpler implementations and lower system size cost.

*Motivation to Write a Book*

While designing high speed computer hardware, I developed several techniques of my own. I wanted to share my ideas with other engineers and scientists. So, I thought that by writing books, I could show with examples how these ideas lead to better logic designs [19]. I hope to get feedbacks from the readers about improving on some of my ideas and about other applications.

In my first book, 'New Fixed-Point Math for Logic Design' [6], I have showed how computations with Fixed Point binary numbers and *rounding* off partial results can lead to problems. I have introduced a new approach that avoid these problems. When fixed-point numbers need to be truncated, '*averaging*' should be used instead of '*rounding*'. There are examples of how math functions can be implemented efficiently with interpolation. The ABAA algorithm presented in this book is a result of applying these concepts to Subpixel computations.

This book, 'New Area-Based Anti-Aliasing for CGI', is the result many years of experience dealing with anti-aliasing. It introduces a new solution that uses Area-Based Computations to solve aliasing problems. It is then compared with the widely used methods that rely on Multi-Point-Sampling.

*Summary of the Chapters*

Chapters 1 to 5 provide understanding about current algorithms for 3D graphics and antialiasing with SSAA, MSAA and BON.
Chapters 6 to 9 describe my new ABAA method for AA.
Chapters 10 and 11 provide information about Flight Simulators and Binary Numbers.
Chapter 10.2.4 has links to 'youtube.com' videos from early RT CGI systems, including the Link DIG and the E&S CT-5

*Description of the Chapters*

In Chapter 1, 'Introduction', there is a description of the evolution of TV, followed by early computer-generated images to the present real-time CGI systems. There is a description of 3D coordinate systems for data base objects, vector analysis and RGB color systems. There is a description of description of 2D coordinate systems and more specifically how they are used in the image coordinate system.
It is advisable to scan thru the last 2 chapters (Flight Simulation and Binary Numbers) to get an idea about CGI systems and computation with binary numbers in computers.

In Chapter 2 there is a description of aliasing in CGI and the physical limitation that cause aliasing. Some of the analytic techniques in this chapter might be new and difficult to understand in the first reading. The reader can skip thru some sections and go back to them at a later time.

In Chapter 3, non-real-time solutions like Super-Sampling (SSAA) as a solution to aliasing are described. Some filtering techniques are also described. Analysis with spatial and frequency domains are presented.

In Chapter 4, real-time solutions like Multi-Sample (MSAA) and Bed-of-Nail (BON) used to fight aliasing are described. The approach using solutions to the 8 Queens puzzle is presented. The solutions, with their short comings, are analyzed with several examples.

In Chapter 5 Image processing in RT CGI systems are presented and analyzed. Area-Based AA (ABAA) is introduced.

In Chapter 6 the evolution of ABAA is presented.

In Chapter 7, the processing to render polygons and triangles is presented.

In Chapter 8 and 9, ABAA with 4 and 8 subpixels is introduced.

### *The Last Two Chapters*
The last two chapters, 10 and 11, don't follow a logical order. For this reason, I have inserted them at the end as general references.

### *Chapter 10, Flight Simulation*
Because of the strong influence of Flight Simulators [81] on RT CGI, the chapter 'Flight Simulation and RT CGI' provides some insight in the evolution of Computer-Generated Imagery in Real-Time during the last 50 years.

### *Chapter 11, Computations with Binary Numbers*
Because of the speed requirements of RT CGI, many computations in RT CGI systems are implemented with Binary Arithmetic. The chapter 'Inside the Binary World' provides basic information on different number representations such a decimal, binary, octal and hexadecimal There is also information in the binary format for fixed-point and floating-point variables.

### *Intended Audience for this Book*

When writing this book, I have consciously tried to make it available to a wide range of readers, from students interested in CGI to Graphics adapter manufacturers. This version of the book, 'New Area-Based Anti-Aliasing for CGI', is well suited for:

- HW and SW students in computer and CGI.
- 3D CGI programmers and designers

The other version, 'Anti-Aliasing with MSAA vs ABAA', is better suited for:

- 3D CGI manager
- 3D game players interested in comparing AA techniques
- 3D game artists and modelers
- Graphics adapter and card manufacturers

- Cell phone and laptop manufacturers

Forgive me when I try to explain some basic concepts that might seem obvious to you, like computing the area of a trapezoid.

*Acknowledgements*

Nowadays, Artificial Intelligence (AI) and Immigration are in the news.

I am often asked about why not using AI to find AA solutions. AI relies on large teams of contributors, large amount of investment and many technologies to develop new products. On the other hand, the AA algorithm described in this book relies on simple math and geometry like computing the area of a trapezoid. It also requires a good understanding and experience in 3D CGI and many iterations in the process.

I am a proud immigrant to the US from Switzerland. During my 20 years at Link Flight Simulation, I have been able to improve the image quality and density of digital visual systems in aircraft simulators. Because of the quality of aircraft simulators, they enhance the efficiency of training for aircraft pilots. I am proud to have saved lives of astronauts and military pilots, extended the life of military aircraft and saved fuel.

First, I am grateful to my parents, *Jakob and Jeanne Rohner*, who have given me the opportunity to learn accordion, piano and bass guitar, and who have supported me to study electrical engineering at the ETH, Zurich. I want to thank my aunt *Yvonne Morf* (my mom's sister) who strongly encouraged me to come to the US to get my Master Degree in EE (MSEE). She had spent many years in the US and she guided me applying for an emigrant VISA. I came to the US in the 1970s, when there was a rapid growth in 3D CGI.

I want to thank my distant relatives in the US who helped me settling in California. Among them, my Swiss born great aunt & uncle *Adele & Louis Panighetti-Aeshliman* in Connecticut, and my cousins *Richard & Michael Gagliasso* (and their family) in San Jose area (Silicon Valey, California. They were instrumental in making the transition easier. Without their help, there would be no book on AA, nor would I have been able to provide a new solution to the aliasing problem. We are all related to two *Panighetti* brothers from Northwest Italy (Piedmontese), who emigrated around 1885, one to Switzerland and one to California.

I also want to mention *Jean Hoerni*, another Swiss scientist who immigrated to the US. He became an important contributor to the development of integrated circuits and microchips.

*Jean Hoerni* first patented his 'planar process' in 1959, during his work at Fairchild Semiconductor. The planar process was critical in the invention of Silicon Integrated circuit by *Robert Noyce*, who built on *Hoerni's* work with his conception of an integrated circuit (IC). *Noyce's* invention was the first monolithic IC chip. This invention is at the base of all the microchips built in the world. These scientists inspired me to come to Silicon Valley. *Noyce* and *Gordon Moore* (Moore's law) left Fairchild Semiconductor to found Intel in 1968. [47]

My first manuscript of this book was ready a year ago. Since then, I have done many iterations and improvements. I thank Gotham books who supported me in the production of this book.

I thank *Dan Weaver* for reviewing my manuscript and for his many suggestions. *Dan* and I have worked together at several companies.

# Chapter 1 Introduction

The field of images generated by computer is referred to as Computer Generated Imagery (CGI) [50]. CGI became feasible during the 1960s. Many algorithms for generating 3D CGI were introduced.

During the 1970s, real-time 3D CGI systems (RT CGI) became available. This field has grown considerably over the years. Nowadays PC graphics adapters can produce 3D RT CGI for many types of applications.

In this chapter, several aspects of TV and CGI are considered.

- 3D CGI
- TV images vs 3D CGI
- Transformations from 3D objects to 2D images
- Pixel with 1 sample point
- Non-Real-Time 3D CGI vs Real-Time 3D CGI
- Introduction to Anti-Aliasing: MSAA vs ABAA

## 1.1 From TV to CGI

There are similarities between TV and CGI. TV is a ubiquitous medium used to broadcast dynamic scenes, TV programs, TV shows and movies. CGI uses digital computers to create synthetic images, simulations and movies.

### 1.1.1 TV Images and Displays

The early black and white TVs were introduced in the 1950s. Color TVs appeared in the 1960s. Color TV technology was limited by the need to keep compatibility. With the color TV standards, the same TV signals are used to transmit black or color TV images. The images were displayed with CRT (Cathode Ray Tube) display monitors. There were several TV standards [41]. In the US, TV images used the NTSC standard. The displayed images consist of 480 interlaced Scanlines (SL), that are transferred and displayed one SL at a time to image displays [42][43]. Images were updated 60 times per second, using alternated even and odd fields. On two subsequent fields, even and odd SLs are interlaced to increase the apparent resolution and reduce flickering. In even fields Scanlines 0, 2, 4, ... were displayed. On odd fields Scanlines 1, 3, 4, ... were displayed. A pair of even and odd field form a frame, displayed at 30 frames per second.

### 1.1.2 TV Images and Movies

*Image Flickering*

On TVs, full images are updated at 30 frames per sec, but they are partially updated at 60 fields per sec, using interlacing. Besides providing more resolution, interlacing solves the problem of flickering.

In the movies, it is acceptable for the eye to capture and display images at 24 frames per sec. But when doing so, the eye perceives image flickering. When images are displayed at 48 times per second, the eye does not perceive image flickering.

Introduction

The flickering problem in the movies is solved by introducing a shutter in front of the projector. The shutter modulates the light at the rate of 48 pulses per sec. Each image is repeated twice. This is not noticeable to the eye, even when the movie images are updated at 24 frames per sec. When there is movement in the scene, the moving scene elements in movies are recorded with 'motion blur'.

## *TV and Display Images*

Although TV displayed images look like Photo or Movie images, they have a rigid structure. Each displayed image consists of a 2-dimensional array of sample points, or Pixels (Picture Elements). The size of this array of Pixels is *PixMax* Pixels Horizontally and *SLMax* Scanlines vertically.

Refer to Figure 1-1.

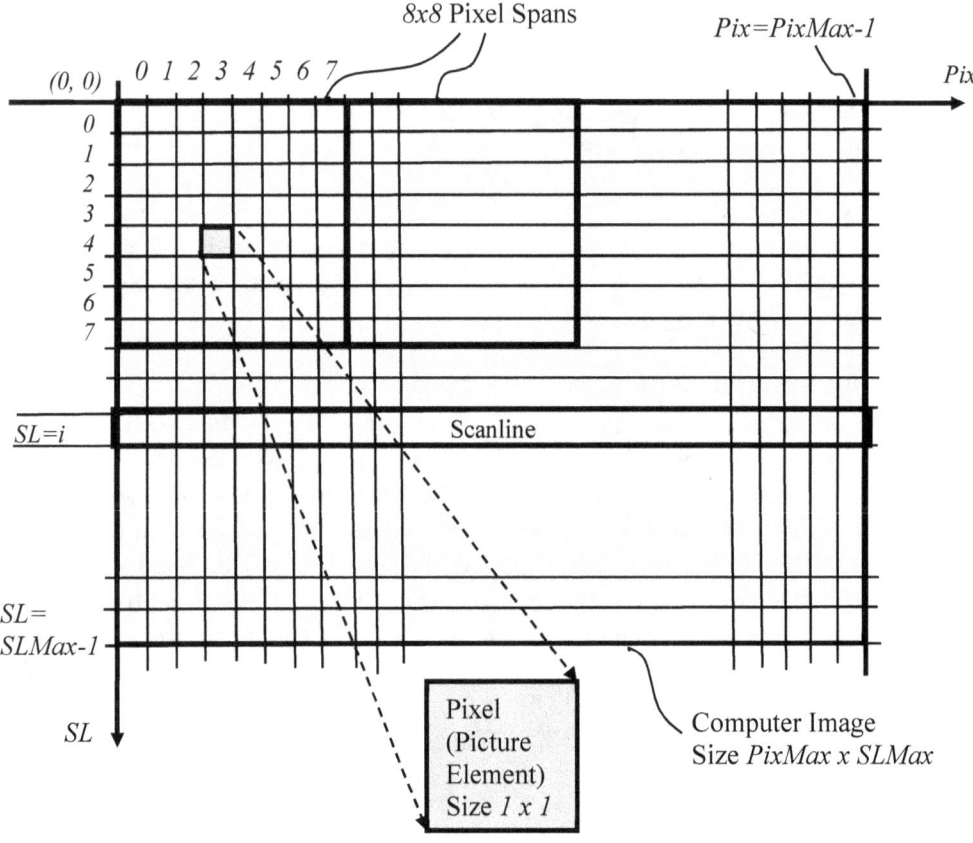

**Figure 1-1 TV Image**

Every 1/60 second, the TV image is refreshed. Pixels are painted one at a time from left to right in the horizontal direction. At the end of the line, the Scanline number is incremented, and the next line is painted from left to right., until the bottom of the image is reached.

In this book the description of Anti-Aliasing deals with images at the Pixel level. In order to have more visibility, the image is decomposed into Spans consisting of 8x8 Pixels only. These Spans are blown up representations of portions of the image They are partial images that will facilitate the descriptions of examples at the Pixel level.

### 1.1.3 Interlaced Display

In TV, the flickering problem is solved with SL interlacing. Half of the image is displayed at 60 fields per sec for NTSC (or 50 fields pre sec for PAL and SECAM TVs in Europe), using alternating even and odd fields. On even fields, only even SLs are displayed. On odd fields, only odd SLs are displayed. When TV images are recorded, the Video Camera records the image the same way as it is displayed, so there is no problem with moving components in the scenes.

Refer to Figure 1-2, 'Interlaced Scanlines in Field0 and Field1'

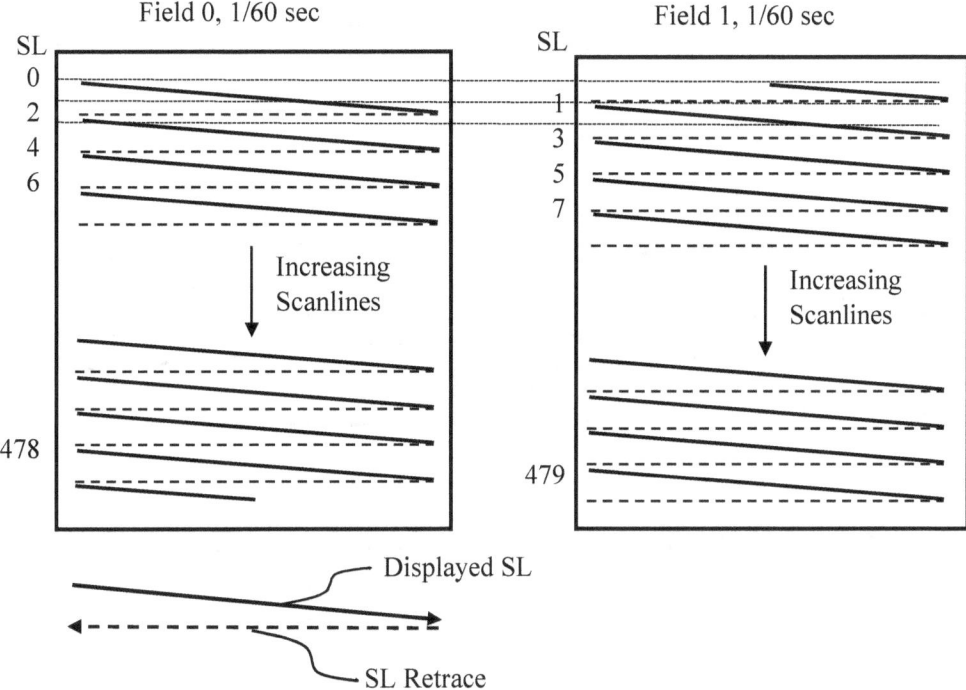

**Figure 1-2 TV Image with Interlaced Scanlines in Field0 and Field1**

For CGI, there is a problem when images are updated at 30 frames per second with interlacing. When the same image is displayed in both fields, objects that move from field to field don't get updated with the correct position. This result in a visual effect referred to as Double Imaging. This can be solved by updating the image at field rate, that is 60 times per sec.
For CGI movies, some algorithms can simulate a 'motion blur' that look similar to the 'motion blur' in movies.

Introduction

## 1.1.4 Progressive Displays

In Progressive displays, all SLs are displayed on every field, 60 times per sec. This requires twice the processing per image, when compared to interlacing.

Refer to Figure 1-3, "Progressive Display'.

With new technologies, most displays and TVs can display interlaced and progressive images as well.

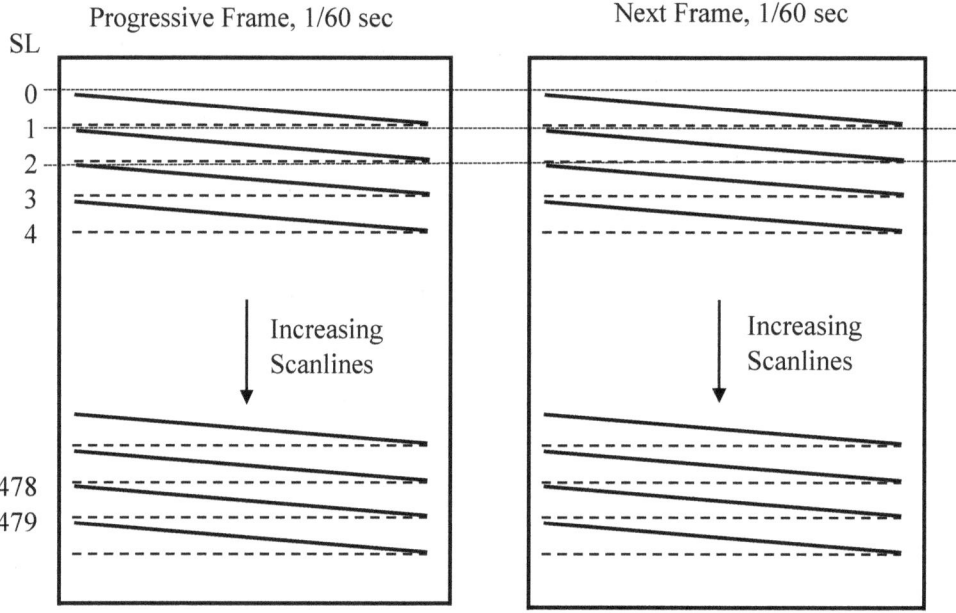

**Figure 1-3 Progressive Display Image (Non-Interlaced SLs)**

## 1.1.5 Color Display Standards

There are several standards for TV and CGI [40] [55]. Refer to Table 1-1, 'TV Standards'.
Refer to Wikipedia 'Standard-Definition Television' [41].
Refer to Wikipedia 'Graphics Display Resolution', 'Refresh Rate' and 'Interlaced Video' [42].

| Standard Definition TV | Display Mode | Resolution *PixMax x SLMax* | Fields/sec |
|---|---|---|---|
| US:   NTSC, 480i | interlaced | 720 x 480 | 60/sec |
| France: SECAM, 576i | interlaced | 720 x 576 | 50/sec |
| Germany: PAL, 576i | interlaced | 720 x 576 | 50/sec |

With the advent of HDTV,
there were interlaced (i) and progressive (p: non-interlaced) standards.

| High Definition TV | Display Mode | Resolution PixMax x SLMax |
|---|---|---|
| 720i | interlaced | 1,280 x 720 |
| 720p | progressive | 1,280 x 720 |
| 1080i | interlaced | 1,920x1,080 |
| 1080p | progressive | 1,920x1,080 |
| 4k | progressive | 3,840 x 2,160 |
| 8k | progressive | 7,680 x 4,320 |

**Table 1-1 TV Standards**

For Graphics Display Standards, refer to examples in Table 1-2 for the Video Graphics Display resolution.

For CGI application, the display resolution can be between 720x576 and 1920x1080. UXGA (Ultra Extended Graphics Array), or UGA, is a display mode in which the resolution is 1600 Pixels by 1200 SLs

| Video Graphics Array | Display Mode | Resolution *PixMax x SLMax* | Fields/sec |
|---|---|---|---|
| VGA | progressive | 640 x 480 | 60/sec and up |
| SVGA | progressive | 800 x 600 | 60/sec and up |
| XGA | progressive | 1024 x 768 | 60/sec and up |
| UXGA | progressive | 1600 x 1200 | 60/sec and up |

**Table 1-2 Graphics Display Resolution**

With the advent of HDTV, the same standards can be used for PC monitors and TV displays. The most common are 720i, 720p, 1018i and 1080p.

### 1.1.6 TV Images vs CGI

There are similarities between TV Images and CGI. The resolution of TV and CGI images are defined horizontally by *PixMax* Pixels (*Pix*) and vertically by *SLMax* Scanlines (*SL*). While Standard Definition TV (SDTV) images use analog signals [41], CGI images are processed with digital signals.

With the advent of High-Definition TV (HDTV) since the 1990s, the TV broadcasts are transmitted with compressed digital signals [44]. The CRT displays have been replaced with larger size high resolution Liquid Cristal Displays (LCD) and Light Emitting Diodes (LED) displays.

In the US, the early TV images were encoded with the NTSC standard with a resolution of 720x480 Pixels. The refresh rate was 60 fields per second, using even and odd fields. NTSC produces 525 lines per frame, where only 480 are visible. The remaining lines are used for control. For CRT monitors, the extra time is used for line retrace, that is moving the display line control from the bottom-right to the top-left of the image. During retrace, the lines are not visible.

In Europe, the color images used the PAL or SECAM standards that have a slightly higher resolution of 720x576, but a lower refresh rate of 50 fields per second. PAL or SECAM produce 625 lines per frame, where only 576 are visible. The remaining *SL* time is used for control.

CGI first appeared in the seventies. Images were usually displayed with monitors similar to TV screen, often with higher resolution. In order to reduce flickering, the monitor also used interlaced images. Although Pixels were defined by the horizontal resolution of 720 Pixels, the TV output consisted of continuous analog signals. For CGI, the computed *SL* Pixels consist of digital signal that are usually stored in SL buffers with *PixMax* locations, each storing one binary color intensity. The SL buffer is then read and converted to analog signals with Digital to Analog Converters (DAC). In the SL buffer, each Pixel is defined by a unique gray shade or color.

For interlaced monitors with *SLMax* Scanlines, even SLs are displayed on even field, and odd SLs are displayed on odd fields. Each field is displayed at 1/60 sec rate to prevent image flickering. By having interlaced (or interleaved) SL, the frame resolution of images at 1/30 sec appears to be double the field resolution at 1/60/sec.

For progressive monitors with *SLMax* Scanlines, all the SLs are displayed on each field. So, for progressive monitors, the image rendering has to be twice as fast as for interlaced monitors.

For more information about TV and Video, there is a good book from Keith Jack: "Video Demystified" [7].

### 1.2 CGI

CGI consists of computer applications for creating images in art, printed media, video games, simulators and computer animation. For CGI, the most generally used approach is to process polygons (mostly triangles) in 3D coordinates, then project them onto a 2D image plane. There are other approaches like 'ray tracing' and 'voxel processing', that are even more computation intensive.

As the processing hardware for RT CGI has evolved with curved surfaces and 3D texture, the last step in rendering still consists of mapping small triangles onto image Pixels. Because of my emphasis on fast processing for 3D RT CGI systems, I am mostly interested in algorithms using polygon (mainly triangle) processing. The algorithms described this book assume polygon processing.

## 1.2.1 Early CGI Contributors

CGI was pioneered in the late 1960s by *David C. Evans* and *Ivan Sutherland* (E&S) at the University of Utah [53]. Many of the early contributors also came from the University of Utah. Among them were *Jim Clark* (founder of Silicon Graphics and co-founder of Netscape), *Ed Catmull* (co-founder of Pixar), *John Warnock* of Adobe, *Scott P. Hunter* of Oracle, *Franklin C. Crow* and *Jim Blinn*. In 1968, *Dave Evans* and *Ivan Sutherland* founded the first computer graphics hardware company, Evans & Sutherland (E&S).

For curved surfaces, there was important developments in the French automobile industry at Citroën and Renault. In 1959, *Paul de Casteljau* (a French physicist and mathematician) developed an algorithm for evaluating calculations on a certain family of curves while working at Citroën. In the 1960s, *Pierre Bézier* at Renault used *Paul de Casteljau's* curves to develop 3D modeling techniques for Renault car bodies. These curves would form the foundation for much curve-modeling work in the field, as curves (unlike polygons) are mathematically complex entities to draw and create models as well. These curves are now called Bézier curves after *Bézier's* work in the field of automotive design. Refer to Wikipedia 'Bézier curves and Bicubic Patches' [13].

The curve algorithms are powerful tools for creating 3D representations with curved surfaces for CGI models. It is important to be aware that these models cannot be processed directly by CGI rendering hardware. First, the 3D models with curved surfaces have to be converted by software applications into polygons (or triangle) meshes in 3D space [14][15]. Note that these conversions could also be implemented in hardware using embedded programs in GPU. Then the triangle meshes in 3D space can be projected onto the 2D image plane for rendering.

## 1.2.2 Non-Real-Time CGI

At first, CGI consisted of static pictures, then movies that were produced in non-real-time.by general purpose computers. Because of the amounts of computations, most of the new algorithms for CGI were executed in non-real-time using the fastest computer systems. These non-RT CGI computers were used to produce beautiful static images and animated scenes for TV commercials and movies.

Most of these implementations used the Z-Buffer approach for rendering. The coordinate Z is the depth coordinate that represents the distance from the viewpoint to sample points in the image. In this approach, the image was computed with 1 triangle sample per Pixel. The triangle sample that is the closest to the observer is selected. The Pixel Color and Z distance are stored into a frame buffer memory (Z-buffer).

## 1.2.3 Real-Time CGI Systems

In the early 1970s, for real-time (RT) CGI applications like virtual reality and flight simulators, fast and special purpose RT CGI systems became feasible. These systems were not available to the general public. They had to be developed from scratch using proprietary special purpose computer hardware They were also expensive and cost above a million dollars.

At that time there was a separation between non-RT CGI using software algorithms running on super computers, and a limited supply of fast RT CGI systems. The favorite computer for non-RT 3D algorithm development was the Cray-1 super computer [73]. Because of its high cost of $8M, it was limited to universities, research labs, animated scenes or special effects in movies.

For the general public, the state of the art in RT CGI were 2D graphics games like Pac-Mac and Space Invaders running on PCs and play stations like Atari and Nintendo. The state of the art in PCs was the Apple II and DRDOS microcomputers, costing around $1k. Later on, there was the Microsoft Flight Simulator [75] with simple graphics for the IBM PC. The images consisted of flight instruments and simple out the window images.

In the 1970s, when RT CGI systems became feasible, only a few companies could manufacture these specialized systems [82] [83]. These RT CGI systems could produce nice CGI at 30 frames/sec, or even at 60 field/sec. They had good image quality and anti-aliasing (AA). They were the grandads of today's 3D graphics chips and graphics cards that are used in high-end PCs. Among them:

- Evans and Sutherland (E&S) in Salt Lake City, Utah [53][86],
  with CT-1 to CT-5 (Continuous Tone) CGI systems.
  There are several patents and publications from E&S about RT CGI in particular about Polygon Clipping [130] to [134].
- General Electric Ground System Division (GE GSD) in Daytona Beach, Florida,
  with CGI CompuScene systems [89].
  There are several patents and publications from GE about RT CGI, in particular about Edge Smoothing from *William M. Bunker* and *Richard G. Fadden* [120] to [127].
- A third company, the Advanced Product Operation (APO) of Link Flight Simulation in Sunnyvale CA, was a late entrant [90] to [99], with DIG CGI Systems.
  Link Flight Simulation had several patents and publications about RT CGI, in particular for High-Speed Sorter, Clipping and Texture from *Judit K Florence*, *Michel A Rohner*, *Johnson K Yan* and *Robert W. Lotz* [100] to [114].

Few people have heard about these RT CGI systems, or have experienced flying in these expensive flight simulators. They were designed under NASA or US military contracts and required security clearances to work on the projects. One of the biggest challenges was to eliminate (or at least reduce) distracting visual artifacts like edge crawling (also referred to as jaggies) and small faces popping in-and-out of scenes.

For the early RT CGI systems designed in the 1970s, the low memory density available at that time prevented implementations with Color-Buffer or Z-Buffer. Instead, they were designed with Edge List and Scanline (SL) computers. In SL Computers, only a few SLs could be stored in local memory at a time. The edges had to be sorted along each SL before being displayed. In the 1980s, the increase in memory density made it feasible to design the rendering with frame buffers.

In 1977, 4 DIG-1 from Link Flight Simulation were delivered to NASA in Houston in preparation of the Shuttle space flights. At around that time, two other computers were announced:
- Cray-1 supercomputer
- Apple II microcomputer.

The Cray-1 [73] supercomputer was designed by Cray Research. It was quite larger (Height: 77", Diam:104") than the Apple II and cost around $8M. When announced, the Cray-1 was the fastest general purpose super computer for 3D graphics and other non-real-time applications. This supercomputer had great 64-bit Floating Point performance and became in high demand all over the world. The first was delivered in the same year as when the first DIG-1 was delivered to NASA [96]. The DIG-1 was of a similar size and cost around $2M.

The Apple II [74] became the most famous microcomputer, until the first IBM PC was introduced four years later. These microcomputers were about the same size as a typewriter and cost around $1.5k. They could generate simple boxy 2D graphics images for games.

*Comparison between DIG-1 and Cray-1 Super Computer*

There are some similarities between the DIG-1 and Cray-1. These systems cost above $1M. They were the fastest at producing 3D Computer Generated Images, but they were designed for 2 different markets:

- Non-Real-Time Applications:
  The Cray-1 was the fastest for *general purpose* applications. For 3D Computer Generated Image rendering, many algorithms were developed in software and executed on off the shelf super computers. Everybody in the 3D community knew about the Cray-1.
  The 1$^{st}$ Cray-1 Super-Computer was announced in 1976. That same year, 1$^{st}$ SMS DIG-1 was shipped to Houston. The non-real-time Cray-1, that was announced at the same time, can be compared with the real-time DIG-1.
- Real-Time Applications:
  The DIG-1 was the fastest RT CGI system in the world for generating 3D graphics scenes used in aircraft simulators, when it was delivered to NASA. It was at least 10 times faster than competitive RT CGI systems at that time. It was 5 years ahead of the competition. On the back page of the book cover, there is an example of image generated by the DIG. The DIG could process up to 12,000 triangle edges (4000 triangles) at the rate of 60 images/sec.
  Because of the limited market and the military applications, practically nobody in the 3D community were aware that RT CGI systems like the DIG-1 existed. Only 10 years later, other companies like Silicon Graphics started to produce such systems with wider distribution.

Although many software algorithms were developed for both non-RT CGI and RT CGI, many of the RT CGI implementations were kind of proprietary. The 3D graphics algorithms for non-RT-CGI were developed using the faster Super Computers at that time. The Cray-1 was the favorite super computer [73] until workstation from Sun Microsystem and Silicon graphics appeared 10 years later.

## 1.2.4 Evolution of AA in RT CGI Systems

### *RT CGI with Edge Smoothing in the 1970s*

During the 1970s, the limitation in memory density prevented RT CGI systems from implementing rendering with Color-Buffer or Z-Buffer. For this reason, the rendering was done one SL at a time in a Scanline Computer. Since the RT CGI systems were used for military and aerospace training, an important requirement was to eliminate visual artifact. In the DIG-1, the edge smoothing with analog circuitry with 4x4 Subpixel resolution implemented by *Robert (Bob) W. Lotz* [108]. For the DIG-2, I implemented a digital version of edge smoothing with 4x4 Subpixel resolution. I am not familiar with the edge smoothing approaches used by GE and E&S.

### *RT CGI with Face Buffer and BON in the 1980s*

During the 1980s, the increase in memory density made implementation with Color-Double-Buffer feasible. This made feasible for companies like Silicon Graphics Inc (SGI) and Computervision Corp in Raleigh, NC, to enter the RT CGI market.

In most RT CGI systems anti-aliasing was handled using up to 16 sample points within a Pixel. The sample points are also referred to Bed of Nail (BON). Refer to Edge Smoothing patent from *Rick Fadden* (Reference [122], 16 sample points and [127], 8 sample points) and the Modular DIG patent from *J. K. Yan and J.K Florence* [111]. Some of these systems show a transition from standard logic circuit modules to ASIC (Application Specific Integrated Circuit).

### *First PC Graphic Adapters with RT CGI in the Mid 1990s*

During the 1990s, there was a big development in ASIC design using RTL (Register Transfer Logic) programming with Verilog. This made implementation of RT CGI systems in a single ASIC chip feasible for the PC market. In the PC graphic adapters, ASIC chips were connected to the PC Bus and a few local memory chips. These 3D RT CGI implementations used a Double-Color-Buffer and a Z-Buffer.

Most of these graphic adapters had no anti-aliasing. The consumers became aware of the artifacts, or jaggies, due to single point per Pixel sampling. One approach to minimize the jaggies was to increase screen resolution.

Using their background designing large RT CGI systems with anti-aliasing, a group of engineers from the leading RT CGI companies (*J. K. Yan, R. G. Fadden, M. A. Rohner*) decided to design a graphic adapter with AA for the PC market at Oak Technology. The result was the Warp5 that implemented AA with 8 Subpixels and was the 1$^{st}$ PC graphics adapter with AA. Prior to joining Oak Technology, I had worked on an early version of my algorithm using Area-Based Anti-Aliasing. Using an adaptation of ABAA, I was going to implement a better version of AA for the Warp5 follow-on, when the project got cancelled. Since then, I have made several improvements and the result is presented in this book.

At the beginning of 2000s, the PC graphic adapters started to implement AA using the Multi-Sample Anti-Aliasing approach (MSAA).

## 1.2.5 Data Base Models

Before CGI can be rendered, 3D models have to be created in a 3D Data Base. The models can consist of single objects or clusters of multiple objects. In most applications, the objects are described with connected triangles. There can be also lines and point lights. There are static models like terrain and buildings and moving objects like airplanes, tanks and living creatures. For moving objects like living creatures and tanks for examples, they can have articulated parts.

The 3D models are inserted into Gaming Areas, where these objects can be rendered by CGI systems in 3D before being projected into a 2D image plane. Depending on the distance between the observer and the models, the projection size of the rendered objects can vary greatly. For this reason, the same Data Base objects can be modeled with different 'Level of Details' (LOD). When the object is close to the observer, the models with higher LODs are processed. When the object is far away the models with lower LOD are processed. When the objects become too small in the scene, they are removed from processing. For example, when the distance to the object increases by a factor of 2, the number of triangles in the next lower LOD could be reduced by a factor of 4. The distances at which the models switch between LOD, are defined as 'Switching Distances'. In order to prevent object LOD to oscillate back and forth during transition, 'Hysteresis' should be applied to the Switching Distances. Distracting effects when objects transition between LODs should be avoided.

## 1.2.6 2D Coordinate Systems

For the CGI computations, a knowledge of geometry, coordinate systems and linear algebra is recommended [20].

### *Triangle In 2D Coordinate System*

Given a 2D drawing area or geographic maps, any point insides of the area can be defined with *(X, X)* coordinates on two coordinate axis x and y. This 2D coordinate defines a 2D space.

For example, a triangle can be defined by 3 vertices *V1, V2* and *V3*.
The 3 vertices are connected by 3 edges: *E1, E2* and *E3*.

Refer to Figure 1-4.

Introduction

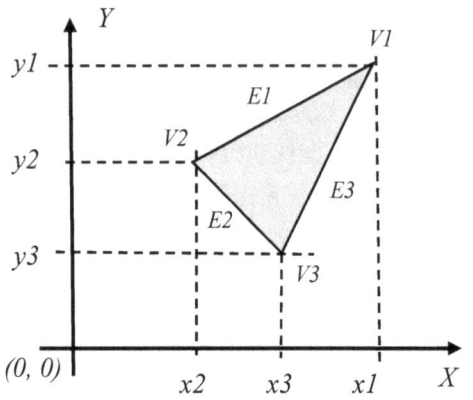

**Figure 1-4 Triangle In 2D Coordinate System**

### 1.2.7 Database Coordinate systems

The image computations are performed in several coordinate systems:
- Database in 3D Coordinate system
- Image in 2D coordinate system

In Figure 1-5, there is a description of 3D coordinate systems in the Gaming Area.

In the three-dimensional coordinate system, the objects need to be rotated using vector and matrix computations. The vectors are defined by the three coordinate components: *(x, y, z)* [20].
The three rotation angles are defined as roll, pitch and yaw, or *(roll, pitch, yaw)*. The 3x3 rotation matrices (*Hr*) are computed from these three angles [23].

Several coordinate systems need to be defined. The gaming area coordinate system, is the reference system *(Xref, Yref, Zref)*.
The coordinate origin for the gaming area, or data base (DB Origin), is at coordinate
  *Vref = (0, 0, 0);*

Since the first RT CGI were designed for aircraft simulation, the viewpoint position is also referred as pilot position. This also defines the plane, or aircraft, position. The viewpoint (or pilot position) is defined as:
  *Vp = (xp, yp, zp);*

The viewed object has a position *Vo* relative to the database origin:
  *Vo = (xo, yo, zo);*

The translated vector, *Vt*, for each object vertex is the difference between the vertex coordinate minus the viewpoint position:
  *Vt = Vo - Vp = (xo, yo, zo) - (xp, yp, zp) = (xo-xp, yo-yp, zo-zp);*

In this figure, the Viewpoint coordinate is defined in aircraft coordinate system, *(Xa, Ya, Za)*.

In this system, the coordinate axes are defined as follows.

- the *Za* coordinate axis points downward,
- the *Ya* axis points in the direction of the right wing
- the *Xa* axis points in the forward direction.

Beside of the Viewpoint position *Vp*, the attitude of the flying aircraft and its coordinate system, *(Xa, Ya, Za)*, must be defined with 3 viewing angles with respect to the fixed data base orientation: such as *roll, pitch and yaw*.

Refer to [20] to [28].

The triangular faces defined by 3 coordinate vertices *Vj = (xj, yj, zj)* relative to the object position. For each face there is also a Face normal vectors *N*, that is used to eliminate back faces.

For each moving object, its attitude and coordinate system, *(Xm, Ym, Zm)*, is also defined with 3 angles (*roll, pitch, yaw*).
There can also be illumination sources defined by a Sun vector, *Vs = (xs, ys, zs)*, and Diffused Illumination, *Id*.

Introduction

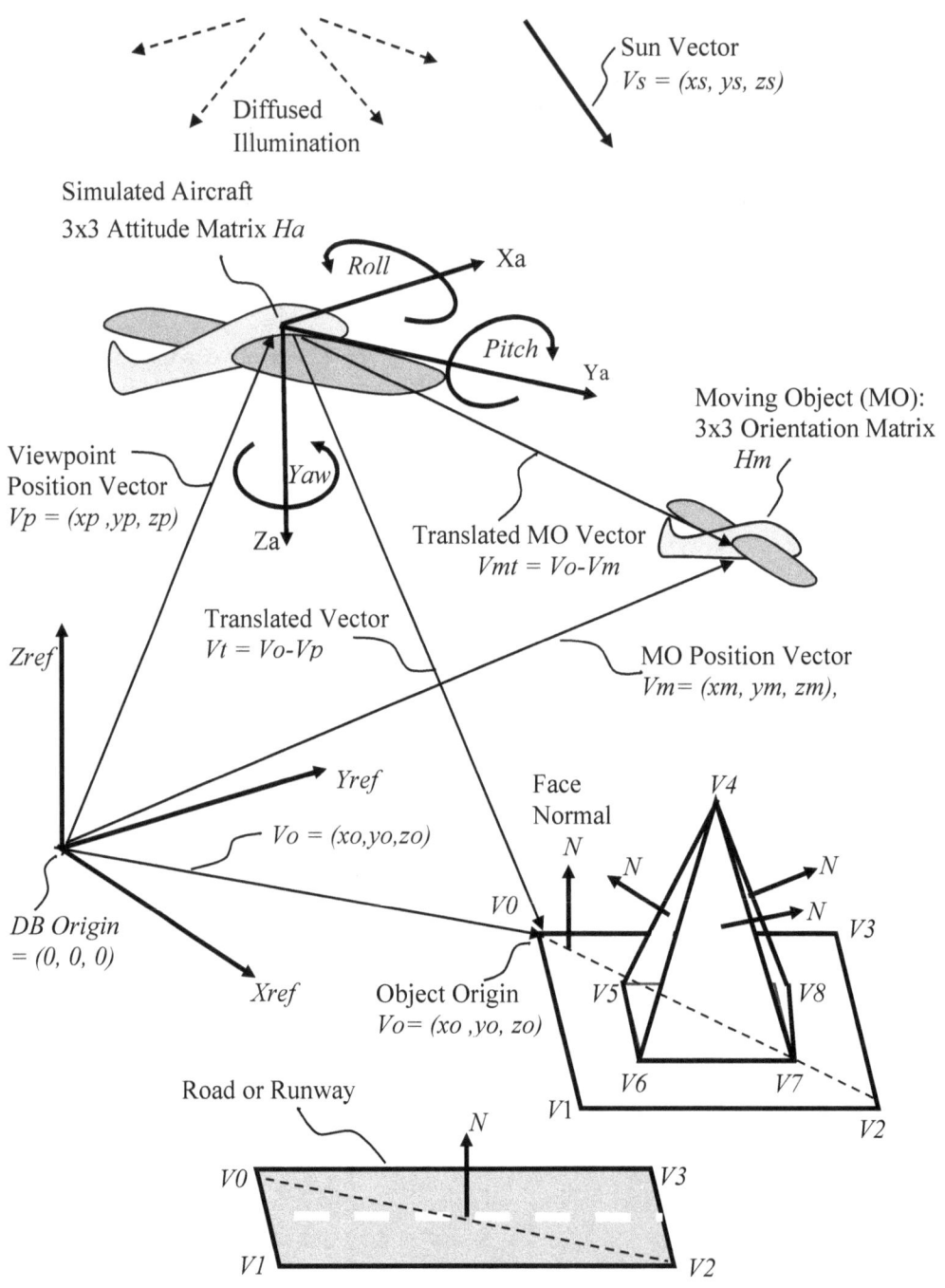

**Figure 1-5 Gaming Area and Coordinate Systems**

# 1.3 Geometry Transformations in 3D and 2D Spaces

## 1.3.1 Objects in 3D Space

The CGI processing deals with objects models defined in 3D space with surfaces made of adjacent triangles. The objects in the vicinity of the observer are stored in an Active Data base. Although general polygons can be processed, the most widely used models use triangles or meshes of triangles. Each object in the data base is defined with an object origin, a list of faces made of triangle and polygon vertices.

In this book, I deal exclusively with 3D images resulting from triangle processing. Each triangle is defined by a sequence of 3 vertices with $(x, y, z)$ coordinates. Triangles can be single triangles or triangle meshes [15]. Triangle meshes can be organized as strips or fans [14].

Refer to Figure 1-6, Triangle, Strip and Fan.

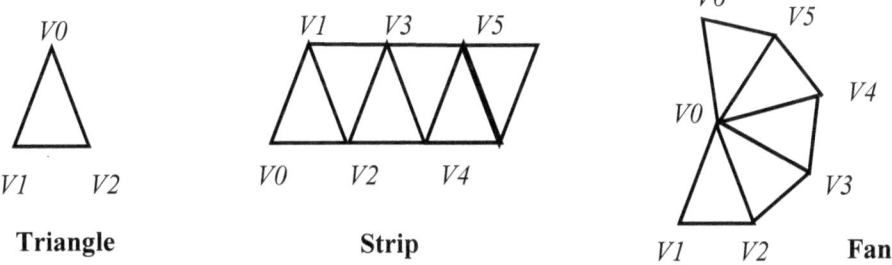

**Figure 1-6 Triangle, Strip and Fan**

## 1.3.2 Object Transformations of from 3D to 2D

The CGI systems consist of 3 main processing blocks:

- Geometric Processor (ex: Frame Calculator in Link DIG systems)
- Image Renderer (ex: Scanline Computer in Link DIG systems)
- Image Display System (ex: Video Generators in Link DIG systems)

The data base objects are defined in 3D space as surfaces made of adjacent triangles. The objects in the vicinity of the observer are stored in an Active Data base. The surfaces of these objects are made of many adjacent triangles. Each triangle is defined by a sequence of 3 vertices with $(x, y, z)$ coordinates.

### *3D Geometric Processor*

The first step in CGI is to access the triangle data from the Active Data Base. The data base consists of faces made of triangles in 3D space. Each triangle is defined by 3 vertices in 3D space. In the Geometric Processor, each triangle is defined by three vertices $V=(x, y, z)$ in the data base. These triangles are first processed with operations in 3D space, including Translations, Rotations and Clipping.

Refer to Figure1-7, 'Vertex Translation'.

Introduction

Refer to Figure1-8, 'Vertex Rotation'.

Refer to Figure1-9, 'Polygon Clipping.

Also, refer to [23]: Rotations in Three-Dimensions, Rotation Matrix, and [24] to [28].

After the 3D operations, the triangles are projected onto a 2D image plane. The Clipping operation makes sure that all the projected vertices are inside of the 2D image.

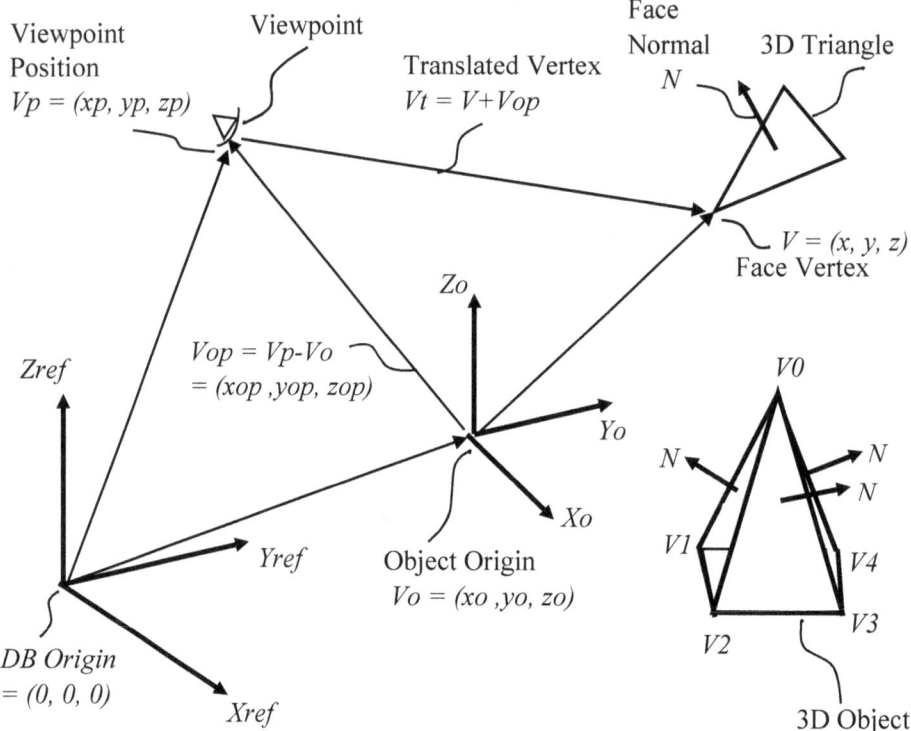

**Figure 1-7 Vertex Translation**

Introduction

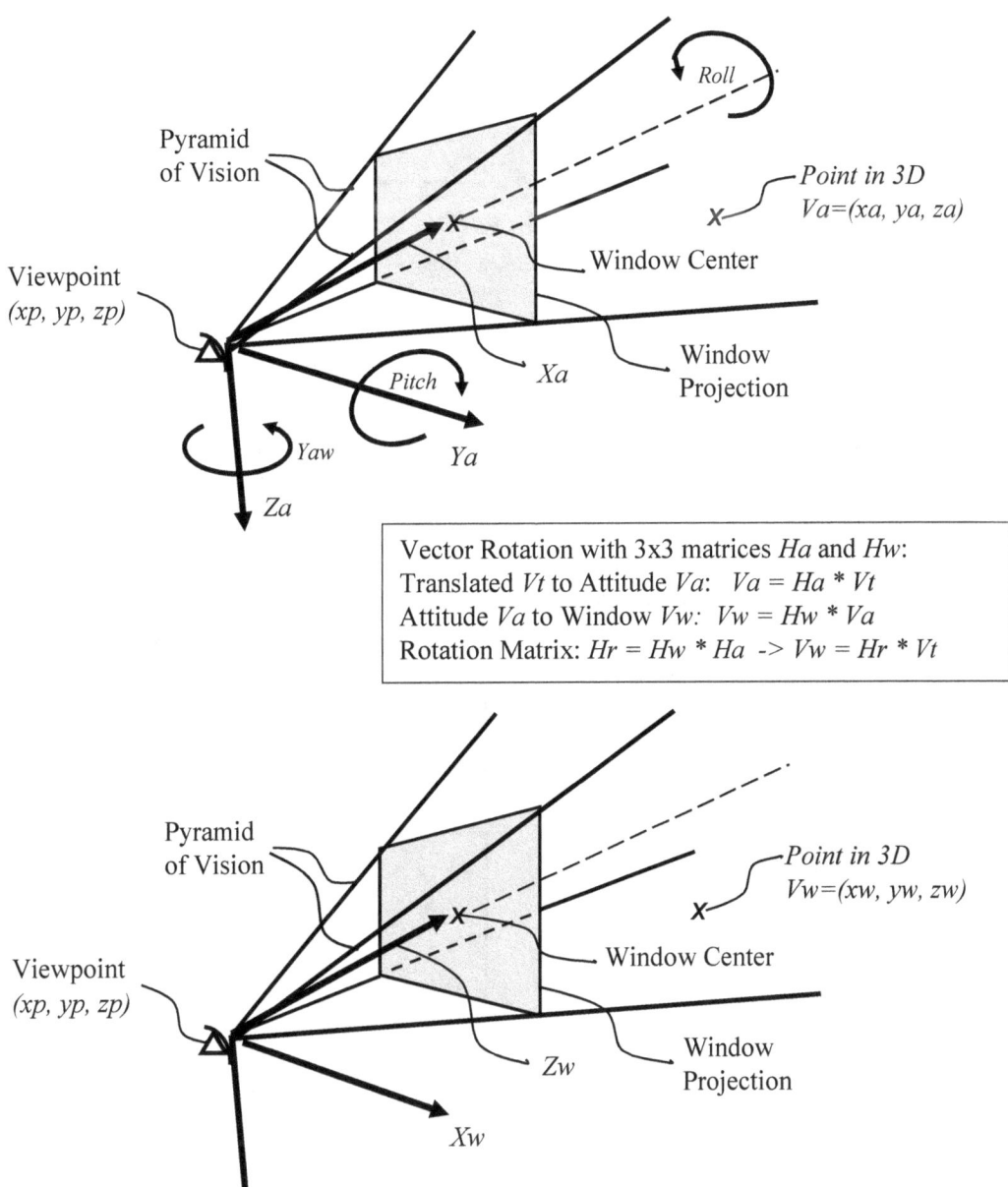

**Figure 1-8 Vertex Vt Rotated into Window Coordinate**

Introduction

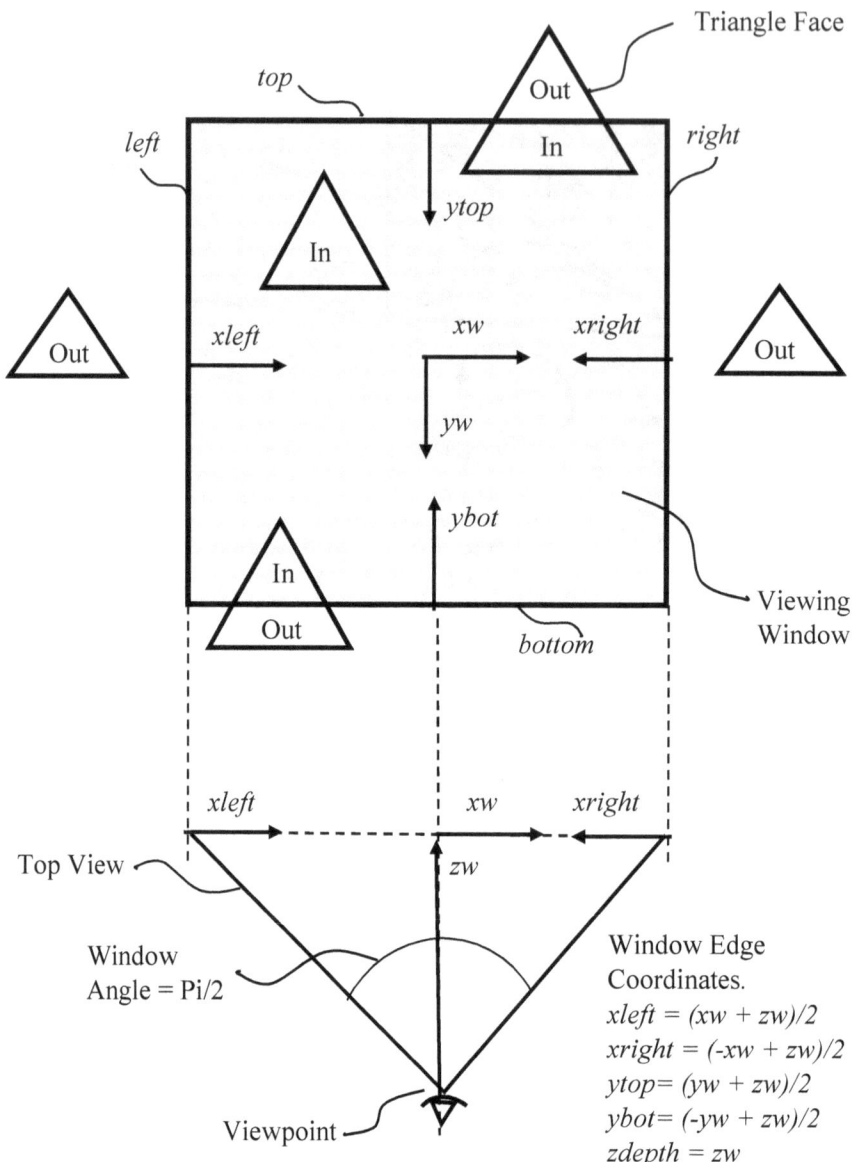

**Figure 1-9 Window Clipping**

Introduction

## 1.3.3 2D Geometric Processor

After several geometric transformations in 3D space, the triangle vertices are projected onto the 2D window space for triangle processing and image rendering. In the 2D image space, the computations are performed in *(Xi, Yi)* image coordinates. Each projected triangle is defined in 2D space with 3 vertices and 3 edges connecting the vertices. The 2D geometric Processor (Face Boundary Calculator in the DIG) generate edge slope and gradients for Image Rendering.

Refer to Figure1-10, Triangle in 2D coordinates

Following the projection of vertices onto the window image plane, the triangle vertices are processed in 2D space. The parameters for the triangle edges are computed.

The projected triangles consist of 3 vertices and edges connecting theses vertices in *(xi, yi)* image coordinates. Each pair of vertices is connected by an edge with a slope *dx/dy* or *dy/dx*.
The output of the Geometric Processor consists of 2D triangles defined by 3 vertices and 3 edges with color and other attributes.

Refer to Figure1-11, 'Triangle In 2D Image Coordinate'.

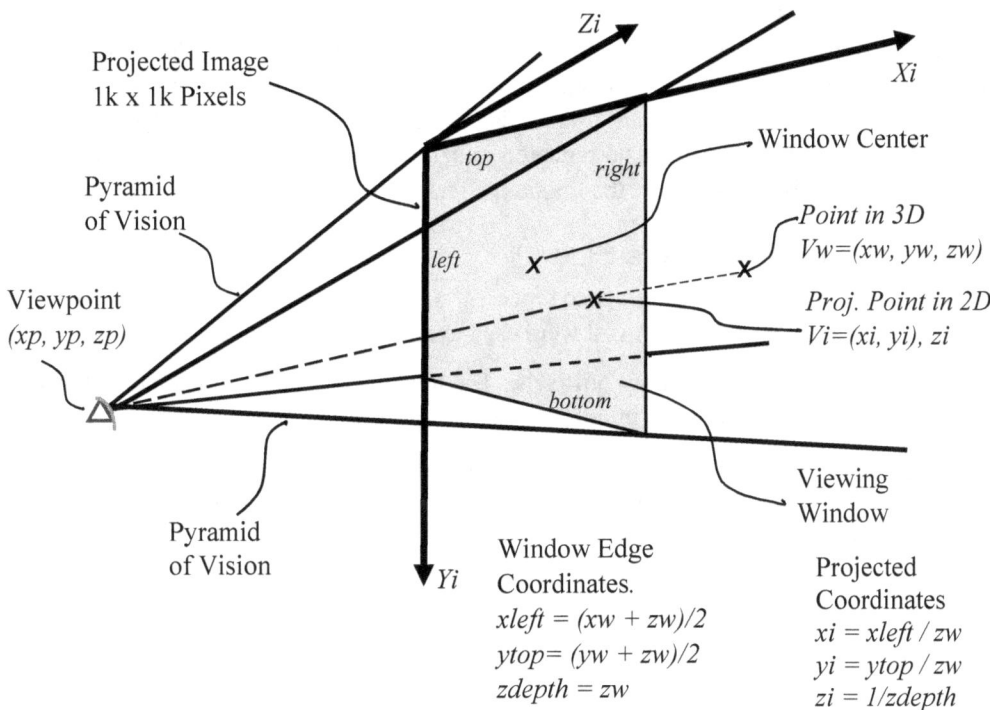

**Figure 1-10 Projection from 3D to 2D**

New Area-Based Anti-Aliasing for CGI

Introduction

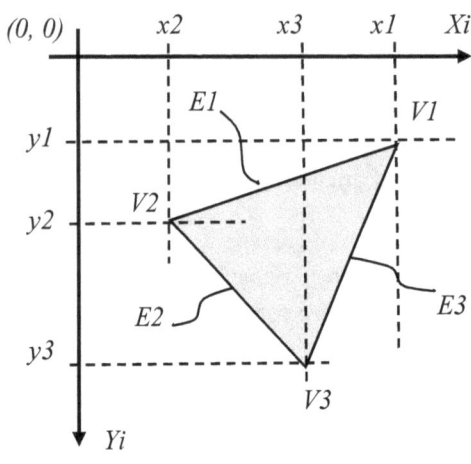

**Figure 1-11 Triangle In 2D Image Coordinates *(Xi, Yi)***

## 1.4 Image Rendering

Following the geometric processing in 2D, triangles are processed by an Image Renderer. The task of the Image Renderer is to draw 2D triangles and maps them into Pixels. Implementation of the Image Renderer can differ. While each triangle is processed separately, all the triangles are put back together to form a 2D image. The rendered image is stored into a Frame Buffer. For each Pixel, there corresponds an address in the Frame Buffer.

### 1.4.1 Image Plane and Image Size

The early approach for CGI rendering was to process triangles with a single sample point per Pixel. Later on, multiple sample points per Pixel were used to reduce aliasing effects.

These 2D images consist of a 2D array of Pixels. The image size is determined by the horizontal and vertical resolution of the display monitor. Refer to Figure 1-12.

The 2D images consist of *PixMax* Pixels horizontally and by *SLMax* Scanlines vertically.
Each image Pixel is of size *1x1* and has a uniform color defined by 3 color components, Red, Green and Blue *(R, G, B)*.

Introduction

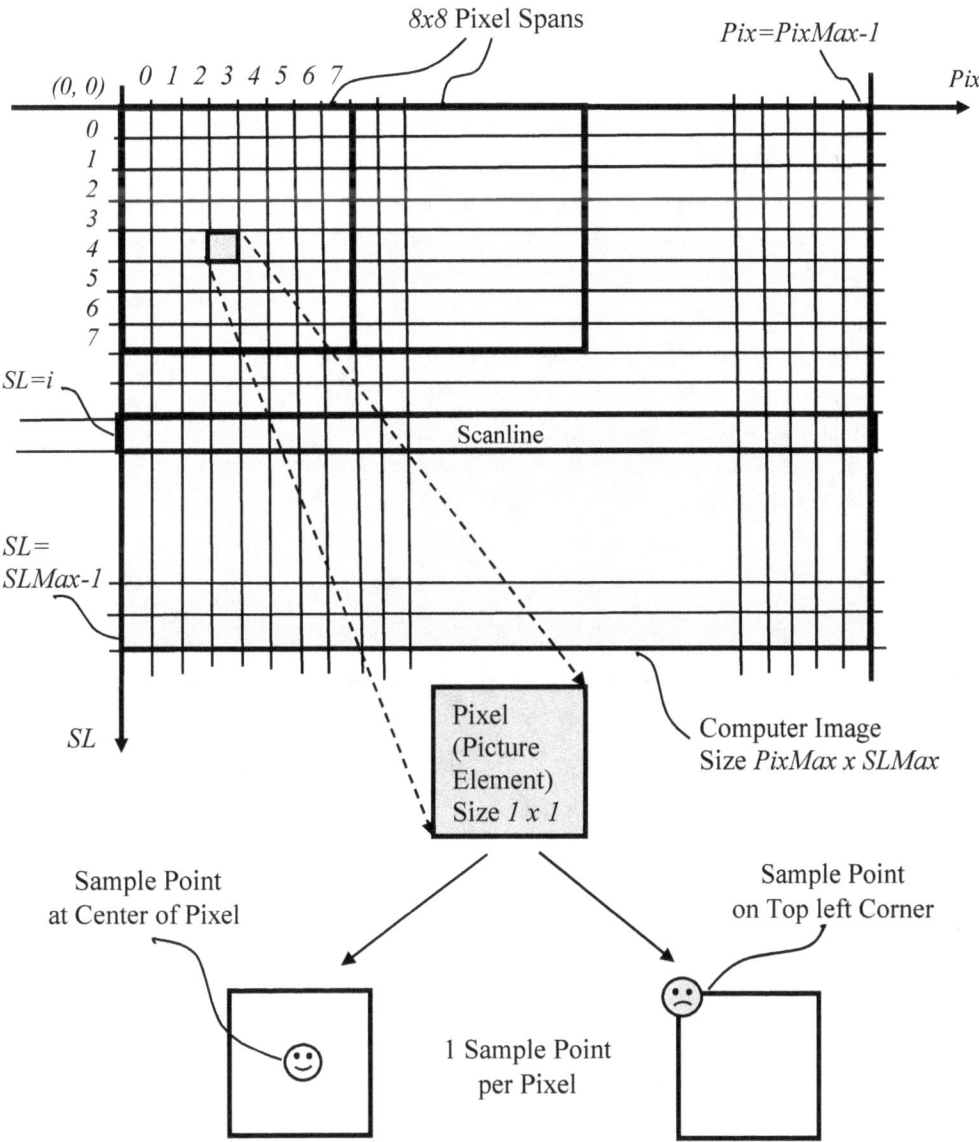

**Figure 1-12 Image Size of *PixMax* Pixels by *SLMax* Scanlines**

For the purpose of transferring the image data or accessing the image data in memory, Pixels are organized horizontally from left to right into SLs. Each SL is a linear array of Pixels. SLs are organized vertically from top to bottom into a two-dimensional array that form the image. So, the image is a linear array of SLs.

Introduction

For the purpose of processing, the image is sometimes organized into small square areas of size 8x8 or 16x16 Pixels, referred to as Tiles or two-dimensional Spans. For image processing, such as image rendering in CGI or data compression for HDTV, there are advantages when the image is decomposed into Tiles.

## 1.4.2 Image Coordinates

The image coordinates are defined by two axes with *x* and *y* coordinates, as follows. Depending on the context, the values on the coordinate axes can be defined with fixed point or with integer numbers. Refer to Figure 1-13.

- Horizontal axis from left to right, using:
  - integer Pixel (*Pix*) coordinate (between *0* and *PixMax*) or
  - fixed-point *xi* coordinate (between *0.0* and *1.0*).
- Vertical axis from top to bottom, using:
  - integer Scanline (*SL*) coordinate (between 0 and *SLMax*) or
  - fixed-point *yi* coordinate (between *0.0* and *1.0*).

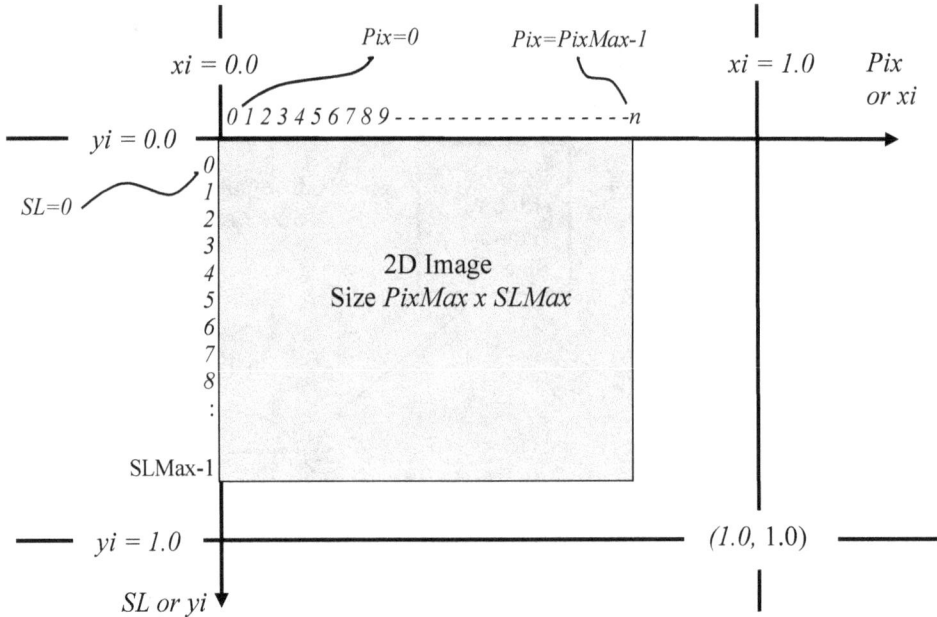

**Figure 1-13 *(Pix, SL)* and *(xi, yi)* Image Coordinates**

In the figure, the image is represented as a two-dimensional array of Pixels of integer size:
*PixMax * SLMax*

As can be seen in these figures, there are 2 image coordinates units on each axis:
- integer (*Pix* or *SL*) coordinates and
- fixed-point (*xi* or *yi*) coordinates

In the Image Display system, the image is retrieved from the Frame Buffer using *(Pix, SL)* coordinates and converted from digital to analog. The image it then displayed on Video Monitors or other image display systems

## *Integer (Pix or SL) coordinates*

*Pix* and *SL* are integer numbers that define Pixel positions in the 2D image.
The horizontal integer coordinate *Pix* ranges from *0* to *PixMax-1*.
The vertical integer coordinate *SL* ranges from *0* to *SLMax-1*.
*Pix* and *SL* Coordinates are used to access the Pixel data inside of the *Pix* and *SL* boundaries. They are also used to access the memory locations in the image buffer.

The range of Pix and SL variables depends on the horizontal and vertical range.

- For ranges up to *511*, they are 9bit integers.
- For ranges up to *1023*, they are 10bit integers.
- For ranges up to *2047*, they are 11bit integers

## *Fixed-point (x or y) coordinates*

The image coordinates *(xi, yi)* represent projection points in the image plane.

For example, for an *800x600* image, the fixed-point coordinates will fit within a *Pix* and *SL* range of *0* to *1024*. This corresponds to *1kx1k Pixels* and can be represented with 10bit *(Pix, SL)* coordinates. For each point in the image, the *(Pix, SL)* coordinates are obtained by multiplying the *(xi, yi)* coordinates by *2\*\*10=1024* then converted to integer values.

$(Pix, SL) = ( integer(1024*xi), integer(1024*yi) )$

For the *(xi, yi)* coordinates, a 16-bit fixed-point format is suitable for an image of *1k x1k Pixels* and an accuracy of 1/16Pixel.
This 16-bit signed fixed-point format for *(xi, yi)* coordinates is:
 *sb.bbbbbbbbbb'bbbb*
where 's' represents the sign bit and 'b' represent a bit. The last 4 characters '*bbbb*' represent a Pixel fraction with Subpixel resolution.
The fixed-point format for Pixel coordinates *(xp, yp)* is: *s.bbbb*
The integer format for Subpixel coordinates *(xs, ys)* is: *bbbb*

## *Conversion from Fixed Point (xi, yi) to Integer (Pix, SL)*

The *(Pix, SL)* coordinates are obtained by shifting the point position 10 places to the right and truncating the 4 bits of fraction.

The values of *xi* and *yi* fixed point numbers can be defined in a range from *-1.0* to *+2.0*.
This range covers a 3x3 image area.
Only the values between *0.0 to 1.0* can be inside of the image.
The values outside of the image are used for interpolation. The portions of triangles that reside outside of the displayed image need to be clipped. Refer to Clipping patents [105][132].

Introduction

## 1.4.3 Rendering Triangles

During rendering, triangle surface defined by vertices and edges is mapped onto image Pixels. For a triangle to be displayed inside of a Pixel, at least one sample point has to be defined inside of that Pixel. In the simpler case, only one sample point is defined inside of each Pixel. Refer to Single Sample Point Selection in Figure 1-14.

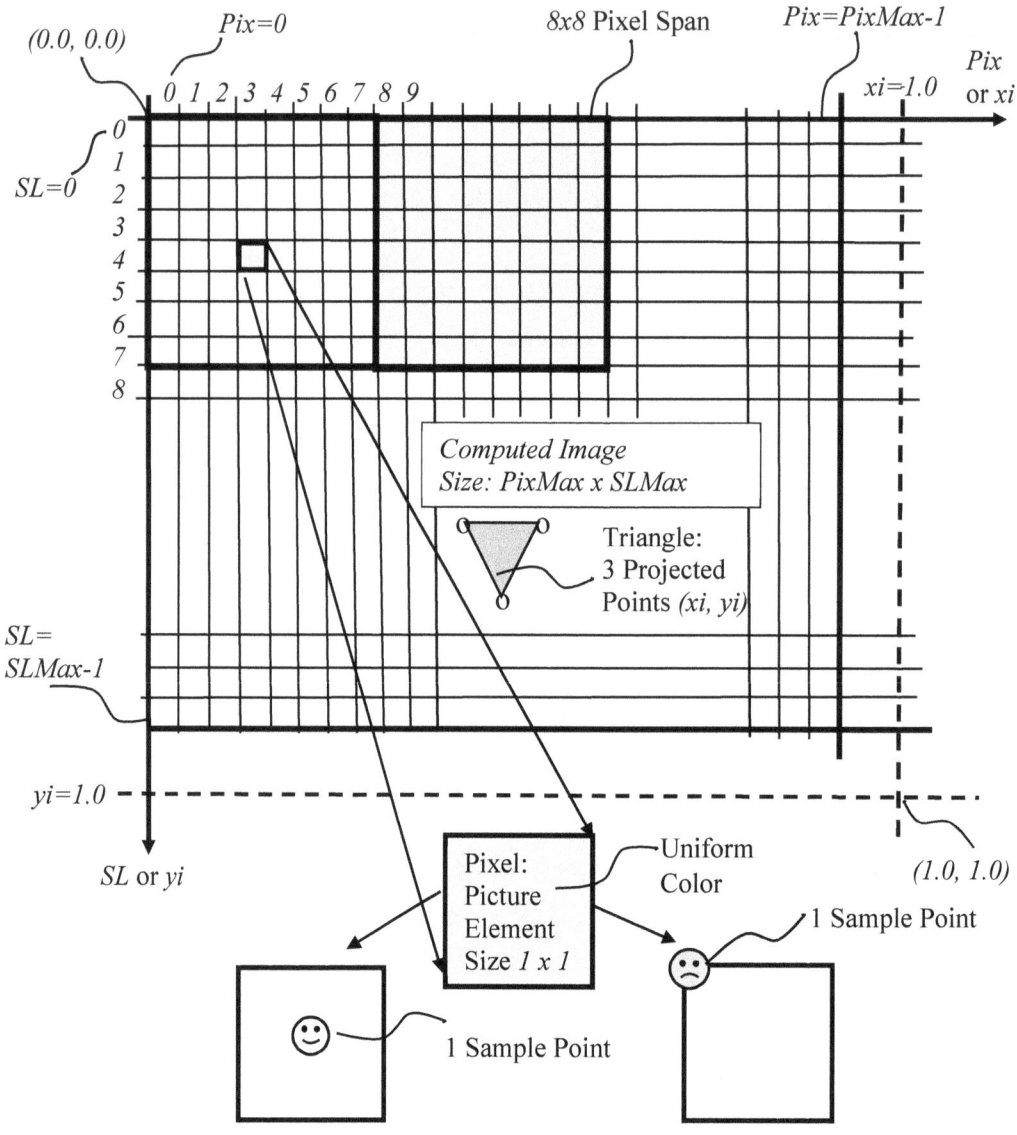

**Figure 1-14 Single Sample Point Selection**

Introduction

When only one Sample Point is used to compute an image, this result into aliasing effects consisting of jaggies (jagged edges), edge crawling and face popping. In order to reduce aliasing effects, several Sample Point should be used inside of Pixels.

In this Figure, there are 2 approaches for selecting a Pixel sample point:
- On the left side, Sample Point at the 'Center' of the Pixel.
- On the right side, Sample Point on the 'Top-Left Corner' of the Pixel.

## 1.4.4 Selecting the Pixel Sample Point

Most of the image rendering algorithms use only one sample point to select whether a triangle is displayed on each Pixel. For real time applications, there are 2 dominant Application Programming Interfaces [76]:

- OpenGL (originally from the proprietary 'Graphics Language' developed by Silicon Graphics)
- Direct3D (from Microsoft).

These application interfaces provide functions to process triangles in 3D and 2D space, and to render the polygon onto the 2D image. But these interfaces ignored antialiasing and decided to select the sample point on the 'Top Left Corner' of the Pixel element.

### *Single Sample Point Selection*

There are two main definitions for selecting a single sample point inside of a Pixel.

Refer to Figure 1-15.

Sample Point
at Center of Pixel:
"happy"

Sample Point
on Top Left corner:
"unhappy"

**Figure 1-15 Sample Point Selection**

I strongly disagree with the Sample Point selection on the 'Top-Left Corner'. For me, the Sample Point should be at the 'Center of the Pixel', for the following reasons.

### *Sample Point on top left corner*

There are disadvantages when selecting the Top Left Corner. It is the result of arbitrary decisions according to the wrong reasons. This is why the selected point on the right side of the figure is unhappy.

Introduction

I can think of three main reasons for selecting the top left corner of Pixels as reference point.

- One of the reasons for selecting the Sample Point on the top left corner is the results of Rounding or Truncating the results of the projection.
- Another reason is the legacy of 2D graphics. Early implementation of 3D graphics used the same approach as used in the 2D graphics games like Pack Man and other 2D graphics game consoles. For these 2D graphics images, the top left corner made sense because Pixels were mapped into memory locations with integer addresses.
- The top left corner is also a legacy of early 3D graphics images using Z-buffer. Because of the memory limitation and cost for Z-buffers, these images did not process Subpixels for antialiasing. The Pixels were only accessed with integer numbers. In the Z-buffer, they are mapped into the *(Pix, SL)* memory addresses used to access the Z-buffer.

Selecting the sample point on the Top Left Corner results in limitations for rendering in 3D graphics.

As I mention in my previous book, 'New Fixed-Point Math for Logic Design' [6], 'Rounding or Truncating' have been the cause of many problems when doing computations in 3D graphics. In this book there are several examples of problems that can be prevented by applying this 'New Fixed-Point Math' approach. Also, I have discovered the 'Area-Based AA' algorithm while applying these fixed-point math concepts.

Later on, Sample Points inside of the Pixels were used for anti-aliasing. For example, an AA technique that uses 'Bed of Nail' (BON) as sample points inside of a Pixel provides good results. This 'BON' approach was used by the early designers of RT CGI since the 1980s. It uses 8 sample points (for example) arranged in a semi-random fashion inside of the Pixel.

### *Sample Point at Center of Pixel*

In 3D graphics, the displayed information consists of real numbers, resulting from the projection of triangles from 3D space onto a 2D screen image. In the displayed image, there are Pixels, Scanlines and projected points. In the 2D image space, the Image Renderer maps the triangles onto Pixels defined in *Pix* and *SL* coordinates. After rendering, the Pixel data is stored in a temporary image buffer using Pixel *(Pix, SL)* coordinates before being sent to the Display system.

For the purpose of computations, the *(xi, yi)* coordinates can be represented with fixed point numbers (instead of floating points). The edge data can be provided in fixed-point format *(xi, yi)*, so that the Pixel geometric information can be processed with Subpixel resolution.

The projected points reside inside of Pixels limited by *Pix* and *SL* boundaries. For the purpose of AA computations, in the area inside of the Pixel the Subpixel positions can be defined with signed 5-bit Pixel coordinates *(xp, yp)=(0.bbbb, 0.bbbb)*, or unsigned 4-bit Subpixel coordinates *(xs, ys)=( (bbbb, bbbb)*.

The displayed points from the computed image consists of **real numbers** that **cannot** be projected onto the **integer numbers** of the Pixel and Scanline grid. When several Sample Points per Pixel are used, the average of all the points within the Pixel boundary converge to a point at the center of the Pixel.

The sample point at the center of the Pixel represents the average of a large number of sample points inside of the Pixel. It is also the center of gravity of the Pixel. This is similar to computations in mechanic, where the motion equations apply to the center of gravity of objects.

The Pixel (*Pix*) and Scanlines (*SL*) integer numbers define a Display Grid on the 2D Image. Each Pixel on the image represents a *1.0x1.0* area inside of Grid Lines. The Grid Lines define thresholds that defined where the projected points transition from Pixel to Pixel. No point that is projected from 3D space onto the 2D image can result into a pure integer point on the Display screen.

There are many advantages for selecting the reference point at the center of the Pixel. This is why the happy Sample Point (on the left) in the previous figure is smiling.

## *Example of Mapping Image Pixels onto Display Screen.*

As I have explained in my previous book, the center of the Pixel represents the average of all the points inside of the Pixel. Rounding or Truncation should not be considered. For more information, refer to my previous book [6]:
'New Fixed-Point Math for Logic Design'

On a Display Screen representation, the lines that represent Pixel and Scanline boundaries have no width. They have integer values and represent boundaries or threshold.

On the other hand, the Pixels that fill the area between these boundaries are the result of projection computations with fixed point numbers with fractions. In order for a fixed point to equate an integer value, it would have a fraction consisting of an infinite number of 0's, which is not practical.

On the image plane, the integer Scanlines and integer Pixels form a grid. The grid lines have no widths, because they represent boundaries (or transition thresholds). So, the Pixel areas cannot touch the integer threshold on the grid lines. Figure 1-16 shows a simplified view of a Pixel grid and Pixel area on a displayed image.

Introduction

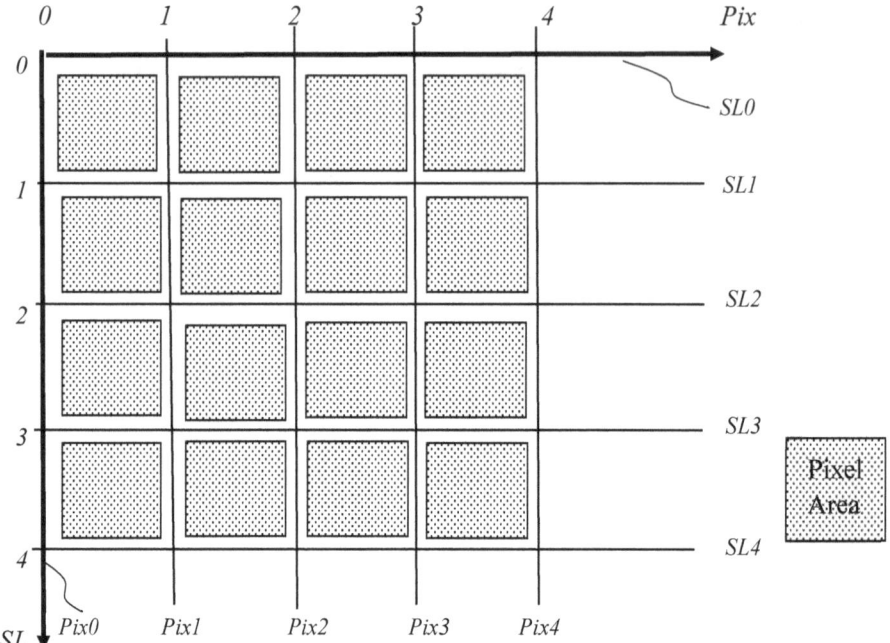

**Figure 1-16 Pixels Located Inside of *SL* and *Pix* Grid**

The Pixel areas form square Tiles surrounded by the grid lines. The Tiles do not touch the gridlines. When the polygon edges are traversing the Tiles, the rendering algorithm compute their intersections with Pixel boundaries and do the processing with fixed-point *averaged* numbers. The intersections of edges with Tile boundaries consist of fixed-point numbers.

When the image is rendered, the Pixels are filled with the computed color components. This simplified view of the image plane represents how the Pixels should be rendered when the edges are processed during the edge traversing phase. After rendering, each Pixel has only one uniform color.

Note that in this example, the grid lines represent static data, while the Pixel information represents dynamic data.

### 1.4.5 Pixel Sampling with Jaggies
*Single Sample Point per Pixel*

When rendering a triangle, the simple approach is to select a single Sample Point inside of Pixels. When the surface of the triangle covers the Sample Point, the color of that triangle is assigned to the whole Pixel. Although this approach can produce decent images, one of the drawbacks is that the assignment of only one triangular color to square Pixels results in aliasing artifacts (jaggies and crawling) in the computed image.

Refer to Figure 1-17 where the color of sample points is assigned to the uniform color of Pixels.

Introduction

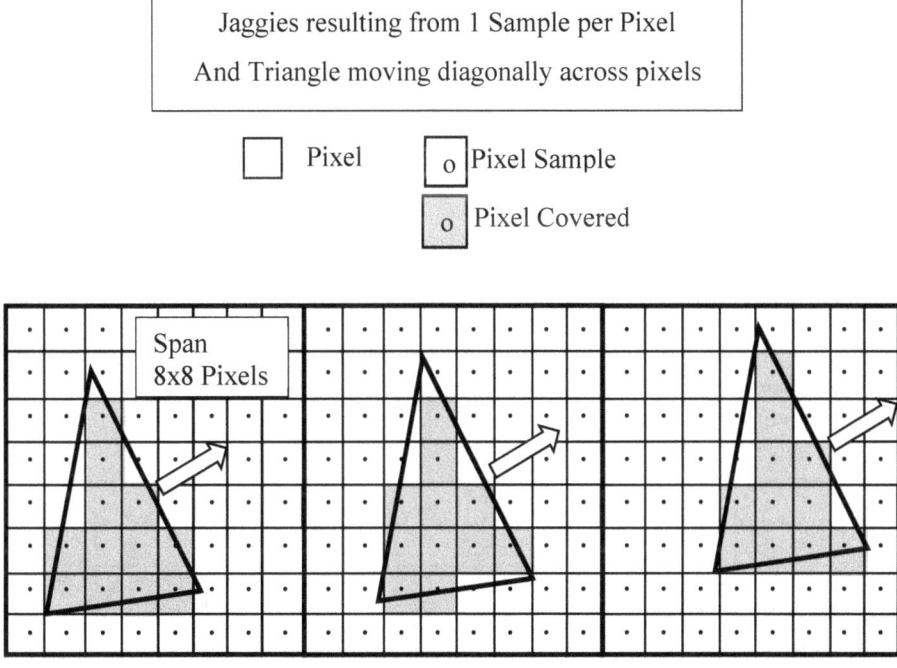

**Figure 1-17 Assign Color Using 1 Sample Point per Pixel**

In this figure, there are 3 identical triangles inside 8x8 Pixel area. From the left to the right triangle, each triangle is displaced by 1 Pixel horizontally and by 1/3 Pixel vertically. The shape of Pixel coverage from left to right shows the effect of crawling.

### *Reducing the Jaggies with Subpixels*

The distracting effect of the jaggies can be reduced by mixing the colors of 2 adjacent triangles in Pixels. In the image in Figure 1-18, the partially covered Pixels are blended with the back ground when the triangle covers between 1/3 and 2/3 of the Pixel area. This image shows the improvement when Subpixel information is used to improve the image quality. The application of Subpixel coverage is referred to a 'edge smoothing', or 'anti-aliasing'.

As a polygon edge moves gradually across a Pixel, the mixed color will result in N incremental steps (N>1). In this document, the Pixel is divided into N Subpixel areas, where N can be 4 or 8. When using N steps, the color of the Pixel changes gradually in N steps increments. With N=4 steps, there is a good improvement over single point sampling. With N=8 steps, there is another noticeable improvement in image quality.

Introduction

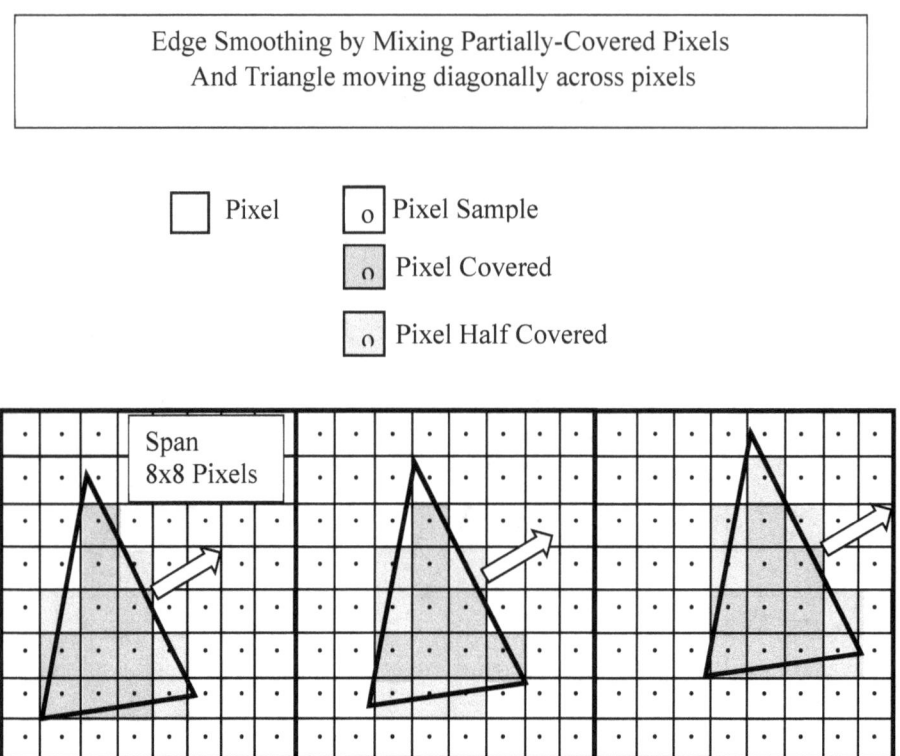

Figure 1-18 Mix Color of Half-Covered Pixels

# 1.5 Color Space

There are several formats for defining colors components in the Color Space. Refer to [45].
For CGI, the color computations are usually done in the *ARGB* format *(Alpha, Red, Green, Blue)*.
*Alpha* is a 4$^{th}$ component that specifies transparency.
For Display Monitors, the PC VGA adapters use the *RGB* format.
For Television, for practical reasons, the colors are defined in the *YCbCr* format.

## 1.5.1 RGB in Color Space

For CGI, the color computations are usually done in the *ARGB* format *(Alpha, Red, Green, Blue)*.
For Display Monitors, the PC VGA adapters use the *RGB* format. Color values are stored as binary numbers consisting of *0's and 1's*. For example, it takes 8 bits to store values between *0* and *255*.

ARGB Color Components
For processing, the *(A, R, G, B)* components can be defined with 16, 24 or 32 bits (binary digits):

- 32 bits with *(A[8], R[8], G[8], B[8])*, where *A* is the alpha transparency.
- 24 bits *(R[8], G[8], B[8])*
- 16 bits *(R[5], G[6], B[5])*

For 32-bit color, the components are defined by 8-bit integer values ranging from *0* to *255*.

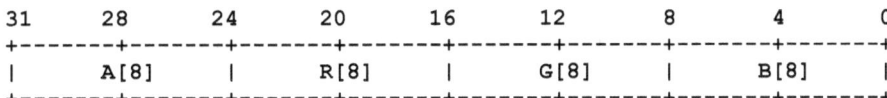

For the 16-bit format:
- *R[5]* and *B[5]* range from 0 to 31.
- *G[6]* Ranges from 0 to 63.

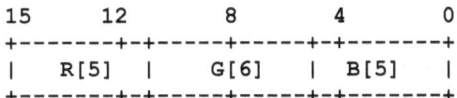

In case of the 16 bits format, the *Green* component has an extra bit because the human eye is more sensitive to the *Green* than the *Red* or *Blue* colors.

When using *RGB*, each Pixel color is defined by four *ARGB* or three *RGB* components. Refer to Figure 1-19.

Introduction

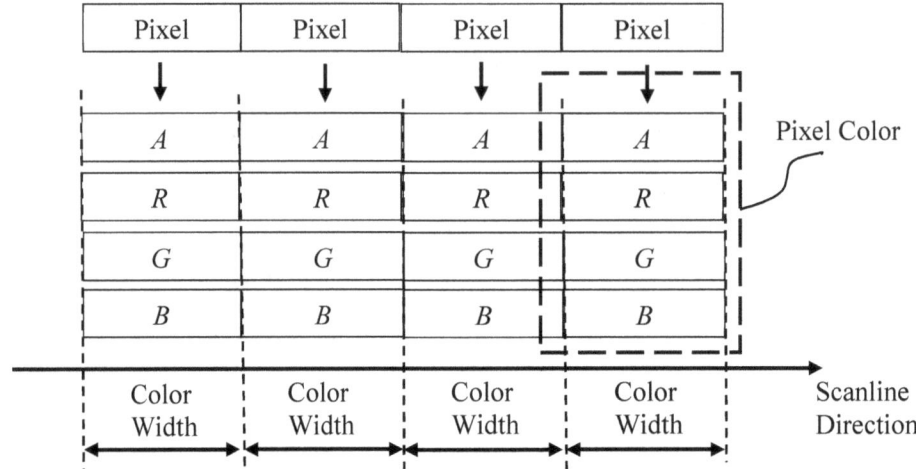

**Figure 1-19 Pixels along SL with *ARGB* or *RGB* Color Components**

### 1.5.2 *YCbCr* in Color Space

For Television, for practical reasons, the colors are defined in the *YCbCr* format.

*YCbCr* Color Components

Refer to Figure 1-20

In the YCbCR format, the *Y* component represents the *Gray* shade.
- The *Cb* represents the *Blue* contribution added to the *Gray* shade.
- The *Cr* represents the *Red* contribution added to the *Gray* shade.

There are advantages to use the *YCbCr* format for TV. In the *YCbCr* format, the *Y* component represents the Intensity or Gray shade. The *CbCr* components represent the color hue in the TV image. Because the eyes are more sensitive to color intensity *Y* than the color hue, the *CbCr* information can be shared between 2 adjacent Pixels.

Another advantage for TV is that the *YCbCr* format can be used for Black & White TV, as well as Color TV. For Black & White TV, the image can be displayed with the Y component only.

For a practical point of view, when you need to adjust the contrast and brightness in a TV set, you are modifying only the *Y* component. When you adjust the color, you are modifying the *Cb* and *Cr* components.

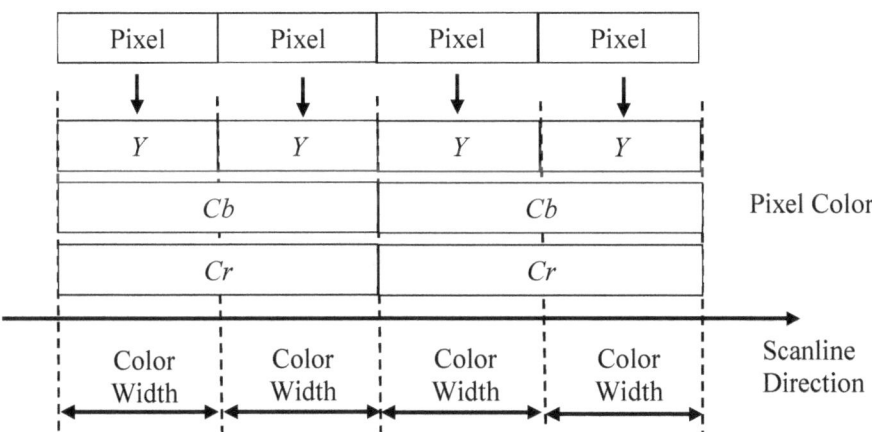

**Figure 1-20 Pixels along SL with *YCbCr* Color Format for Television**

## 1.5.3 Color Space and Conversion

The *RGB* and *YCbCr* components are related by the following equations. Depending on the application, these equations can vary slightly.

Refer to [45].

*RGB to Gray Conversion*:
  $Y = 0.299R + 0.587G + 0.114B$

*RGB to YCbCr Color Conversion*
  $Y = 0.299\ R + 0.587\ G + 0.114B$
  $Cb = (B-Y) * 0.564 = -0.168935\ R - 0.331665G + 0.50059\ B$
  $Cr = (R-Y) * 0.713 = -0.499813\ R - 0.418531\ G + 0.081282\ B$

*YCbCr to RGB Color Conversion*
  $R = Y + 1.403\ Cr$
  $G = Y - 0.344\ Cb - 0.714\ Cr$
  $B = Y + 1.773\ Cb$

In the book Dirty Pixels from *Jim Blinn* [3] (Chapter 8), there is a simpler set of equations for *RGB to YCbCr*. Refer to Figure 1-21.

Introduction

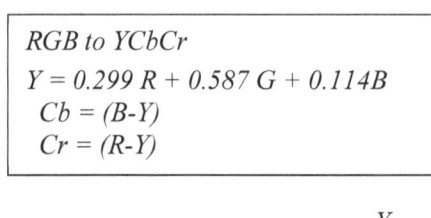

*RGB to YCbCr*
*Y = 0.299 R + 0.587 G + 0.114B*
*Cb = (B-Y)*
*Cr = (R-Y)*

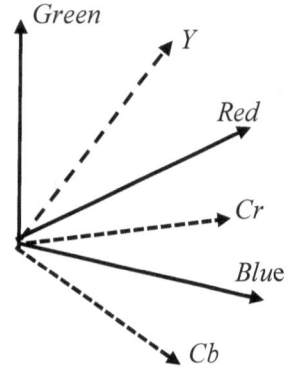

3D View of
*Rd, Green and Blue*

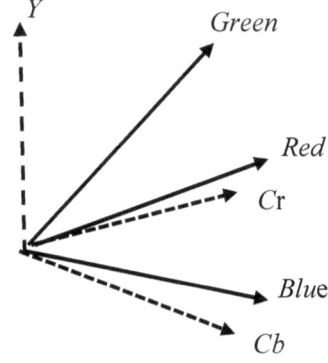

Color Coordinates Converted into
*Y Cb Cr* Coordiantes

**Figure 1-21 *RGB* and *YCbCr* in Color Space**

# Chapter 2 **Aliasing**

The early computer-generated images were static rendering and usually had only one Sample Point per Pixel. Edges of the rendered triangles had stairsteps. This resulted into aliasing effects, referred to as 'Jaggies'. Many algorithms got developed to remove the Jaggies.

Some of the analytic techniques in this chapter might be new to the reader and difficult to understand in the first reading. But do not get discouraged. For the first reading, just scan through the titles and figures.

Also refer to the cited reference numbers shown in brackets like [xx]. After going back and reading a few times, you'll be surprised that you can understand most of it.

## 2.1 Aliasing and Anti-Aliasing

### 2.1.1 Aliasing

In CGI, television and movies, Aliasing is also referred to as: Jaggies, Face Popping, Edge Crawling, Narrow Faces Breakup, Moiré patterns and Distracting Artifacts [61].

*Jaggies and Edge Crawling*

Jaggies and Edge crawling occur when polygon edges transition vertically or horizontally and jump from Pixel to Pixel. Jaggies appear in static and dynamic images, when only one Sample Point per Pixel is used during rendering.

*Face popping*

Face popping in-and-out of scenes occurs when some dimensions of displayed polygon faces are smaller than the Pixel size. Face popping also occurs when new polygons are introduced into a scene, or removed from a scene.

*Moiré patterns*

Repetitive patterns in CGI can cause aliasing and Moiré patterns.
Moiré patterns aliasing occurs when using polygons to render repetitive patterns.
When modeling repetitive patterns in CGI, aliasing can be avoided by using texture maps [32].
Texture mapping can display repetitive patterns using several levels of resolution.

*Distracting Artifacts*

All these effects are considered as Distracting Artifacts.

### 2.1.2 Anti-Aliasing and Edge Smoothing

Anti-Aliasing (AA) consists of the methods that are used to prevent, or at least, minimize the unwanted effects of Aliasing. Such methods include Subpixel processing, Edge smoothing and also image filtering. Several methods for AA are presented in this book. .These methods are related to Digital Signal Processing.

Aliasing

### 2.1.3 Digital Signal Processing
When processing electronic signals, there are 2 kinds of signals: **analog** and **digital** signals.

*Analog Signals*

In nature, the signals are usually analog continuous signals. In the earlier days of electronics, these signals were processed with analog electronic circuits. A sound amplifier is a good example of analog circuit. The sound is converted to an analog electric signal by a microphone. It is amplified by an analog amplifier with a volume control to adjust loudness. Finally, it is converted back to sound by a speaker.

One of the problems with analog circuits, is that they have limited accuracy precision and may require frequent tuning. In the earlier TV, the circuits were all analog. They usually required periodical adjustments referred as 'tuning'.

With the advances in integrated circuit the encoding and decoding of TV signals have been replaced with digital circuits. At the input, the signals are converted from analog to digital (A2D). The A2D conversion consists of sampling the continuous analog signals and converting the measurements into sequences of binary numbers. After digital processing, the digital signals are converted back to analog signals with digital to analog converters (D2A).

*Digital Signals*

In CGI, the image data consist of digital signals consisting of sequences of binary numbers, that is numbers in base 2 consisting only of sequences of *1's* and *0's*.

Although these numbers could also be represented with decimal numbers in base10, inside of a computer, all the processing is done with binary numbers. Refer to later chapter '*Inside the Binary World*'.

Digital signals are represented with binary numbers and they accuracy is only limited by the number of bits that represent these signals. For processing TV signals, the number of bits to represent these signals is in the order of 10 to 12 bits. This corresponds to an accuracy of 1/1024 to 1/4096. As an example of digital signals, the sound and images are captured and recorded on CD and DVD compact discs. Another advantage of digital signal is that they can be compressed. The signals stored on CD and DVD are compressed digital signals. After being converted to digital, the signals are stable and don't need regular tuning.

## 2.2 Simple Example of Signal Sampling
As an example of signal sampling, let's consider a sprinter running *100m* in *10 sec*. This can be represented by a function $f(t) = d(t)$ where:
- $f(t)$ is a function of time
- $d(t)$ is the distance in *meter* (*m*).
- $t$ is the time in *second* (*s*).

While running, the function *d(t)* of the sprinter running *100 meters* in *10 seconds* is an analog continuous function. This function describes the increasing distance at any time during the *10 seconds*. But in order to represent that function in a graph, the distance has to be recorded at regular intervals to get sample points. In Figure 2-1, there are 2 examples with 2 different sample intervals.

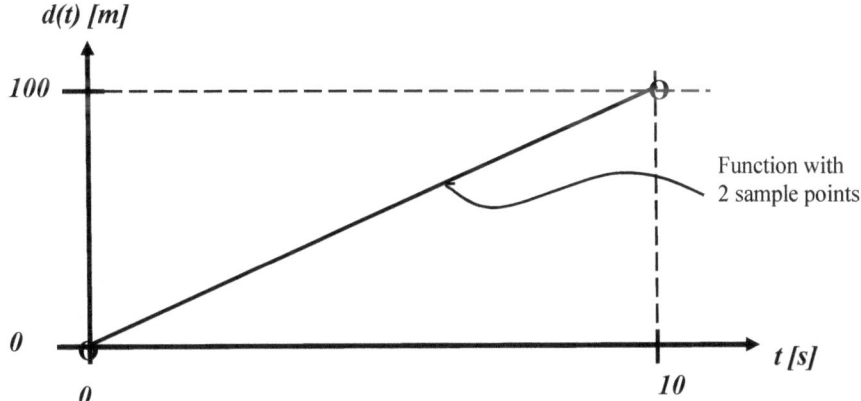

Function *d(t)* with 1 sample per *10 seconds*

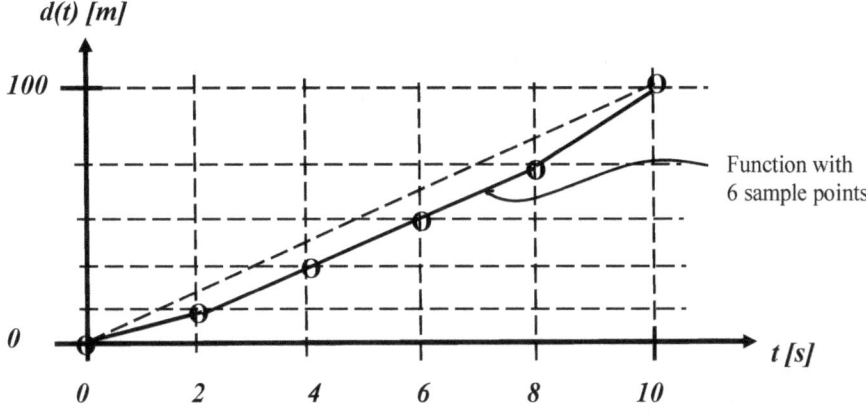

Function *d(t)* with 1 sample per *2 seconds*

**Figure 2-1 Sampling Example of Sprinter Running *100 meters* in *10 seconds***

Usually, the time at the beginning and is measured at the end. This corresponds to 2 samples points. In the first graph the function *d(t)* is drawn using 2 sample points. Since there is no information about the function behavior between the samples, the function can be represented with a straight line.

If we want more information, the distance can be sampled every *2 seconds*. In the 2$^{nd}$ graph, the function is drawn with the results of 6 measurements, the first measurement being *0 meter* at time *0 second*, the last one being *100 meters* at *10 seconds*. This graph represents a more detailed description of the sprinter progress.

During the first *2 seconds*, the progress is slower, because the sprinter starts at a speed of *0 m/s*. He accelerates until he reaches cruising speed. From *2 to 8 seconds*, he runs at almost constant cruising speed. During the last *2 seconds*, from *8 to 10 seconds*, the speed increases because of the sprint to the finish line. Again, there is no information about the behavior between samples, so the sample points are connected with straight lines.

Note that, if the sprinter was recorded in a movie at 24 samples per *second*, there would be 240 sample points from start to finish. In this case, the progress of the sprinter would be more complete and would be closer to the analog curve.

In this example, the samples are taken at equal time intervals. This can be referred as temporal sampling.

In another example, the sampling can be done by reading the times at equal distance intervals. This can be referred as spatial sampling. As example, a runner run 10 miles in a circular track, and the time samples are taken after every lap.

## 2.3 Anti-Aliasing in Real Time CGI Systems

The early RT CGI systems appeared in the 1970s. They were expensive and limited to NASA and US Military market. These customers wanted RT CGI Systems with good Anti-Aliasing features. For these systems there is a broader definition of 'Aliasing'.

### 2.3.1 Definitions of AA for RT CGI with the 5 A's

In 1980, the 'US Army Material Development and Readiness Command' produced a report about 'Computer Generated Imagery (CGI) Current Technology' [82]

From this report, there are several good definitions for the 5 A's.

*Aliasing*

In communications theory, the generation of spurious signals caused by sampling for a signal at a rate lower than twice its frequency. In a CGI scene, sampling refers to the spatial frequencies involved in both the computation of the scene and its display. The result is spatial and/or temporal image defects. Manifestations of aliasing include edge stair-step, scintillation of small scene surfaces, breakup of long narrow surfaces, positional or angular motion of edges in discrete jumps or steps, Moiré patterns in regions where there is periodic structure, double imaging, and loss of dynamic image integrity due to field tracking induced by edge motion perpendicular to the scanning direction.

*Anti-Aliasing*

Image processing techniques, usually involving low pass filtering, that reduce spatial and/or temporal aliasing phenomena. To avoid significant reduction in image resolution, it is generally necessary to perform the anti-aliasing on an image with higher resolution than the one to be displayed.

# Aliasing

## *AOI*
Area of Interest. Part of the visual display that contains a high-resolution terrain video presentation. The remainder of the display can be low-resolution supporting information such as featureless sky/earth or sky / checkerboard patterns.

## *Arc Minute*
A measure of resolution as applied to human perception or acuity. One (1) minute of arc is equal to 1/3000th of the distance to an object or 12 inches at 3000 feet.

## *Artifacts*
With respect to CGI systems, artifacts are those phenomena which are encountered in the engineering, operation and use of CGI visuals such as aliasing, flicker and the 'jumping' changes involved in dynamically changing the level of detail.

## 2.3.2 Spatial and Temporal Image Artifacts

In the following figures there are examples of Aliasing in CGI. These aliasing artifacts are very noticeable when the images are rendered with only one Sample Point per Pixel. Aliasing can be caused by Spatial and Temporal artifacts.

### *Spatial Artifacts*:
Spatial Artifacts are the unwanted effect caused by limited sampling resolution. These effects are noticeable in static or still pictures.

### *Temporal Artifact*:
Temporal artifacts are caused objects with spatial artifacts moving in the scene over time.

### *Edge Stairsteps and Crawling*
In this example, depending on their slopes triangle edges are categorized as Horizontal (*HE*) and Vertical (*VE*).

In Figure 2-2, there are 2 examples with triangles. Each triangle has 2 *HEs* and 1 *VE*.

These 2 examples illustrate Spatial and Temporal Artifacts.
In both examples, the triangles edges are rendered with Stairsteps.
In the second half, the triangle has moved ½ Pixel left and ½ Pixel down.
When the triangle moves, the Stairstep pattern changes, resulting in Edge Crawling.

Aliasing

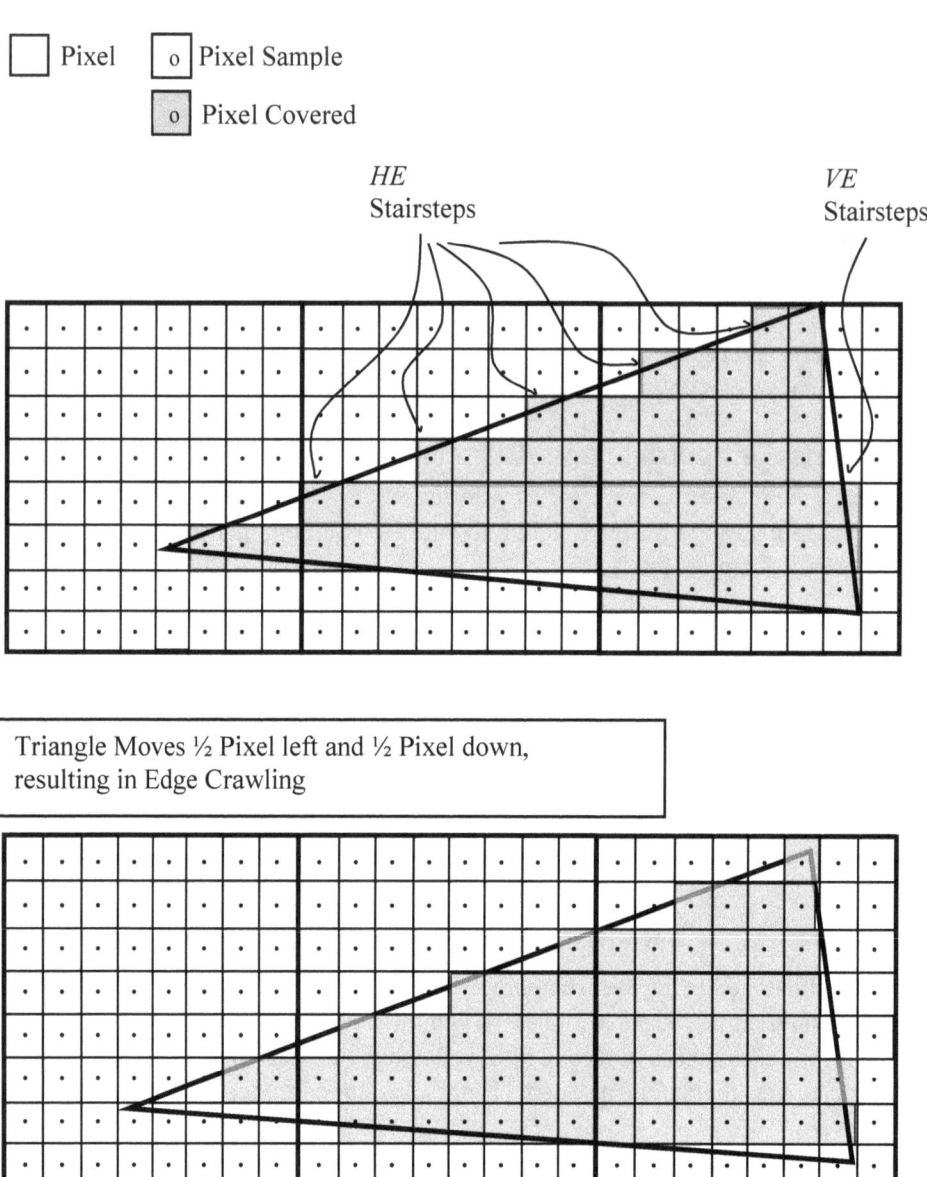

**Figure 2-2 Edge Stairstep and Edge Crawling**

# Aliasing

## *Narrow Face Breakup*

In Figure 2-3, there are 2 examples of Narrow Face Breakup.
When the width of narrow faces is near of smaller than the Pixel size, the rendering results in Face Breakup.

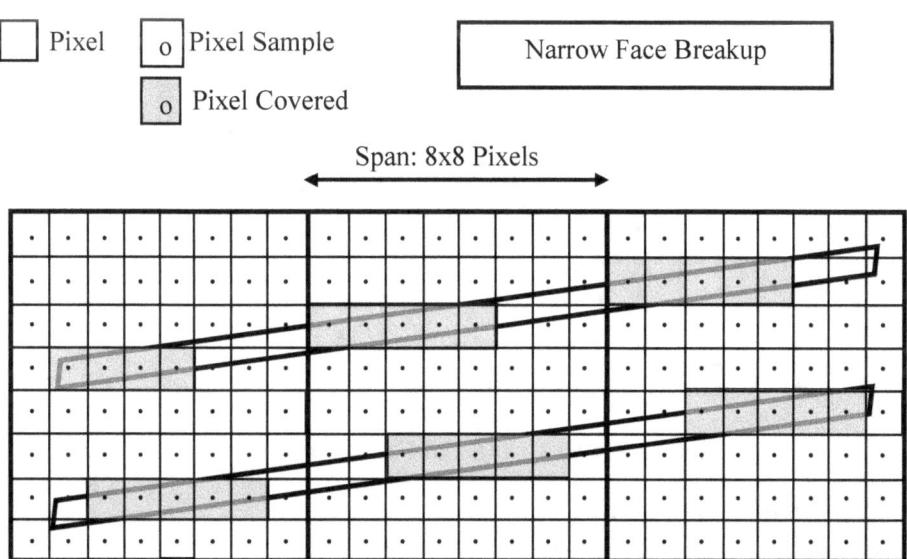

**Figure 2-3 Examples of Narrow Face Breakup**

## *Face popping*

Face popping is a temporal artifact. It shows with objects going in-and-out of scenes when some dimensions of displayed polygon faces are smaller than the Pixel size.

In Figure 2-4 there are examples of face popping. These tiny faces are displayed only when the Pixel sample point is inside of the faces. In a moving scene, this result into faces popping in-and-out of the scene.

In the Link DIG, a special patented feature provided the capability to remove small face before their projected size reach the Pixel size [105]. This capability was especially effective with runway stripes during landing or take-off, and with windows on buildings.

For coplanar faces, a new type of face was introduced: Detail Faces. Detail Faces are nested inside of coplanar Mother Faces. For coplanar Detail Faces, the contrast with their mother faces can be gradually reduced from full contrast to zero between size 4 Pixels to size 1 Pixel. At size 1 Pixel, the contrast reaches zero and the detail face can be gracefully introduced or removed in the scene without popping in-and-out of the scene.

Aliasing

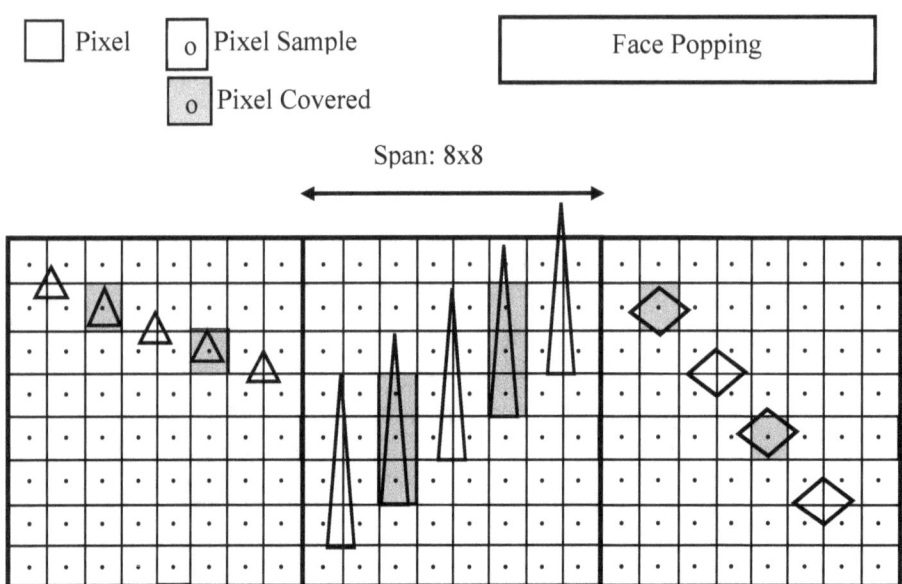

**Figure 2-4 Examples of Face Popping**

### *General Example of Moiré pattern [61]*

In Figure 2-5, there is a general example of Moiré pattern.

In this example, a set of concentric circles is repeated. These overlapping concentric circles result in various Moiré patterns. In particular, in the lower part of the image, there is a pattern looking like a dragonfly or a spider. This was not intended. It is the result of Moiré pattern.

While this example does not relate to CGI, there are many examples of Moiré patterns in CGI. A typical example consists of displaying checkerboards or arrays of small repetitive pattern. This results in Moiré pattern when the size of the projected patterns become smaller than the Pixel size. Refer to the next examples.

### *Moiré Pattern when Displaying Checkerboard In CGI*

All kinds of artifacts like squares or rectangles popping in-and-out of scene can occur when displaying a checkerboard pattern. The appearance of Moiré patterns depends on the projection size, viewing angle and movement of the checker board pattern.

**Figure 2-5 Example of Moiré Pattern**

*Size of Checkerboard Squares when Compared with Pixel Size*

When squares in checkerboard pattern are of the **same size or larger** than the Pixel size, they are displayed properly, but can show stair steps and crawling.

When they are **smaller** than the Pixel size, the under sampling produces squares or rectangles that can be much larger than the projected size. These squares or rectangles can pop in-and-out of scene.

Here are several examples displayed of checkerboards, some of them resulting in Moiré patterns. In these examples, a mask the size of an 8x8 Pixel Span is used to select the color at the center of each Pixel. Refer to the mask on the left side of the figures. In these masks, little holes at the center of Pixels select the color to display on the rendered Pixels. On the right side, the Pixels are displayed with the selected Pixel color.

When squares in checkerboard pattern are of same size or much larger than Pixels, they are displayed properly. Refer to Figure 2-6.

Aliasing

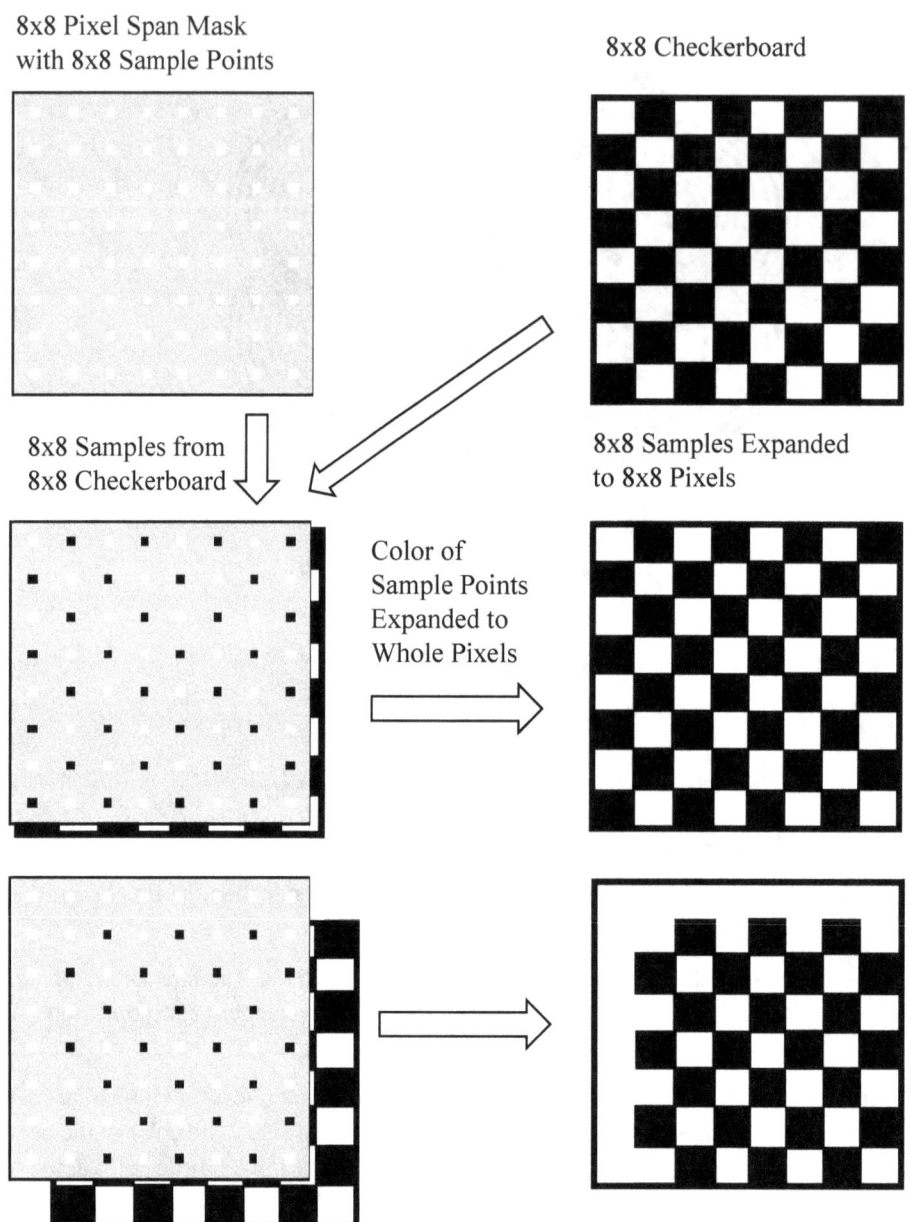

**Figure 2-6 Checkerboard with Squares Equal to Pixel Size**

# Aliasing

## *Checkerboard Squares Greater than Pixel Size*

When the checkerboard squares are greater than the Pixel size, the size of square or rectangle array of size NxN is unchanged. Refer to Figure 2-7.

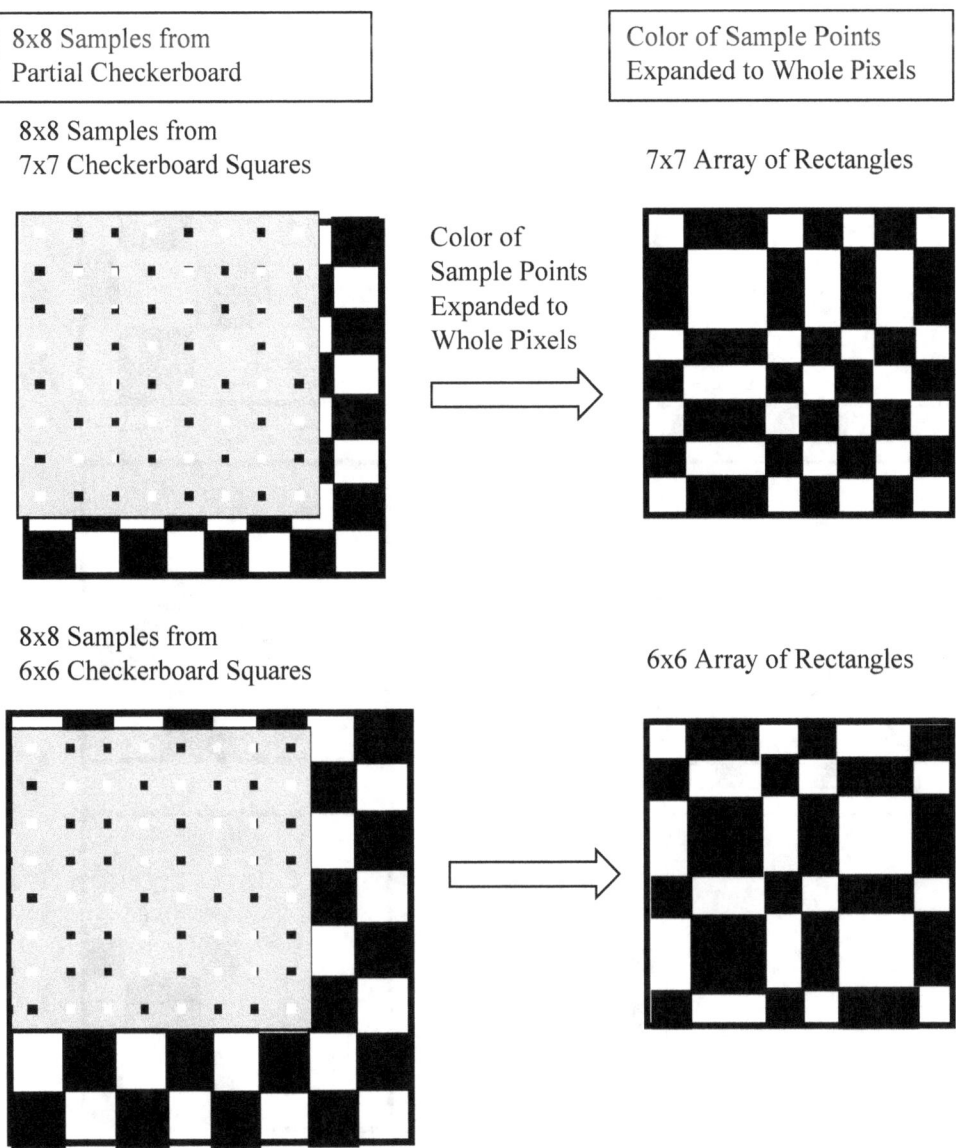

**Figure 2-7 Checkerboard with Squares Greater than Pixel Size**

New Area-Based Anti-Aliasing for CGI

Aliasing

*Checkerboard Squares Smaller than Pixel Size*

When they are smaller than the Pixel size, they start showing aliasing problems with Moiré patterns. In Figure 2-8, the small checker board moves in steps of ¼ Pixel to the right. The displayed squares jump from one pattern to another.

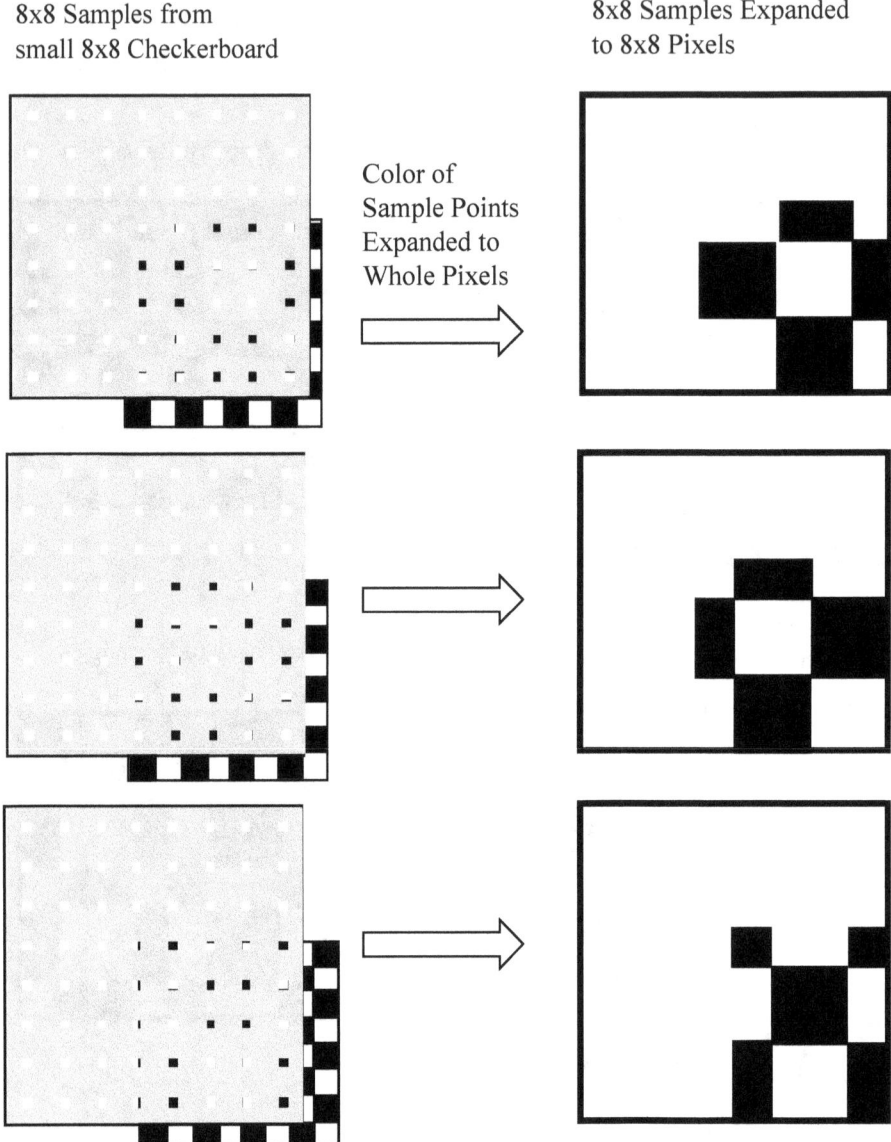

**Figure 2-8 Small Checkerboard Moving 1/4 Pixel to the Right**

When the checkerboard squares get much smaller the size of Pixels, the size of the displayed squares or rectangles can become much larger than their projected size. They also produce Moiré patterns. The aliasing also shows as the size of the displayed rectangle array decreases from NxN to smaller than NxN. Refer to Figure 2-9.

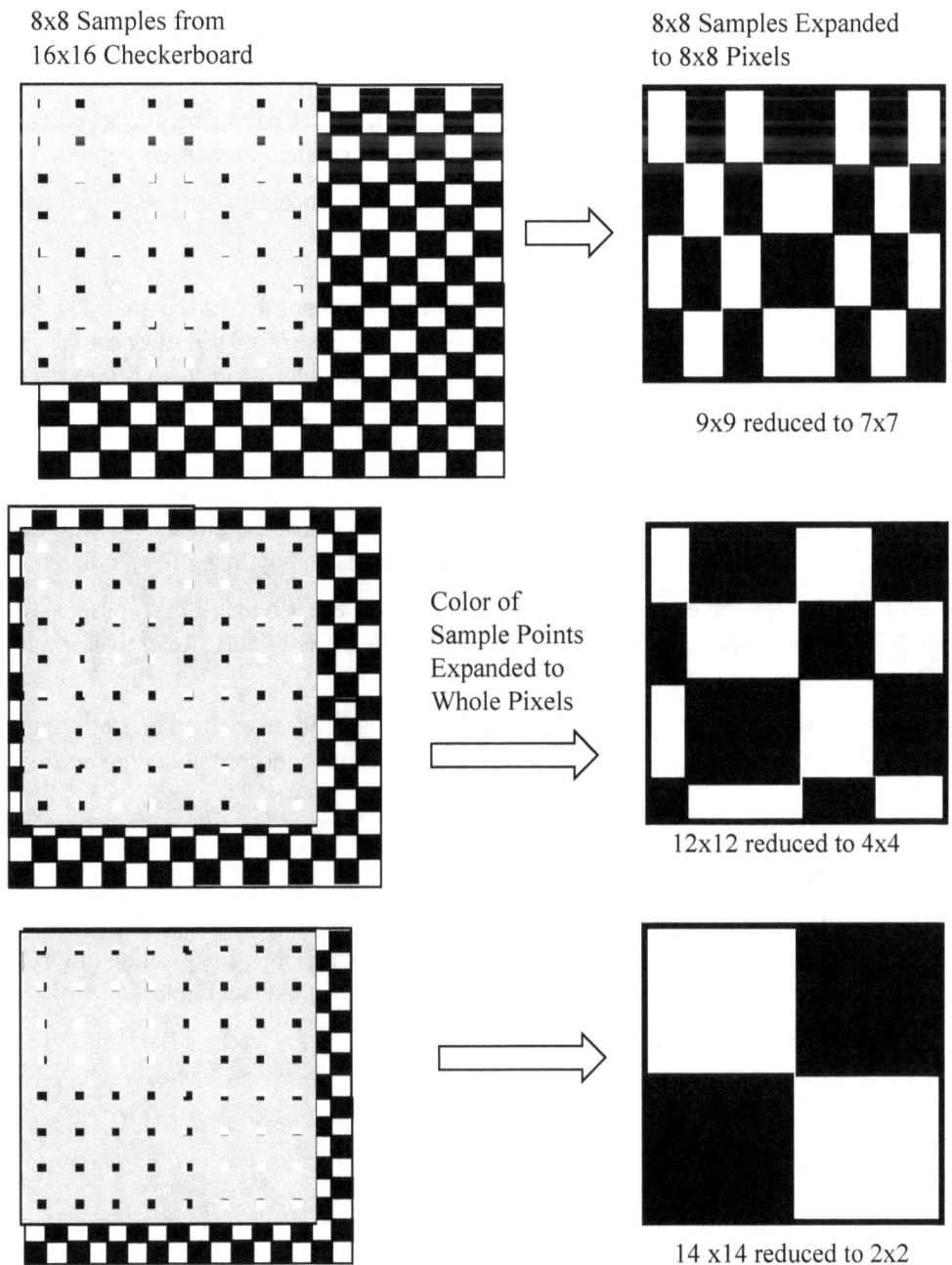

**Figure 2-9 Displayed Squares from Shrinking Checkerboard.**

### *Display Checkerboard using Texture Maps.*

Instead of modeling checkerboard patterns with polygons and repetitive patterns, it could be implemented with texture maps. With texture maps the level of details would minimize and correct these Moiré patterns.

For example, texture maps of size MxN can be reduced by successive averaging into several level of details, starting at M/2xN/2, and reducing the dimension by a factor of 2 at each step.

The CGI system will select the proper texture size during image rendering.

## 2.3.3 Double Imaging

The Double Imaging effect shows up when displaying dynamic scenes that are computed at frame rate of 1/30 sec and displayed with interlaced Scanlines at field rate of 1/60 sec. Because the same image is computed only once and displayed twice a 1/60 sec interval (although on alternate Scanlines), double imaging effect can be observed in fast moving scenes. For example, this can happen when doing a quick left or right turn, or a roll in an airplane.

Double Imaging can be observed when displaying 2 objects in the scene while their relative positions change noticeably on the display. For example, assume that the human eye is tracking one Object #1 (Obj1) in the scene while Object #2 (Obj2) moves rapidly in a different direction.

While tracking Obj1, both objects are projected in the viewer eye's retina. Let's consider what happens in 2 successive frames, each consisting of 2 fields: field0 and field1. Refer to example in Figure 2-10.

In the field0 of 1st Frame, the 2 objects have a relative position between each other. Let's assume that the observer is tracking Obj1. When Obj2 moves, the eye moves according to the tracking of Obj1.

After 1/60 sec, when field1 of the same frame is displayed, the 2 objects in the computed image still have the same relative position as in field0.

But after 1/60 sec, when field1 of the same frame is displayed, Obj2 has moved relatively to Obj1. In the retina, Obj1 is still in focus. But because the eye is tracking Obj1, the position of Obj2 in retina is recorded at a different position after the 1/60 sec between field0 and field1.

But since Obj2 is moving relative to Obj1, the projection of Obj2 in the retina at field1 of 1st frame is expected to have moved at the middle of distances between 2 subsequent frames.

The expected position Obj2 at field 1 is different from the repeated position at field1. This result in having 2 images of Obj2 in the retina.

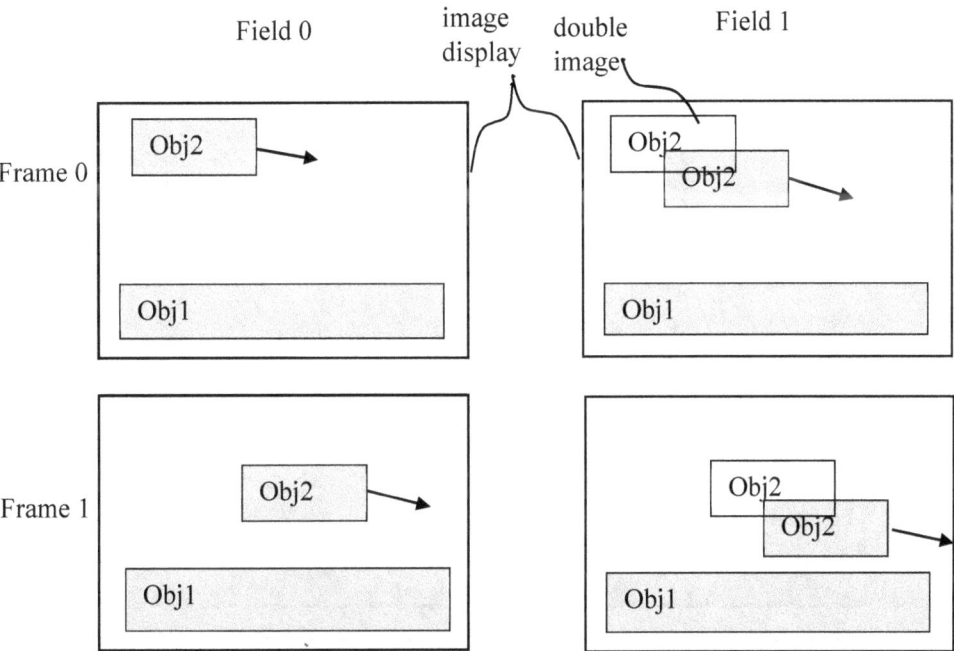

**Figure 2-10 Example of Double Image**

*My experience with Double Imaging*

I could not find a reference about Double Imaging in Wikipedia. Instead, I will describe my own experience to describe this effect.

When we started to evaluate our R&D DIG prototype at Link, it did not take long to observe Double Imaging in the CGI system for the first time in our CGI prototype system.

For the DIG testing and evaluation, we had a one window setup with a split screen display and parabolic mirror that presented the image at infinity. This setup was enclosed into a little black tent. We could control a flying airplane with switches and a simple joystick [81]. With this simple setup, it was like flying in the cockpit of a real plane.

We had designed the DIG prototype to compute the dynamic scenes at frame rate, that is the images were updated each 1/30 sec, while the same image was displayed in the two fields (1/60 sec each) on the interlaced display. It did not take long to observe Double Imaging and jerky images when doing quick left or right turns. For example, when an airplane does a turn, it first does a small roll, then turns. When doing turns in the simulated flight, the image also does a roll.

In this case, I observed this effect while my eyes were concentrated on the image display. The horizontal horizon changed to around a 30 degree angle and I was able to observe Double Imaging in my eyes' peripheral vision. It was a jerky motion, similar to the 'ta-ta-ta' of a machine gun. Refer to the 'hill' in Figure 2-11.

Aliasing

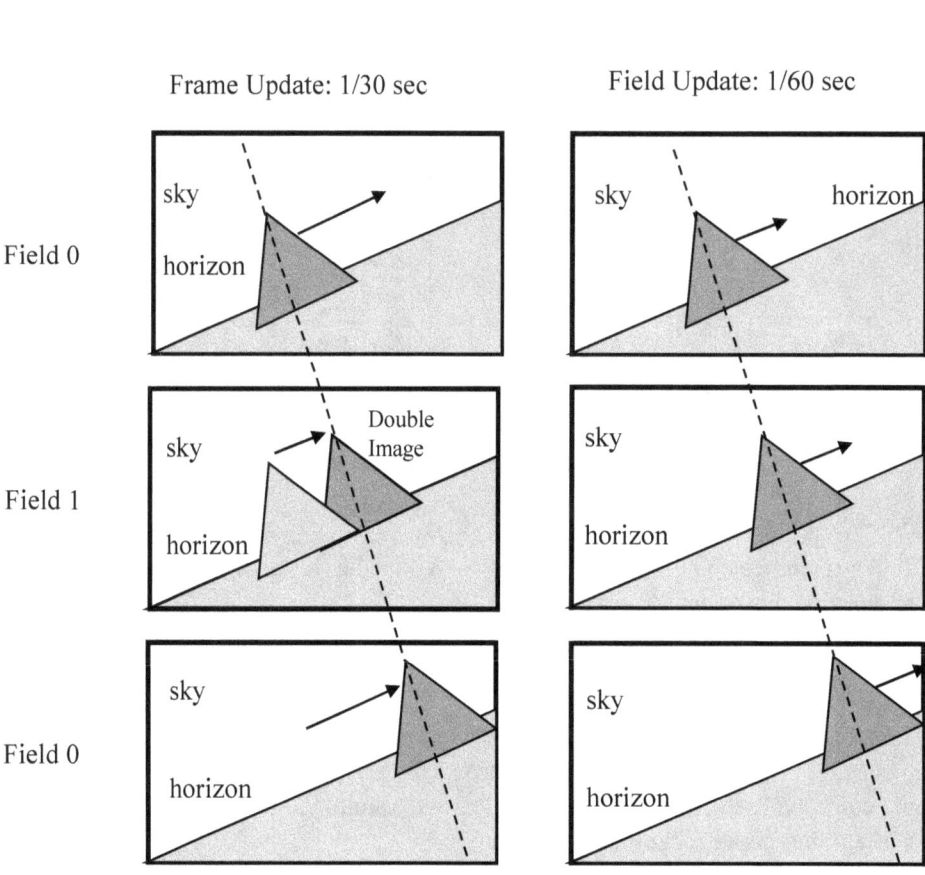

**Figure 2-11 Double Imaging During Plane Roll**

*Double Imaging can be elusive*

Since the Double Imaging effect depends on what object you are focusing on in the dynamic scene (or in the display surrounding), it is not always reproduceable. When repeating the experiment while looking at the scene elements that caused Double Imaging, this distracting effect disappears.

Double Imaging was a disappointment. We made small modifications to the DIG prototype in order to run at field rate of 1/60 sec. To our satisfaction, we observed no Double Imaging when using field update rate. We decided that all DIGs should be delivered with Field Update rate as the default. This also means that the number of edges per field would be roughly half the number of edges per frame. Because of this decision, the scene density was reduced by half. Also, the production DIGs had to compute 3 independent windows: front, left and right. This corresponds to reduction by 3 for the edge count per window.

For the production DIG, I made significant improvements in the frame Calculator (Geometric Processor) by improving the processing units and removing major bottle necks. With minor increase in circuitry, the edge processing rate was increased to >10'000 edges per field.

While the competition tried to improve the processing rate by using parallel processing, all the DIGs were able to achieve these performances with a single Geometric Processing pipeline.

### *Link DIGs Were Updating Images for 3 Windows at 1/60 sec Field Rate*

I was heavily involved in the debugging and bring up of the Link CGI prototype. After analyzing the processing of the subsystems in the Geometric Processor, I was able to improve the processing rate of the Frame Calculator for the production DIG to NASA. The edge processing capability was increased by a factor between 6 and 10, depending on the scene complexity. The bottle neck in the Frame Calculator was the Rotations Subsystem. With the improvements, it could rotate each vertex (or edge) in 6 cycles at 4.5 MHz (220 ns cycle).
This corresponds to 1320 ns/vertex
The field update time is 1/60 = 16.667 ms.
The maximum # vertices/field is 16'666'667/1'320=12626 edges/field (250k triangles/sec).
Assuming a 20% efficiency for real-time systems: 12626*0.8=10100 edges/field.
We were able to demonstrate the 10k edges per field to the customer for the helicopter program.

What I find interesting is that by doing now a single chip design similar to the DIG system designed 45 years ago, the clock frequency could be 45MHz, instead of 4.5MHz. This corresponds to 100k edges per field, or 2M triangles per sec.

During a period of 10 years, the Frame Calculators in all DIGs used the same Vector Multiplier boards for rotating vertices or matrices, and the same Clipping processor boards for window clipping. Most improvements in the Frame Calculators during that 10-year period were due to more efficient processing. For the B-52 program, a bubble test was added to the Object Processor, so that objects clearly out of the window could be eliminated early in the processing. For the Apache Helicopter program, a new front-end HW box, the Priority and Sectoring Processor (PSP), added the capabilities of the DIG Controller to select objects from the Active Data Base in hardware at a much higher rate. The PSP provided the capability to update the scene components several times per second to keep up with the helicopter high turn rate.

## 2.4 Aliasing Examples with Analog Signals

### 2.4.1 Definition of Aliasing in Broadcast TV

Before the advent of CGI, aliasing was observed on images produced by broadcast TV and even movies. On TV, a typical example can be seen when presenters wear ties or shirts with repetitive patterns of size of around a few *mm* or a fraction of an inch (around *1/8"*). In movies it can be observed when wheels of carriages seem to turn backward.

Aliasing

Here is a definition of 'Aliasing', according to Mariam Webster Dictionary [60]:

'Aliasing is an error or distortion created in digital images. It usually appears jagged outlines. We commonly observe aliasing on television. This occurs when there is an insufficient magnification produced by the lens of a TV camera focused on periodic structures such as the pattern of pinstripes in an announcer's shirt, bricks in the wall of a house, or seats in an empty stadium.'
- *Douglas B. Murphy*, Fundamentals of Light Microscopy and Electronic Imaging, 2001

## 2.4.2 Sine Function and Frequency

The most common repetitive analog signal is the sine function. For more details, refer to sine and cosine functions [46].

The sine and cosine functions are periodical functions. Ther repeat at equal intervals referred to as cycle or period. The frequency of periodic analog signal is measured in cycles per second [cyc/sec], or Hertz with symbol [Hz]. For example,

*1Hertz:*        *1 Hz = 1 cyc/sec*
*1 kilo Hertz:*  *1 kHz = 1000 cyc/sec*
*1 Mega Hertz:*  *1 MHz = 1000 kHz = 1000'000 cyc/sec*
*1 Giga Hertz:*  *1 GHz = 1000 MHz = 1000'000'000 cyc/sec*

The cycle is measured in arc angles. The unit of arc angle is degrees *[deg]* or radians *[rad]*. For example, the angle for a full circle is:
*1full circle = 360 deg*
*1full circle = 2Pi rad, where Pi = 3.14159265...*

The constant Pi is an irrational number with an infinite non-repetitive and unending fraction. For example:
50 fraction digits of Pi: *Pi = 3.14159265358979323846264338327950288419716939937510...*

The cosine function precedes the sine function by 90 degrees, or Pi/4. Refer to Figure 2-12.

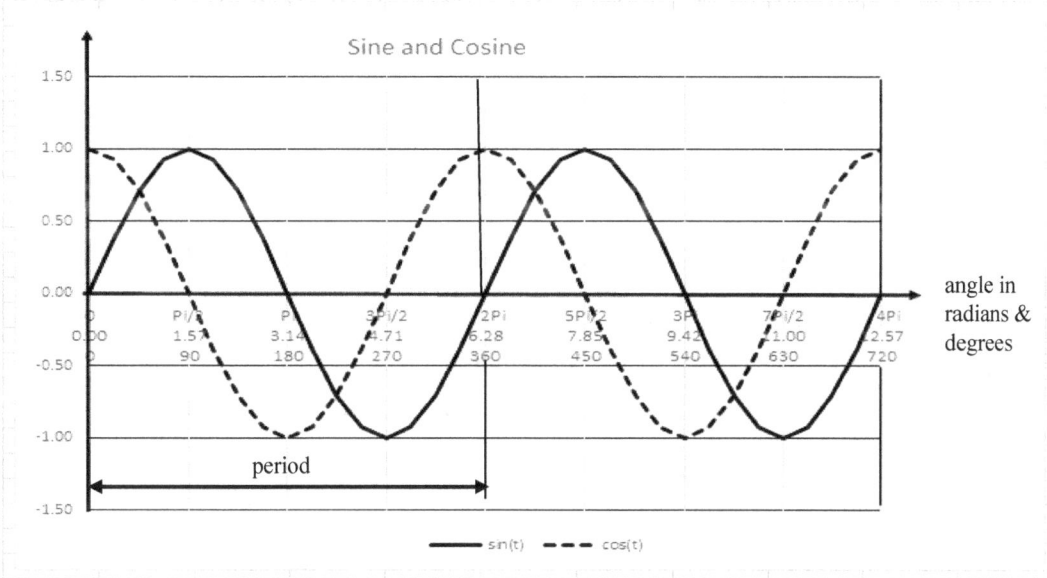

**Figure 2-12 Sine and Cosine Functions**

### 2.4.3 Aliasing when Sampling a Sine Function

In electronics, there are analog and digital signals. An example of analog signal is the processing of sound with a microphone, analog amplifier and speaker. The sound is converted from sound wave into electric signal in a microphone. It is then amplified with analog circuits and converted back into sound waves in a loud-speaker.

One of the weaknesses of analog signals is that their levels and amplitudes can drift and need to be calibrated. In older TV, the signal processing was done with analog circuits that needed calibration.

On the other hand, digital signals consist of numbers that are processed with digital circuits. The advantage of digital processing is that the numbers have stable values and can be safely reproduced. The CD and DVD are good examples of digital processing. Since sound and music are analog signals, they have to be sampled and converted to digital values before they can be stored in CDs or DVDs. Digital compression algorithms are then used to increase the density of data in CD and DVD (like JPEG, MPEG2, MPEG3, MP3 and HDTV).

### 2.4.4 Sampling Frequency and Nyquist Frequency

Aliasing is often caused when analog signals levels are digitized and the sampling frequency is not high enough to sample all the signal transitions. The critical sampling frequency for signal sampling is defined by the Nyquist frequency. For more info, refer to the Nyquist–Shannon sampling theorem [62].

When sampling periodic signal, there is no frequency aliasing when sampling frequency $fS$ is at least twice the signal frequency $f$. The Nyquist Frequency defines the minimum Sampling Frequency to prevent frequency aliasing [62].

# Aliasing

> Definition of Nyquist Frequency:
>
> The Nyquist Frequency $fN$ is defined as 2 times the frequency $f$ of the sampled signal: $fN = 2f$
>
> When sampling a signal, the sampling frequency $fS$ should be at least greater than the Nyquist Frequency $fN$ to prevent aliasing: $fS > fN = 2f$

When the highest frequency of a signal is less than the Nyquist frequency of the sampler, the resulting sample sequence is said to be free of the distortion known as aliasing, and the corresponding sample-rate is said to be above the Nyquist rate for that particular signal.

> What is Frequency Aliasing:
>
> The Nyquist Sampling frequency is a requirement for preventing 'Frequency Aliasing'. There are other aliasing effects such as jaggies (edge stairsteps and crawling), faces popping and other distracting artifacts. For this reason, the definition of Nyquist frequency should be rephrased like:
>
> When sampling a signal, the sampling frequency $fS$ should be at least greater than the Nyquist Frequency $fN$ to prevent 'frequency aliasing'.

## *Frequency Aliasing when $f/fN > 0.5$*

When the ratio of Signal frequency to Sample frequency $f/fS$ is greater than 0.5, this results in aliased frequencies in the sampled signals. The frequency of the aliased sampled signal consists of a down and up mirror pattern limited by the Nyquist frequency.

The graph in Figure 2-13 shows how the frequency of a sampled results into aliased frequencies when $f/fN > 0.5$.

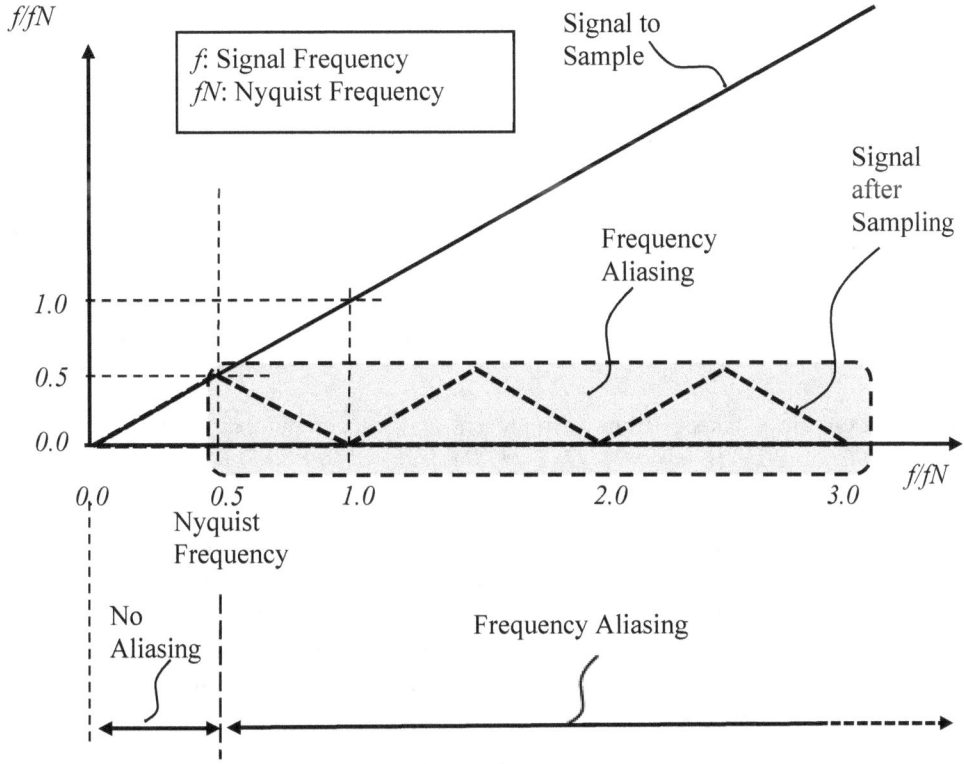

**Figure 2-13 Signal to Sample and Signal after Sampling**

## 2.4.5 Sampling of a Sine Function as Aliasing Example

Here is a typical example of aliasing that is caused by under-sampling.

A sine function is defined by its Amplitude ($A$), Phase ($t$) and offset Phase ($dt$):
$f(t) = A * sine\ (t + dt)$

The sine function is a periodic function, where a *Period* $P=2*Pi$ is the time before the function repeats with the same values. A period, or cycle corresponds to an angle of *2Pi* (or *360 degrees*).
$f(t) = A * sine\ (t) = A * sine\ (t + P)$

When a point rotates around a circle of radius 1 and centered a $x=0$ and $y=0$, its projection on the $y$ axis describes a *sine* function, and the projection on the $x$ axis is a *cos*ine function.

The sine function repeats with the same values after each period. The 'frequency' is defined as the number of 'periods per second', measured in *cyc/sec,* or *Hz.*

The sine function represents an analog signal. Its values are continuous. For example, the early TVs were implemented with analog circuits, using vacuum tubes or transistors. The signals were continuous and their amplitude could be observed and measured with analog oscilloscopes. The new TVs use mainly digital circuits and a few analog circuits for interfaces.

Aliasing

On the other hand, digital computers deal only with binary numbers instead of continuous analog signals.

For more info about binary numbers and binary logic, refer to later chapter:
*'Inside the Binary World'.*

Binary logic consists of logic blocks separated by holding registers. Data in computers consist of bits (binary digits). Each bit can have only 2 states: *0* and *1*. For example, it takes 8 bits to represent and integer number from decimal *0* (binary '*0000'0000*') to *255* (binary '*1111'1111*'). Since the number of bits can be very large, groups of 8 bits are organized into bytes (B). Here, the quote symbol (') inside of number is used to facilitate reading. The value of each byte is between *0* and *255*. When bits are stored into memories, they are usually stored as 1, 2, 4 or 8 bytes.
For example:  *32 bits = 4 bytes = 4B.*

As another example it takes 10 bits to represent and integer number from decimal *0* (binary '*00'0000'0000*') to *1023* (binary '*11'1111'1111*'). Binary '*100'0000'0000*' = decimal '*1024*' is often referred as *1 kbit,* since the value is close to digital '*1000*'.

The computer operations are controlled by their main clock, which is a square wave of frequency around 1GHz. Registers data can change at the end of each clock cycle. The computer clock oscillates between *0* and *1*. The clock frequency corresponds to the number of clock transitions from *0* to *1* in a second. Generally, a computer can perform one operation per clock. The clock frequency of modern computer is around 1 GHz, that is computers can perform 1000 million (1billion) operations per second.

In the newer TVs, the processing of TV signals is also implemented with digital circuits. In order to accomplish this, the sine functions have to be sampled with analog to digital converters (AC to DC) to produce the sine function with a sequence of measured amplitudes. At the end of the processing, the signal can be converted back from digital to analog with DC to AC converters. Current display monitors can be driven by analog or digital RGB color signals.

As mentioned above, there is an important requirement for sampling analog signals. In order to prevent 'aliasing', the 'sampling theory' defines the critical (or minimum) sampling frequency to be at least twice the largest frequency of the signals to sample. The minimum sampling frequency is the referred to as the **Nyquist frequency**.

*Example of Sampled Sine Function*

In these examples, a sine function is sampled with six different frequencies. The highest sampling frequency corresponds to 12 samples per period. Then the number of samples are divided by 2 in each subsequent case.

Refer to Table 2-1.

# Aliasing

| Sine Functions at Time t and Offset dt. | Number of Samples per Period | Frequency of Sampled Function | Aliased Function |
|---|---|---|---|
| sine( ( t+dt) * Pi/6) | 12 | F | Non-Aliased |
| sine( ( t/2 +dt) * Pi/6) | 6 | F | Non-Aliased |
| sine( ( t/4+dt) * Pi/6) | 3 | F | Non-Aliased. But near critical frequency. |
| sine( ( t/8+dt) * Pi/6) | 1.5 | F/2 | Half the frequency |
| sine( ( t/16+dt) * Pi/6) | 0.75 | F/4 | One Quarter of F |
| sine( ( t/32+dt) * Pi/6) | 0.375 | F/8 | One 8th of F |

**Table 2-1 Sampling of a Sine Function**

The corresponding graphs are shown in Figures 2-14, 2-15 and 2-16.

The examples in these graphs have been generated with Excel spreadsheets. There are 3 similar graphs, each displaying 6 sampled signals. In each graph, the same sine function is sampled by six different frequencies.

The 3 graphs differ by varying the offset *dt*. By changing the offset, the shapes of the aliased functions differ. The effect of *dt* is represented by crawling in the aliased function samples.

The relationship between the Signal before Sampling and the Signal after Sampling shows the aliasing effect when the sampling frequencies is below the Nyquist frequency (aliasing when *fS/fN > 0.5*).

Aliasing

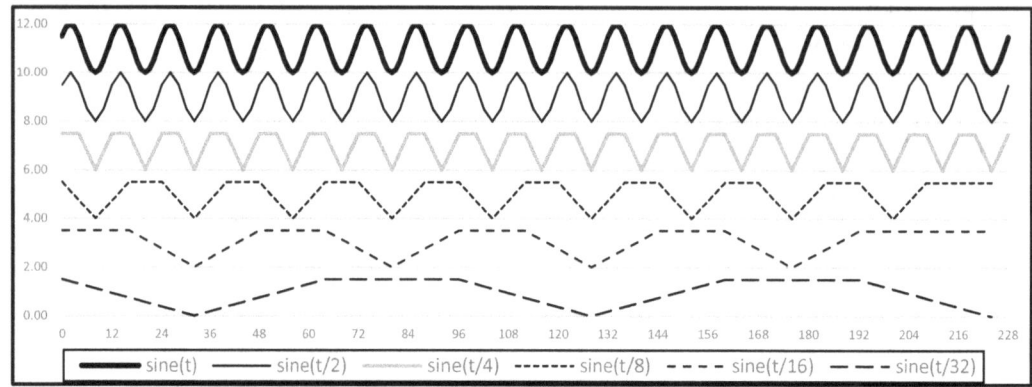

Figure 2-14 Function with Aliasing: *Sine((x+1) * Pi/6)*

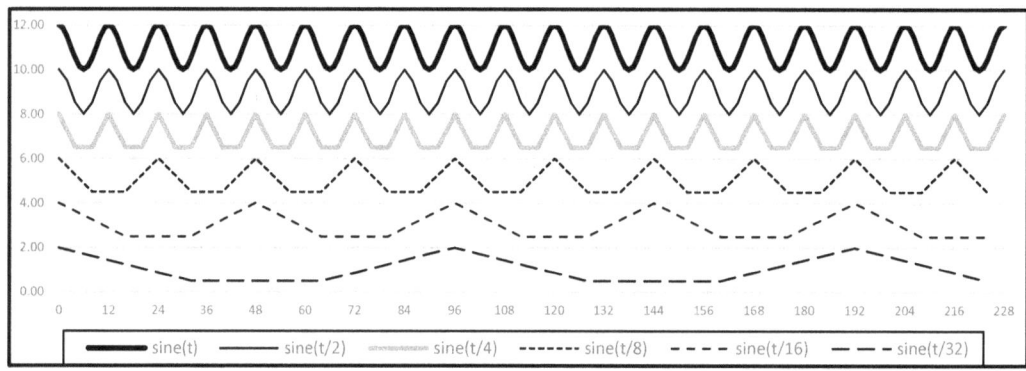

Figure 2-15 Function with Aliasing: *Sine((x+3) * Pi/6)*

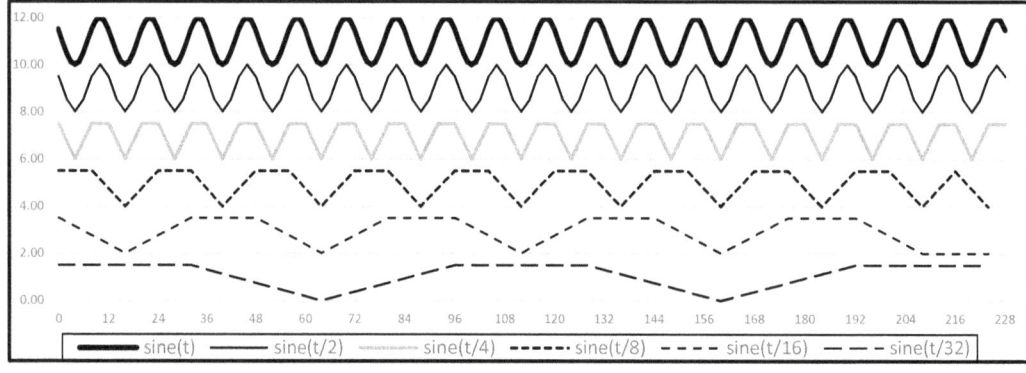

Figure 2-16 Function with Aliasing: *Sine((x+5) * Pi/6)*

# Aliasing

## 2.4.6 Aliasing when Sampling a Sine or Cosine Function

Here is another example of aliasing when sampling *sin()* and *cos()* functions.

In Figure 2-17, there are 6 examples of a *sin()* function sampled with 6 different frequency ratios *fS/fN*.

In Figure 2-18, there are 6 examples of a *cos()* function sampled with these 6 different frequency ratios *fS/fN*.

There is no frequency aliasing for sampling ratios of *fS/fN* < 0.5. There is no interest in showing sampling frequencies below the Nyquist frequency. So, the lowest ratio starts at *fS/fN* = 0.5. In these Figures, the Signals after sampling are compared with the Signals before sampling.

For the *sin()* function, the sampling at frequency ratios *fS/fN*= 0.0, 0.5, 1.0, 1.5, 2.0, ... would be all 0.0. So, the sampling is delayed by 0.25.

For *fS/fN*=0.25, 0.75.1.25.1.75,2.25, ,..., the non-zero samples are *1.0, -1.0, 1.0, -1.0, 1.0, ....*

Since the *cos()* function starts at *cos(0)=1*, there is no need to delay the sampling.

For *fS/fN*= 0.0, 0.5, 1.0, 1.5, 2.0, ..., the non-zero samples are *1.0, -1.0, 1.0, -1.0, 1.0, ....*

The sample points are indicated with 'up-arrows'.

- *fS* is the Signal frequency
- *fN* is the Nyquist frequency
- *fS/fN* = 0.5 at the Nyquist frequency

In the sequence of examples, the ratio of sampling intervals is incremented in steps of *1/8=0.125*, starting at the Nyquist frequency of
   *fS/fN = 4/8 = 0.5*.

Note that the indexes on the left of the graph is used only for identifying the cases.

Aliasing

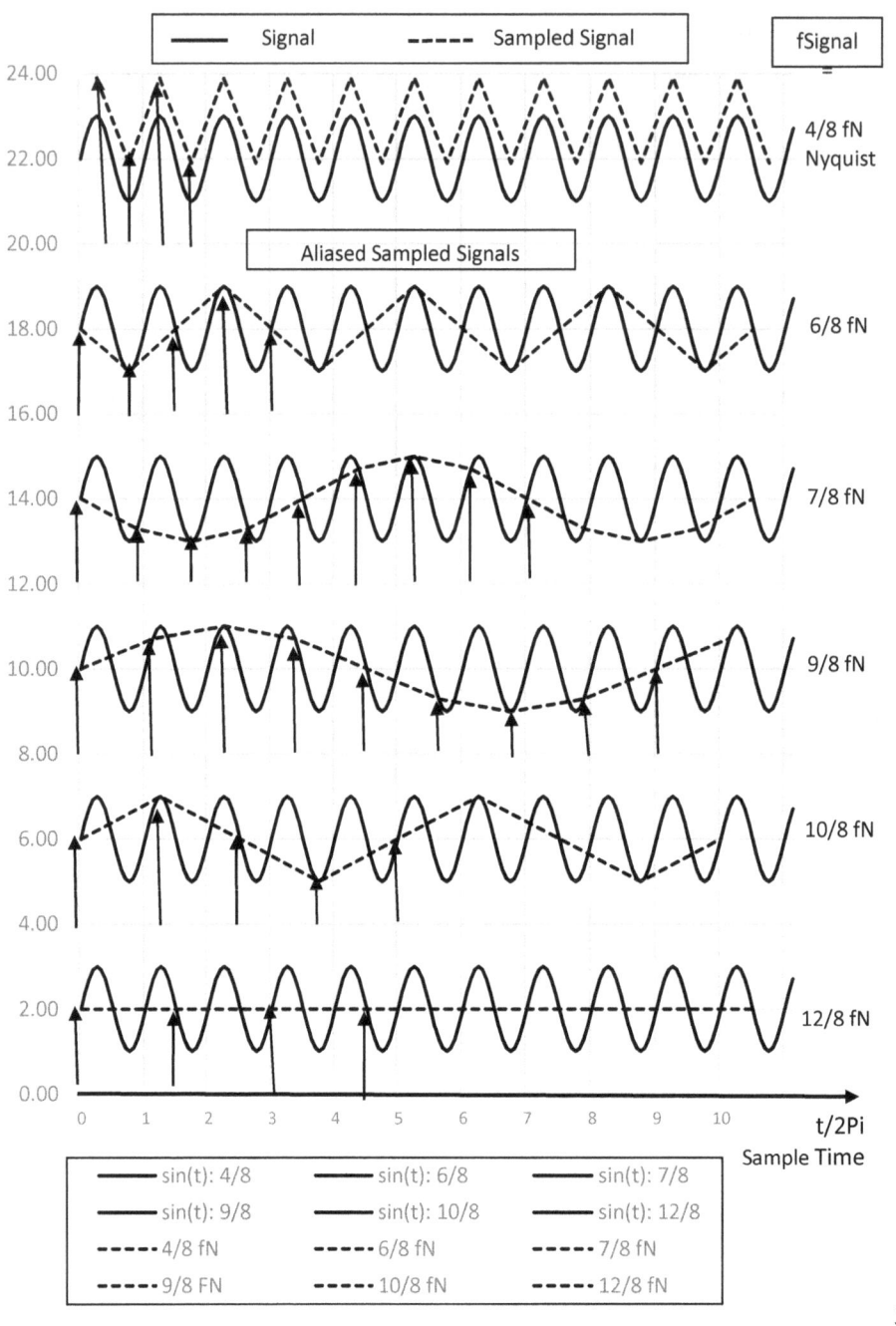

**Figure 2-17 Aliasing when Sampling Sine Function**

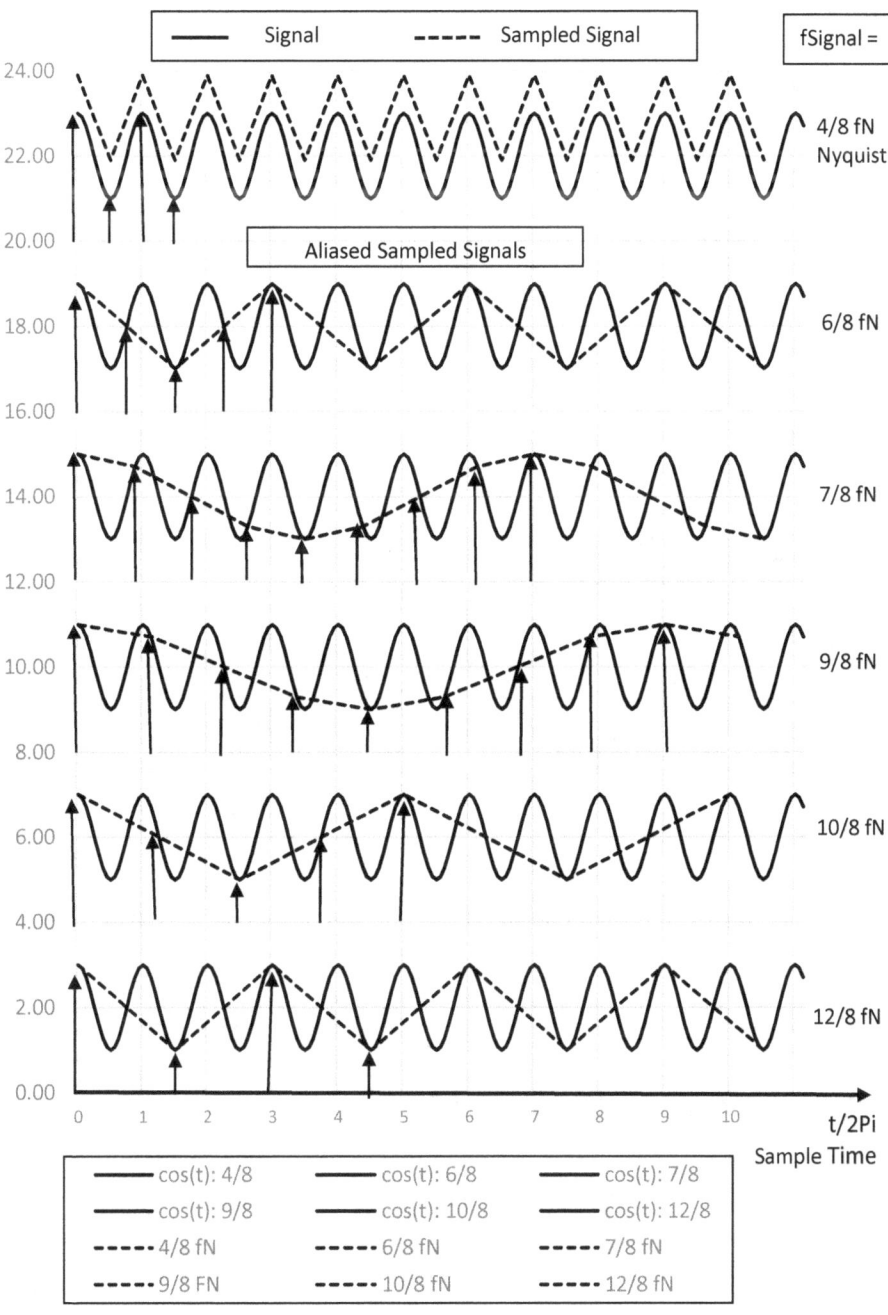

**Figure 2-18 Aliasing when Sampling Cos Function**

Aliasing

The results of the examples in the previous figure are plotted in Figure 2-19. In this figure, the frequencies for ratios of *f/fN* are shown before and after sampling.

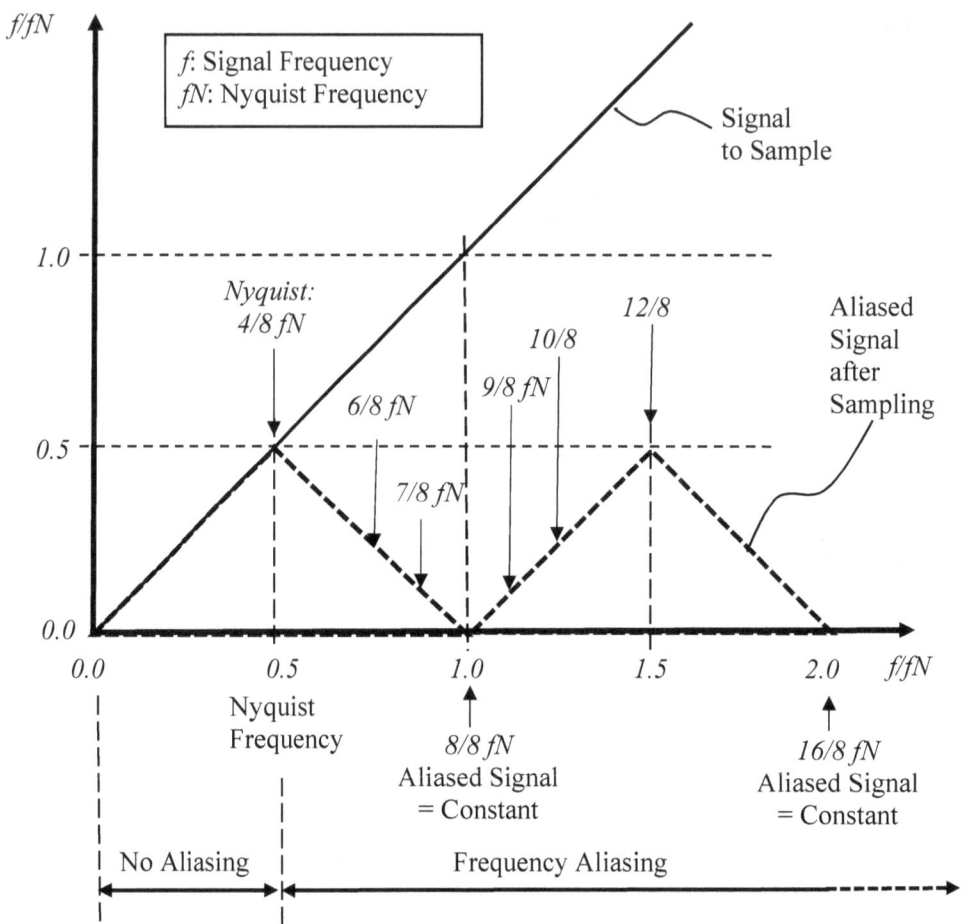

**Figure 2-19 Signal to Sample and Signal after Sampling**

For other examples where the frequency ratios have integer values, like *f/fN* = 0, 1, 2, 3, ..., the aliased output samples would have a constant value of *1*.

For the *cos( )* function examples, when starting with *cos(0)=1*, the aliased samples would be all *cos(n\*2Pi)* = *1*, for *n*= 0, 1, 2, 3, .... For other examples, starting with an *offset* value, the sampled output would have a constant value ranging from *-1 to +1*.
 *cos(n\*2Pi + offset)* = *constant*, for *n*= 0, 1, 2, 3, ....

### 2.4.7 Sine and Cosine Functions after Sampling

In the examples above, the sampled values are shown connected with line segments. In reality, the sampled functions consist of sequences of unconnected points. In case of signals consisting of sine and cosine functions after sampling, the analog signals can be recovered by applying filters or scaler functions.

But there is a problem when sampling at the Nyquist frequency $fN = 2fS$.

Depending on the sample point, the output could be a constant value.

Refer to Figure 2-20.

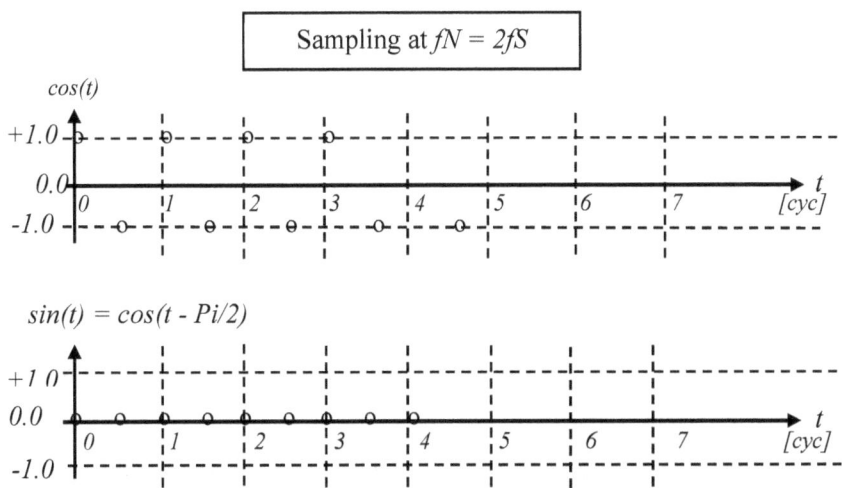

**Figure 2-20 Cosine Function Sampled at Nyquist Frequency (fN=2*fS)**

For example, the samples of function $cos(t)$ for $fN=2*fS$, or $fS/fN=0.5$, consist of 2 points per cycle

When the amplitude at points is maximum, there is enough information for reconstructing the sine and cosine function by applying filters. But, note that in the case of $cos(t - Pi/2)$, the output amplitude of the samples are all zero. This is what happens at the Nyquist frequency. There is no aliasing. The frequency of the output signal is the same as the frequency of the input signal, although the amplitude is zero.

So, the Nyquist frequency is no warranty for the output amplitude being the same as the input amplitude. It is only the limit for output without frequency aliasing. In order to have the same amplitude, the frequency limit should be $fN = 4*fS$. In this case, the output amplitude would be the same as the input amplitude. Refer to Figure 2-21.

Aliasing

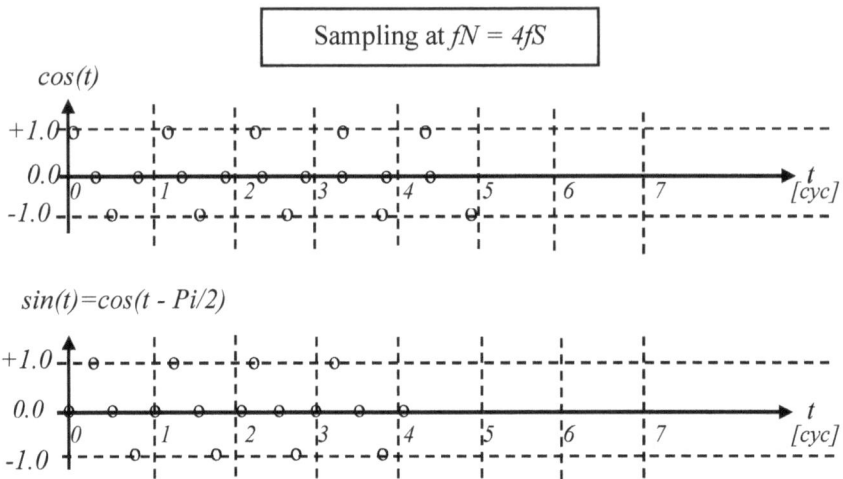

**Figure 2-21 Sin and Cos Func Sampled at Twice the Nyquist Freq (*2fN=4\*fS*)**

## 2.5 Sampling of TV Signals

As mentioned earlier, there are different TV standards in the world. In particular the image refresh rate (or field rate) is 60 Hz in the US and 50 Hz in the European countries. On top of that, the detail standards can vary from country to country. In order to exchange TV programs across different countries, the ITU (International Telecommunication Union) developed standards to store TV images into a common digital format.

### 2.5.1 Standard TV

There are two recommendations documents from the ITU to define the standard of exchanging TV signals between different analog TV formats [43].

ITU-R BT.601 (or its former name CCIR 601) is a standard originally issued in 1982 by the CCIR for encoding interlaced analog video signals in digital video form. It includes methods of encoding 525-line 60 Hz and 625-line 50 Hz signals, both with an active region covering 720 luminance (intensity info) samples and 360 chrominance (blue and red color info) samples per line.

BT.601 provides interlaced video data, streaming each field separately, and uses the *YCbCr* 4:2:2 color encoding system. The sampling frequency for Pixels is 13.5 Mz. The Luminance is transmitted at 13.5MHz. The Color info is also transmitted at 13.5 MX, but with alternating component. The resulting transmission rate for *Cr* and *Cb* is 6.75 MHz.

ITU-R BT.656 describes a digital video protocol for streaming uncompressed PAL (Germany, 50 Hz and 625 lines) or NTSC (US, 60 Hz and 525 lines) Standard Definition TV signals. The protocol builds upon the 4:2:2 digital video encoding parameters defined in ITU-R BT.601,

BT.656 data stream is a sequence of 8-bit or 10-bit words, transmitted at a rate of 27 Mword/sec. The transmitted word sequence of Pixel pairs consisting of 4 words '*Y, Cr, Y, Cb*' is transmitted at 6.75 MHz. (4*6.75 Mword/sec)

The ITU (International Telecommunication Union) is based in Geneva, Switzerland. Its global membership includes 193 countries and around 900 business, academic institutions, and international and regional organizations.

The CCIR is the 'Comité Consultatif International pour la Radio', a forerunner of the ITU-R.

Although the number of Line for PAL and NTSC are different, it is compensated by having 25 frames/sec and 30 frame pre sec, respectively.

In Table 2-2, there is the list of parameters for the NTSC (US), PAL (Germany) and SECAM (France) standards.

| Parameters | 525-line, 60 field/s | 625-line, 50 field/s |
|---|---|---|
| Standard | NTSC | PAL, SECAM |
| Coded signals | Y, $C_B$, $C_R$ | Y, $C_B$, $C_R$ |
| Number of samples per total line for each signal | 858 | 864 |
| # Lines /Frame | 525 | 625 |
| # frames/sec | 30 | 30 |
| Total #cycles/sec | 2*858*525*30 = 27'027'000 | 2*864*625*25 = 27'000'000 |
| Transfer frequency | 27.0 MHz | 27.0 MHz |
| Sampling frequency for each Pixel | 13.5 MHz | 13.5 MHz |
| Sampling frequency Y | 13.5 MHz | 13.5 MHz |
| Sampling frequency Cb or Cr | 6.75 MHz | 6.75 MHz |
|  |  |  |
| Form of coding | 8 or 10 bit samples | 8 or 10 bit samples |
| Duration of the digital active line expressed in number of samples | 720 | 720 |
| Form of coding | Y, Cb, Y, Cr | Y, Cb, Y, Cr |

**Table 2-2 TV Digital Encoding**

In Figure 2-22, there are examples of the data sampling and transfer for *Y, Cb*, and *Cr*.

For the color information, TV images use the *YCbCr* color format instead of *RGB*, for the following reason. In the *YCbCR* format, the *Y* component represents the intensity or gray shades. For Black and White TV, the image can be displayed with the *Y* component only. The *YCbCr* format could be used for Black and White TV, as well as Color TV.

For a practical point of view, when you need to adjust the contrast and brightness in a TV set, you are modifying the *Y* component. When you adjust the color, you are modifying the *Cb* and *Cr* components. It would be hard to adjust the image brightness if you had to manipulate the three *RGB* components.

It was determined through experiments that the human eye is more sensitive to gray shade changes than color changes. This allowed sampling the *Y* component at the Pixel frequency and the *Cb* & *Cr* components at half the Pixel frequency. The French went one step further by alternating the sampling of the *Cb* and *Cr* component from *SL* to *SL*. Each component was sampled on one *SL* then sent a 'one *SL* delay line' so that it could be reused on the next *SL*. At that time, it allowed the colors in the SECAM standard to be more stable than in the NTSC US standard.

By using the *YCbCr* format the color can be represented in a 16-bit format when the *Cb* and *Cr* components are sampled at half the frequency of *Y* component. During the transfer of color data, the *Cb* and *Cr* components alternate from Pixel to Pixel.

While the Standard TV standards have been replaced by HDTV standards since the early 2000s, they are still used for transmitting TV image in local TV surveillance and monitoring systems. While working at MetaVideo in Los Gatos CA, I have designed several chips for TV surveillance camara systems.

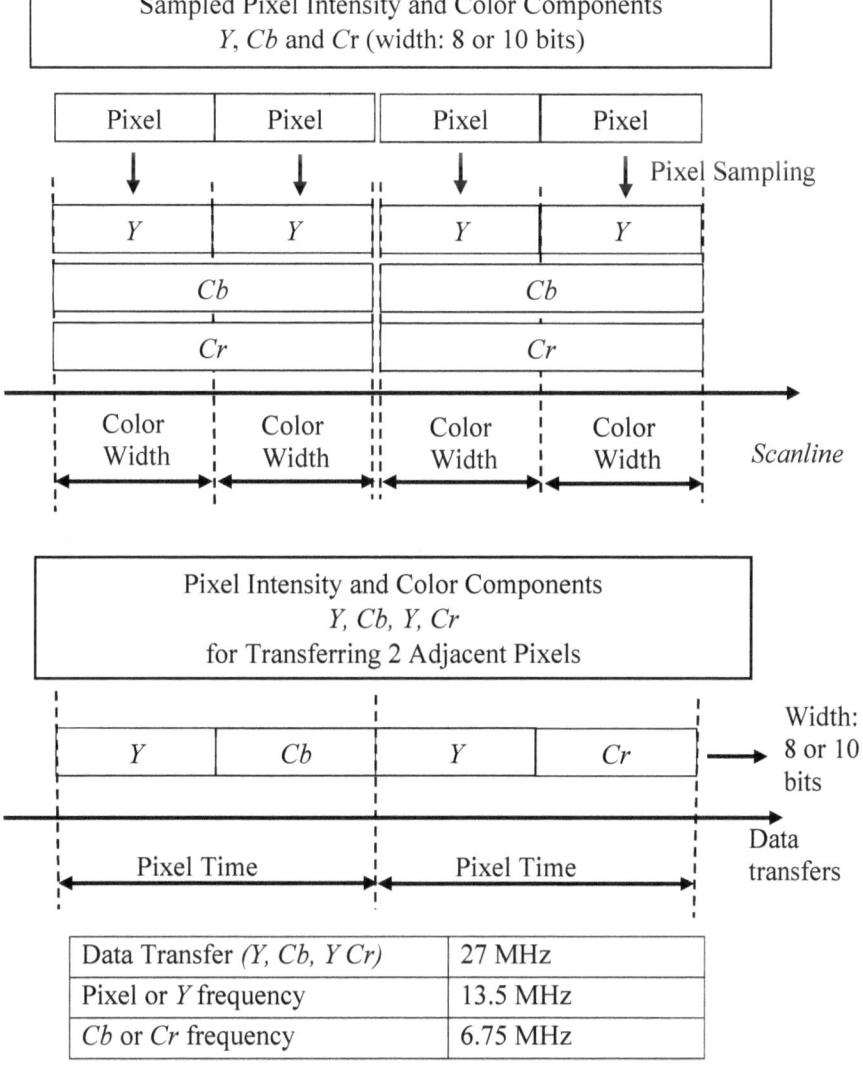

**Figure 2-22 Pixel Data Sampling and Transfer**

## 2.5.2 High-Definition TV (HDTV)

HDTV as is known today first started official broadcasting in 1989 in Japan. It was widely adopted worldwide at the beginning of the 2000s.

HDTV has a better image quality and resolution than Standard TV. Another advantage of HDTV is that it can be broadcast within a smaller bandwidth. The TV channels for Standard TV occupy a bandwidth of 8 MHz per channel. HDTV signals are compressed and can send more detailed images with 8 time less bandwidth. HDTV can be transmitted within the same channels, but instead of 1 channel of STV, up to around 8 HDTV channels can be transmitted within this bandwidth.

# Aliasing

With HDTV, the ITU standards (ITU-R BT.601 and 656) have been replaced by HDTV standards like H.264 and H.265. Refer to [44].

## *H.264*

Advanced Video Coding (AVC), also referred to as H.264 or MPEG-4 Part 10, Advanced Video Coding (MPEG-4 AVC), is a video compression standard based on block-oriented, motion-compensated integer-DCT coding on block size. It is by far the most commonly used format for the recording, compression, and distribution of video. It supports resolutions up to and including 8K.

H-264 Block Sizes: 4x4 or 8x8 Pixels

## *H.265*

High Efficiency Video Coding (HEVC), also known as H.265 and MPEG-H Part 2, is a video compression standard designed as part of the MPEG-H project as a successor of Advanced Video Coding (AVC, H.264)

While AVC uses integer discrete cosine transforms (DCT) with $4\times4$ and $8\times8$ block sizes, HEVC uses integer DCT and DST transforms with varied block sizes between $4\times4$ and $32\times32$.

When compare to AVC, HEVC offers from 25% to 50% better data compression at the same level of quality or substantially improved video quality at the same transmission rate.

H-265 Block Sizes: 4x4, 8x8, 16x16 and 32x32 Pixels

## 2.6 Aliasing with Digital Signals

In CGI, instead of sampling analog signals, the samples are taken from scene elements consisting of 3D triangles projected onto a 2 D image. During rendering, the image is constructed by sampling triangles in 2D geometric space to assign colors to the image Pixels. Only one color can be assigned to each Pixels. When taking only one Sample Point per Pixel, aliasing occurs where triangles cover only portions of Pixels.

### 2.6.1 Point Sampling and Z-Buffer

*Single Sample Point and Z-Buffer*

In the 1960s, with the advent of minicomputers, several universities started to produce 3D images from computers. Because of the amounts of computations, the images were simple. But soon many algorithms were developed and the images became quite complex and realistic.

For images generated by computer, the color and depth of the computed Pixels are saved in a frame buffer in computer memory. The frame Buffer consists of a Color-Buffer and a Z-Buffer. When 2 objects that are projected onto the image overlap in depth, the hidden portions of these object have to be ignored. When rendering the triangles on the image, for each Pixel, the Z-depth is used to select the triangle closest to the viewpoint. Because of the memory requirement, only one Sample Point can be saved in memory. When selecting only one sample, the quantization effect produces stairsteps on the edges of projected triangles or breakup of narrow faces. These stair steps are also referred to as Aliasing or Jaggies. This can be fine for static images, but not for dynamic images and movies.

When only one Sample Point inside of a Pixel (*Pix*) is used to produce dynamic scenes in CGI, the lack of resolution amplified these adverse distracting effects. The edge stairsteps results in edge crawling and small faces popping in out of the scene.

*Multiple Sample Points*

One of the AA methods for reducing the jaggies consists of taking several samples to render each Pixel. There are several ways for selecting these samples. For example:

- Render an image at higher resolution, then reduce the image to a lower resolution with filtering. This is the approach used by Super Sampling AA (SSAA). This approach is equivalent to taking NxN Samples to render each image Pixel.
- Another approach is to sample several points inside of image Pixels, referred to as Subpixels and construct several images using these Subpixels. The final image is obtained by taking the average of these images. The array of Subpixels within a Pixel is often referred to a Bed of Nails (BON). This is the approach used by Multi Sample AA (MSAA). This approach is equivalent to taking Nx1 Samples to render each image Pixel.
- The ideal solution would be to process the Subpixels in one pass, without rendering an image for each Subpixel. This is the approach proposed with Area-Based AA (ABAA). This approach is equivalent to sampling N Subpixel-Areas to render each image Pixel.

## 2.6.2 Sampling Frequency and Nyquist Frequency

In a previous section, the Nyquist frequency was introduced for periodic analog signal. Here, the Nyquist frequency is introduced for Pixel sampling with Pixel frequency ($fP$).

During rendering, the decision to display polygons depends on their displayed size and the sample points. The sample points can be the Pixel center, or, several Subpixel sample points. In general, there is no frequency aliasing when the polygon width is greater than the distance between 2 Sample Points. The Nyquist Sampling Frequency ($fN$) defines the minimum frequency ($f$) of the sampled signals to prevent frequency aliasing [62].

> Definition of Nyquist Frequency:
>
> The Nyquist Frequency $fN$ is defined as 2 times the frequency $f$ of the sampled signal: $fN = 2f$
>
> When sampling a signal, the sampling frequency $fS$ should be at least greater than the Nyquist Frequency $fN$ to prevent aliasing: $fS > fN = 2f$

When the highest frequency of a signal is less than the Nyquist frequency of the sampler, the resulting sample sequence is said to be free of the distortion known as aliasing, and the corresponding sample-rate is said to be above the Nyquist rate for that particular signal.

> What is Aliasing:
>
> The Nyquist Sampling frequency is a requirement for preventing 'Frequency Aliasing'. There are other aliasing effects such as jaggies (edge stairsteps and crawling), faces popping and other distracting artifacts. For this reason, the definition of Nyquist frequency should be rephrased like:
>
> When sampling a signal, the sampling frequency $fS$ should be at least greater than the Nyquist Frequency $fN$ to prevent 'frequency aliasing'.

### *Nyquist Frequency and Pixel Frequency*

When sampling signal and displaying these signals, several frequencies need to be defined:

- $f$: Signal frequency or Pattern frequency
- $fP$: Pixel frequency
- $fS$: Sample frequency
- $fN$: Nyquist frequency

## 2.6.3 Checkerboard Pattern with 1 Sample per Pixel

In the following examples, the Pixel color is obtained with only 1 sample per Pixel. A checkerboard pattern is used to illustrate how the Nyquist Frequency applies to Pixel sampling.

### *Rendering a Checkerboard Pattern*

When rendering a checkerboard pattern, the pattern frequency is the frequency of the repeating pattern. The pattern period consists of '1 white square and 1 black square'.

So, the Sample frequency of the checkerboard pattern should be at least 1 sample per square.

- $f(pattern) = 2 squares/period$.

In order to sample a pattern without aliasing, the sampling frequency should be at least greater than twice the Signal frequency, or Pattern frequency.
That is $fS = 1\ sample/square$.

### *Checkerboard with Squares Equal to Pixel Size*

When sampling with 1 Sample Point per Pixel, the Nyquist frequency should be at least equal to the Pixel frequency is. It takes 2 cycles to represent a cycle of white and black squares.
When sampling the checkerboard pattern at 1 sample/Pixel and 1 square per Pixel, the Pattern frequency is $f(pattern) = fP/2$
where $fP = Pixel\ frequency$.

Refer to Figure 2-23.

In Figure 2-24, there is an example of a checkerboard where each square is equal to 1 Pixel. There are 2 samples, 1 taken on the bottom-right moving and 1 taken on the top-left. As can be seen, the rendered 8x8 pixel-span is unchanged. This is different from the sine being sampled across a half cycle (180 degrees or Pi radians). Compare with analog 'Sampling a Sine Function' in a previous section.

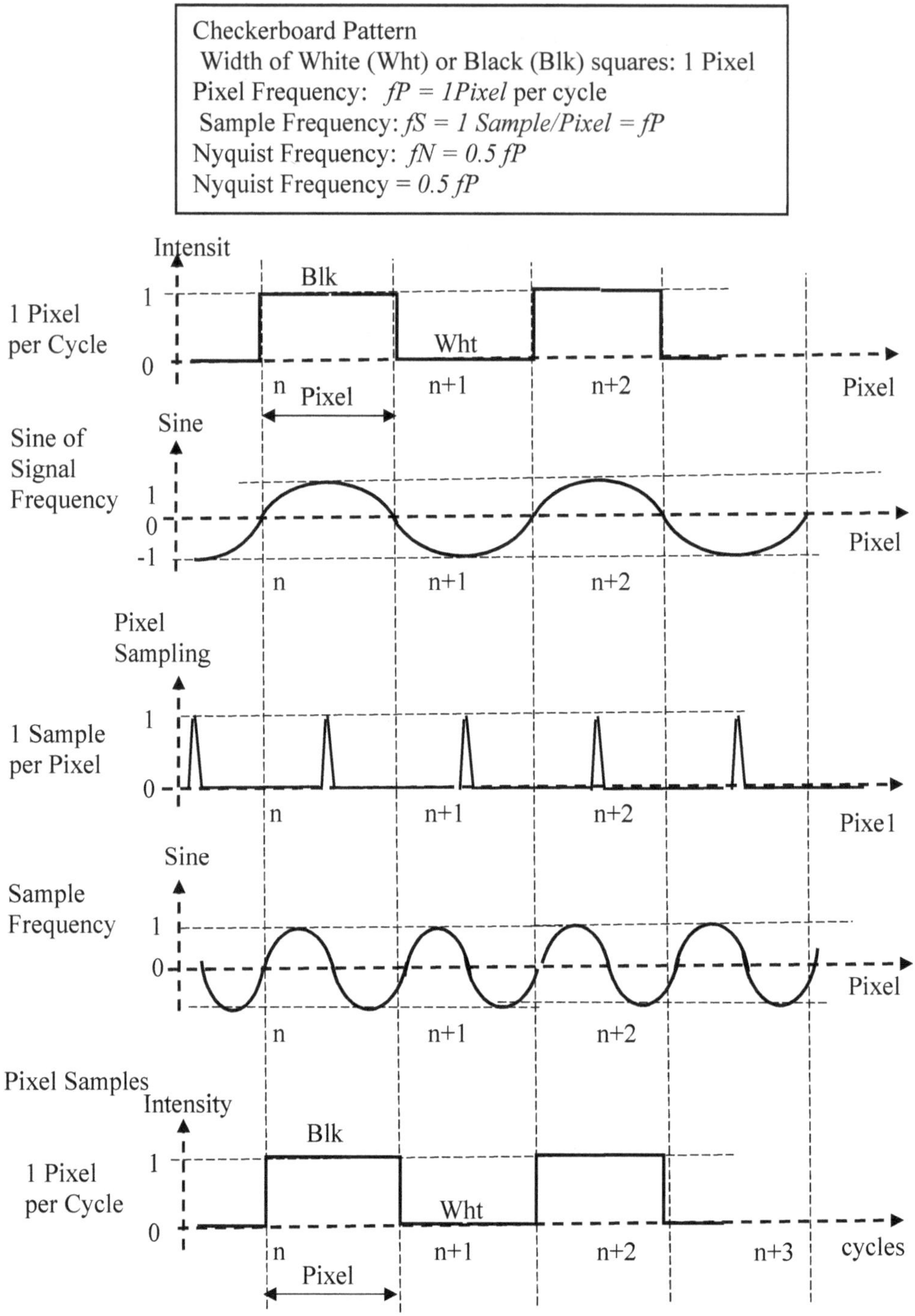
Checkerboard Pattern
Width of White (Wht) or Black (Blk) squares: 1 Pixel
Pixel Frequency: fP = 1Pixel per cycle
Sample Frequency: fS = 1 Sample/Pixel = fP
Nyquist Frequency: fN = 0.5 fP
Nyquist Frequency = 0.5 fP
Intensit
1 Pixel per Cycle
1
0
Blk
Wht
n
Pixel
n+1
n+2
Pixel
Sine
Sine of Signal Frequency
1
0
-1
n
n+1
n+2
Pixel
Pixel Sampling
1 Sample per Pixel
1
0
n
n+1
n+2
Pixel
Sine
Sample Frequency
1
0
n
n+1
n+2
Pixel
Pixel Samples
Intensity
1 Pixel per Cycle
1
0
Blk
Wht
n
n+1
n+2
n+3
cycles
Pixel

**Figure 2-23 Sampled Signal with 1 Sample per Pixel**

# Aliasing

> Using 1 Sample per Pixel: Nyquist Frequency = Pixel Frequency
> Checkerboard Pattern Frequency = 1 square per pixel = NyquistFrequency /2
> Nyquist Frequency = 2* Pattern Frequency

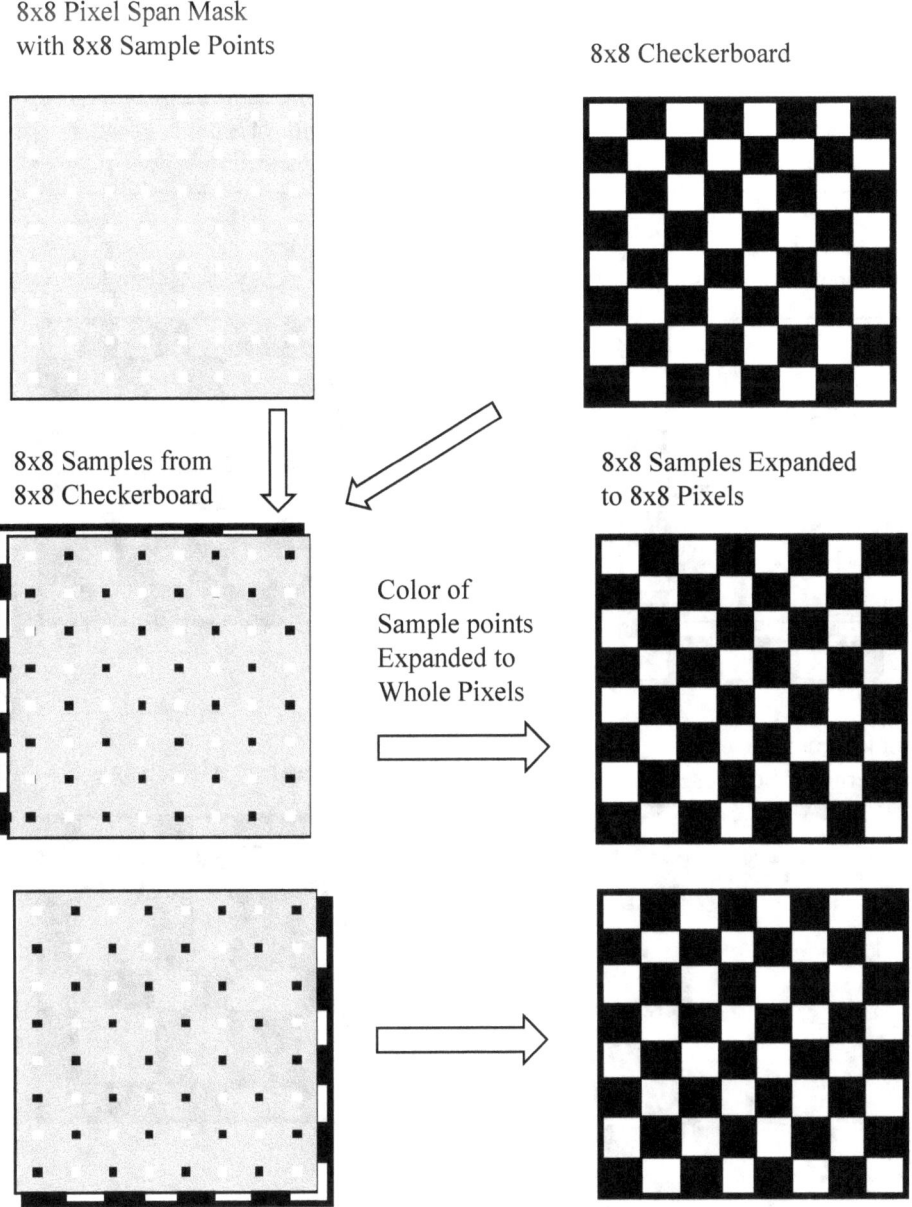

**Figure 2-24 Checkerboard with Squares Close to the Pixel Size**

Aliasing

## *Checkerboard Squares Greater than Pixel Size*

There is no frequency aliasing when there is at least 1 sample per Pixel.

When squares in checkerboard are larger than Pixels, the squares are displayed properly (as squares or rectangles). In this case when the pattern frequency is less than half the Pixel frequency, there is no 'frequency aliasing; In the sampled image, there is either a square or a rectangle for each sampled square. Refer to Figure 2-25

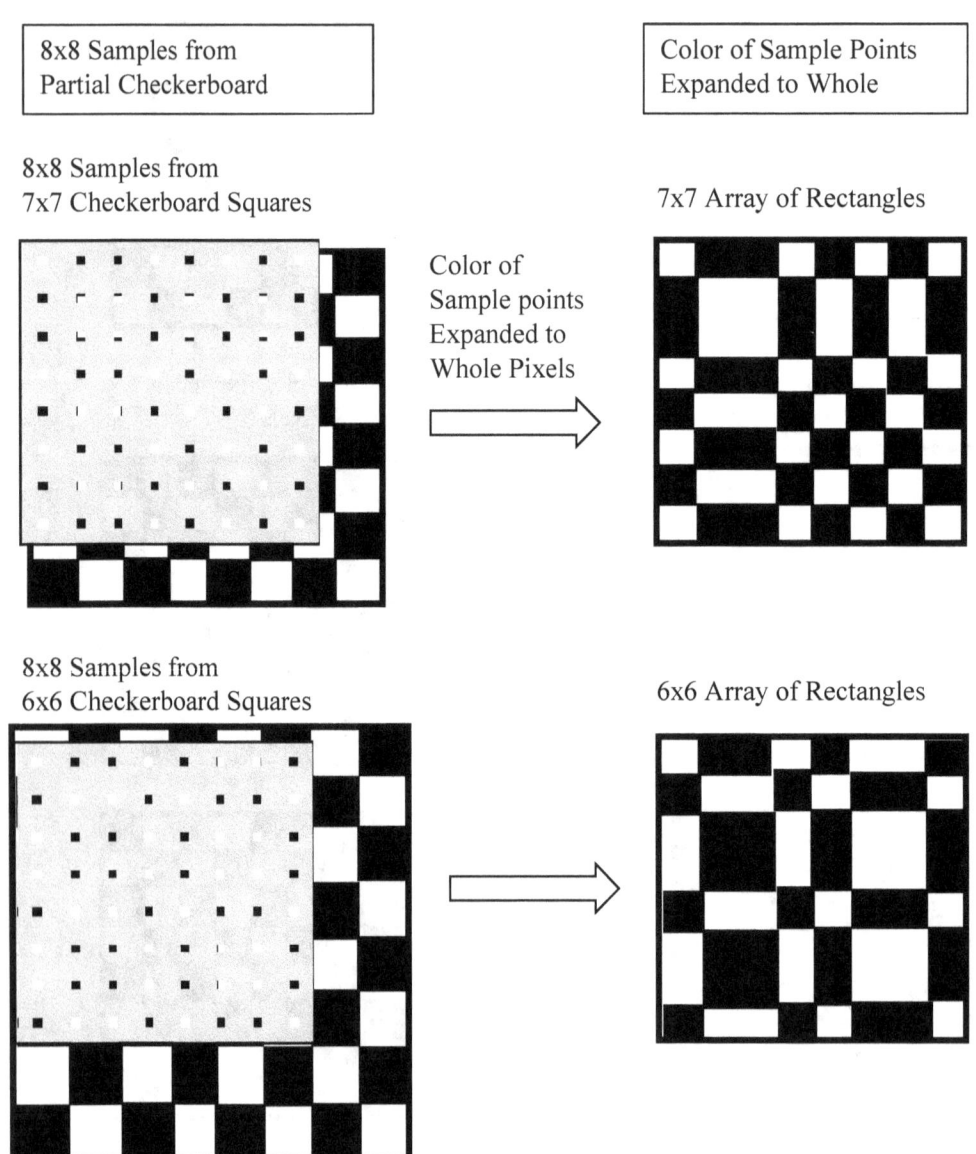

**Figure 2-25 Sampling when Sample Freq > Nyquist Freq**

## *Checkerboard Squares Near Pixel Size*

- When the rendered squares in checkerboard pattern are **larger** than the Pixel size, they will show no frequency aliasing.
- When the rendered squares in checkerboard pattern are **equal** to Pixel size, they is no frequency aliasing.
- When the rendered squares in checkerboard patterns are **smaller** than Pixel size, they show frequency aliasing. The under sampling produces squares that are larger than the projected size. They also produce Moiré patterns.

Refer to Figure 2-26 with Example when Sample Frequency is near the Nyquist Frequency

# Aliasing

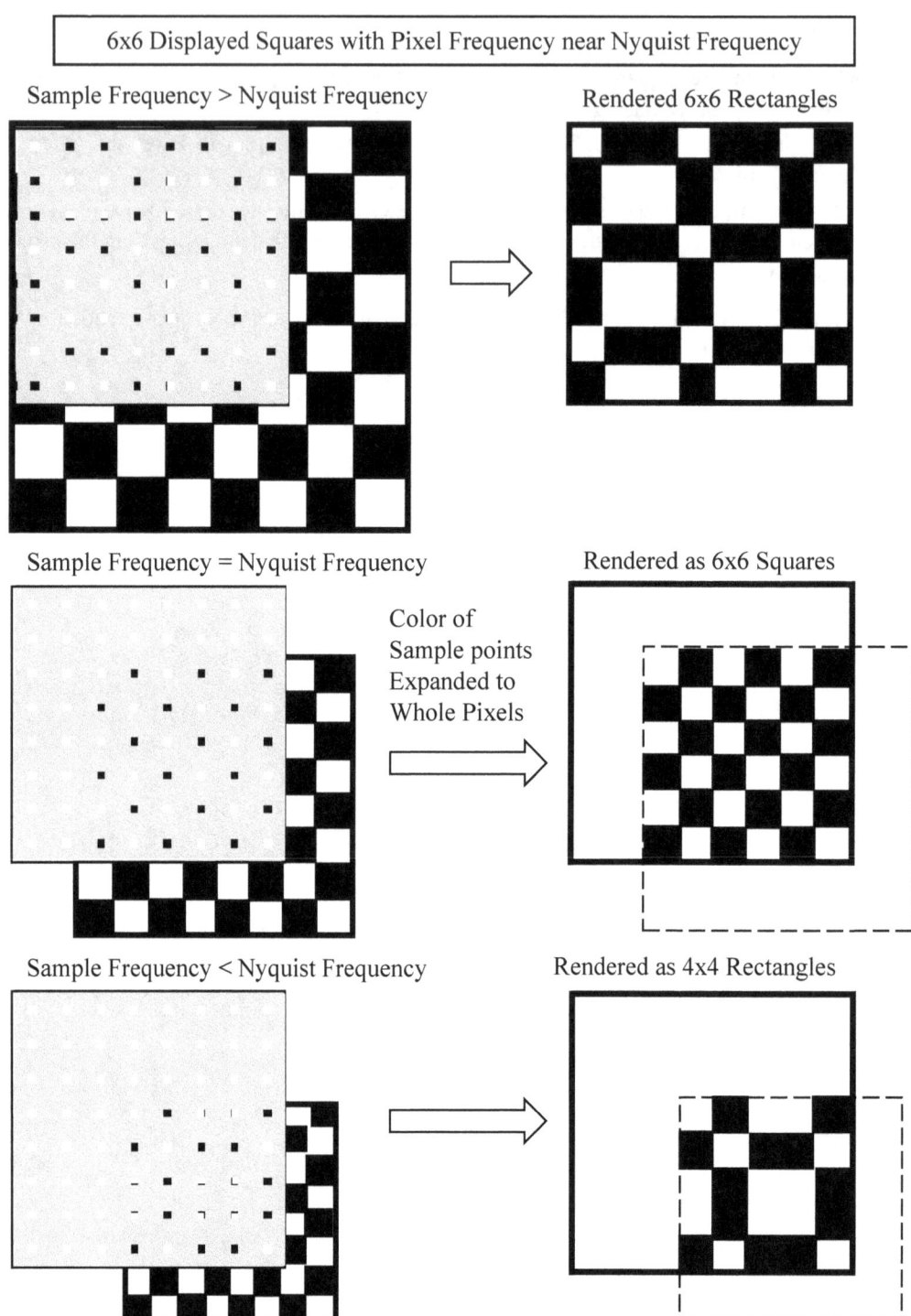

**Figure 2-26 Checkerboard with Squares near the Pixel Size**

# Aliasing

## *Checkerboard Squares Smaller than Pixel Size*

When checkerboard squares are smaller than the Pixel size, many distracting aliasing effects occur.

- In-and-out face popping
- Edge Crawling
- Moiré patterns

Refer to 3$^{rd}$ example in the figure, when the Sampling Frequency < Nyquist Frequency

## *Checkerboard Squares Equal to Half Pixel Size*

There is an interesting case when the checkerboard squares are equal to half the Pixel size. In this case the sample frequency is equal to ½ Nyquist frequency: $fS = fN/2$.

Refer to Figure 2-27.

In this example the sampled array of 6x6 checkerboard squares results in a display of a Black or White square of size 3x3 Pixels.

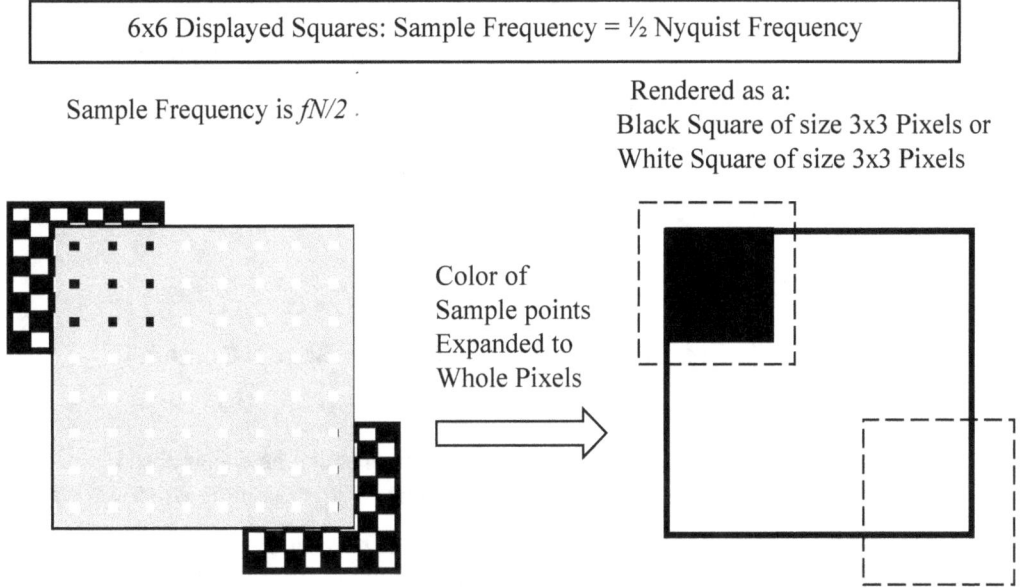

**Figure 2-27 Pixel Frequency Equal to 1/2 Nyquist Frequency**

## 2.6.4 Box Filter and Frequency Response

In Sample Theory, the sampling region in the image is referred to a Fourier window [63]. Within the window the weights to the Sample Points are represented by a function. Outside of the window, the sample weights are '0'. When the image is rendered with N Sample Points per Pixel and all the samples have the same weight, the sample window is a square window. This square window represents a 'Box Filter'.

Refer to Figure 2-28.

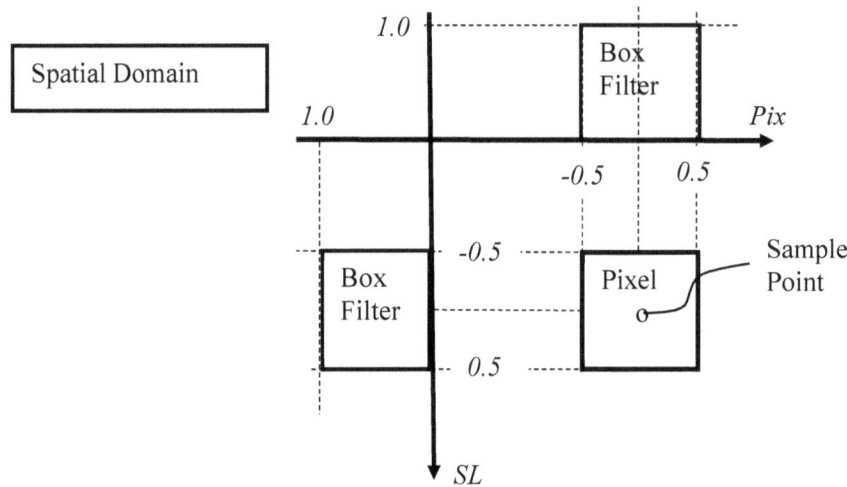

**Figure 2-28 Two-Dimensional Box Filter in Spatial Domain**

*Frequency Response*

As an example, when an image is rendered, the image elements can be decomposed in a sum of signal at different frequencies. This is the frequency response of the sampling window.

The sampling window has a frequency response that indicates how the frequency of the signal will be rendered. The single point sampling (N=1) can be represented by a Box Filter in the 'spatial or time domain'. The frequency response is represented by a *sinc()* function in the 'frequency domain':

$sinc(Pi * x) = sine (Pi * x) / (Pi * x)$, where $x$ is the signal angle in radian.

Refer to Figure 2-29, 'Box Frequency Response with *sinc()* Function'.
Refer to 'Nyquist and sinc() function' in Wikipedia [62].

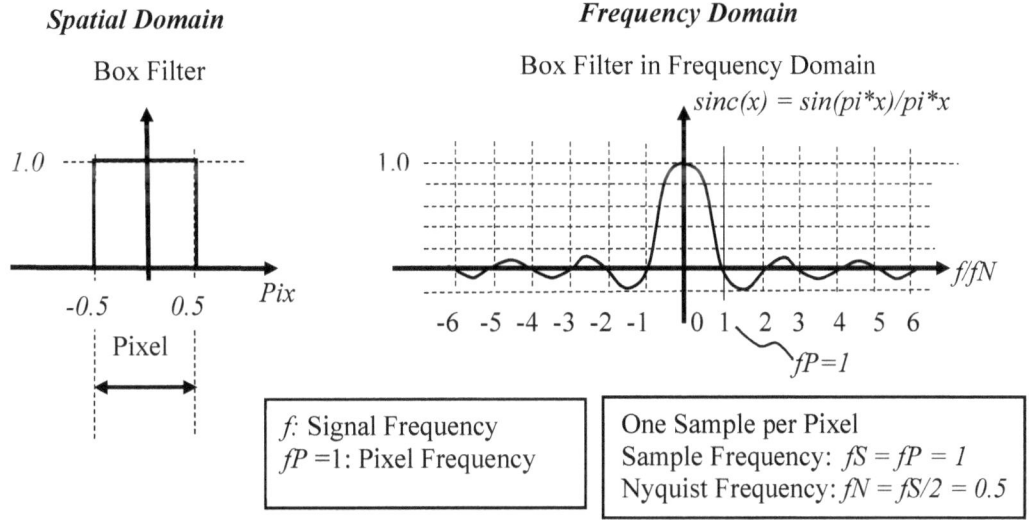

**Figure 2-29 Box Filter in Spatial Domain and Frequency Domain**

*Frequency Aliasing and Aliasing Effects*

According to the sampling theory, aliasing occurs when the frequency of the signal is more than half the Nyquist frequency. This is what I will refer to as 'Frequency Aliasing'. In CGI, other distracting artifacts are also referred to as 'Aliasing'. I will refer these as 'Aliasing' or 'Aliasing Artifacts'.

When sampling within a Pixel, the Pixel frequency($fP$) is equal to 1:

$fP = 1$;

With 1 Sample Point per Pixel, the sample frequency ($fS$) is equal to the Pixel frequency ($fP$).
$fS = fP$

To prevent aliasing, the sample frequency ($fS$) should be no less than twice the Nyquist frequency ($fN$).
$fN = fS/2$

To prevent aliasing, the signal frequency ($f$) should be no more than the Nyquist frequency.
$f < fN = fP/2$

The signal frequency ($f$) is limited to half the Pixel sample frequency ($fS$).

Refer to Figure 2-30 and 2-31.

When considering the frequency response, there is significant 'Frequency Aliasing' when the signal frequency ($f$) becomes greater than the Nyquist frequency of $fN=0.5$. This explains the Moiré patterns with the checkerboard when the size of the squares becomes smaller that the Pixel size.

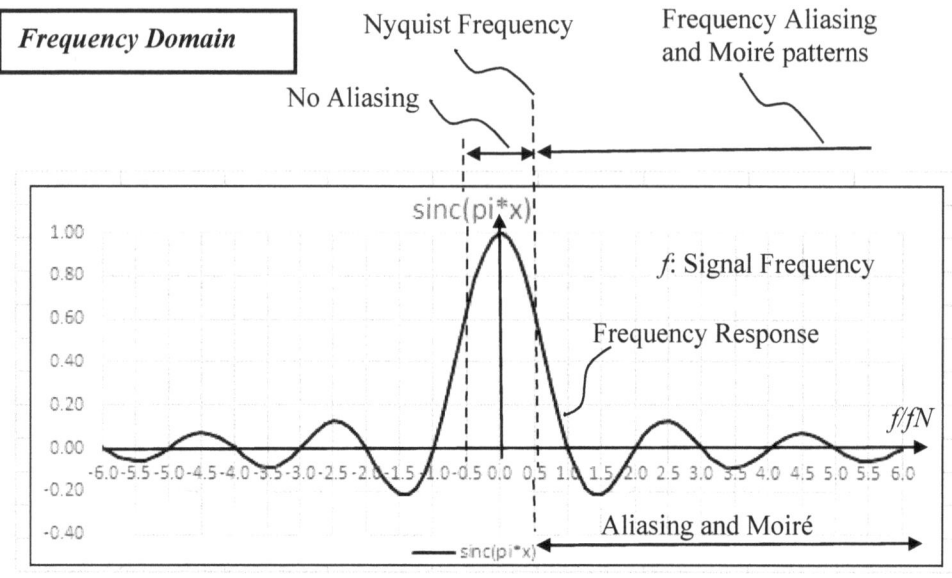

One Sample per Pixel: $fP = 1.0$; $fN = fP/2$;

**Figure 2-30 Box Frequency Response with sinc() Function**

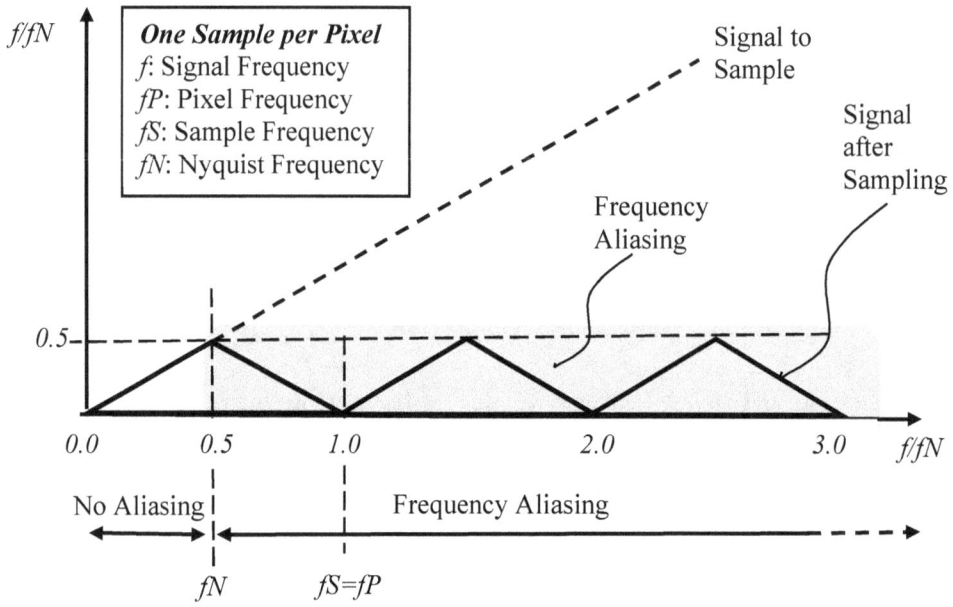

**Figure 2-31 Signal to Sample and Signal after Sampling**

# Chapter 3 **Anti-Aliasing with Super-Sampling**

AA algorithms for CGI described in this book assume that the images are rendered with triangle or polygon processing. There are other approaches like 'ray tracing' and 'voxel processing'. These are usually more computation intensive. These techniques can produce beautiful images, but they require too much processing for use in real time applications. For this reason, for speed reason when processing RT CGI, the preferred approach is to process triangles with one or more Sample Points per Pixel.

As mentioned earlier, for curved surfaces, there are algorithms for creating models with curved surfaces using bicubic patches. They can produce more realistic images. But these models still have to be converted into triangle meshes [13][14][15] in 3D space before the projection onto the 2D image plane. Then the projected triangles can be rendered by the computer hardware.

In CGI, instead of sampling analog signals, the samples are taken from projected geometric features. During rendering, triangles are projected onto the image and colors are assigned to the Pixels covered by these triangles. When a Pixel is covered by a triangle, its color is derived from samples taken within that Pixel. Aliasing occurs when Pixels are only partially covered by triangles. When taking only one Sample Point per Pixel, aliasing occurs when there are abrupt transitions of color.

When considering CGI processing, several approaches to AA have to be considered.
- General algorithms for AA
- Non-Real-Time CGI (Non-RT CGI)
- Real-Time CGI (RT CGI)

## 3.1 Super Sampling AA (SSAA)

For non-RT CGI, one approach is SSAA. This is accomplished by computing an image at a higher resolution than that of the target image using one Sample Point per Pixel. Then the high-resolution image is reduced to the desired resolution with filtering. Since there are no time constraints, large images can be computed offline using high-speed general-purpose computers. For example, when doing a Super-Sampling at 4x4 resolution, an image of 2048x2048 Pixels is computed. It is then reduced to a 512x512 Pixels image thru filtering. In this case the computing time will be roughly 4x4=16 time larger.

### 3.1.1 SSAA Examples

I am an *IEEE Society* life time member. When *IEEE* started a special publication about 3D graphics in 1981, 'IEEE Computer Graphics and Applications' (IEEE CG&A), I became an early subscriber. In the first issue, there was a very good article from *Franklin C. Crow*, 'A Comparison of Antialiasing Techniques' [5]. There were many images comparing different SSAA techniques with and without Filtering. There was also a 3D Graphics image on the front cover that used *Franklin C. Crow* Bartlett Window Filter. The results of this article are analyzed in more details in a later section of this chapter about 'Two-Dimensional Super-Sampling' and 'Selecting AA

Filters'. One small problem with this article is that the reproduced images are too small to really evaluate the effect of SSAA and filtering.

*Franklin C. Crow* has published several articles comparing AA algorithms and filters. These non-RT AA algorithms used Super Sampling by computing the image at a higher resolution like 2048 Pixels per line and 2048 SLs per frame. The anti-aliased image at lower resolution is obtained by reducing the image to 512 Pixels per line and 512 SLs, using averaging or filtering. For each Pixel, the contributions of NxN Pixels were combined into one Pixel color in the lower resolution image.

Refer to *Franklin C. Crow* publications [5]:
'The Aliasing Problem in Computer-Generated Shaded Images.', Comm ACM, 1977
'A Comparison of Antialiasing Techniques', IEEE CG&A, 1981

### 3.1.2 SSAA with Filtering

When downscaling the image with SSAA, different types of filters can be applied. When taking the average of Pixels samples in, the filtering can be done with a simple average or a weighted average of the samples. When all the samples have the same weight the resulting the AA filter is a square, or' Box Filter'. Another approach is to assign weights to the samples that linearly increase from edge of the Pixel to the center of the Pixel. The resulting filter is a "triangle', 'Tent' Filter' or 'Bartlett' Filter.

When it comes to high quality AA, fancy filters can be used to render the triangles with Subpixel information. *Jim Blinn* has written many articles about image filtering. I am a big fan of *Jim Blinn*. On the last pages of most issues of *IEEE CG&A*, there was my favorite subjects about 3D Graphics and Math in the '*Jim Blinn's Corner'* section. I enjoyed reading these articles. They gave me a good insight about AA and other aspects of 3D graphics. So, when *Jim Blinn* decided to publish a collection of these articles in books, I rushed to buy his books.

For non-RT CGI processing and AA, there is a good source of information about AA filters in the book '*Dirty Pixels'*, from *Jim Blinn*. In particular the following Chapters:

Blinn, James F.: Jim Blinn's Corner: Dirty Pixels [3]
   Chapter 2: 'What We Need Around Here is More Aliasing'
   Chapter 3: 'Return of the Jaggy'

Other Books of interest from *Jim Blinn*:
Blinn, James F.: Jim Blinn's Corner: A Trip Down the Graphics Pipeline.[2]
Blinn, James F.: Jim Blinn's Corner: Notation, Notation, Notation.[4]

## 3.2 One-Dimensional Super-Sampling

One AA method for reducing the jaggies consists Super-Sampling (SSAA).

In this approach, the image is rendered at a higher resolution, then reduced to a lower target resolution with filtering.

With SSAA, the color of each Pixel is the result of sampling a group of Pixels, then combining their contributions into a single color by doing a simple or a weighted average of these contributions. There are several ways to select the groups of Pixels such as:

- One-dimensional array of Pixels, with group size Nx1
- Two-dimensional array of Pixels, with group size NxN
- Random group of Pixels, with group size N

Also, with SSAA the sample point is assumed to be at the center or the top left corner of Pixels. But there could be some advantages by varying the selection of Sample Points within Pixels.

In the trivial case of Single Point Sample, the group size is $N=1$. There is only one way to select the Pixel color. The sampling in Horizontal and Vertical dimension is 1x1. When considering the two dimensions, their no difference since the sampling is still *1x1*.

When considering Pixel array sizes with $N>1$, there is an advantage to consider these cases in one-dimension (*Nx1*) first, then to generalize cases in two dimensions (*NxN*).

## 3.2.1 Sampling Image with One Sample per Pixel

The case of $N=1$ was evaluated with a checkerboard pattern in the previous section, with the following results.

### *Trivial case of Super-Sampling with 1x1 Pixel*

Pixel frequency: $fP = 1$;
Sample frequency: $fS = fP = 1$;
Nyquist frequency to prevent aliasing: $fN = fS/2 = 0.5$;
Signal frequency (f) to prevent aliasing: $f < fN = fP/2$;

The next step is to consider Super-Sampling with 2x1 samples. This consist of taking 2 Pixel samples in one direction.

## 3.2.2 One-Dimensional Super-Sampling with *2x1*

The rendering of the checkerboard example can be improved with Super-Sampling (SS). The improvement with SS can be evaluated step by step by increasing the number of samples. In order to compare the results, the SS operation can be scaled down using Subpixels within a Pixel.

The first step is to consider a one-dimensional *2x1* Super-Sampling of the Checkerboard Pattern with 2 Samples per Pixel.

### *Replacing Downscaling Operation by Using Subpixels*

When considering image Super-Sampling with $N>1$, the operation of selecting a group of *Nx1* or *NxN* Pixels, followed by downscaling the image can be simplified in most cases.

For RT CGI, the computation of higher resolution images followed by downscaling, can be too time consuming. The most common approach is to use a Selection of Sample Points within a Pixels. The samples within Pixels are also referred to Subpixels or Bed of Nail (BON). The final Pixel color is obtained by taking the average of the Subpixel contributions. This approach is also referred to Multi-Sample AA (MSAA)

The image Super-Sampling use for AA (SSAA) can be replaced by sampling within the target image size and sampling within single Pixels with Nx1or NxN Subpixels (MSAA). For example, sampling of a *2x1* group of Pixels can be replace by sampling *2x1* Subpixels in a single Pixel. In this case, the Subpixels within the Pixel will be positioned in a pattern similar to the Group of Pixel samples they represent. Refer to Figure 3-1

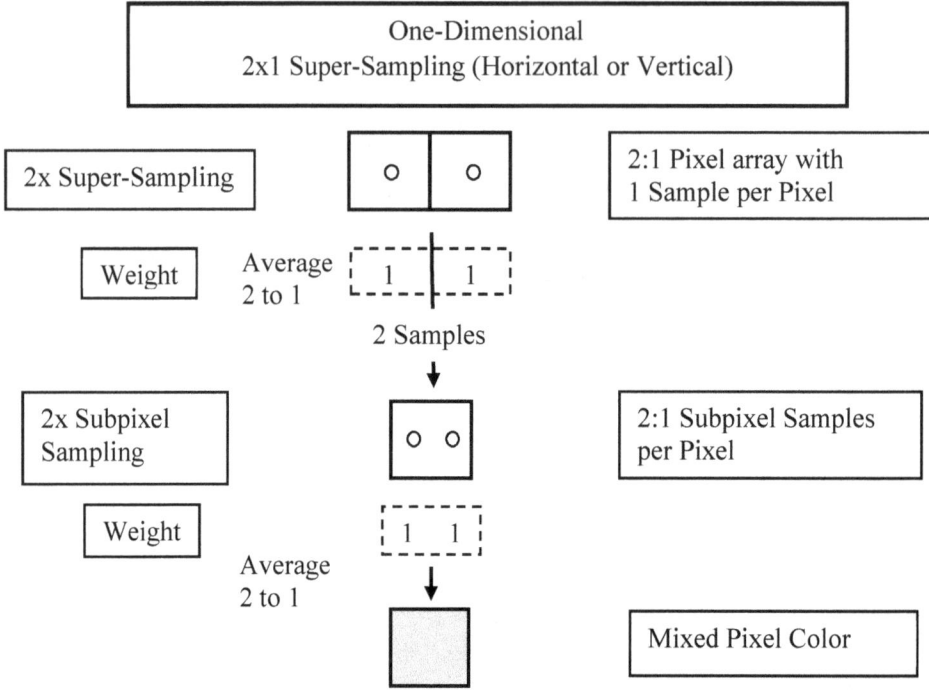

**Figure 3-1 One-Dimensional 2x Super Sampling and 2x Subpixel Sampling**

When sampling within a Pixel, the Pixel frequency is always equal to: $fP=1.0$;

Because only one color is assigned to each Pixel, no matter how many samples contribute to the Pixel Color, each Pixel is still displayed with a single intensity or color.

With Super-Sampling 2x1, the Sample and Nyquist frequencies become:
Sample frequency: $fS = 2fP = 2.0$ (two Subpixels per Pixel);
Nyquist frequency: $fN = fS/2 = 1.0$;
Signal frequency to prevent aliasing: $f < fN = fP$;

By using 2 samples per Pixel, the checkerboard is displayed with 2x Super-Sampling. The Nyquist frequency has doubled when compared to one sample per Pixel. When reduced to 1 Pixel, their color contribution is averaged. Each to these 2 samples contribute to half the color of the single Pixel. By introducing a gray-shades in the combined pixels, the aliasing due to sampling is reduced.

Refer to Figure 3-2, 'Square Width = 1 Pixel; $f = fP/2$' (checkerboard same size as 8 Pixels)

For 2 Sample Points per Pixel, depending on how the checkerboard squares line up with the Sample Points, the resulting picture color will be either alternating black and white, or a uniform gray color.

# Anti-Aliasing with Super-Sampling

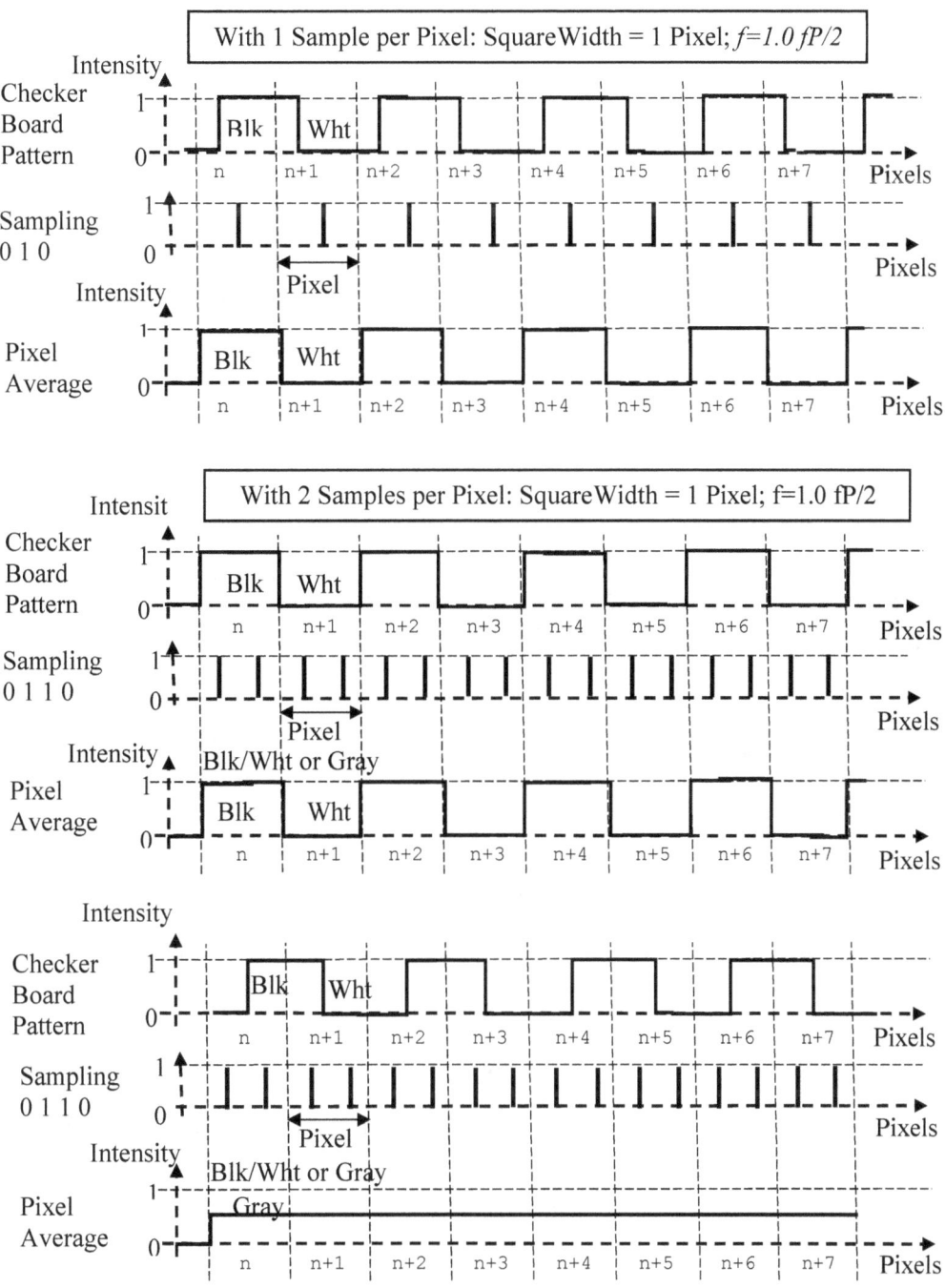

**Figure 3-2 Squares of Width=1, with 1 and 2 Samples per Pixel**

### 3.2.3 Checkerboard Pattern with 3 Samples per Pixel

The 2x Super-Sampling can be improved by taking 3 samples per Pixel with unequal weights of '1, 2, 1'. Refer to Figure 3-3, '3 Samples per Pixel', on the right side.

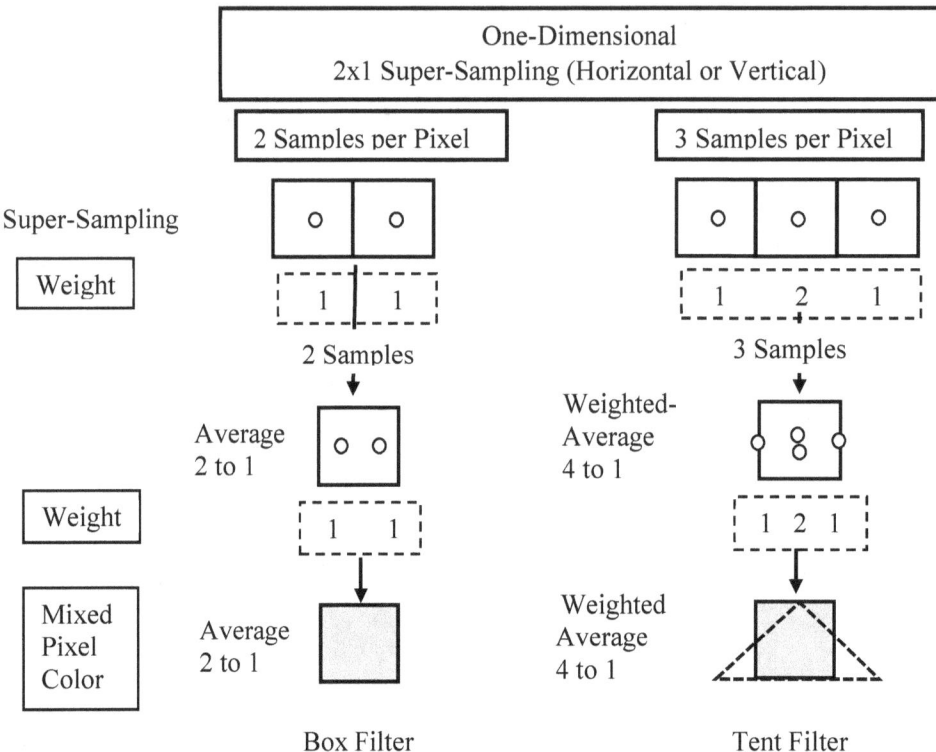

**Figure 3-3 One-Dimensional 2x Super Sampling**

For 3 Sample Points per Pixel, the Pixel center is Sampled twice. This corresponds to a weight of 1+2+1 = 4. In the image, they contribute to 2 adjacent Pixels. When reduced to 1 single Pixel, their contribution is averaged. Their contribution to resulting Pixel is (1+2+1)/4 =1.

Although there are 3 samples per Pixel, the distance between Subpixels is the same as the distance with 2 Subpixels. The Subpixels on the edge are shared with the adjacent Pixels. So, with the Tent filter with 3 Subpixels it is still a 2x1 Super-Sampling. The color assigned to each Pixel is the weighted average of the contributing samples.

For 3 Sample Point per Pixel, depending on how the checkerboard squares line up with the sample points, the resulting picture color will be either alternating black and white, or alternating 2 gray colors.

Refer to Figure 3-4, where checkerboard squares are projected as 1 square per Pixel. In this case: for Square Width = 1 Pixel, $f = fP/2$.

# Anti-Aliasing with Super-Sampling

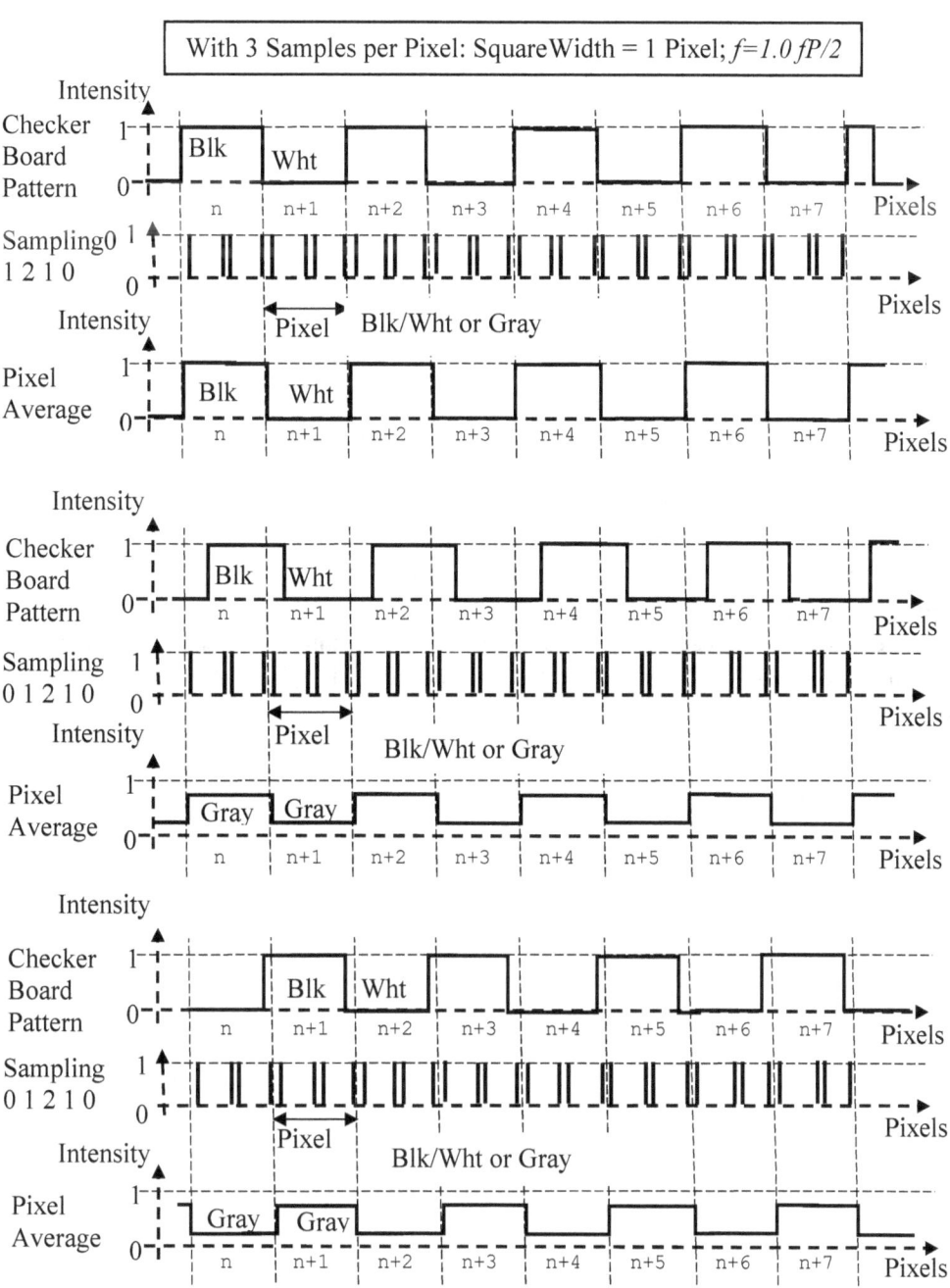

**Figure 3-4 Squares of Width=1, with 3 Samples per Pixel**

### 3.2.4 Checkerboard Sampling from ½ to 1 Pixel.

When the size of the checkerboard pattern decreases from 1 square/Pixel (half the Pixel frequency) to 2 squares per Pixel (Pixel frequency $fP$) it reaches the Nyquist frequency ($f=fN$).

  1 square/Pixel: $f = fP/2 = fN/2$
  2 squares/Pixel: $f = fP = fN$

When the size of the checkerboard squares is smaller than a Pixel but greater a half Pixel, the overlapping squares in the sampled Pixels will be replaced with gray shades.

As the size of the squares decreases, the image will have an increasing number of gray squares until the checkerboard color reaches a uniform gray color at half a Pixel.

***Figures in Spatial (Time) Domain***

For Width = 1, refer to the 2 examples in the previous section.

For Width < 1, refer to following figures in 'spatial domain'. In each of the following figures, there are 3 examples in 'time domain', for 1, 2 and 3 samples per Pixel.

Figure 3-5 SquareWidth = 7/8 Pixel; $f = 1.14\,fP/2 = 0.57\,fP$;
Figure 3-6, SquareWidth = 6/8 Pixel; $f = 1.33\,fP/2 = 0.67\,fP$;
Figure 3-7, SquareWidth = 5/8 Pixel; $f = 1.60\,fP/2 = 0.80\,fP$;
Figure 3-8, SquareWidth = 1/2 Pixel; $f = 2.0\,fP/2 = fP$;

As can be observed in these figures, when the number of samples increases, the number of gray shades in the averaged Pixels also increases. At the frequency $f=fP$, all the Pixel have the same color or shade.

# Anti-Aliasing with Super-Sampling

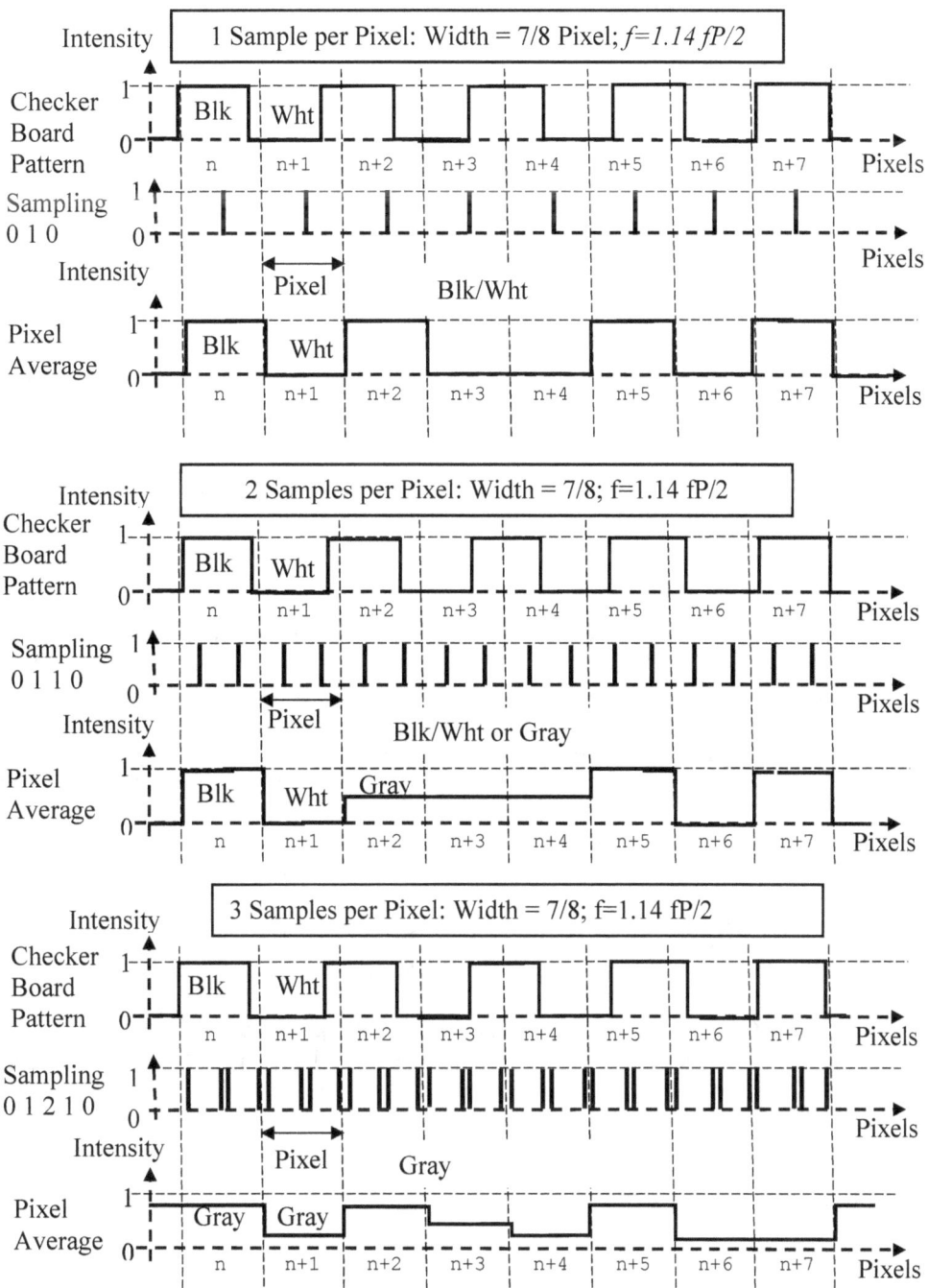

**Figure 3-5 Checkerboard with *f* = 1.14 fP/2**

New Area-Based Anti-Aliasing for CGI

Anti-Aliasing with Super-Sampling

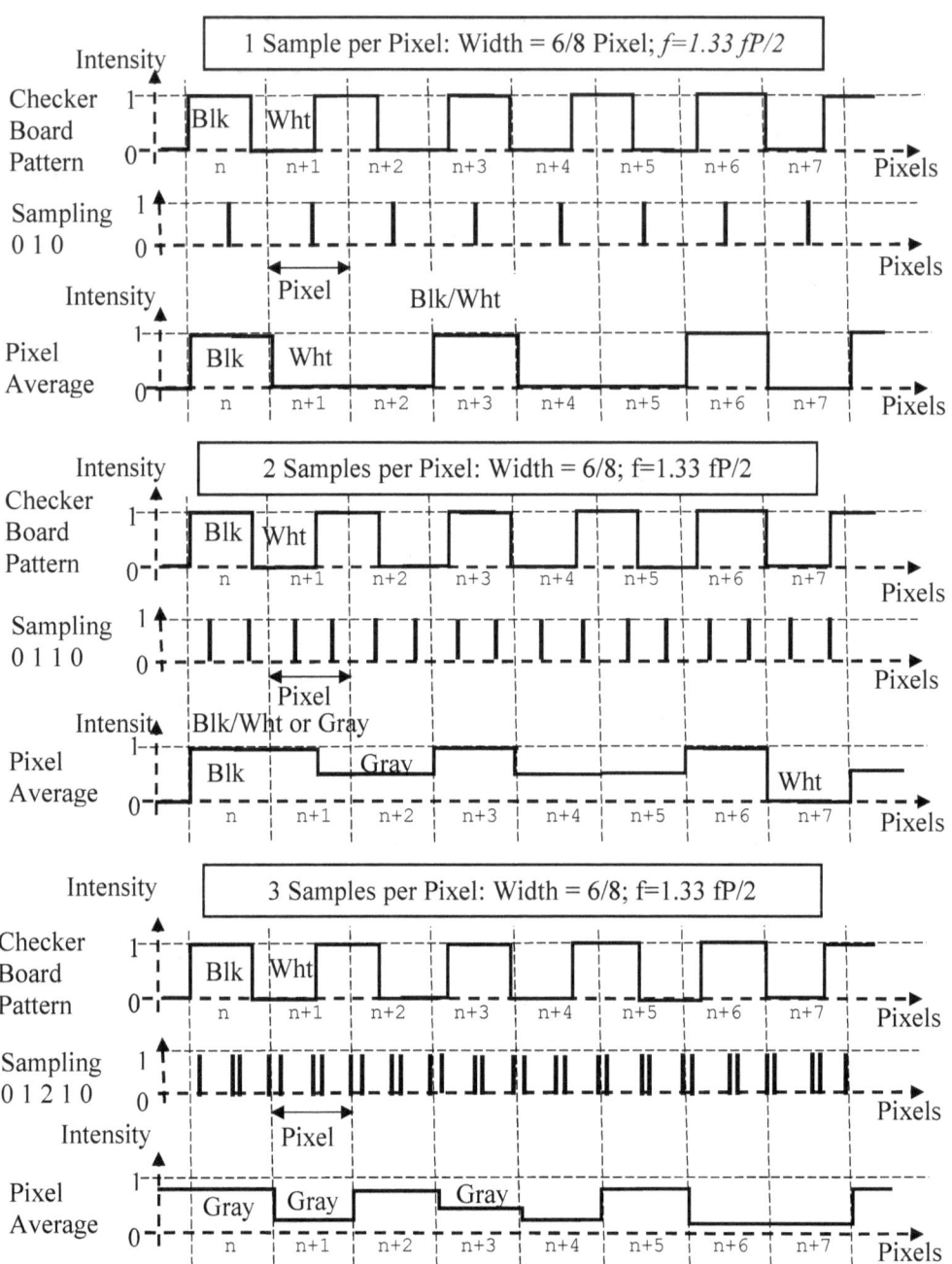

**Figure 3-6 Checkerboard with *f* = 1.33 fP/2**

Anti-Aliasing with Super-Sampling

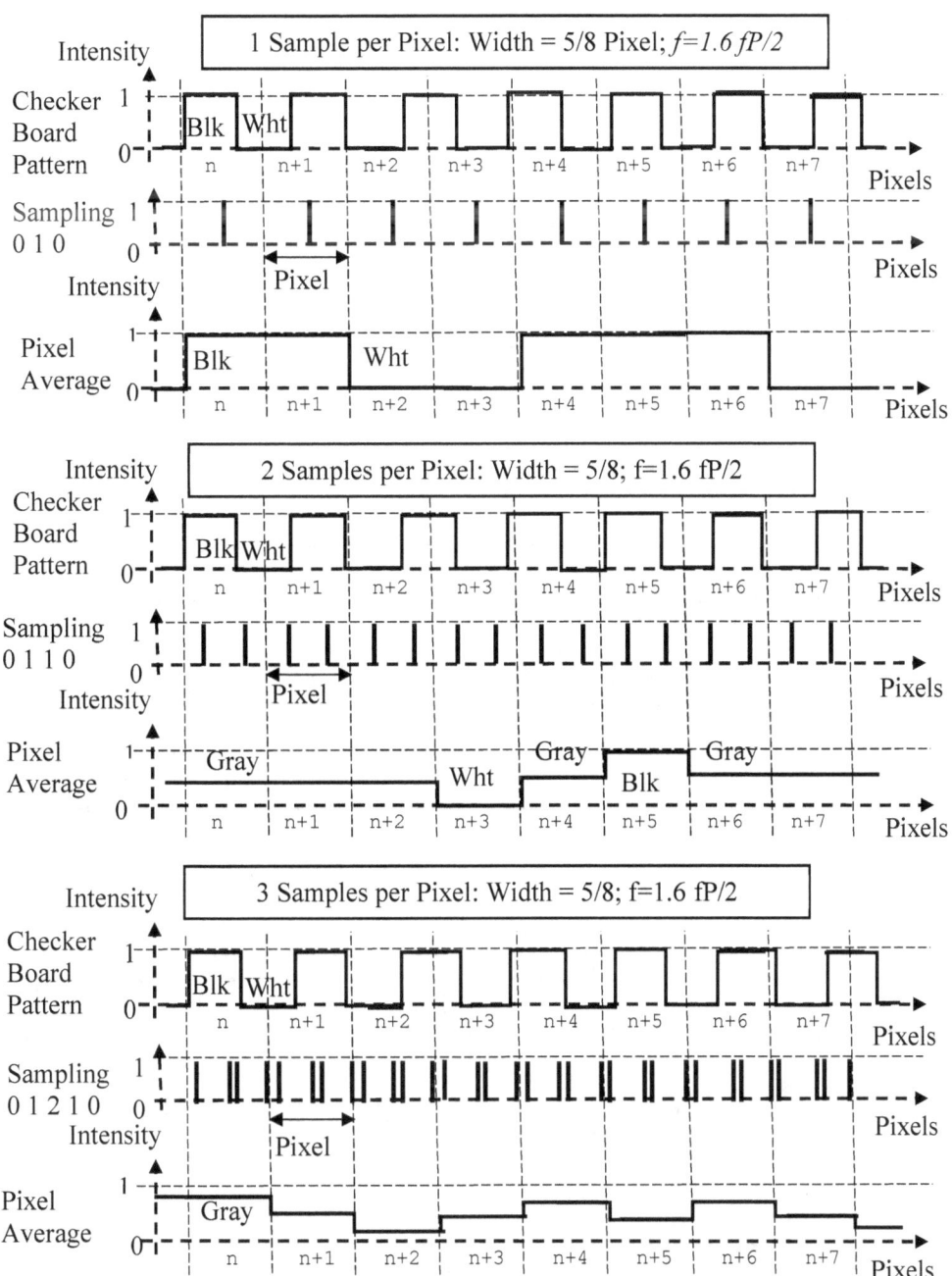

**Figure 3-7 Checkerboard with *f* = 1.60 fP/2**

New Area-Based Anti-Aliasing for CGI 91

Anti-Aliasing with Super-Sampling

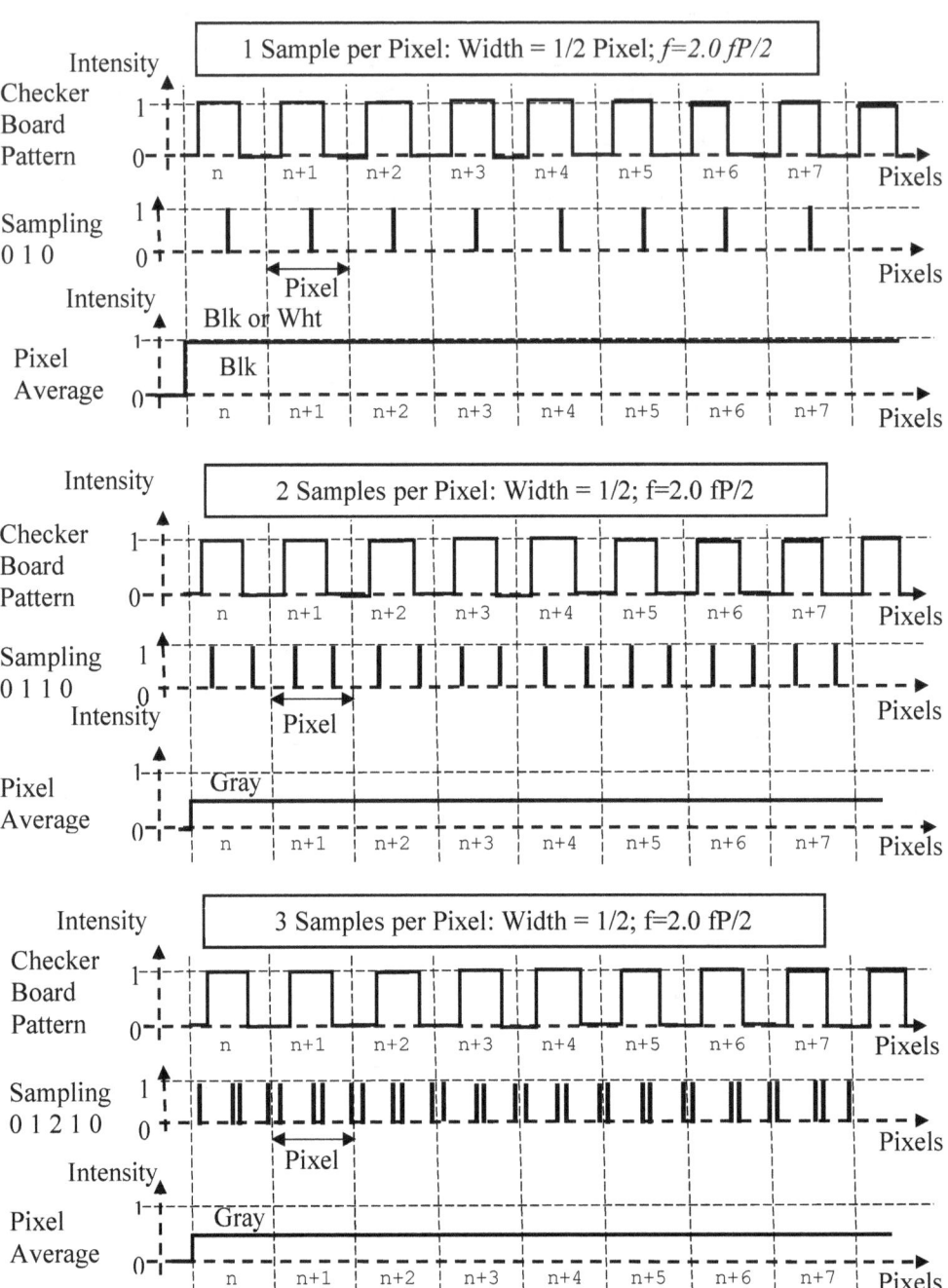

**Figure 3-8 Checkerboard with *f* = 2.0 fP/2**

## 3.2.5 Box Filter and Tent Filter

For the 2 sample per Pixel with weight '1, 1', the filter is referred to a Box Filter.
For the 3 sample per Pixel with weight '1, 2, 1', the filter is referred to a Tent, Triangle or Bartlett Filter.
For a comparison of the Sampling frequency $fS$ vs the Nyquist frequency $fN$, refer to Table 3-1.

| # Samples per Pixel | Weight | Sample Freq $fS$ | Nyquist Freq $fN$ | Super-Sampling | Filter |
|---|---|---|---|---|---|
| 1 | 0 1 0 | $fS = fP$ | $fP/2$ | 1x | Box |
| 2 | 0 1 1 0 | $fS = 2fP$ | $fP$ | 2x | Box |
| 3 | 0 1 2 1 0 | $fS = 2fP$ | $fP$ | 2x | Tent |

**Table 3-1 Sample Frequency vs Nyquist Frequency**

For 1 sample per Pixel, the sampling frequency $fS$ is equal to the Pixel frequency $fP$.
So: *$fN=fP/2$*

For 2 samples per Pixel, the sampling frequency $fS$ is equal to the Pixel frequency $2fP$.
So: *$fN=fP$*

The sampling of a pair of Pixels with equal weights '0 1 1 0' is a 2 Pixel wide Box Window. The result is a Box filter. When reduced to 1 Pixel, the result is a 1 Pixel wide Box Window.

The sampling of a 3 of Pixels with weights '0 1 2 1 0' is a 3 Pixel wide Tent Window. The result is a Tent filter. The 3 sample points is the result of 2 overlapping pairs of Pixel. It is the result of a convolution of 2 pairs of Pixels.

Horizontally, the convolution of 2 pairs of Pixels box windows with coefficients '0, 1, 1, 0' and '0, 1, 1, 0' results in a tent window with coefficients '0, 1, 2, 1, 0'. An example of convolution of two '0 1 1 0' sampling window into a '0 1 2 1 0' sampling window. Refer to Figure 3-9.

The aliasing resulting from these filters can be analyzed from their frequency response. For the Box filter, the frequency response is the '*sinc()* function'. The Bartlett filter is the result of the convolution of 2 Box filters. The frequency response for the Bartlett window is obtained by applying the Convolution Theorem.

*Convolution Theorem*
The convolution theorem states that the Fourier transform of a convolution of two signals or functions is the product of their Fourier transforms.

According to the Convolution Theorem, the frequency response of the Tent (or Bartlett) filter is the square of the *sinc()* function, that is *sinc()^2 = sinc() * sinc()..*

Refer to Figure 3-10, 'Frequency-Response of Box and Bartlett Filters'.

As can be observed, the Bartlett Filter is efficient at eliminating aliased frequencies

Anti-Aliasing with Super-Sampling

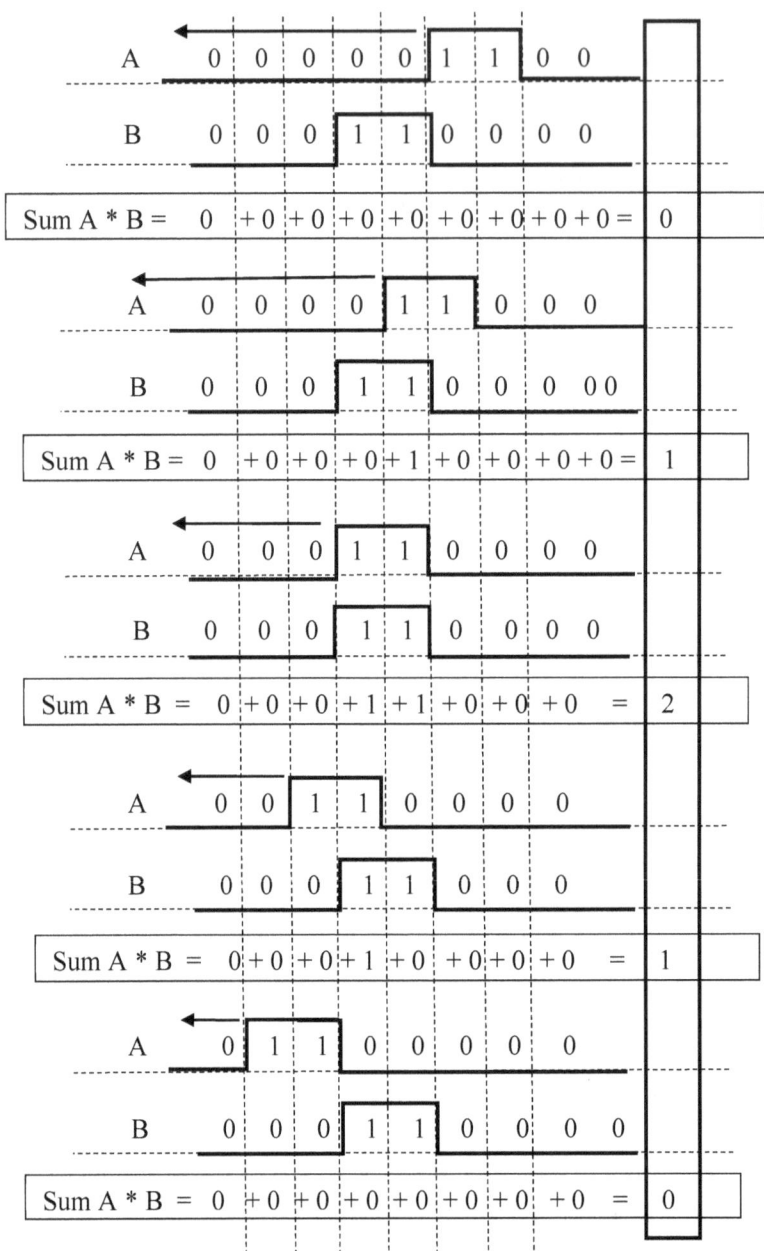

**Figure 3-9 Convolution of 2 Pairs of Pixels '0, 1, 1, 0' and '0, 1, 1, 0'**

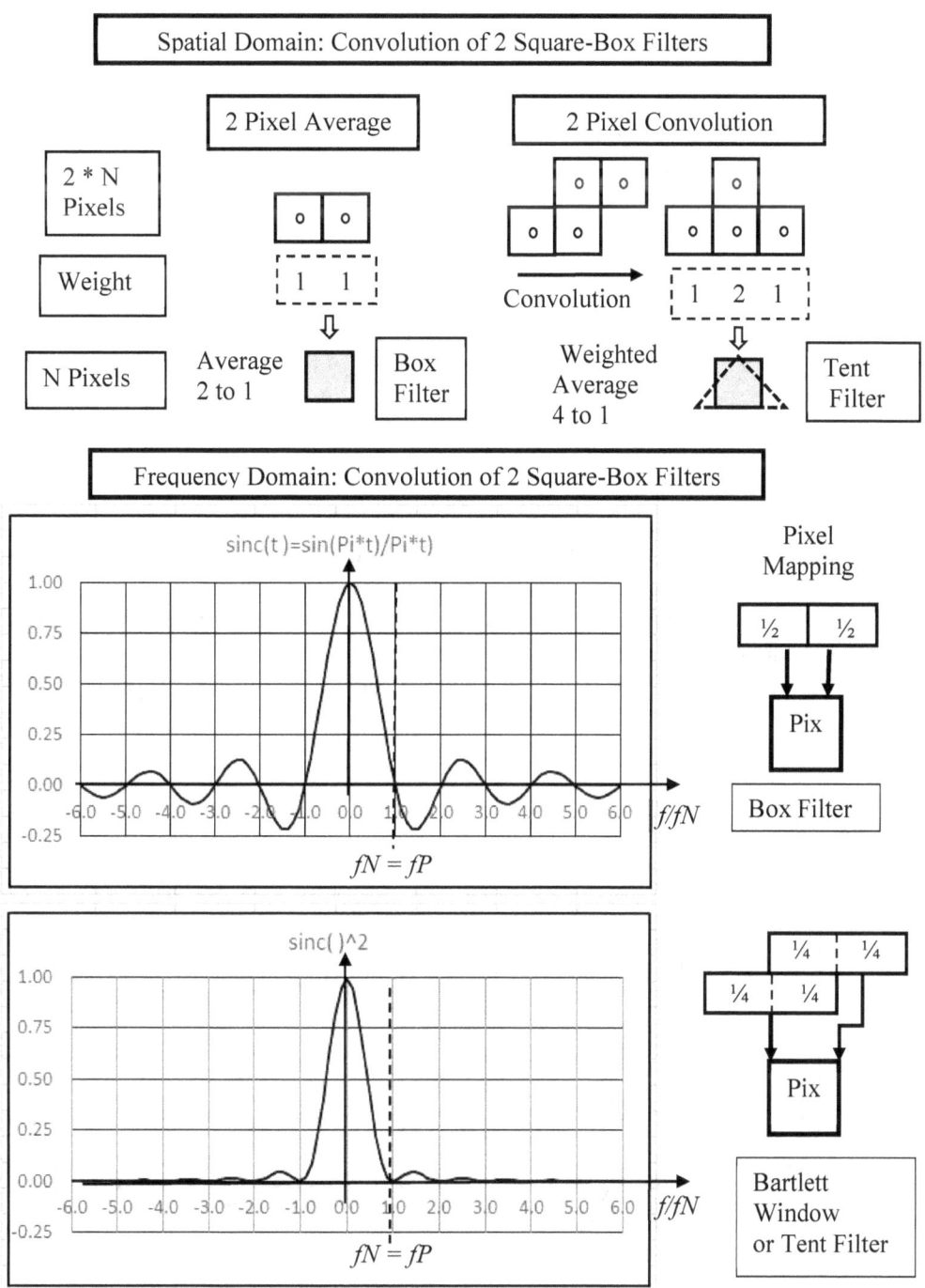

**Figure 3-10 Frequency Response of Box and Bartlett Filters**

## 3.2.6 Frequency Response for 1 to 3 Sample Points

When sampling Subpixels for computing the Pixel color, there is a constant that can be used as a reference for comparing AA filters. For all filters, the Pixel frequency is constant.

*fP = 1.0*;

So, the filters for 1, 2 and 3 samples per Pixel can be compared relative to the Pixel frequency, that is *f/fP*. Also, the Nyquist cut-off frequency can be used to estimate the cut-off frequency for aliasing.

**Figures in Frequency Domain**

In each of the following figures, there are examples in 'frequency domain'.
The frequency response *f* of the filter is shown as a function of the frequency relative to the Pixel frequency, that is *f/fP*.
The relationship of frequency before and after sampling is super imposed on top the filter frequency response.

**1 Sample per Pixel**

Reger to Figure 3-11, Freq Response for 1 Sample per Pixel, using a Box Filter.
In this figure, the Nyquist frequency is *fN=fP/2*. Since there many frequencies beyond the Nyquist frequency of *f>0.5*, this should explain the Moiré pattern with the checkerboard when the squares become smaller than the Pixel size,
When looking at the frequency response, there is no protections for frequencies beyond the Nyquist frequency of *fN=0.5*.

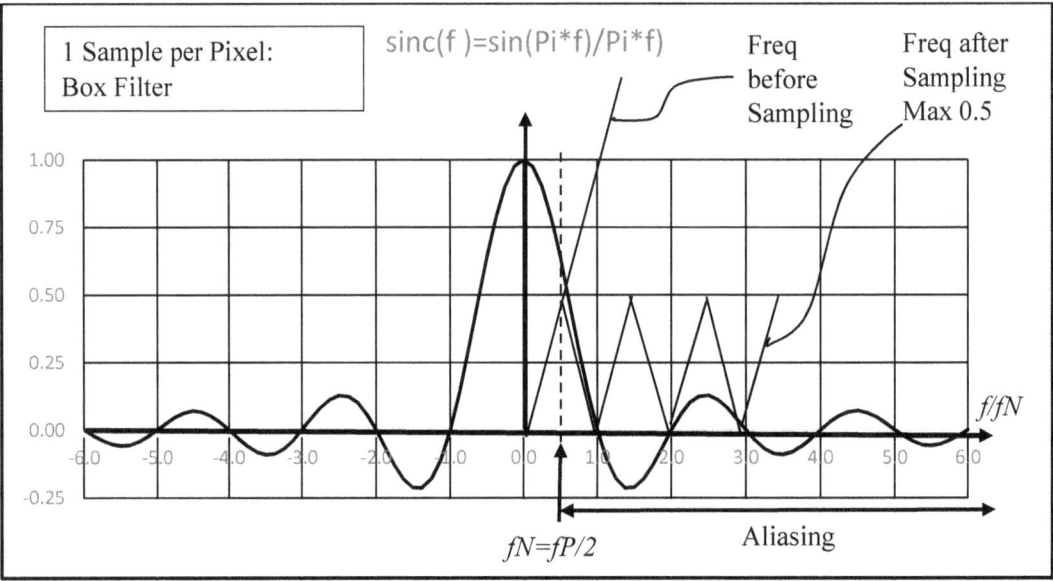

**Figure 3-11 Freq Response for 1 Sample per Pixel**

## 2 Samples per Pixel

Reger to Figure 3-12, Freq Response for 2 Sample per Pixel, using a Box Filter
In this figure, the Nyquist frequencyis $fN=fP$. With this filter, there significant sideband frequencies when $f>1.0$ (negative and positive) that will produce aliasing effects.

When looking at the frequency response, there is no protections for frequencies beyond the Nyquist frequency of fN=fP. This is an improvement from 1 sample per Pixel. The frequencies from 0.0 to 1.0 are rendered properly.
Refer to Figures 3-12

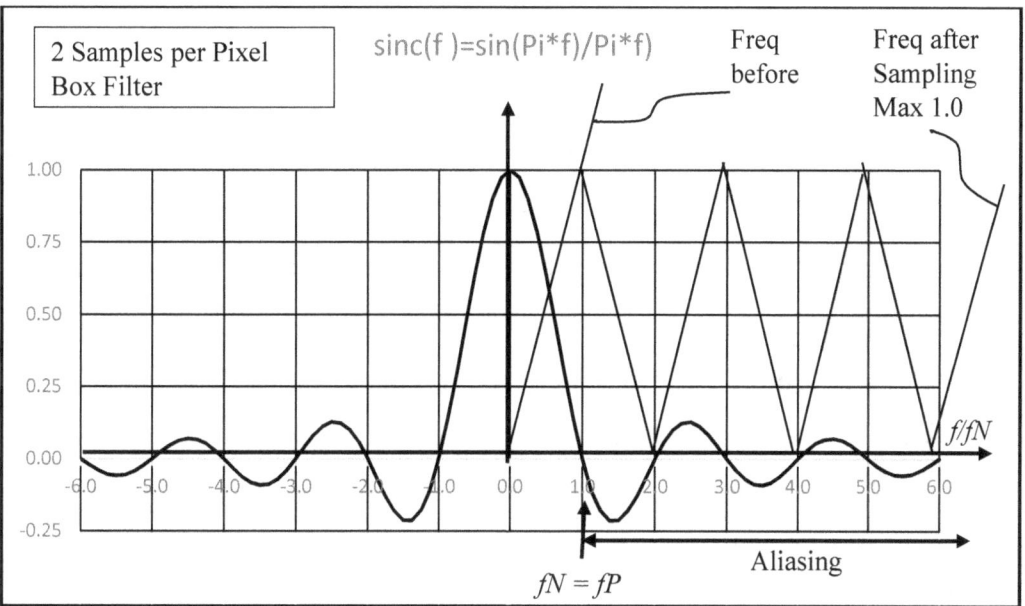

**Figure 3-12 Freq Response for 2 Samples per Pixel**

## 3 Samples per Pixel

Reger to Figure 3-13, Freq Response for 3 Sample per Pixel, using a Tent Filter
In this figure, the Nyquist frequency is $fN=fP$. With the Tent filter, the sideband frequencies when $f>1.0$ Are greatly reduced. This should reduce aliasing effects considerably.

The tent filter behaves as a low-pass filter. Whith this filter, most of the aliased higher frequencies beyond fN=1.0 are greatly attenuated.

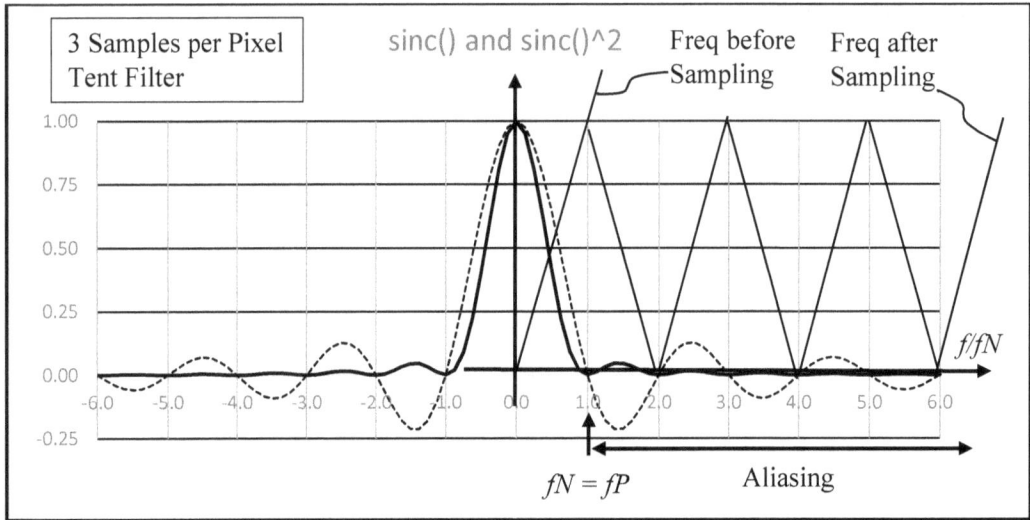

**Figure 3-13 Freq Response for 3 Samples per Pixel**

## Checkerboard example with Box Filter

When considering the frequency response, the window for a single Pixel is a Box Window. The frequency response for the Box window is a '*sinc* function' and the unit is the Pixel frequency, $fP=1.0$. For $fP=1.0$, the cycle is equal to the Pixel width. Note that by using the Box window as a filter here, there is no assumption about the number of samples in the Pixel.

Previously in the checkerboard example where white and black squares occupied a whole Pixel, the signal frequency was $0.5f/fP$. or a cycle per 2 Pixels. According to the Nyquist theorem, a signal with higher frequency would have frequency aliasing, as shown in the checkerboard example. This behavior can be explained because there was only 1 Sample Point per Pixel.
- For a single Sample Point per Pixel, the Nyquist frequency was $fN=0.5fP$.
- For 2 Samples Points per Pixel, the Nyquist frequency is at the cut-off frequency at $fN=1.0fP$.

When taking 2 samples per Pixel, the Nyquist cut-off frequency is $fN=1.0fP$. This means that for a signal with a cycle time equal the Pixel time, a sine function or a square wave function would go through a full cycle within the Box window. The positive and the negative areas of the function would cancel and the sum of the sampled signal is zero, as expected.

*Checkerboard example with Tent Filter*

For the Bartlett window, the tent extends to a half Pixel on each side. The unit on the frequency response is also the Pixel frequency, *fP=1.0*. This is a low pass filter. The cut-off frequency is at around *f=0.80P*. It should allow a Checkerboard with a lower frequency to be displayed without aliasing. That corresponds to a cycle of 1.25.

*Interpretation of the Frequency Response*

In order to interpret the frequency response charts above, using Pixel frequency *fP=1.0*, it is necessary to consider the assumption about the sample distribution. These curves make no assumptions on the number of samples per Pixel. They assume that there is an infinity of samples that are averaged. That is, they consider the area inside of the sample.

The tent filter reduces the effect of the stairsteps since it results into more steps spread over more Pixels. By attenuating the contrast in the stairsteps, it does reduce their distracting effects.,

## 3.2.7 Selecting an AA Filter with Subpixels

In order to facilitate comparison of SSAA approach, the filters are applied to Subpixels within a Pixel instead of Pixels inside of a SS image.

For non-RT CGI, there is more freedom in selecting AA algorithms and the selection of Subpixels. Besides the Subpixels that reside inside of the Pixel, Subpixels that surround it can also contribute to the filter. Different weights can be applied to Subpixels, In the book '*Jim Blinn's Corner: Dirty Pixels*', *Jim Blinn* presents a 'Nice Filter' in section 'Building a Nice Filter', refer to pages 28 and 29. This filter uses an array of Subpixels, like a 'bed of nails' to sample several points in order of implement the filter. Refer to page 30. This filter also uses Subpixels from the 4 surrounding Pixels to compute the Pixel color. Different weights are applied to each Subpixel depending on their distance from the center of the Pixel. There are examples of 2x2, 4x4 and 8x8 Subpixel arrays inside of each Pixel. Clearly, this approach is not well suited for real-time applications.

*'Box Filter' compared to 'Nice Filter'*

The 'Box Filter' and the 'Nice Filter' in spatial domain are compared in Figure 3-14. In this figure, the filters are applied in H and V directions. For the 'Box Filter', only Subpixels inside of the Pixel are selected and all the Subpixels have the same weight.

The 'Nice Filter' is in some way similar to a Tent filter, except that it has two negative lobes. Also, the Nice Filter needs the contribution of Subpixels outside of the Pixel.

For the Nice Filter, there are problems when we consider the memory access in 3D RT CGI systems.

For real-time applications, the Pixels are organized into blocks and are stored as such in image memory. For the Pixels at block boundaries, the application would require to access the blocks for the surrounding Pixels on the 4 adjacent sides. This is too inefficient for high-speed real-time rendering.

Another question is the number of Sample Points required in order to get an accurate rendition of the filter.

# Anti-Aliasing with Super-Sampling

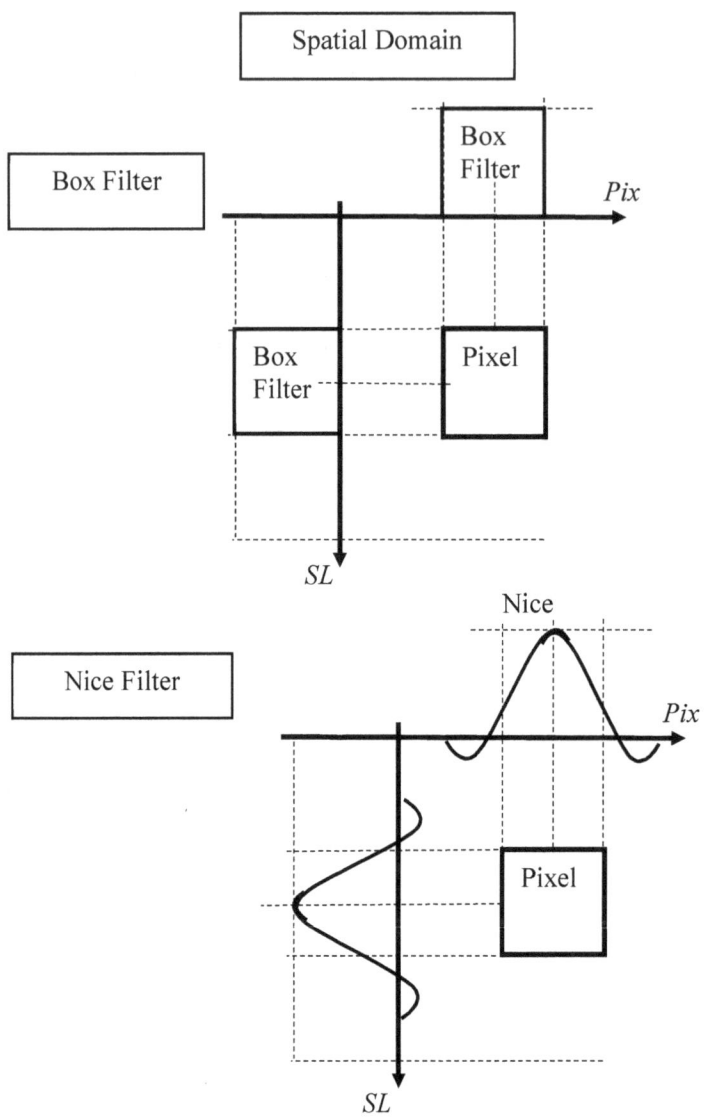

**Figure 3-14 Box Filter and Nice Filter**

## 3.2.8 AA Filter Comparison

A good filter can be evaluated by looking at the frequency response. In Figure 3-15, the frequency response of the Nice Filter is compared with that of the Box Filter and the Tent Filter.

### *Aliasing and Nyquist Frequency*

In order to avoid true aliasing, the frequency of the sampled signal should be less than twice the Nyquist frequency. In the frequency response chart, the Nyquist frequency is represented by the frequency of *0.5* and *-0.5*. The frequencies outside of *-0.5* and above *+0.5* represent 'aliasing'. In the frequency domain, the Pixel frequency is 1.0. The desired frequency lies between *-0.5* and *+0.5*. That means that under *-0.5* and above *+0.5*, there are under-sampling frequencies that will cause aliasing. For example, the frequencies at *0.6* and *1.4* will alias at *0.4*. The frequencies at *0.9* and *1.1* will alias at *0.1*.

### *Nice Filter*

In the frequency domain, the Nice Filter proposed by *Blinn* eliminates the frequencies outside of the range of *-0.5 to +0.5*. Also because of its square shape, it does not reduce the signal that are not aliased. This should result in a sharper image.

### *Box Filter*

On the other hand, the Box Filter has some aliasing as shown in the side lobes outside of *-0.5 to +0.5*.

### *Tent Filter*

The Tent Filter is obtained by a convolution of 2 Box Filters. In the frequency response of the Tent Filter, the side lobes are greatly reduced. It is clear that the convolution of two square Box Filter' is a better approximation of the 'Nice Filter'. The frequency response of the square Box Filter shows higher frequencies in the side lobes.

The coefficients of the Bartlett can be compared with the Nice Filter. Refer to Figure 3-15, 'Comparison of 3 Filters'. The tent distribution has a wider frequency range (*1.5 \* Nyquist Freq=0.75*). The frequency response if also similar to a triangle. In comparison, the Nice Filter has an almost square frequency response within the Nyquist frequency (*Nyquist Freq=0.5*).

The advantage of the Tent Filter is that it is closer to the Nice Filter. It is also easier to implement than the Nice Filter.

# Anti-Aliasing with Super-Sampling

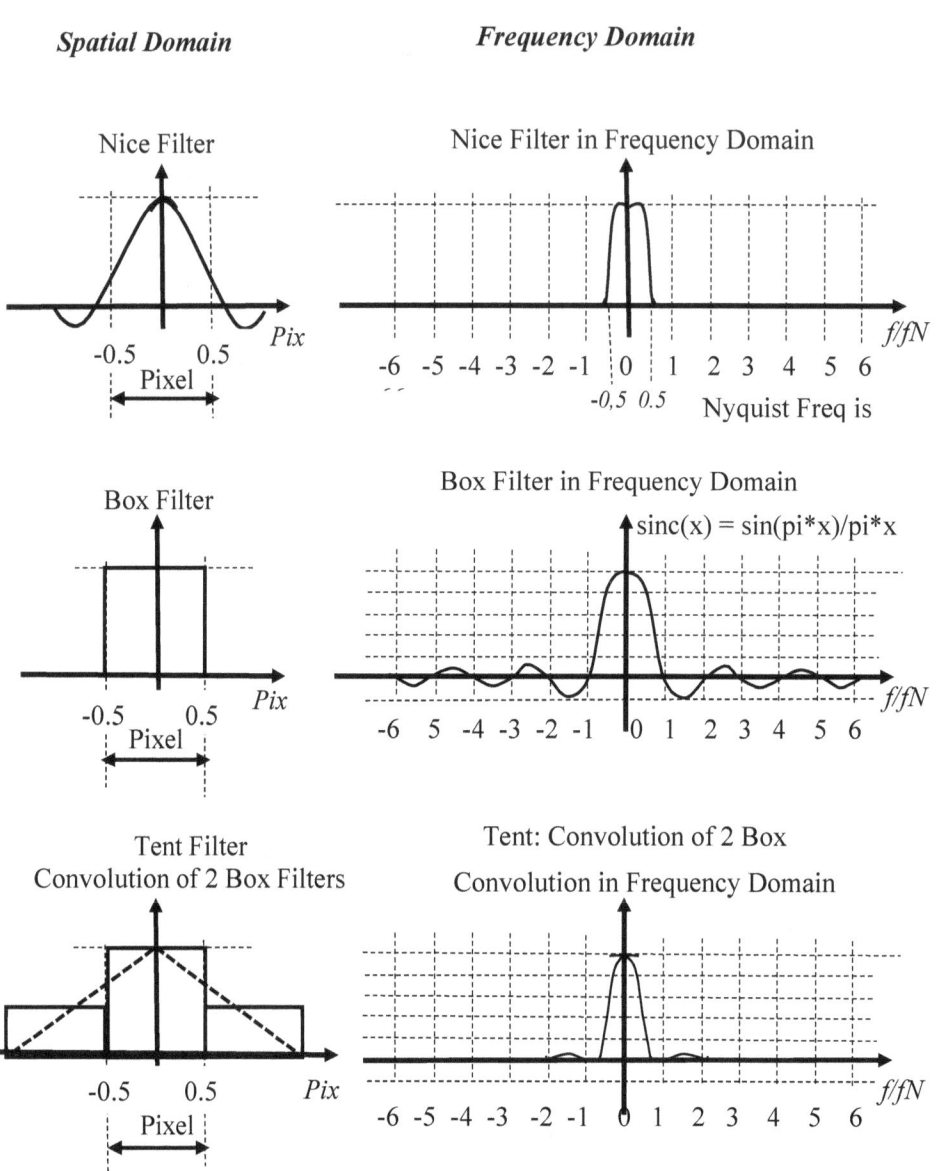

**Figure 3-15 Filters in Spatial Domain Frequency Domain**

## 3.3 Two-Dimensional Super-Sampling

In the previous sections, several cased of Pixel sampling have been considered:

- Two-dimensional sampling of a checkerboard with 1 sample per Pixel
- One-dimensional sampling of a checkerboard with 2 and 3 samples per Pixel

### 3.3.1 Two-Dimensional Box Window

The two-dimensional Box window is obtained by expanding the one-dimensional array of N Pixels with weight '0 1 1 0' into a two-dimensional array of NxN Pixels with weights:

```
'0 0 0 0'
'0 1 1 0'
'0 1 1 0'
'0 0 0 0'
```

***Replacing Downscaling Operation by Using Subpixels***

When considering image Super-Sampling with N>1, the operation of selecting a group of Nx1 or NxN Pixels, followed by downscaling the image can be simplified in most cases.

Just like in the one-dimensional case of SS, in the two-dimensional case, the SS of Pixels with 1 sample per Pixels can be replaced with sampling Subpixels within a Pixel.

Using Subpixels, the sampling within the target image can be done with Nx1 or NxN Subpixels per Pixel. In the two-dimensional case, sampling of a 2x2 group of Pixels can be replace by sampling 2x2 Subpixels in a single Pixel. In this case, the Subpixels within the Pixel will be positioned in a pattern similar to the Group of Pixel samples they represent.

Refer to Figure 3-16.

# Anti-Aliasing with Super-Sampling

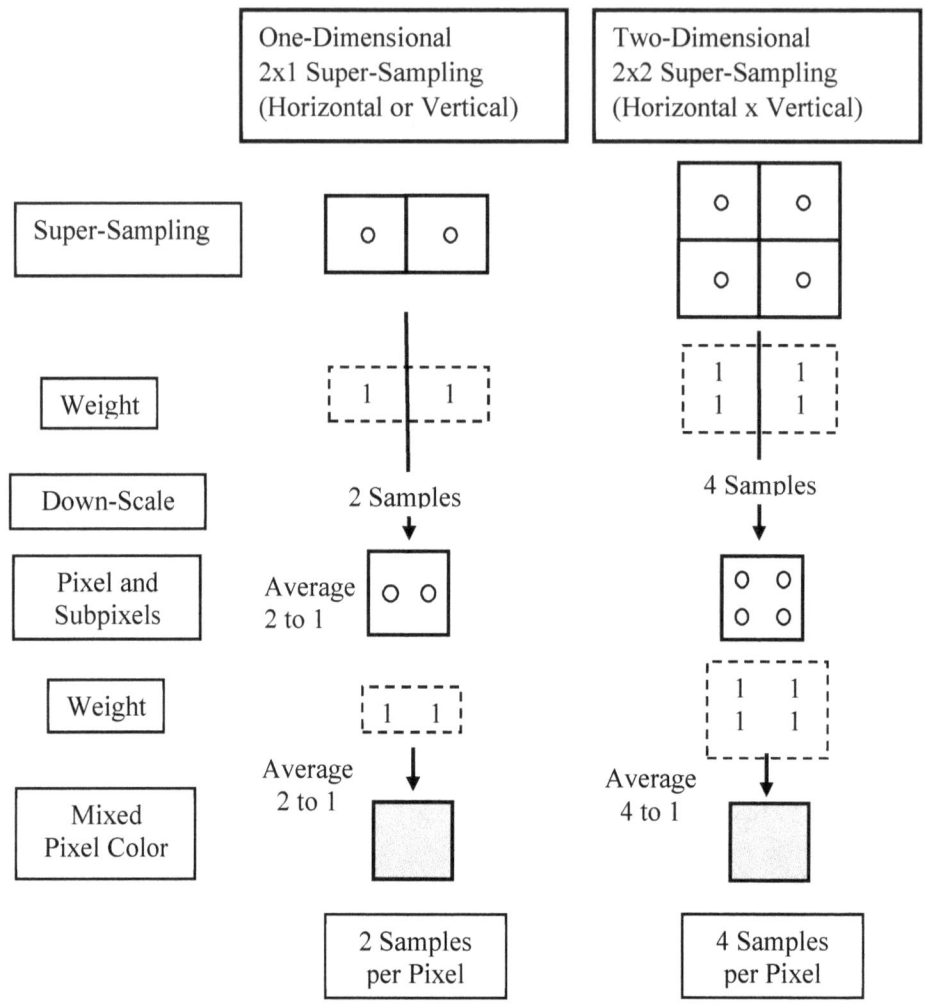

**Figure 3-16 One- and Two-Dimensional Super-Sampling**

2 Samples per Pixel in Horizontal or Vertical Dimension.

When considering the two-dimensional contribution of 2 samples per Pixel is each dimension, there are actually 2x2=4 samples within the Pixel area. The examples in the previous section have shown horizontal or vertical slices with 2 or 3 samples per Pixel each.

When selecting a 2x2 array of sample points there are 3 approaches:

1. Select the Sample Points aligned in the horizontal (H) and vertical (V)direction.
   This solution results from Super-Sampling at 2x2 resolution using 1 sample per Pixel, then downscaling with uniform averaging.

# Anti-Aliasing with Super-Sampling

2. Select Sample Points that don't align horizontally or vertically.
   This solution is also the result from Super-Sampling at 2x2 resolution using 1 sample per Pixel, then downscaling with uniform averaging. But in this case, each Pixel within groups of 2x2 sampled Pixels will use different and preassigned Sample Points within a Pixel.
3. Select the sample points as random as possible.

Refer to Figures 3-17 and 3-18.

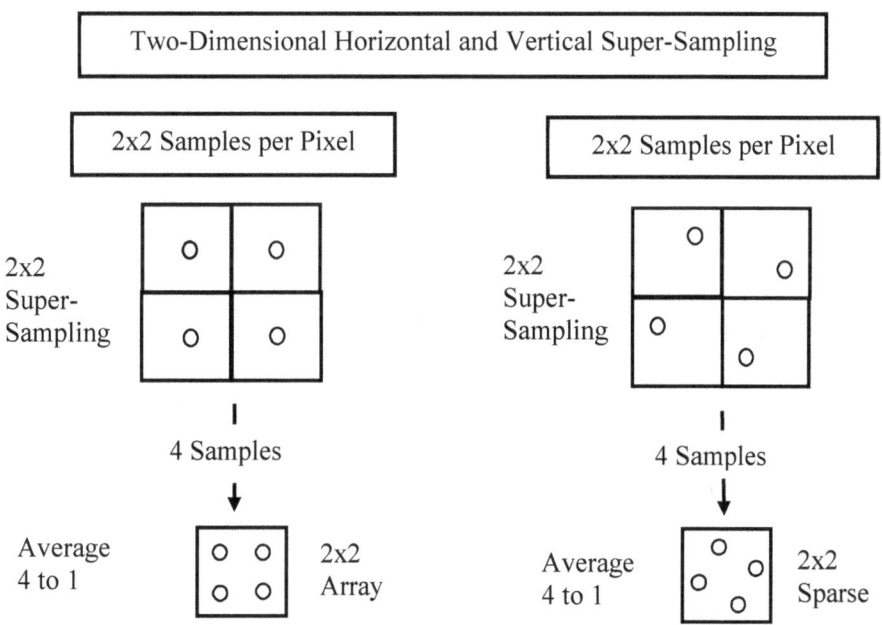

Figure 3-17 Two-Dimensional Super Sampling

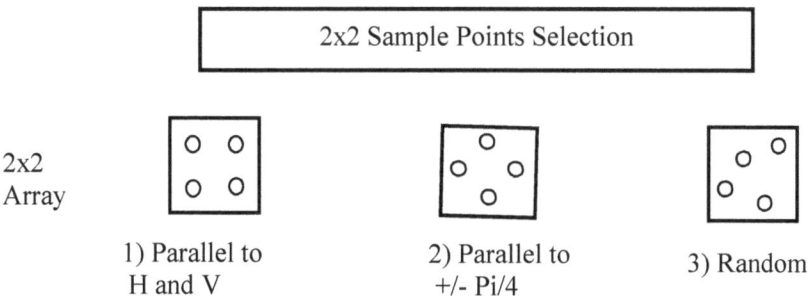

Figure 3-18 Selection of 2x2 Sample Points

### 3.3.2 Two-Dimensional Bartlett Window

The two-dimensional Bartlett window is obtained in 2 steps as follows.

For example, for the 2x2 window, the convolution of 2 horizontal slices is obtained by shifting then adding the coefficients. The result is a 3x3 window.

Horizontally, the convolution of 2 pairs of Pixels box windows with coefficients '0, 1, 1, 0' and '0, 1, 1, 0' results in a tent window with coefficients '0, 1, 2, 1, 0'.

In the $2^{nd}$ step, the results from the horizontal convolution are used for the vertical convolution. From 2 rows with coefficients '0, 1, 2, 1, 0' and '0, 1, 2, 1, 0' we obtain the 2-dimensional tent window with a vertical convolution of 3 vertical slices as follows:

Slice:     _1_2_3_
$1^{st}$ row:  '0, 1, 2, 1, 0'
2ne row: '0, 1, 2, 1, 0'

The 2-dimensional tent is obtained with 3 vertical convolutions:
Vertical Slice 1: '0, 1, 1, 0' and '0, 1, 1, 0' result in vertical tent '0, 1, 2, 1, 0'
Vertical Slice 2: '0, 2, 2, 0' and '0, 2, 2, 0' result in vertical tent '0, 2, 4, 2, 0'
Vertical Slice 3: '0, 1, 1, 0' and '0, 1, 1, 0' result in vertical tent '0, 1, 2, 1, 0'

The 2-dimensional tent look like a pyramid, with the difference that the middle of the sides is slightly elevated.

For the tent filter with 3x3 array of Sample Points, an analysis similar to that of the 2x2 filter can be done.

Starting from these results, a computer simulation could provide additional results.

## 3.4 Selecting AA Filters

The early images generated by computer were static image and usually had only one Sample Point inside of Pixels. Since the edges of rendered triangles had stairstep, the aliasing effect was referred to as jaggies. Many algorithms got developed to remove the jaggies

When selecting AA Filters, there are several parameters that affect the selection:

- Non-RT vs RT AA Filters
- Number of Subpixels from N=1 to N>1

### 3.4.1 Non-RT AA Solutions with Super-Sampling

One approach to AA is to compute an image at a higher resolution, then downscale the image by combining the contributions of selected Pixels into a single Pixel of lower resolution. When using NxN Pixel sample arrays, the AA method is referred to Super-Sampling AA, or SSAA.

With a Box Filter, the combined Pixels can have all the same weight. In this case, the final Pixels are the average of the Pixel selection.
With a tent filter different weights can be applied to the selected Pixels and the resulting Pixel is obtained by a weighted average.

### 3.4.2 Pixel Averaging with Box and Bartlett Windows

As Mentioned earlier, *Franklin C. Crow* did a good analysis of Super-Sampling in an article that appeared in the first issue of IEEE CG&A. He showed several images produced with simple average (Box window) and weighted averages (Bartlett Window) of Sample Points.

Refer to [5] 'A Comparison of Antialiasing Techniques', IEEE CG&A, 1981

'The simple average corresponds to filtering by convolution with a Fourier window. We can achieve somewhat better results with a Bartlett window. The Bartlett filter can be approximated by expanding the domain of Pixels from which each reduced Pixel is averaged and weighting the central Pixels of that domain more heavily than the peripheral ones.' *Franklin C. Crow*

In the write up from *Franklin C. Crow*, there are 2 types of filters: the Box and the Bartlett Filters. These filters use a square area of Pixels in the high-resolution image. The square Pixel area is also referred to a Fourier Window. Inside of the window, the colors of the Pixels are averaged with weights defined by a function. Outside of the window, the coefficients are '0'.\

*Box Filter*

For the Box Filter, all the coefficients inside of the Fourier window are equal to 1. All samples have the same weight. In Super-Sampling, the filtering is done by sampling a window of NxN Pixels and adding the contributions. Then the NxN window is reduced to a single Pixel by dividing the sum of the contributions by N*N.

The super-sampled image is reduced from *N*PixMax x N*SLMax* to *PixMax x SLMax*

## Anti-Aliasing with Super-Sampling

### *Bartlett (or Tent) Filter*

The Bartlett filter is also referred to a Tent, or Triangular Filter. In a 3-dimensional space, where the weight represents the height, the Tent Window looks like a pyramid.

For the Bartlett Window, the function has linear increasing weights as the samples get closer to the square center. In each dimension (horizontal and vertical), the 'Tent' Filter is obtained by doing a convolution of 2 identical Box Filters. In Super-Sampling, the filtering is done by sampling a window of *(N+N-1) x (N+N-1)* Pixels and adding the contributions according to the sample weights. Then the window is reduced to a single Pixel by dividing the 'weighted' sum of the sample contributions by the sum of all the weights.

The super-sampled image is reduced from *N\*PixMax x N\*SLMax* to *PixMax x SLMax*.

Note that in both cases the image reduction is the same. For the Bartley Filter, the sampling windows of (N+N-1) x (N+N-1) Pixels is greater than the NxN size of the Box filter.
In the Box window, the coefficients of adjacent windows don't overlap. In the Bartlett window, the coefficients of adjacent windows overlap. The value of the coefficients increases as the Sample Points get closer the center of the window.

In Table 3-2, the examples of Box and Bartlett windows a summarized.

The Box Windows are defined in NxN square area of Pixels with equal weights. The contributions of the Box Windows 2x2, 3x3 and 4x4 are obtained by averaging the Pixel contributions.

The Bartlett (or triangle or tent) Windows are defined in *(N+N-1) x (N+N-1)* square area of Pixels with weights increasing as the distance of the sample get closer to window center. The contributions of the Bartlett Windows 3x3, 5x5 and 7x7 are obtained by a weighted sum of the Pixel contributions.

In Figure 3-19 and 3-20 there are examples of these filters, showing the horizontal, or vertical slices for box windows 2x2, 3x3 and 4x4.

When considering the weighted coefficients for the Bartlett Windows, the sum of weighted coefficients for the 3x3, 5x5 and 7x7 windows amount to 4, 9 and 16 for the first rows, respectively. For the two-dimensional Tent, the sums of the 9, 25 and 49 weighted coefficients amount to 16, 81 and 256, respectively.

Note that in these 2 figures, the filter coefficients are for horizontal or vertical slices through the edges of the filters. The value of the coefficients increases as the slices get closer to the center of the window.

The corresponding Bartlett windows with weighted coefficients in 3x3, 5x5 and 7x7 windows are obtained in 2 steps from the box window. In the first step a convolution of the horizontal coefficients produces a horizontal window slice. In the second step a convolution of the vertical coefficients produces a vertical window slice

Weighting used for Computing Filtered Images

| Resolution | 1024/SL | 1536/SL | 2048/SL |
|---|---|---|---|
| Reduced to | 512/SL | 512/SL | 512/SL |
| Image reduction | 2 to 1 | 3 to 1 | 4 to 1 |
| | | | |
| For Box Window | Pixel Average Box Window | Pixel Average Box Window | Pixel Average Box Window |
| NxN Array | 2x2 | 3x3 | 4x4 |
| # Coefficients | 4 | 9 | 16 |
| Coefficients Sum | 4 | 9 | 16 |
| Coefficients for Averaging Windows | 1 1<br>1 1 | 1 1 1<br>1 1 1<br>1 1 1 | 1 1 1 1<br>1 1 1 1<br>1 1 1 1<br>1 1 1 1 |
| Pixel Ratio NxN to 1x1 | 2x2 to 1x1 | 3x3 to 1x1 | 4x4 to 1x1 |
| # Stairsteps | 2 per Pixel | 3 per Pixel | 4 per Pixel |
| | | | |
| For Tent Window | Bartlett Window | Bartlett Window | Bartlett Window |
| NxN Array | 3x3 | 5x5 | 7x7 |
| # Coefficients | 9 | 25 | 49 |
| Coefficients Sum | 4*4=16 | 9*9=81 | 16*16=256 |
| Coefficients for Weighted Average using Bartlett Windows | 1 2 1<br>2 4 2<br>1 2 1 | 1 2 3 2 1<br>2 4 6 4 2<br>3 6 9 6 3<br>2 4 6 4 2<br>1 2 3 2 1 | 1 2 3 4 3 2 1<br>2 4 6 8 6 4 2<br>3 6 9 12 9 6 3<br>4 8 12 16 12 8 4<br>3 6 9 12 9 6 3<br>2 4 6 8 6 4 2<br>1 2 3 4 3 2 1 |
| Pixel Ratio (N+N-1) x (N+N-1) to 1x1 | 3x3 to 1x1 | 5x5 to 1x1 | 7x7 to 1x1 |
| # Stairsteps | 3 per 2 Pixels | 5 per 2 Pixels | 7 per 2 Pixels |

**Table 3-2 Comparison of Filtering with Box and Bartlett Windows**

Anti-Aliasing with Super-Sampling

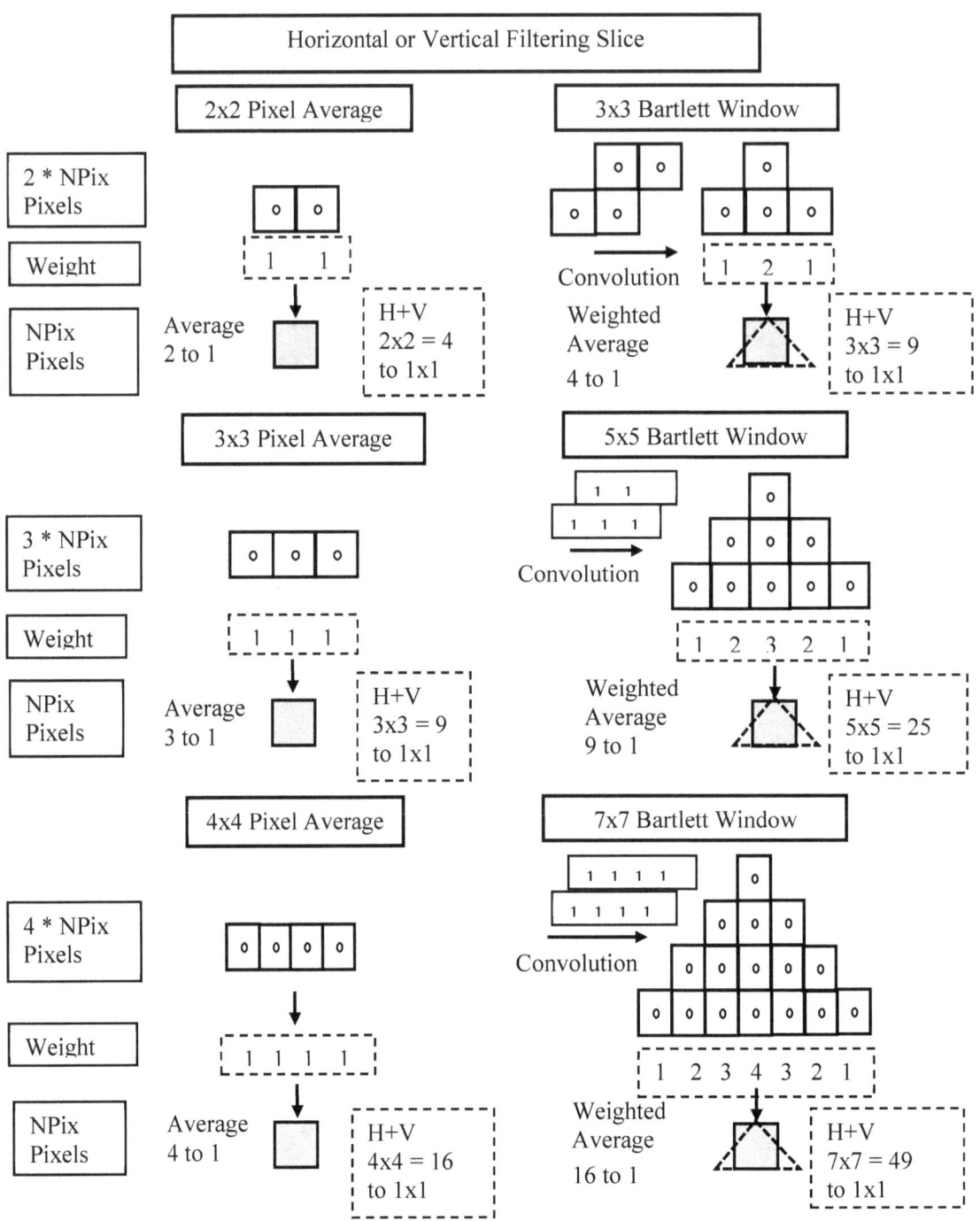

Figure 3-19 Comparison between Box and Bartlett Windows

New Area-Based Anti-Aliasing for CGI

Anti-Aliasing with Super-Sampling

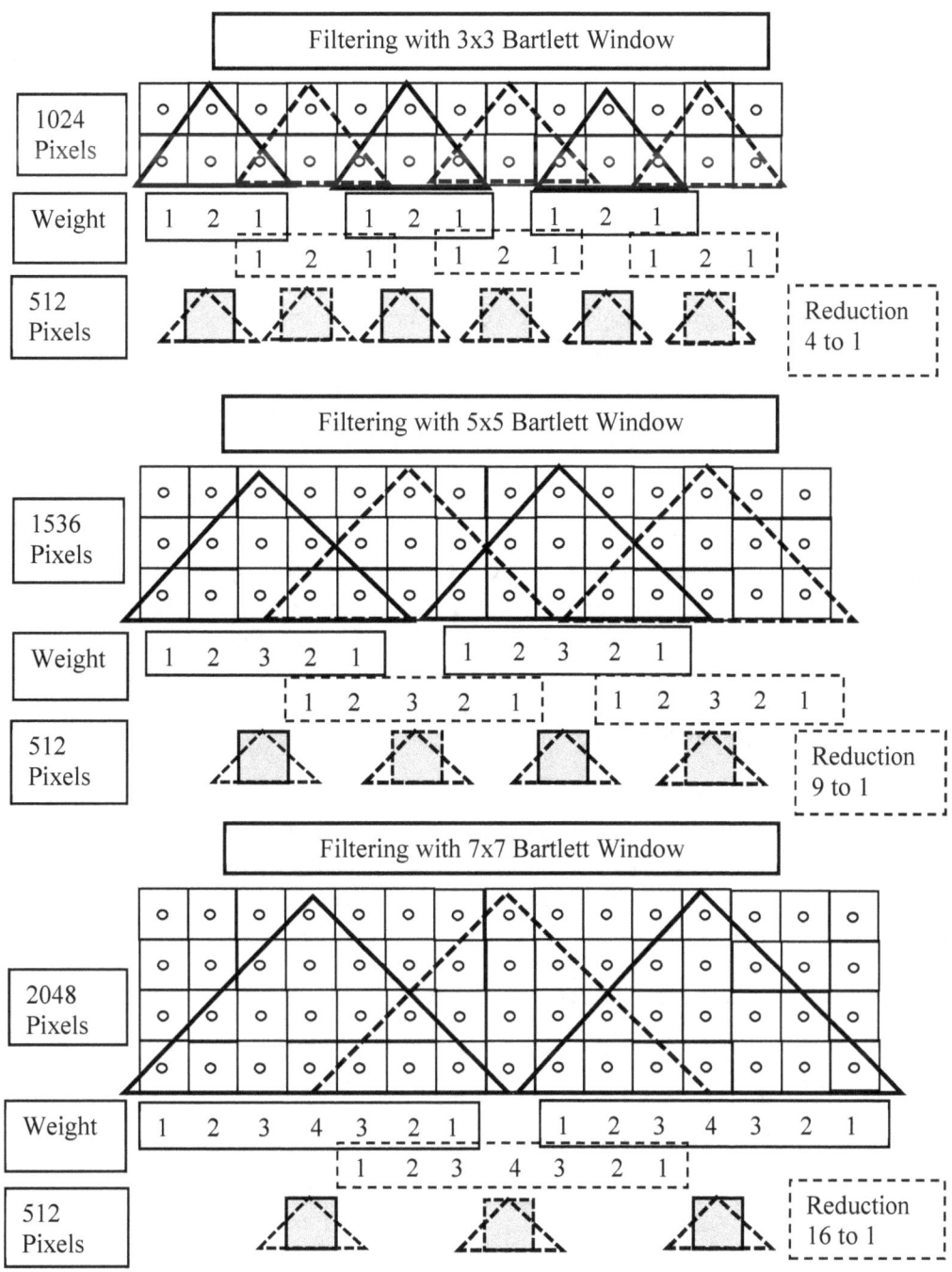

**Figure 3-20 H or V Slices for Tent Windows 3x3, 5x5 and 7x7 to 1x1**

## Non-Real-Time Solution

For his study, *Franklin C. Crow* computed images at higher resolutions like 1024, 1536, 2048 and even 4096 using one Sample Point per Pixel. Then he downscaled the image by computing a simple or weighted average the contributions of square groups of Pixels for the final image. There are examples of final images with Pixel resolution of 512. This was a non-real-time solution. It looks like this study was very computation intensive.

## Box Window

For the Box window, averaging is done on square windows of sampling size NxN, where N=2, 3 and 4. The total of samples consist of NxN = 4, 9 and 16 samples. Since all Pixels have a weight of 1, the sum of the weights is also 4, 9 and 16. The sampling using the same weight for all NxN samples forms a two-dimensional square Box Filter with NxN samples. Since the Super-Sampled images of 1024x1024, 1536x1536 and 2048x2048 Pixels are filtered and downscaled to a 512x512 image, the result should be similar to taking multiple samples in single Pixels containing 2x2, 3x3 and 4x4 arrays of Subpixels.

## Bartlett (or Tent) Window

For the Bartlett window, averaging is done on square windows of sampling size NxN, where N=3, 5 and 7. The total of samples consist of NxN = 9, 25 and 49 samples with various coefficients. When looking at horizontal and vertical cross-sections of the Bartlett Coefficients, they have a triangular distribution, forming a pyramid or tent on top of the NxN square area. Using this distribution, the highest weight for the samples is at the center. For the Bartlett window, a downscaling similar to the Box window occurs. The Super-Sampled images of 1024x1024, 1536x1536 and 2048x2048 Pixels are filtered and downscaled to a 512x512 image.

## Super-Sampling with Box and Bartlett Windows

The two-dimensional Bartlett window is obtained from a convolution of two box windows. For this reason, it occupies more sample points than the box window. But the triangular windows overlap. So, that the Super-Sampled image still keeps the same SS ratio as the box window it is derived from. Refer to Table 3-3.

| Filter | Size of Super-Sample | #Pixels | Sum of Weights | SS Image Ratio | SS Image Size |
|---|---|---|---|---|---|
| Box | 2x2 | 4 | 4 | 2x2 | 4x |
| Bartlett | 3x3 | 9 | 16 | 2x2 | 4x |
| Box | 3x3 | 9 | 9 | 3x3 | 9x |
| Bartlett | 5x5 | 25 | 81 | 3x3 | 9x |
| Box | 4x4 | 16 | 16 | 4x4 | 16x |
| Bartlett | 7x7 | 49 | 256 | 4x4 | 16x |

**Table 3-3 Super-Sampling with Box and Bartlett Window**

# Chapter 4  Multi-Sample AA (MSAA)

Processing NxN array of samples for SSAA is computation intensive. For RT CGI, a more efficient method is to use smaller number of random (or sparse) Subpixel samples. The Multi-Sample Anti-Aliasing (MSAA) approach for RT CGI AA relies on taking Multiple Sample Points (or Subpixels) within image Pixels. Also, see references [60] to [69].

## 4.1 From SSAA to MSAA

This MSAA approach is derived from SSAA. With SSAA, the samples are organized in uniform array. With MSAA a decimated set of samples is selected and spread inside of the Pixel in a non-uniform, or sparse, distribution.

For CGI, the most common algorithm has been to divide the Pixels into several Subpixels (2, 4, 8, 16, 32 or 64) and use a variety of filters. For RT CGI, the most common algorithm is to divide the Pixels into 4 or 8 random (non-arrayed) Subpixels and use a Box Filter. Most algorithms assign Subpixels inside of a Pixel and use Subpixel point sampling. The resulting Pixel color is the color mix that is the average of the selected Subpixel contributions. For RT CGI, the square Box Filter is the fastest approach and it produces good results.

For MSAA, when all Subpixels have the same weight, the sparse distribution of N Subpixels is more efficient for a Box Filter than an array of NxN Subpixels. But as will be shown, the performance of MSAA depends on the polygon edge directions.

## 4.2 Selecting Subpixels for Sampling

In the previous Chapter, AA filtering was done by Super-Sampling, that is computing an image at a higher resolution. Then an image of lower resolution was produced by applying a Box Filter or a tent filter to square areas to the higher resolution image.

A similar result can be obtained by sub-dividing Pixels into an array of Subpixels that have same relative positions within the Pixel. This way, there is no need to use a 2 step-process that require producing a high-resolution image before being downscaled and filtered into a lower resolution image. By using Subpixels, the sampled image and displayed image have the same number of Pixels. In Most implementations, the Pixel color is obtained by the average of the Subpixel contributions. This corresponds to a Box Filter.

*Pixel Divided into Subpixels*

This is the solution used for real-time AA. In most approaches the Pixel is divided into a number of Subpixels. Here, N indicates the number of Subpixels. In the simple implementation, there are no Subpixels, that is N=1. There is only one Sample Point at the center of the Pixel. As demonstrated, this approach is unsuited for most applications.

In Figure 4-1, there are examples of Pixels divided into Subpixels.

## Multi-Sample AA (MSAA)

### *Single Sample Point: N=1*

When N=1, this is the worse-case for aliasing. For this reason, the image rendering with 1 Sample Point per Pixel shows many artifacts caused by aliasing.

### *N>1: N and NxN Subpixels*

When N>1, there are many possibilities for dividing a Pixel into Subpixels. The Subpixels can be organized as sparse N Subpixels or into an array of NxN Subpixels. After the image is computed for all Subpixels, the final image is obtained by averaging all these images. This approach is similar to the Super-Sampling of Pixels described in the previous Chapter. These methods can also be described as:

- Super-Sampling AA (SSAA)
  In order to avoid confusion, when doing Super Sampling by replacing Pixels with square arrays of NxN of Pixels, or square arrays of NxN Subpixels inside of Pixels, the process will still be referred to NxN SSAA.
- Multi-Sample AA (MSAA).
  The MSAA refers to sampling a one-dimensional array of N random or sparse Subpixels within a Pixel.
- Bed of Nail (BON) can be SSAA or MSAA,

### *Box Window*

When the filter is a Box Filter, all Subpixels have the same weight. In this case, the final image is obtained by straight averaging. In this case the use of Sparse Subpixel is more efficient.

### *Bartlett Window*

For other algorithms, the Subpixels within the Pixel are weighted according to their distance to the center of the Pixel. This is the case with the Bartlett Window. In this case, the final image is obtained by doing a weighted average of the computed images. In this case the use of arrays of Subpixel produces more accurate results.

Multi-Sample AA (MSAA)

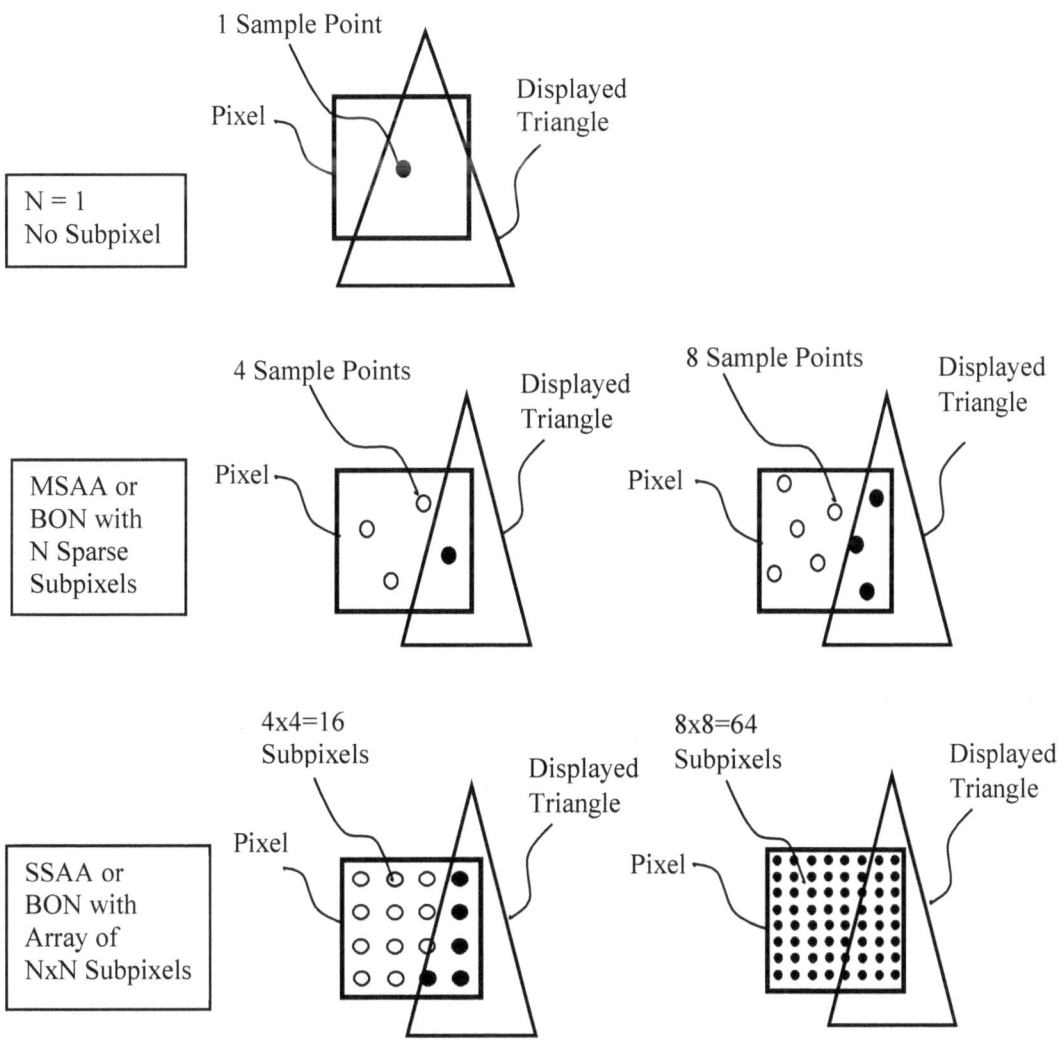

**Figure 4-1 Examples of Pixel divided into Subpixels or Bed of Nails**

Multi-Sample AA (MSAA)

## 4.3 Processing Subpixels as Bed of Nails

The BON approach is similar to MSAA, but instead of computing multiple frame buffers followed by averaging these buffers, the covered Subpixel or BON can be detected in one or a few cycles.

The covered Subpixel are detected as follows.

Refer to Figure 4-2, Edge to Subpixel Distance in *(xi, yi)* Image Coordinate System

In this figure, there is a Pixel and an Edge defined in an *(xi, yi)* coordinate system. The Subpixel Distance is defined from the Edge to the Sample Point at the center of the Pixel.

In the *(xi, yi)* coordinate axis system, the edge can be represented by its equation:
$axi + byi + c = 0$

The normal to the edge can be derived from this equation:
$N = (a, b)$.

The normal distance of any point *(xi, yi)* on the line edge can be obtained by replacing the point coordinates in the equation. The normal distance of the line edge to the origin *(0, 0)* is: $c$.

The normal distance of the Pixel center *(x1, y1)* the line *(xi, yi)* can be obtained by replacing the point *(x1, y1)* in the line equation. The normal distance $d$ of the Pixel center *(x1, y1)* to the line edge is:
$d = a*x1\ b*y1 + c$.

Since the edge belongs to a triangle, there is an in-side (visible) and out-side of the edge. In this example, the points on the left of the edge are *outside* of the triangle. The points on the right side of the edge are *inside* of the triangle. So, if $d>0$, the point is *inside,* else it is *outside*.

When there are several Subpixels, each Subpixel is tested against the edge.

# Multi-Sample AA (MSAA)

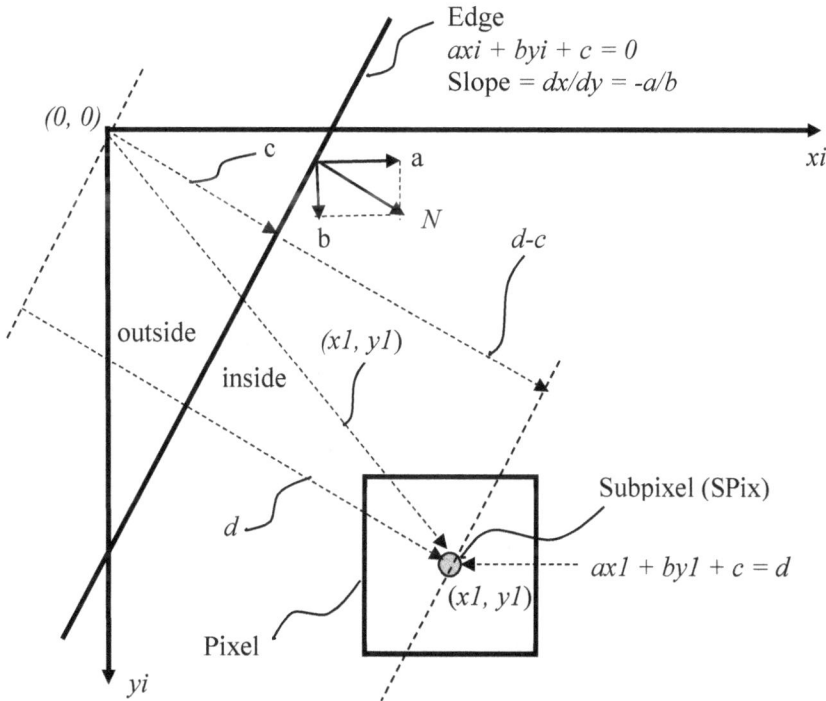

**Figure 4-2 Edge to Subpixel Distance in *(xi, yi)* Image Coordinate System**

In the next Figure 4-3, there are 4 Subpixels that get tested inside of each Pixel. For 8 Subpixels, the approach is similar.

Multi-Sample AA (MSAA)

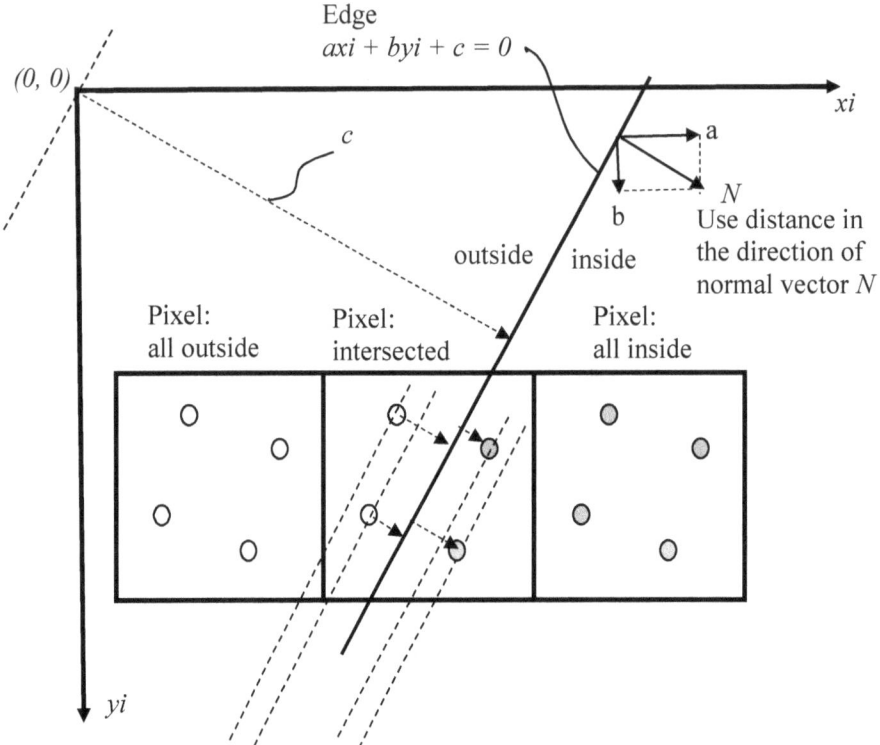

**Figure 4-3 Edges vs 4 Subpixels in *(xi, yi)* Image Coordinate System**

## 4.4 MSAA and the 8 Queens Puzzle

When implementing MSAA, there are several factors that affect the image quality and performances. The quality of the MSAA implementation depends on the number of Subpixel and how they are distributed within the Pixel.

- How many Subpixels to select.
- How to select Subpixels the Subpixel distribution for optimum performances.
- Do all Subpixels have the same weight?

The performance depends on how and when the distances to Subpixels are computed. The distance can be computed in real-time, or precomputed and stored into a look-up table. That table is then accessed using the entry and exit points of the edge intersecting the Pixel.

In this section, the selection of $N=8$ Subpixels will be analyzed. All Subpixels have the same weight. Assuming that the triangle has an intensity $i$, where $i$ can be a RGB color component on the triangle area. When the Pixel is fully covered by this triangle, the triangle contribution is *100% \* i*. Each Subpixel will have a contribution of *i/8*. One approach is to use solutions to the '8 Queens Puzzle' [61].

## The 8 Queens Puzzle

In the literature, the selection of Subpixel within a Pixel is often referred to as "Solutions to the 8 Queens Puzzle". The idea is to position 8 Queens on a chess board, so that no Queen can attack another Queen. This algorithm provides good solutions for MSAA, but there are acceptable solutions that do not satisfy as solution to the '8 Queens Puzzle'.

## Selecting 8 Subpixels as a Solution to the 8 Queens Puzzle

The distribution of 8 Subpixels inside of a Pixel can be simulated with a chess board with *8x8=64* square locations. In this approach, each of the 8 Subpixels will be assigned one of the 64 squares and reside at the center of the assigned square. For simulation purpose, all 8 Subpixels will be assigned the same set of moves or properties from one selected chess piece, such as: Queen, Rook, Bishop or Knight. Since the Queen has access to moves from the Rook (0 degrees and 90 degrees, and Bishop (+/- 45-degree diagonals), the Rook and Bishop are not considered. For this reason, the Queen is a good choice for selecting Subpixels. When all Subpixels are considered as Queens, none of them is under a Queen threat. The Knight is another chess piece of interest since it can attack a Queen without being under Queen attack. Although the Queen has more power than Knights, the Knights can be useful in looking for good solutions.

## Knights and Queens

Refer to Figure 4-4, Knights and Queens

In this figure, there are 2 solutions that satisfy the 8 Queens Puzzle. For each solution, a Pixel is organized as an array of 8x8 Subpixels locations. For a solution with 8 Subpixels, only 8 locations are selected among the possible 64 locations.

On the left Pixel, the 8 Subpixels are identified with the K letter. Although this arrangement is a solution to the 8 Queens Puzzle, the K is selected to show the Knight threats capability. The Knight moves 2 horizontal or 2 vertical spaces, followed by 1 diagonal space.

On the right Pixel, the Subpixels are identified with the Q letter, to show that it is a solution to the 8 Queens Puzzle.

What is interesting with these 8 Queens assignments is that the Queens on the right figure are obtained from the left figure **by swapping 4 Knights in lower half with the 4 Knights in upper half.**

Both are solutions to the 8 Queens Puzzle. But after a quick analysis, it turns out that the assignment with the Queens on the right side is better. In order to identify the Subpixels that are aligned, the lines that connect pairs of Subpixels are assigned a number. The sets of parallel lines that connect Subpixels are identified with the same number.

Refer to Table 4-1

In this table, the cases with aligned Subpixels are identified. For each line direction, the number of parallel cases is counted. The best selection for AA should have the minimum of aligned Subpixels and the minimum number of parallel cases.

## Multi-Sample AA (MSAA)

In the 8 Knights assignment, 4 Knights are aligned, which would make it a bad selection for an AA solution.

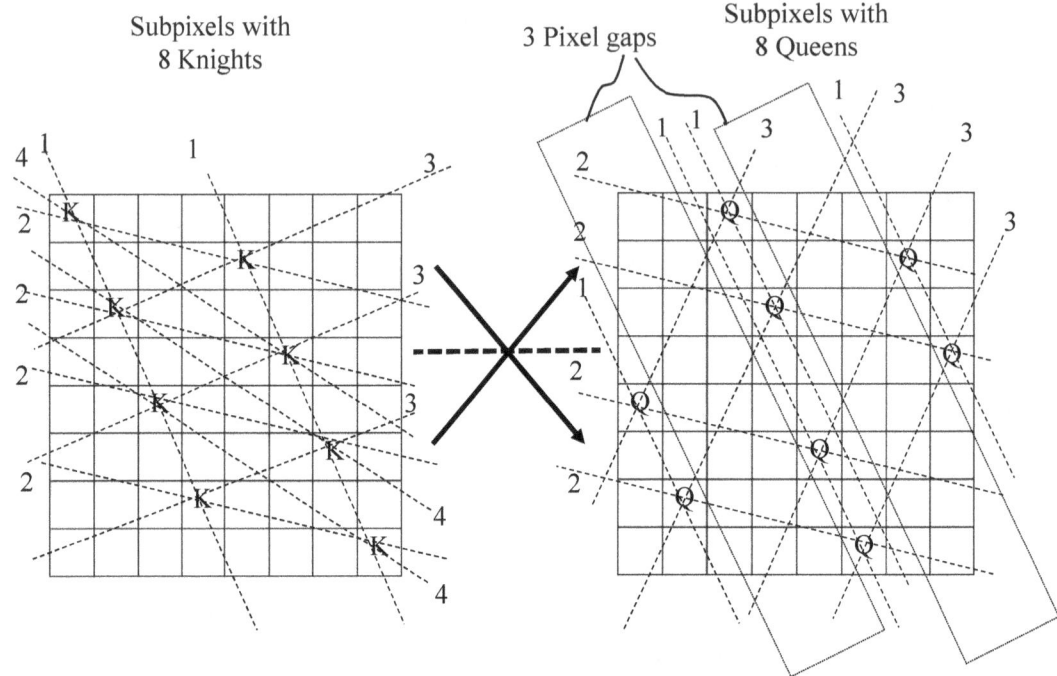

**Figure 4-4 Knights and Queens**

Subpixels with 8 Knights

| Case | #Cases | #SPix | di |
|---|---|---|---|
| 1 | 2*4=8 | 4 | 1/2 |
| 2 | 4 pairs | 2 | 1/4 |
| 3 | 3 pairs | 2 | 1/4 |
| 4 | 3 pairs | 2 | 1/4 |
| 5,6 | 2*2pairs=4 | 2 | 1/4 |
| 7..10 | 4*1 pair | 2 | 1/4 |
| total | 28 | | |

*di* is fractional intensity jump

Subpixels with 8 Queens

| Case | #Cases | #SPix | di |
|---|---|---|---|
| 1 | 4 pairs | 2 | 1/4 |
| 2 | 4 pairs | 2 | 1/4 |
| 3 | 4 pairs | 2 | 1/4 |
| 4..7 | 4 * 2 pairs | 2 | 1/4 |
| 8..19 | 12 *1 pair | 2 | 1/4 |
| total | 28 | | |

*di* is fractional intensity jump

**Table 4-1 Intensity Jumps for Knight and Queens**

## 8 Knights Solution

In the case of Knights, there are 2 parallel cases (1) where 4 Knights are aligned.
When 2 sets of 4 Knights are aligned, there are only 2 steps per Pixel. Each group of 4 Knights correspond of 5 pairs. So, these 2 sets of 4 Knights amount to 10 pairs.
There is 1 case (2) with 4 parallel pairs of Knights. This results into 4 steps per Pixel (4 pairs.)
There are 2 cases of 3 parallel pairs of Knights (3, 4). This result into 5 steps per Pixel (6 pairs.)
Then, 6 cases remain with 1 or 2 aligned pairs (5…10), which corresponds to 6 or 7 steps per Pixel.

## 8 Queens Puzzle's Solution Derived from 8 Knights Solution

In the case of the Queens, there are 3 cases where 4 pairs (1,2,3) are aligned. This amount of 12 pairs. There remain 16 pairs where 1 or 2 pairs are aligned.

The solution with the Queens on the right Pixel is better than the solution with the Knights on the left Pixel. The 8 Queens Puzzle has 16 cases where 1 or 2 pairs are aligned (4…19). This is better than the 8 Knights solution where there are only 6 cases where 1 or 2 pairs are aligned (cases 5..10).

One of the weaknesses of this solution, is that there are 2 parallel gaps of around 3 Pixel wide. For edges parallel to these gaps, there will be a degradation of antialiasing. When an edge that is parallel to these gaps moves from left to right the following behavior is expected.
There is no transition for a distance of 3 Pixels, followed by 4 transitions across 4 sample points in the space of ½ Pixel, followed by no transition for a distance of 3 Pixels.

## Best Case

No matter how the Subpixels are selected, it cannot be avoided that at least 2 Subpixels can be aligned along some random triangle edge. When 2 Subpixels aligned with a triangle edge, this will reduce the number of intensity steps by 1.

In the best case, each line connects only 2 Subpixels. The minimum set of lines can be counted as follows.

Counting Subpixel pairs:
Subpixel 0, 7 pairs: 0-1, 0-2, 0-3, 0-4, 0-5, 0-6, 0-7
Subpixel 1, 6 pairs: 1-2, 1-3, 1-4, 1-5, 1-6, 1-7
Subpixel 2, 5 pairs: 2-3, 2-4, 2-5, 2-6, 2-7
Subpixel 3, 4 pairs: 3-4, 3-5, 3-6, 3-7
Subpixel 4, 3 pairs: 4-5, 4-6, 4-7
Subpixel 5, 2 pairs: 5-6, 5-7
Subpixel 6, 1 pairs: 6-7
Given 8 Subpixels, there are: 7+6+5+4+3+2+1= 28 possible pairs

## Selecting a Solution

In order to analyze the solutions, the following criteria will help in finding a good solution.

Avoid solution where there are more than 2 sets of parallel Subpixels pairs.
Select the solution where there is a maximum of 1 or 2 pairs of aligned Subpixels.

# Multi-Sample AA (MSAA)

Avoid solutions with large gaps.

## *Non 8 Queens Solutions*

While looking at information on websites, I have found 2 solutions from reputable source that do not satisfy the 8 Queens Puzzle. Refer to Figure 4-5, Non-8-Queens Solutions

- Solution from Rick Fadden's Patent 6445392 [127]
- Solution from Nvidia, according to article from Tom's Hardware [67] (Part1, Pg4)

These 2 solutions look pretty good according to my criteria enounced above.

In the example on the left, the Subpixel looks pretty good.
In the example on the right side, because of the bunching of 4 subpixels within ½ Pixel, at 45 degrees, there is a problem similar to the one described in the $1^{st}$ example:
There is no transition for a distance of 3 Pixels, followed by 4 transitions across 4 sample points in the space of ½ Pixel, followed by no transition for a distance of 3 Pixels.

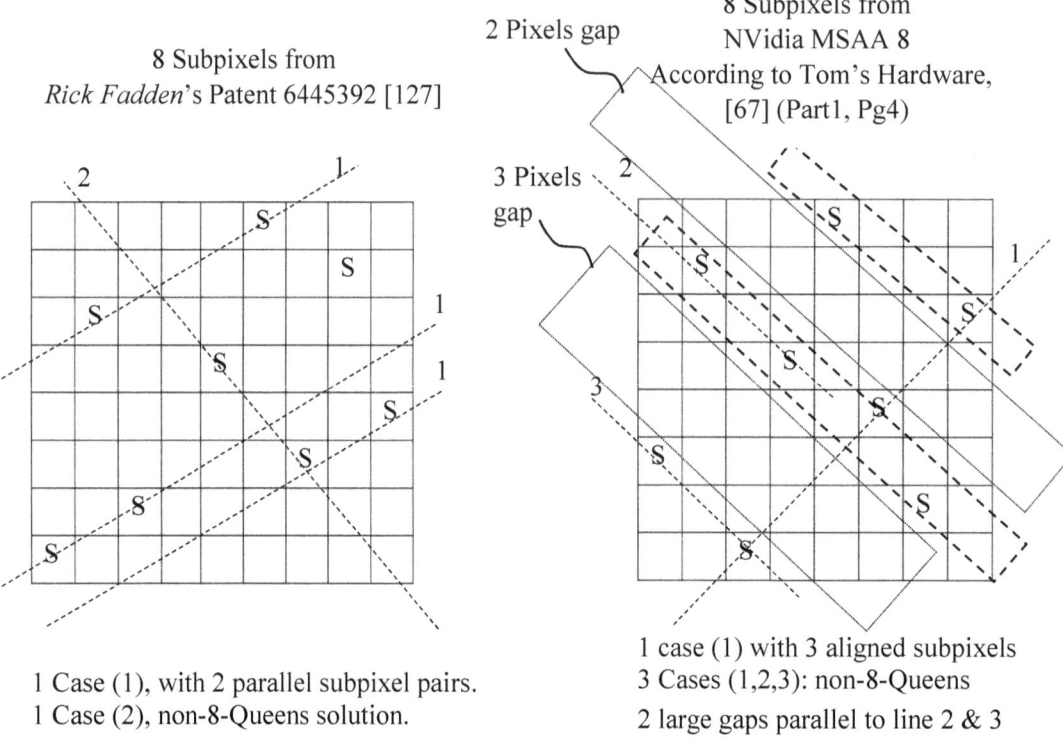

**Figure 4-5 Non-8-Queens Solutions**

## *Other Examples of 8 Queens Solutions*

In Figure 4-6, there are four Examples of 8 Queens Solutions

In each of these four 8 Queens examples, there are at least 2 cases with 2 pairs of parallel Subpixels. In examples 1 to 3, there is at least are one case with 3 aligned Subpixels (2 cases in example 1).

In example 4, there are only 2 cases with 2 aligned Subpixels. So, the Subpixel distribution in example 4 should be the best approach.

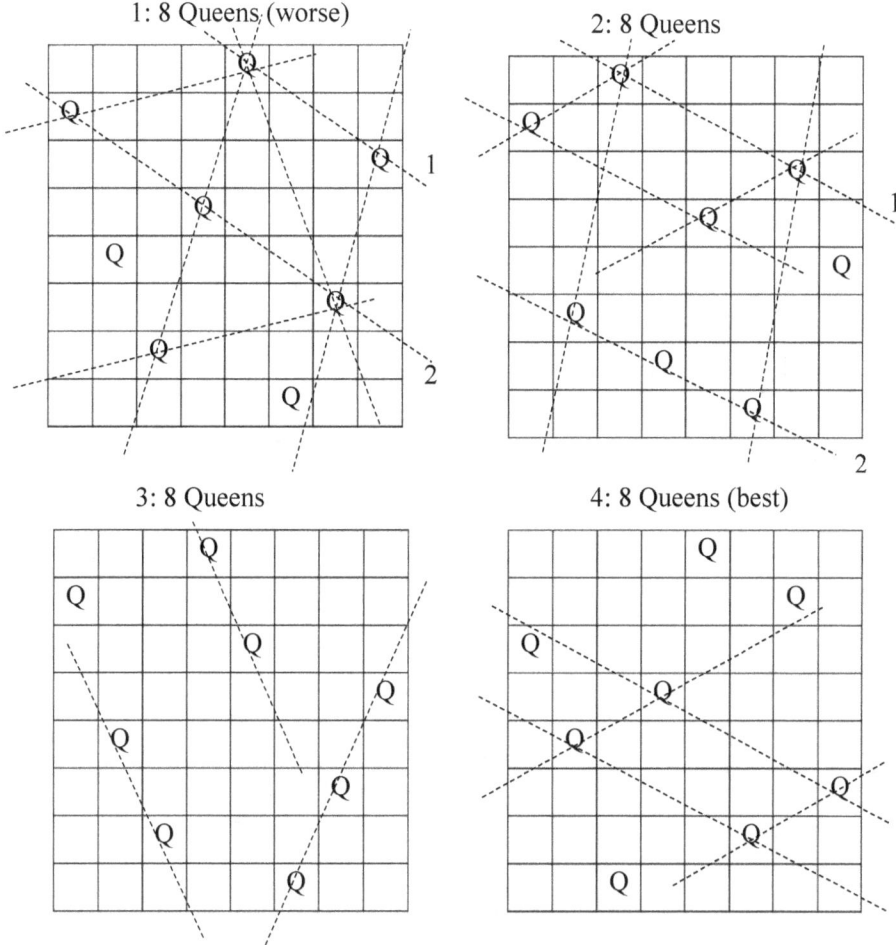

**Figure 4-6 Four Examples of 8 Queens Solutions**

Multi-Sample AA (MSAA)

### *Gaps > ¼ Pixel in 8 Queens Solutions*

Besides aligned Subpixels, the gaps between aligned Subpixel should be considered. When there are gaps > ¼ Pixel between groups of Subpixels, narrow faces < ¼ Pixel wide would pop in-and-out of scenes.

In Figure 4-7, several gaps are identified in these four 8 Queen Solutions

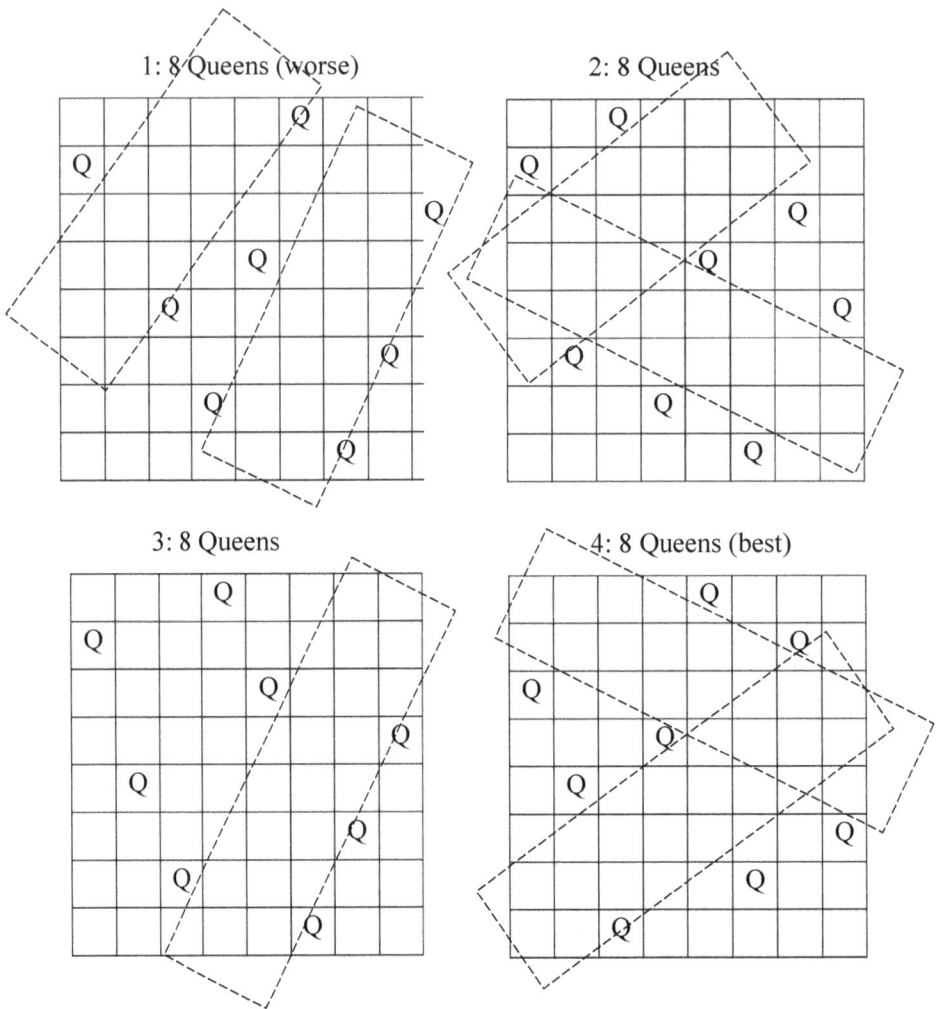

**Figure 4-7 Identified ¼ Pixel Gaps in 8 Queens Solutions**

# Chapter 5  RT CGI with Anti-Aliasing

This Chapter is divided into the following sections:
- Anti-Aliasing: ABAA vs MSAA
- Early RT CGI Systems
- Covered Area Computation

## 5.1 ABAA vs MSAA

In RT CGI, AA is implemented by processing Subpixels. The most widely used approach is MSAA. In this book I have introduced a new approach, ABAA, that samples Subpixel areas instead of Subpixel point samples. I have already presented several advantages of ABAA over MSAA. In this section, several aspects of accuracy between ABAA and MSAA are presented. Refer to Figure 5-1.

In this figure, there are examples of Pixel subdivided into 4 and 8 Subpixels using two 2 different approaches: ABAA vs MSAA.

*Subpixel Areas with ABAA*

On the left side, using ABAA, each Pixel is decomposed into 4 or 8 Subpixel Areas. There many ways to represents the Subpixel Areas. A few examples are shown here.

- Example of Pixel with 4x4 Subpixel Areas. This approach was used by the Link DIG, one of the first special purpose Super Computer that was used to train the Space Shuttle astronauts before their missions in space. Of interest, this RT CGI system used an early version of ABAA, using 4x4 Subpixel areas.
  In this approach, edges are separated into 2 slope types. Depending on their slope, they are Vertical Edges (*VE*) when |slope|<1.0, else they are Horizontal Edges (*HE*).
- Example of Pixel with 4 Subpixel Areas
- Example of Pixel with 8 Subpixel Areas

As will be shown in the next chapter, the 4 & 8 Subpixel Areas solutions are derived from the 4x4 Subpixel Areas of the DIG. This was made possible by changing the shape of the Subpixels, so that the same Subpixel area can be used for both *HE* and *VE*.

*Subpixel Sample Points with MSAA*

On the right side, MSAA uses Subpixel Sample Points for Super-Sampling. In the MSAA approach, each Pixel is subdivided into 1, 4 or 8 Subpixel Sample Points. There are many ways to arrange Subpixels as Sample Points. Two examples are shown here.

- Pixel with 1 Sample Point
- Pixel with 4 Sample Points
- Pixel with 8 Sample Points

In the MSAA approach, several images are computed using different sample points within a Pixel. The AA image is obtained by the average of these images.

# RT CGI with Anti-Aliasing

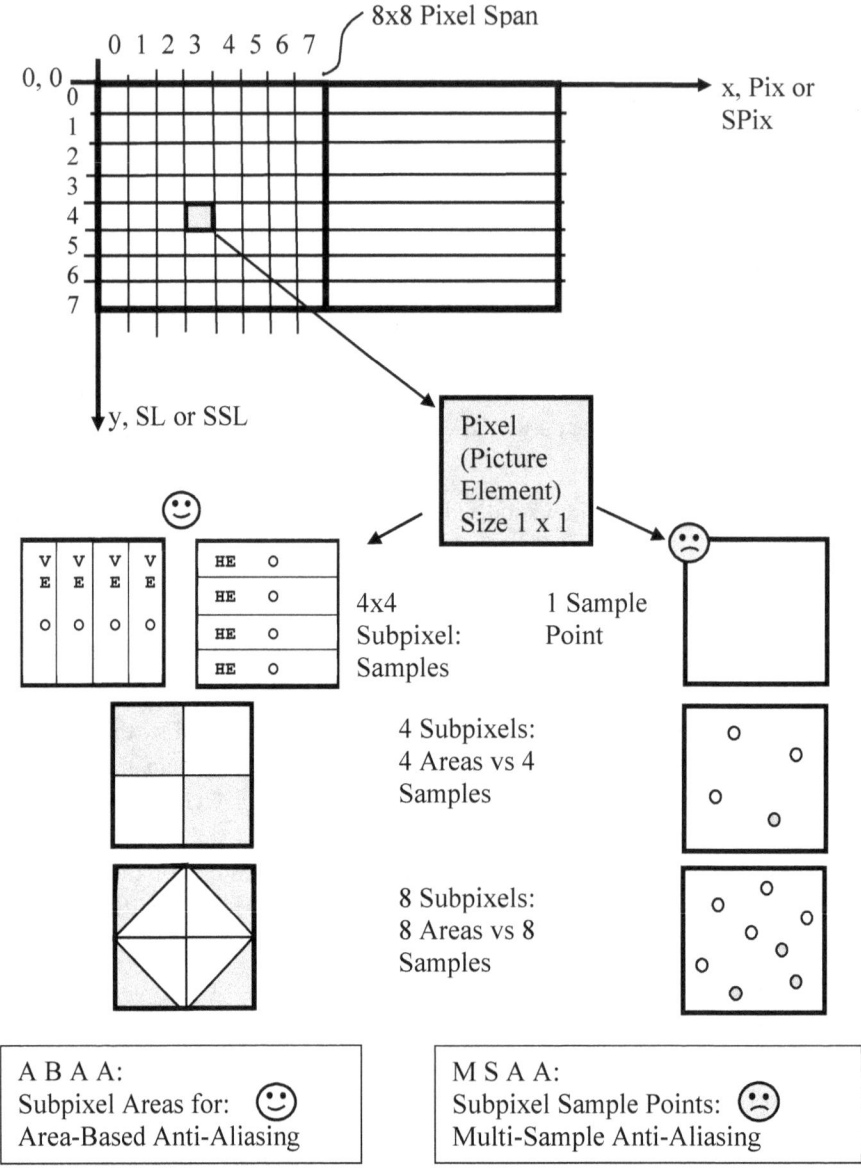

**Figure 5-1 Comparison of Subpixels with ABAA and MSAA**

MSAA evolved as follows. When I was designing 3D graphics systems, we used 3D Graphics workstations for the development of our 3D data base. These workstations came from Evans Sutherland or Silicon Graphics. During the design, we used these workstations to preview the 2D images created from our data base. Initially, the 2D images were computed using only one Sample Point per Pixel. Of course, we could see the stairsteps on the displayed images.

While looking at static images, the workstations were idling. Then, the workstation programmers realized that instead of idling, the workstation waiting time could be better used by computing multiple images while moving the sample point within the Pixels. This can be done by adding a Pixel fraction and a SL fraction to the projected Pixel (before rounding!). Then several images were averaged. Soon, after about 5 seconds, the point sampled images were replaced with an anti-aliased image consisting of 4 or 8 Subpixels. This is a neat solution, but costly if it has to be implemented in real-time for 3D RT CGI. For this reason, most of the early RT CGI systems did not have good anti-aliasing. Another solution for reducing aliasing was to compute images with higher resolution, using SSAA.

## 5.2 AA in Early RT CGI Systems

Before Silicon Graphics and the PC 3D graphics adapter, only a handful of companies were designing 3D RT CGI systems for NASA and the US military.

Around 1980, these RT CGI systems were used for Flight Simulation and Training. The customers were NASA and the US Military. The 2 most important requirements were 'Speed' and 'Anti-Aliasing'.

These 3D RT CGI systems are referred to as "Big Iron" because they were big and filled a full room of computing hardware. This hardware was contained in several steel cabinets the size of refrigerators, and costed above $1M.

- General Electric Company
- Evans and Sutherland/Redifon
- McDonnell Douglas Electronics Company
- Singer Company - Link Division

As a solution to AA, the Link DIG from the Link Division of the Singer Company had 4x4 Subpixel Edge Smoothing. After 1980, most of these companies adopted a Bed of Nail (BON) approach similar to MSAA

There is more information about these systems in a later chapter of this book about 'Flight Simulators and RT CGI'.

The BON approach was usually used with Tile architectures, where the image is subdivided into Span consisting of 8x8 Pixels. In the BON approach the Pixel coverage by Subpixel is identified in one operation and the mixed color computed at once within Spans.

In my new ABAA implementation, the Pixel coverage is also decoded with high accuracy in one operation.

In the following sections, the accuracy of these approaches will also be evaluated

### 5.2.1 Link DIG AA Implementation with 4x4 Subpixels

The Link DIG used a Scanline Computer for image rendering. In this approach, the image is rendered one SL at a time. For the purpose of edge smoothing, edges were divided in two types:

- Vertical Edges (*VE*) when the slope *dx/dy* < *1.0*.
- Horizontal Edges (*HE*) when the slope *dx/dy* >= *1.0*.

In the following figure, there is an example where a triangle is rendered with VE and HE Subpixels. A Subpixel Area is covered when its center is covered by the triangle. For the Pixels that are not

## RT CGI with Anti-Aliasing

intersected, their color is either the Pixel color or the Background color. For each partially covered Pixel, the triangle color of the covered area is mixed with the Background color, in step of 1/4 increments.

Using this approach, there can be only 2 face contributions per Pixel:
top face and face behind top face.

In the example of Figure 5-2, the triangle defined by 2 VEs and 1 HE is rendered using a combination of *VE* and *HE* Subpixels

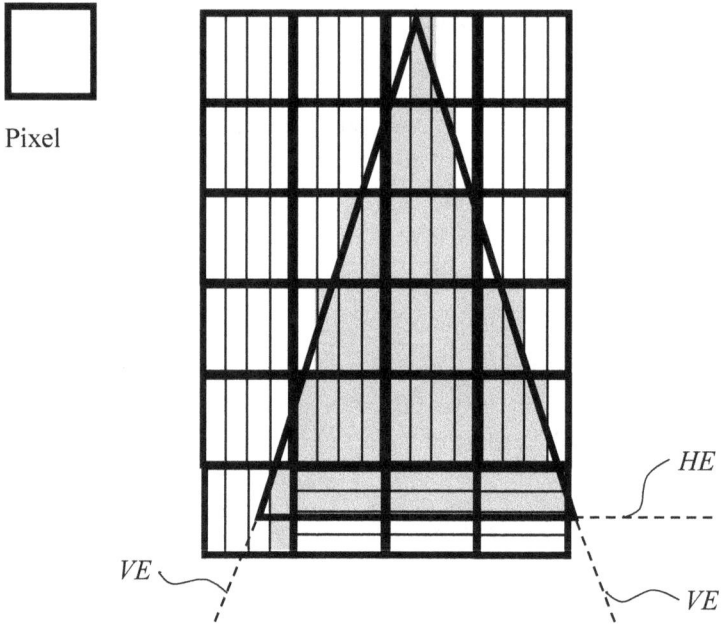

**Figure 5-2 Triangle with 2 *VEs* and 1 *HE* Rendered with Subpixels**

In the Link DIG, this method produced good results. This approach works well when only 2 colors are blended in a Subpixel. In case when there are a VE and HE in the same Pixel, the last intersecting edge, VE or HE, determines the Subpixel type.

In the DIG, I implemented an important feature to prevent small projected faces from popping in-and-out of the dynamic scenes.

The DIG systems had the capability to accurately compute the projection size of faces in the 3D space. The narrow faces were detected dearly in the geometry processing and handled gracefully. Refer to my patent [105] on Face Resolvability Test.

## 5.2.2 RT CGI AA Implementation with Bed of Nails (BON)

A few years after the Link DIG introduction, the increase in memory density made face buffer implementation feasible. In the 1980s, some manufactures of RT CGI systems adopted 'Tile based' architectures using a face buffer. In one approach, the image is subdivided into Spans consisting of 8x8 Pixels. Within a Span, the Subpixel were arranged in a BON configuration similar to the MSAA approach. The Pixel coverage by Subpixel were identified in one operation and the mixed color computed at once within Spans. In the mid 1990s, this approach was implemented in the Warp 5 from Oak Technology in Sunnyvale [78] for the PC add-on graphic card market. When it was introduced, the Warp 5 was the only 3D graphics chip with AA.

One approach to the BON implementation is to use the edge entry and exit points to the Pixel. Then the covered Subpixels can be derived from a table.

## 5.2.3 Accuracy of Pixel Entry and Exit Points

As mentioned above, when knowing the edge entry and exit points to the Pixel, the covered Subpixels can be derived from a table. But the output of the table is only as precise as the accuracy of the input and exit points. When there are 4 entry points and 4 exit points to a Pixel, the accuracy on each side is +/- 1/8.

In the following example, a Vertical Edge type enters on the top and exit on the bottom of Pixel. For Horizontipe Edge type, the cases are similar. The entry point would be on the left side and the exit point would on the right side of the Pixel. In Figure 5-3, 'Edge Accuracy at Pixel Boundaries', there 2 examples of edges entering and exiting a Pixel.

- Edge1 represents the most common case. Edge1 enters the Pixel on the top boundary and exits on the bottom boundary of the Pixel with and accuracy of *+/- 1/8*. This is the worst case. The difference between the difference between the maximum area, *Amax*, and the minimum area, *Amin*, is:
  *Amax – Amin = ¼ Pixel*
- Edge2 enters the Pixel on the top boundary and exits the Pixel on a side boundary. This is an intermediate case. The difference between *Amax* and *Amin* is:
  *Amax – Amin = 1/8 Pixel -1/32 Pixel = 3/32 Pixel*
- In the best case, the edge enters on top at segment 0 and exits on the left side at segment 0. The difference between *Amax* and *Amin* is:
  *Amax – Amin = 1/32 Pixel -0/32 Pixel = 1/32 Pixel*

So, in the worst case, the error is ¼ *Pixel*. In the case of 8 Subpixels, each Subpixel has a weight of 1/8 Pixel. So, the fluctuation is:
*BON ACCURACY = +/- one Subpixel weight*. When the 2 Subpixels don't line up
*BON ACCURACY = +/- two Subpixel weight*. When the 2 Subpixels line up
In the worst case, when an edge lines up with a Subpixel pair, this corresponds to 4 Subpixel weights.

The most important case is that when a vertical edge type enters on the top side and exits on the bottom side of a Pixel or Pixel pair. A similar case consists of a horizontal edge type enters on the left side and exits on the right side of a Pixel or Pixel pair. These cases are similar to Edge1.

# RT CGI with Anti-Aliasing

The computation of the edge distance using normal vectors is another accuracy factor that need to be considered, In the case of multiple samples, the accuracy of the number of Subpixels will depend on the entry point and the accuracy of the normal vectors.

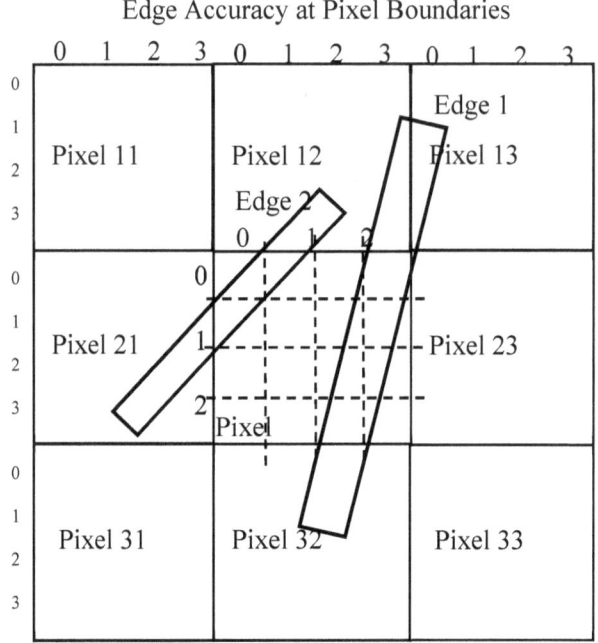

**Figure 5-3 Edge Accuracy at Pixel Boundaries**

Comparison between MSAA and ABAA Accuracy

In Figure 5-4, the accuracy of the Subpixel assignment is compared between MSAA and ABAA.

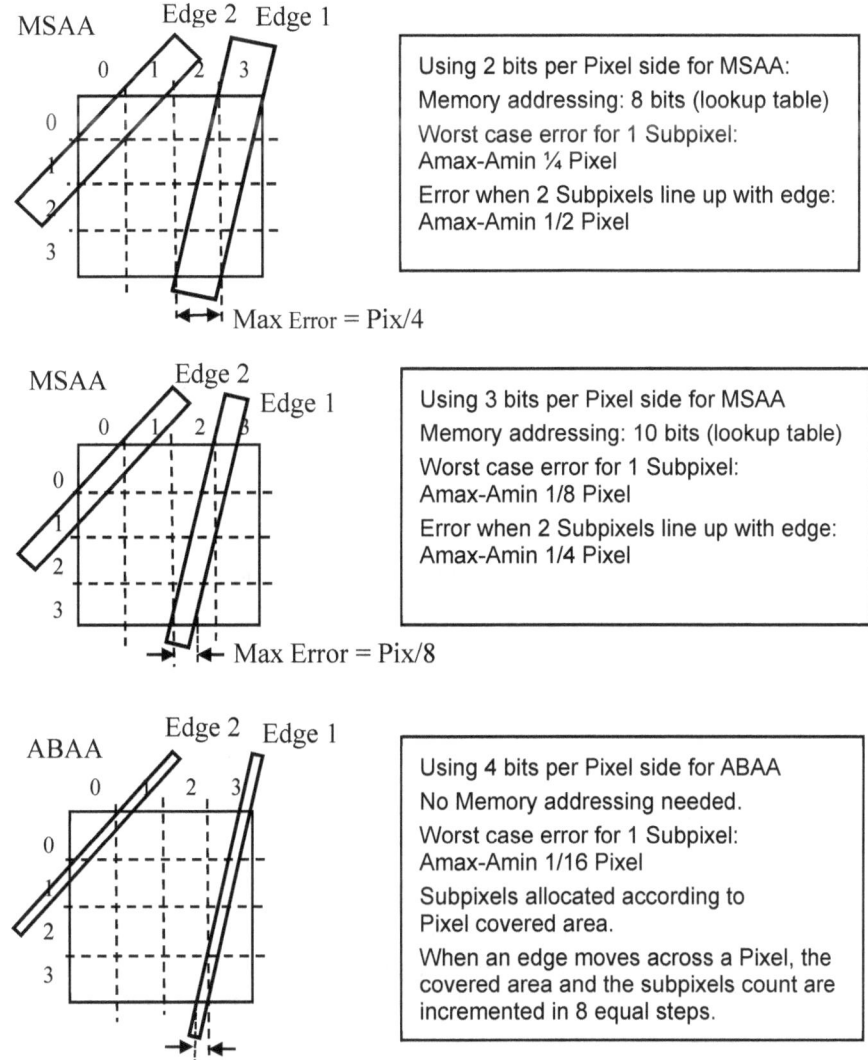

**Figure 5-4 Comparison between BON and ABAA Accuracy**

It is assumed that the AA is implemented with 8 Subpixels.

- For BON, two cases for Pixel sides accuracy are considered. It is assumed that the accuracy at Pixel entry and exit is 2 bits or 3 bits.
- For ABAA, the accuracy at Pixel entry and exit is 4 bits.
  More details about the implementation will be presented later.

As can be see in the previous figure, ABAA is more accurate than the BON with lookup table. Akso, it does not have the disadvantage of 2 Subpixels lining up with triangle edges. It is assumed that the Subpixels are selected so that there a no cases of 3 Subpixels lining up with edges.

With BON, just like MSAA, when 2 Subpixels line up with an edge, the there will be a jump of 2 Subpixels when the edge crosses the 2 Subpixels. In this case, the 8 Subpixel AA will behave like 4 Subpixel AA. For true horizontal edges, vertical edges, and diagonal edges at 45 degrees (i.e. *angle = N\*Pi/4*), the 8 Subpixels are selected so that they will not align with such edges. For other angles like *N\*Pi/4 +Pi/8*, the 8 Subpixels could also behave like 4 Subpixels.

### 5.2.4 Use Edge Distance to Detect Covered Subpixels.

In the BON and MSAA implementation, the covered Subpixels can be detected by computing their distance to the edge.

Refer to Figure 5-5, 'Edge to Subpixel Distance in *(xp, yp)* Pixel Coordinate System'.

In this figure, there is a Pixel and an Edge defined in *(xp, yp)* Pixel coordinate system. The Subpixel Distance is defined from the Edge to the Sample Point at the center of the Pixel.

***Line Equation***

In the *(xp, yp)* Pixel coordinate axis system, the edge can be represented by its equation:
  *axp + byp + c = 0*
The normal to the edge can be derived from this equation:
  *N = (a, b).*

The normal distance of any point *(xp, yp)* on the line edge can be obtained by replacing the point in the equation. The normal distance of the line edge to the origin *(0, 0)* is: *c*.

The normal distance, *d*, of the Subpixel center *(x1, y1)* to a line edge *axp + byp + c = 0* can be obtained by replacing the point *(x1, y1)* in the line equation *d = ax1 + by1 + c*. The normal distance of the Pixel center *(x1, y1)* to the line edge is *d-c*.

Since the edge belongs to a triangle, the is an in-side (visible) and out-side of the edge. In this example, the points on the left of the edge are *outside* of the triangle. The points on the right side of the edge are *inside* of the triangle. So, if *d>c*, the point is *inside,* else it is *outside*.

When there are several Subpixels, each Subpixel is tested against the edge.

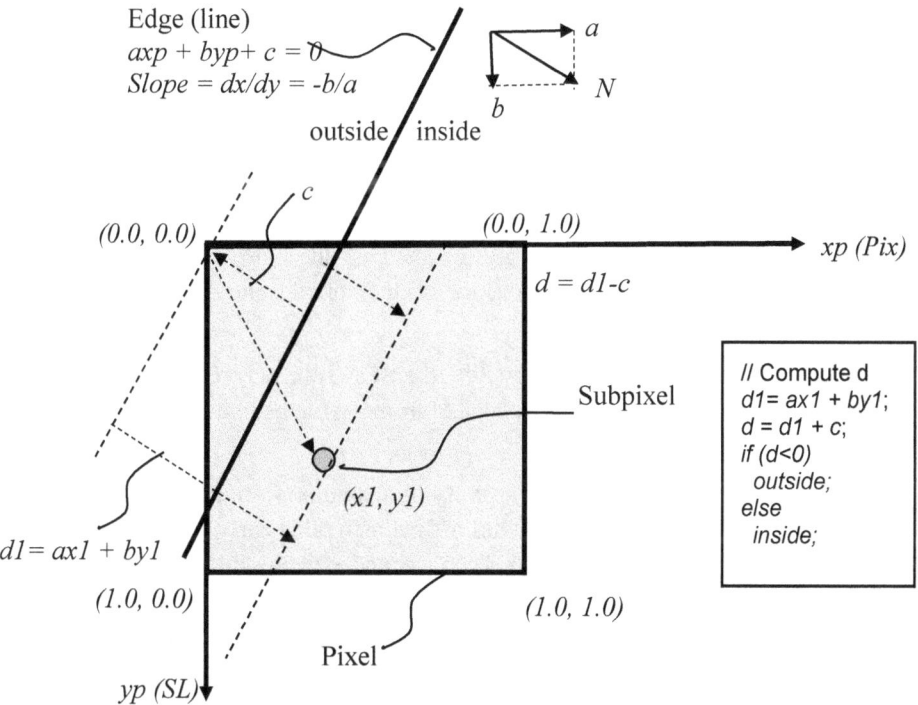

**Figure 5-5 Edge to Subpixel Distance in *(xp, yp)* Pixel Coordinate System**

*Accuracy of Distance Computation*

The distance computation $d = ax1 + by1 + c$ consists of 2 multiplications and 3 additions. There is no error is $x1$ and $y1$ since they are constants defining the Subpixel position. Assuming that the error in $a$, $b$ and $c$ is $e$, the error in the $d$ equation is $3*e$

If the resolution inside of a Pixel is 1/16, then the error in the distance will be: $dmax - dmin = 3*e$. The order of magnitude of the error is close to *1/8,* which represents a Subpixel.

*Comparison with ABAA Error*

As will be shown later on, with ABAA, the covered area can be computed with a resolution of *1/16*.

So, the maximum error will be:
$e = +/- 1/16$

## 5.3 Comparison of MSAA with ABAA

### 5.3.1 My Experience with MSAA and ABAA

When I worked at Link, the ModDIG (nex gen DIG) designers did simulations and came up with 8 Subpixels as the preferred solution. It looks like at GE they came up with the same conclusion as they designed AA solutions with 8 Subpixels. At that time the solutions with 4 and 8 sample points were referred to as Bed of Nail (BON). Although the BON approach is similar to MSAA, in the BON approach, the covered Subpixels are detected in one path and only one image is computed. With MSAA, one image is computed for each Subpixel and the final image is the average of these images.

When we designed the Warp 5 at Oak Technology [78], the BON solution consisted of 8 Subpixels, or Bed of Nails. The Subpixel assignment were decoded from a table using the Pixel entry and exit points of edges.

While working on the next generation of the Warp5, I did a simulation of an early version of my ABAA algorithm. Then I generated dynamic scenes offline using this early ABAA algorithm and the same scenes using the Warp5 BON algorithm. Then we made side by side comparisons of these simulated dynamic scenes. In the comparions, my ABAA approach looked significantly better than the version implemented in the Warp5. May be twice better. Unfortunaltly, there was no follow on to Warp5, because the project got cancelled.

Using my analysis of the MSAA algorithm and the results form the Warp5 comparison, I suspects that an ABAA method using only 4 Subpixels should produce results at least as good MSAA with 8 Subpixels.

***Understanding Binary Numbers***

The ABAA algorithm will be explained in the following Sections. But, in order to have a full understanding of the algorithm the reader should have some understanding of binary numbers. In order to describe the algorithm, the image is decomposed into small square areas of size 8x8 Pixels. These square areas of 8x8 Pixels are referred to as 'two-dimensional Spans', or simply 'Spans'. In the final steps of the AA hardware implementation (and also software implementation), the operations are performed with binary numbers.

### 5.3.2 MSAA and ABAA with 4 or 8 Subpixels

Given a Pixel with $N$ Subpixels, as an edge moves across a Pixel, that should result into N distinct intensity increments. When the Pixel intensity (or color) is considered, these corresponds to N intensity steps. With ABAA, there are always $N$ distinct intensity increments.

1. With MSAA, there are always several cases where 2 Subpixels are aligned with a polygon edge. When a moving edge that is aligned with a pair of Subpixels crosses these Subpixels, the Subpixel count jumps by 2. Consequently, the Subpixels sequence will increment by 1 and sometimes 2 or more Subpixels at a time.
   For 4 Subpixels, there are *3+2+1=6* Subpixel pairs.
   For 8 Subpixels, there are *7+6+5+4+3+2+1=28* Subpixel pairs.

With ABAA there is no case where the number of Subpixels will jump by *2*.
2. With MSAA the *N* increments are not evenly spaced.
With ABAA, the *N* increments are evenly spaced.
3. With MSAA, the detection of covered Subpixels is not always accurate.
With ABAA, the detection of covered Subpixels is accurate (*1/16 Pixel*)
4. With MSAA the covered Subpixels are detected with multiple operations.
With ABAA, for each edge position, the number of covered Subpixels is derived in one operation, according to the sampled area. There is no need for Multi Sampling.

### 5.3.3 Advantages and Limitations
*Problem to be solved*

All 4 approaches, SSAA, MSAA, BON and ABAA try to solve the Aliasing problem to the best of their ability. They use different approaches based on available information, assumptions and design constraints. With these tools, the following Facts and Illusions can be derived.

*Available Information*

The geometric information consists of a set of polygons (mainly triangles) that partially cover a Pixel. The covered areas are also referred as fragments. If there was no limitation or constraints about the implementation, the exact area could be computed and applied to the computation of the resulting Pixel mixed color. The following two solutions could most accurately accomplish the area computation:
- The SSAA approach with sufficient resolution, such as 8x8 Subpixels for example, could provide area distributions with accuracy of 1/8 to 1/64. A disadvantage of SSAA is that it is very inefficient. For example, with 64 samples, there are only 8 horizontal and only 8 vertical transitions. There is an advantage of SSAA for non-uniform filters, because different weights could be applied, depending on the sample location.
- ABAA is the next best approach. Given a limitation of 4 or 8 Subpixel Areas, it can provide a fairly accurate approximation of quantized fragments areas. The advantage of ABAA is that it is a real time solution.

*Assumptions*

With point sampling, the following assumptions are made:

- The Sample Points accurately represent the size of their surrounding area. Although all the sample points have the same weight, the sample area that they represent is undefined.
- When an edge moves across a Pixel, the incremental covered area is accurately accounted for. This is probably true when edges are parallel with the *x* or *y* axis, but not for other edge directions. In the worst case, when an edge crosses two aligned sample points, the incremental covered area is double.
- for the SSAA approach, the number of Subpixels is *NxN (4x4 or 8x8)*.
- for MSAA, BON and ABAA, the number of Subpixels is *N (4 or 8)*
- the accuracy of the computations is limited by the accuracy of the slope computation. It can be estimated at *1/16* (half the Subpixel resolution).

## Constraints

For real time implementation there several constraints:
- Limited time for the mixed color computations.
- Limited number of Subpixels due to local storage limitation.
- Limited accuracy in the computations.

## SSAA

When doing SSAA using Pixels, the image is computed with a higher resolution, there are more accuracy bits available. It is more accurate than when doing SSAA with Subpixels.

## Limited Accuracy with MSAA

The accuracy of the sample points and the edge positions is around 1/16 Pixel
Due to the limited accuracy of the edge position, the cumulative error between Sample Point and edge depends on the edge slope parameters (a, b, c) and the edge positions (with 1/16 accuracy). This could amount to 3/16, which is between 1/8 and 1/2 of the Pixel size.
Also, the sizes of sampled areas vary greatly. For 8 Sample Points, they vary between 0 and ¼, while the expected area should be 1/8.

## Conclusion

According to this discussion, the ABAA approach is the best for RT CGI applications. For non-RT CGI, both SSAA and ABAA can produce acceptable results.

# 5.4 Selecting Subpixels for AA

In this section, there are several examples comparing ABAA with SSAA and MSAA.

For RT CGI, most algorithms assign Subpixels inside of a Pixel and use Subpixel point sampling. The resulting Pixel color is the color mix that is the average of the selected Subpixel contributions. Both MSAA, BON and ABAA use a similar approach, where all the Subpixels have an equal weight. The filter corresponds to a square box. This is a fast approach that produces good results. For MSAA, when all Subpixels have the same weight, the sparse distribution of Subpixels is more efficient for a Box Filter than SSAA with arrays of *NxN* Subpixels.

In the following figures, there are several examples of Subpixel distributions within Pixels and the expected result when a triangle intersects that Pixel. The Subpixels can be organized into an N*N array of Subpixels, or as sparse N Subpixels. In each of the following examples, there are 4 displayed triangles intersecting a Pixel. The same triangles are used for the 4 examples. On the left side, the first triangle intersects the Pixel, but all Subpixels are covered. So, the Pixel is completely covered. In the other 3 cases, the Pixels are partially covered. The triangles cover various fraction according to the covered Subpixels. As can be observed, the fraction of covered Subpixels can be different, depending of the Subpixel distributions and the triangle position. Depending of the organizations of the Subpixels, the Pixel coverage can vary for the same triangle vs Pixel geometry.

In the first three figures, the Subpixels are assigned using the SSAA and MSAA approach. The same four triangles are shown intersecting Pixels consisting of 16, 64, 32 and 8 Subpixels. Each Subpixel is represented by a Sample Point within the Pixel.

In the fourth figure the Pixel is divided into 8 Subpixel Areas of equal size. The Subpixels are assigned using the Area-Based AA algorithm. With ABAA, the area allocated to the 8 Subpixel Areas is equivalent to the covered area of the Pixel.

*SSAA with array of 4x4 or 8x8 Subpixels*

In Figure 5-6, there are SSAA examples of with an array of 4x4 Subpixels, for a total of 16 Subpixels. As can be seen, for thin vertical triangles, the number of Subpixels can jump from 0 to 4, when the triangle moves sideways (or thin horizontal triangles moving upward). This is a disadvantage of Subpixels organized in array form. On the other hand, square arrays of *NxN* Subpixels are well suited for AA filters when different weights are assigned to Subpixels, depending on their position relative to the center of the Pixel.

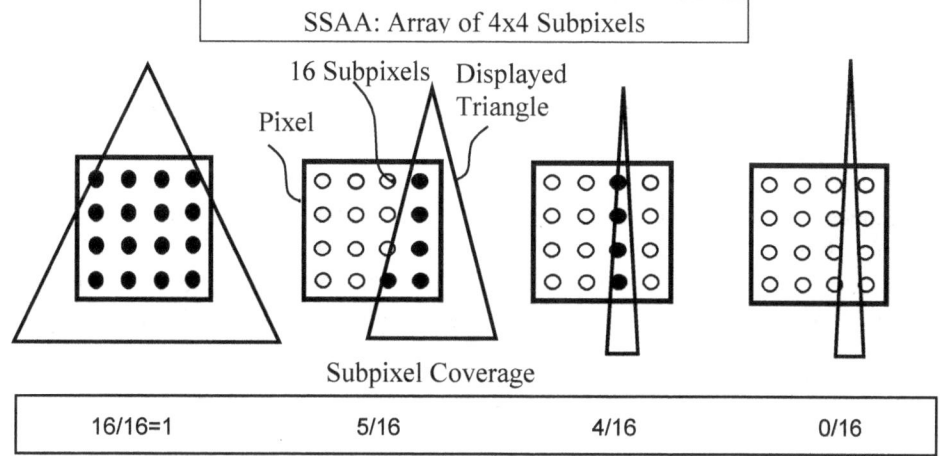

**Figure 5-6 SSAA Examples of Triangles and 4x4 Subpixels**

*SSAA with array of 8x8 Subpixels*

When using a larger array of Subpixels, such as 8x8=64 Subpixels, the problem with narrow triangles is reduced. Refer to Figure 5-7.

There is a better solution using only 32 Subpixels, as shown in the next example.

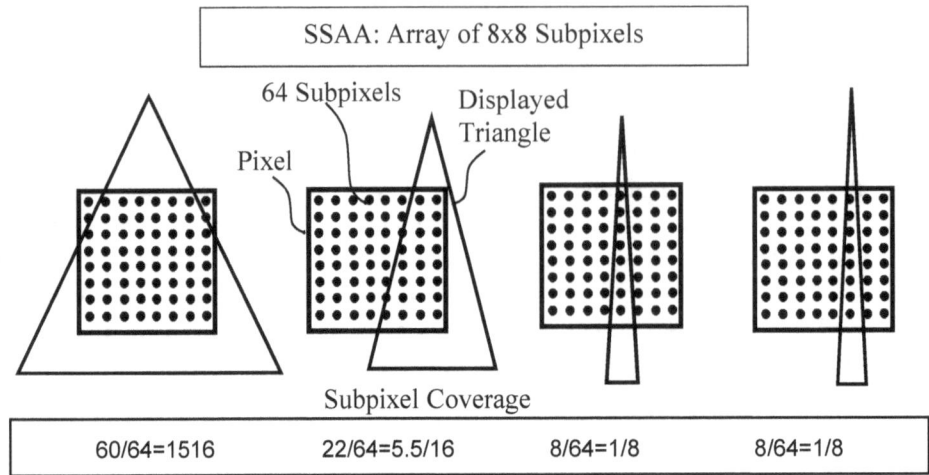

**Figure 5-7 SSAA Examples of Triangles and 8x8 Subpixels**

### SSAA with array of 4x8 Subpixels

In Figure 5-8, there are SSAA examples with an array of 4x8 Subpixels, for a total of 32 Subpixels. The 4 rows of 4 Subpixels are repeated with an offset from their original position. This is an improvement over the array of 4x4 Subpixels, without using 8x8 Subpixels. For thin triangles, the number of covered Subpixels is more stable, when the triangle moves vertically or sideways.

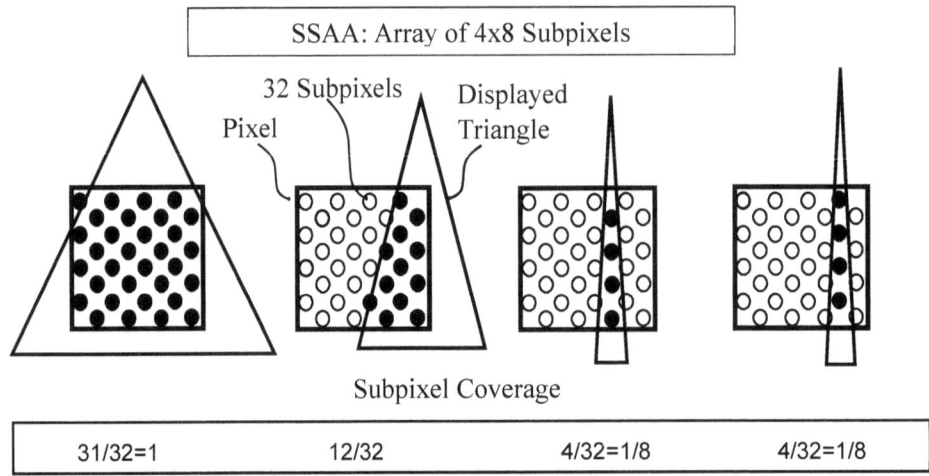

**Figure 5-8 SSAA Examples of Triangles and 4x8 Subpixels**

### MSAA and BON with array of 8 sparse Subpixels

In Figure 5-9, the same triangle examples are shown with MSAA (or BON), using only 8 sparse Subpixels. Here, the Subpixels a positioned so that no more than two are aligned. This results into a more efficient use of Subpixels. But there is still a problem when some triangle edges are aligned with pairs of Subpixels. In this example, the number of Subpixels can jump from 0 to 2, when triangles move across the Pixel.

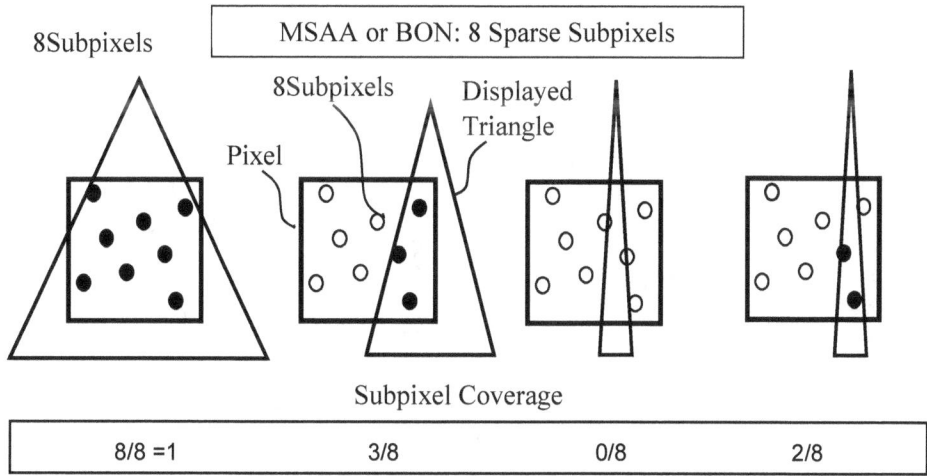

Figure 5-9 MSAA or BON: Examples of Triangles and 8 Sparse Subpixels

*ABAA with array of 4 and 8 Subpixel Areas*

In Figure 5-10, using the same triangle example, the 4 triangles intersect a Pixel divided into 4 Subpixel Areas of equal size, using the Area-Based AA algorithm.

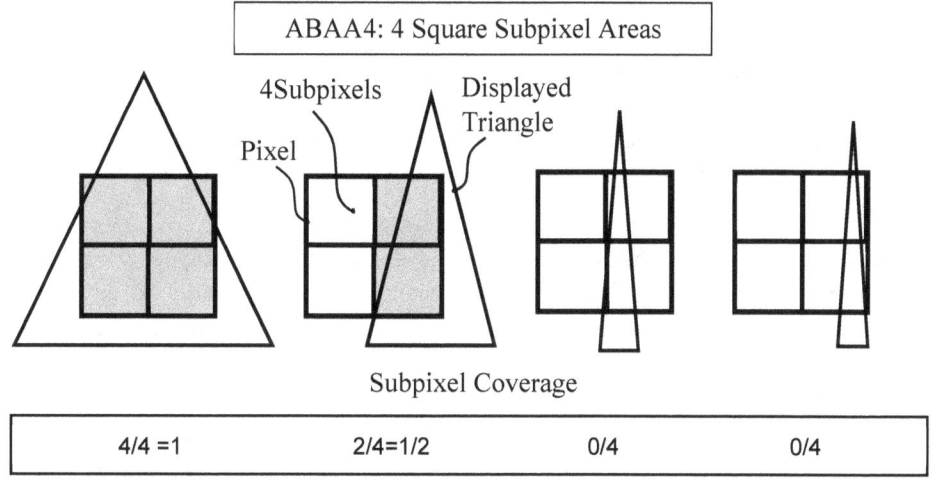

Figure 5-10 ABAA4 Examples of Triangles and 4 Subpixel Areas

In Figure 5-11, using the same triangle example, the 4 triangles intersect a Pixel divided into 8 Subpixel Areas of equal size When compared with the example of 8 Subpixels with MSAA, the

Subpixel assignment with ABAA is more accurate and continuous. Also, the location of the covered Subpixel Area is close to the original covered area.

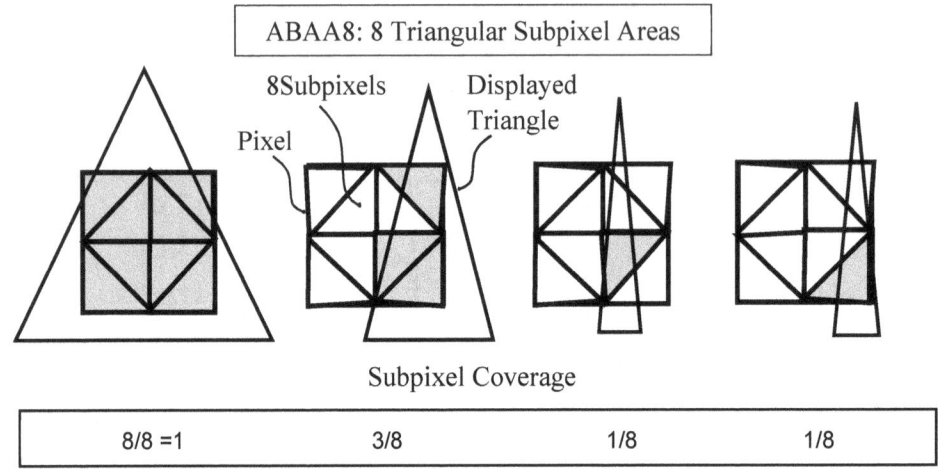

Figure 5-11 ABAA8 Examples of Triangles and 8 Subpixel Areas

### 5.4.1 Advantages of ABAA over MSAA

As of this writing, and to my knowledge, the most commonly used method for anti-aliasing in RT CGI relies on taking Multiple Sample Points. It is referred to Multi-Sample Anti-Aliasing (MSAA). It is a legacy of the traditional Z-buffer approach for rendering 3D Computer Generated Images (3D CGI).

While most methods are based on Point Sampling, in this book a new method that relies on Area Sampling is introduced. It is referred to as Area-Based Anti-Aliasing (ABAA). This method divides the Pixel into N Subpixel areas. It consists of computing the Pixel area that is covered by a polygon and assigning this area to N Subpixel areas. ABAA is much simpler and more accurate than MSAA and is less computation intensive.

There are many advantages of ABAA over MSAA. As discussed previously, there are serious weaknesses of MSAA with N Subpixels. When a triangle edge is parallel to any segment connecting 2 Subpixels, there is an increment of *di=2/N* (instead of *1/N*) when the edge transitions from one side to the other side of that segment. With 8 Subpixels there are:

*1+2+3+4+5+6+7 = sum(1 to 7) = 28* cases of Subpixel pairs

that can be aligned with a polygon edge. When an edge is crossing one of these segments, the intensity will have an increment of *1/4*, instead of *1/8*. Implementations with more than 2 aligned Subpixels should be avoided. Implementations with 2 aligned Subpixels should be worst case.

*Comparisons of Intensity Steps Between SSAA, MSAA and ABAA*

One way to compare the AA methods described in this book is to count the intensity steps as edges move across Pixels. This is done for edge slopes that vary over a 90 degree angle. For this comparison, 2 group of edges are used in the comparison: *HE* and *VE*.

In a later chapter, 'ABAA with 8 Subpixel Areas', the performances of ABBA8 with MSAA8 are compared with a computer simulation. Inside of an 8x8 Pixel span, several thin triangles with a base of 1 Pixel and a height of 8 Pixels are organized as a fan. Part of the results for 0 to 90 degrees are reproduced here. Refer to Figure 5-12, 'Number of Intensity steps for ABAA8 and MSAA8'.

In Table 5-1, the AA methods are compared when edges move accross a Pixel as vertical edge slopes $VSlp=dx/dy$ or horizontal edge slopes $HSlp=dy/dx$ vary between *0.0* and *1.0*.

What is interesting is that for vertical and horizontal edges *(Slp=0.0)*, all of these methods produce 8 equal steps.

As can be seen, ABAA is the most consistant and most efficient approach. With ABAA, the number of steps is always 8, independently of edge slope, as the covered area changes linearly across pixels.

The SSAA solution is the most expensive. For 0 degree *(Slp=0.0)* and 45 degrees angles *(|Slp|=1.0)*, the results are similar to MSAA. For other slope angles, the resolution increases with SSAA, while it decreases with MSAA.

With MSAA, the number of steps can vary between 4 and 8 for slopes between 0.0 (horizontal or vertical) and 1.0 (45 degrees).

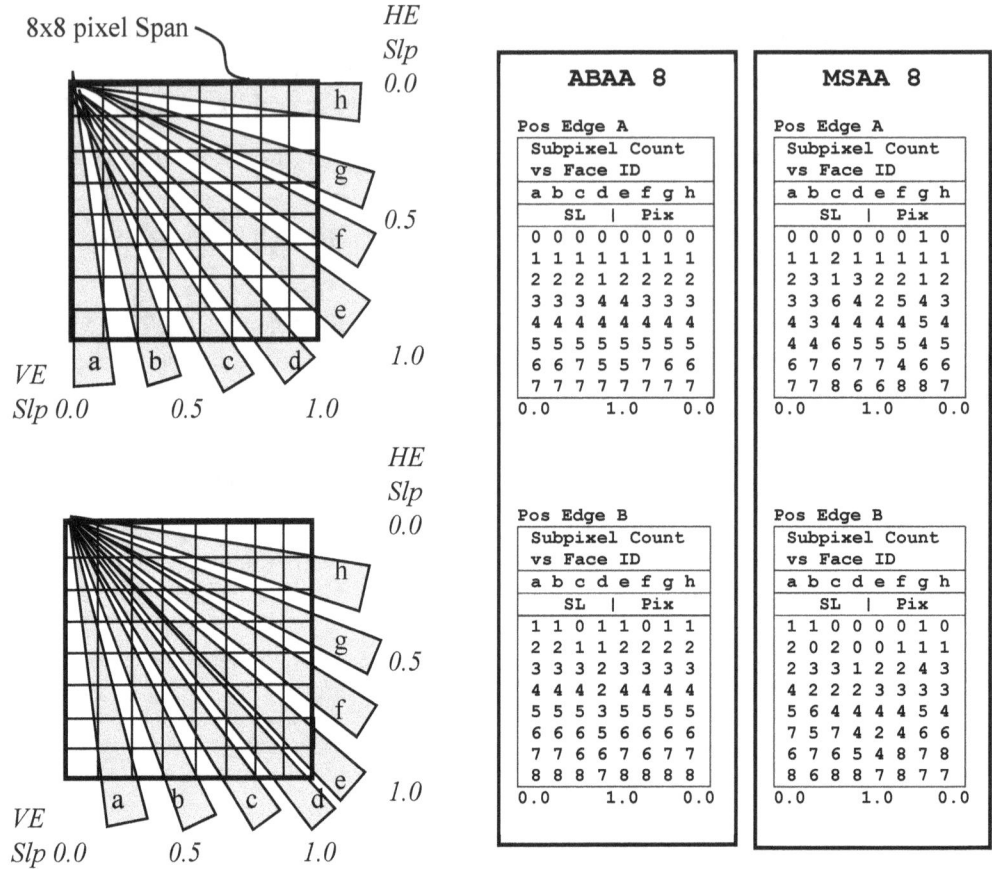

Figure 5-12 Number of Intensity steps for ABAA8 and MSAA8

| #Steps vs Edge Slope | VSlp=0, HSlp=0 (Slp=0.0) | VSlp=1/8, HSlp=1/8 | VSlp=1/4, HSlp=1/4 | VSlp=1/2, HSlp=1/2 (Slp 0.5) | VSlp=1, HSlp=1 (Slp =1.0) |
|---|---|---|---|---|---|
| **AA Method** | | | | | |
| SSAA, 8x8 | 8 | 64 | 32 | 16 | 8 |
| SSAA, 4x8 | 8 | 32 | 8 to 16 | 8 to 16 | 8 |
| MSAA, 8 Queens | 8 | 4 to 8 | 4 to 8 | 4 to 8 | 8 |
| ABAA, N=8 | 8 | 8 | 8 | 8 | 8 |

Table 5-1 Comparison of Intensity Steps vs Edge Slopes

Note that for *Slp=1.0*, ABAA does not show 8 steps in all cases. This is due to the interaction of the left and right triangle edges in the fans. But, for each left and right triangle edges, there will be 8 transition steps (by definition).

In most cases, SSAA and MSAA provide a decent approximation of the Subpixel Areas. As edges move across the Pixel area, they provide a gradual increment of Subpixel count. With MSAA, the thin triangle examples with edge *Slp* around *0.5* show poor results. The subpixel increments jump back and forth (Ex: 0 2 1 6 4 6 6 8).

## 5.5 From SSAA to ABAA

In this section, a gradual conversion from SSAA to ABAA is presented.

### 5.5.1 Convert SSAA Sample Points into ABAA Areas

With SSAA, when a Pixel consisting of MxM sample points (M=8) is converted into a N-Subpixel areas (N=4), the operation can be explained with the following process.

In Figure 5-13, a Pixel divided into 8x8 Subpixel Sample Points (M=8). Using the information from the Sample Point counts from SSAA, a conversion of these counts into 4 Subpixel Areas (N=4) is attempted.

Using an array of 8x8 Sample Points inside of an SSAA Pixel, the covered areas of an equivalent ABAA Pixel can be evaluated by counting the Subpixels inside each area.

1. Divide the 8x8 super-Sample Points used for SSAA into 4 equal areas (4x4 =16 Super-Sample Points).
2. Identify the SSAA areas that are fully covered. These areas are converted into Subpixel Areas for ABAA.
3. Next, sort the other SSAA areas that are partially covered.
4. Then the mostly covered area is identified and it is filled from Super-Sample Points from least covered areas.
5. Continue until most areas are filled. Add a half area of Super-Sample Points (16/2=8) for rounding.
6. This completes the conversion of Super-Sample Points into N Subpixel Areas.

# RT CGI with Anti-Aliasing

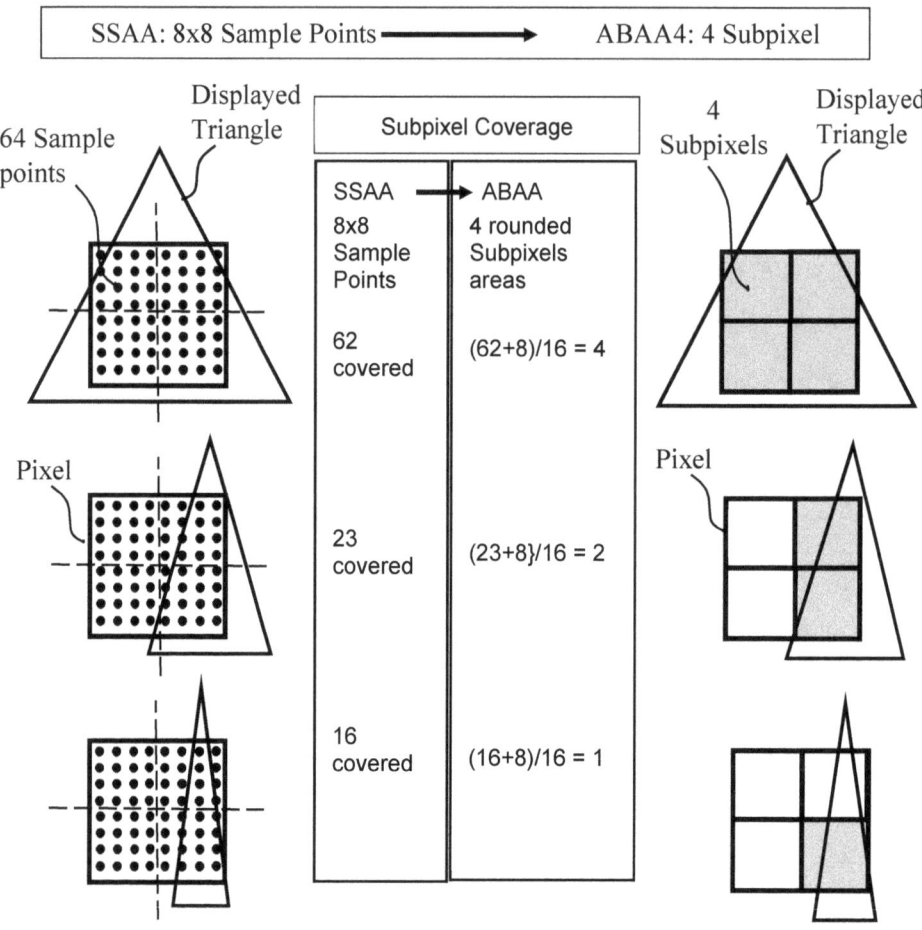

**Figure 5-13 From SSAA to ABAA4**

This operation can be compared to using weights in an old fashion weight scale, just like the scale that is shown as a 'blind symbol of justice'.

Refer to Figure 5-14.

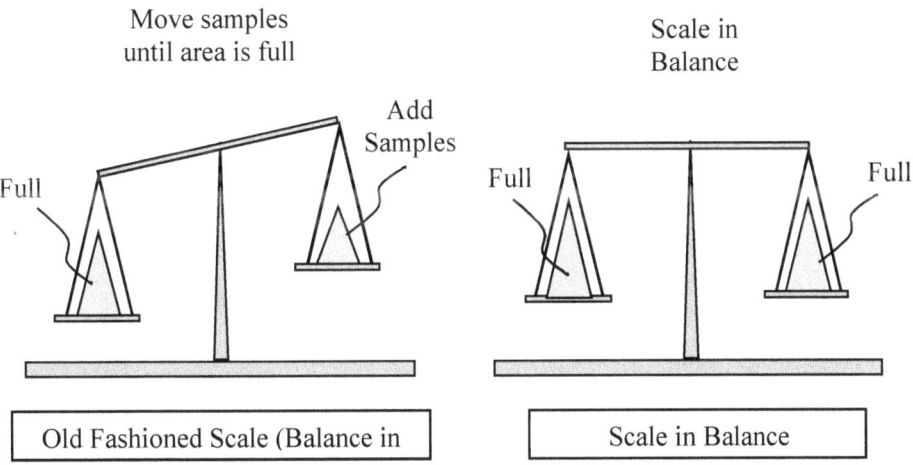

**Figure 5-14 Old Fashioned Weight Scale**

## 5.5.2 Identify Shortcomings of MSAA

*About Scale in Balanced State*

As edges move across Pixels, there is a change of state in the Super-Sampled Points. The Super-Sampled Points are moved gradually from one side of the scale to the other side. When the scale reaches a 'balanced state' this corresponds to a critical moment where the balance tips and the ABAA assigned Subpixel-Area transition to other Subpixel Areas. When the scale is balanced, the position of the crossing edge represents a 'Critical Edge Transition Threshold' (CETT).

*MSAA Jump at CETT*

In case of MSAA, when an edge crosses a pair of aligned Subpixel-Sample Points, the Subpixel contribution jumps by 2 Subpixels instead of 1.

With ABAA, when an edge moves across a CETT, the Subpixel count will not change by more than 1. For ABAA, a transition of 2 Sample Points at once is not allowed.

*With ABAA, the 'Winner Takes it All'*

When I think about the 'Winner Takes it All', it reminds me of the song recorded by the Swedish pop group ABBA [29]. It works in a way similar to the lyrics in ABBA's song "The Winner takes it all, the Loser has to fall" (no pun intended). With ABAA the Subpixels with higher Subpixel-Sampled Points take it all. The remaining Subpixels have to fall from the covered Subpixel count.

# Chapter 6  Evolution of ABAA

Although the term "Area-Based Anti-Aliasing" might seem new to you, this approach actually predates the other approaches like SSAA, MSAA and also BON (bed of nails). In the early RT CGI Systems, "anti-aliasing" was referred to as "edge smoothing".

*Early Need for RT CGI Systems with AA*

In the 1970s, the early RT CGI systems used in simulators for aircraft training were required to have AA. Aliasing artifacts were considered as negative training. The purpose of these high-speed RT CGI systems was to generate 'Out The Window' (OTW) scenes used in aircraft and spaceship trainers/simulators. These systems could not use the Z-Buffer approach, because of the low density of memory and the limitation of single sample per Pixel in Z-Buffer implementations. Also, because the basic Z-Buffer approach uses 1 sample per Pixel, it results in jaggies and polygon popping in-and-out of scenes.

While I worked at Link Flight Simulation, the main product of the company consisted of flight simulators. Our Division in Sunnyvale, CA, was responsible for delivering special purpose computers and RT CGI systems for these simulators. The DIG was our first RT CGI system and was highly successful with orders and deliveries to NASA and the US military. Its implementation for AA, or edge smoothing, was actually an area-based AA method.

In the 1980s, most companies adopted the MSAA or BON approach. As other companies were offering competitive systems, the Link company faced increased competition. By the end of 1980s, the Link company gave up in developing new RT CGI systems and closed its offices in Sunnyvale. MSAA and BON have been in use for around 40 years, with inconsistent results. The quality of AA depends on edge orientation. Now it is time for a better approach.

Before leaving the Link company, I was working on developing a tiled approach to RT CGI, similar to the approach used at the GE GSD company. I realized that with the shrinking of electronic circuits and semiconductor memories, it was now possible to develop an RT CGI graphics adapter for the PC with AA. For a couple of years, I tried developing such a system at a startup, with friends from Link. Although I was able to develop and simulate an early version of the ABAA approach presented in this book, we could not get financing because the market was not aware of the importance or AA. So, I had to abandon the idea for a while.

## 6.1 First 3D RT CGI Systems Had AA

In flight simulators with RT CGI, the pilot is flying through a terrain database. The data base objects have to be retrieved from a database and processed in a fraction of second. The 3D RT CGI systems have to produce images at the rate of 30 (frame rate) or 60 images (filed rate) per second. These systems needed to drive at least three window images (for left, front and right windows) in real-time to train pilots for aircraft take-off to landing, special missions and emergency situations. For the RT CGI systems used in these simulators, an important requirement was that they have edge smoothing. The images have to be smooth and stable. Edge crawling and polygons popping in-and-out of scenes were not acceptable. In mission simulations, distracting image artifacts would result in negative training. The RT CGI systems have to do some kind of Subpixel processing to avoid edge crawling and polygon popping.

### *Need for Special Purpose RT CGI Systems with AA*

In the in early 1970s, when 3D CGI became available, there was a need for high-speed RT CGI systems that could produce images in real-time for training [82][83][94][96]. These RT CGI systems had to produce 3D CGI with smooth interlaced images at 60 fields per second. They were mostly limited to US military and NASA applications. An important requirement was that they had AA.

Since there were no such systems available in the market, the companies in this market had to develop and build their own proprietary special purpose RT CGI computers, this includes HW, real-time SW and database development. In early 1970s, this task was accomplished by proprietary RT CGI systems from a few companies. These systems were quite large. Typically, the special purpose hardware occupied 6 cabinets, each cabinet being the size of a refrigerator. They were driven by a 16 or 32-bit minicomputer. For example, these minicomputers were designed by from Digital Equipment Corp (DEC) or InterData from Perkin Elmer. The size of the large removable hard disks was 300Mbyte. They consisted of several magnetic plateaux (between 10 and 20), 16in in diameter. The size of these minicomputer was also similar to the size of refrigerator. To be fair, cost of these systems was above $2 million.

When I started to work on a RT CGI prototype at Link, in Sunnyvale, CA, only a few computer companies were able to produce such RT CGI systems. At first, 2 companies had produced proprietary RT CGI systems in the early 1970s that could produce 1000 to 2000 edges per field:

- Evans and Sutherland (E&S) in Salt Lake City, Utah, with
  CT-1 to CT-4 (Continuous Tone) CIG systems
- General Electric Ground System Division (GE GSD) in Daytona Beach, Florida, with CompuScene CIG systems
- A third company, the Advanced Product Operation (APO) of Link Flight Simulation in Sunnyvale CA, was a late entrant. At Link APO, we were able to build the R&D DIG (Digital Image Generator), an RT CGI system that could produce around 1500 edges/field. Then the production Link DIG had improved performances and could produce 12,000 edges/field. I was involved early on the Link prototype and continued to make improvements thru several generations of DIGs.

Although E&S and GE had produced RT CGI in the early 1970s, these systems were low performance, limited to around 1000 edges per frame. Then, NASA requested bids for RT CGI systems for training astronauts in its Space Shuttle Simulators. By the mid 1970s, the Link Flight Simulation Company was able to demonstrate such a system with its R&D DIG. It won the contract for 4 production DIGs to be used in the Shuttle Mission Simulator program.

For non-RT applications, like advertising and motion pictures, the most common approach at that time used the Z-buffer approach. Because of the low memory density at that time, the DIGs used a Scanline Computer as Image Renderer. There was no Image or Z buffers. The image storage was limited to Scanline double buffers. The digital images were processed in Scanline order with storage limited to Scanline double buffers.

Ten years later, in the 1980s, the density of memory had increased by a factor of 32x ($2^5$x for 10yrs, according to Moor's Law). The use of frame buffer became feasible for RT CGI systems and opened the door to Tiled architecture.

By the mid 1990s, the increase in chip and memory density made it possible to implement RT CGI systems fitting in add-on cards for Desktop PCs.

There is more information about the Link DIGs and other RT CGI systems in a later chapter about "Evolution RT CGI".

## 6.2 Edge Smoothing in the Link DIG Systems

The edge smoothing implementation in the Link DIGs used an area-based Subpixel solution. This approach can be described as 4x4 Subpixel anti-aliasing, or 4x4 ABAA. Depending on the triangle edge slopes the edges were categorized as Horizontal (*HE*) and Vertical (*VE*) edges types. Each pixel could be subdivided into 4 horizontal or 4 vertical Subpixels, depending on the edge type of the top triangle (i.e., triangle closest to the observer). Edge type transitions between *HE* and *VE* occurs when their orientation is near a 45 degrees (*PI/4*) angle.

In Figure 6-1, there is an example where a triangle is rendered with *VE* and *HE* Subpixels. The triangle is defined by 2 *VEs* and 1 *HE* and is rendered using a combination of *VE* and *HE* Subpixels Also, edges are defined as beginning edges (*BE*) or ending edges (*!BE*). For *VEs*, the scan is left to right. For *HEs*, the scan is top to bottom. A Subpixel is covered when its center is covered by the triangle. For the Pixels that are no intersected, their color is either the Pixel color inside of the triangle or the background color outside of the triangle. For each partially covered Pixel, the triangle color of the covered area is mixed with the background color, in step of 1/4 increments.

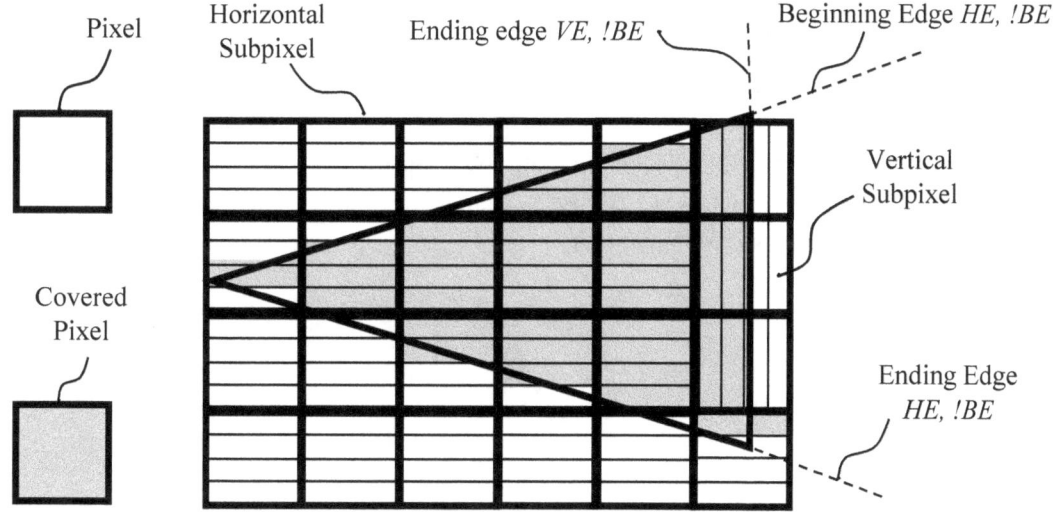

**Figure 6-1 Triangle with 1 *VE* and 2 *HEs* Rendered with 4 Subpixel Areas**

Evolution of ABAA

This approach works well when only 2 colors are blended in a Subpixel. In case there are a *VE* and a *HE* in the same Pixel, the last partial edge, *VE* or *HE* determines the Subpixel type.

In the Link DIG, this method produced good results. An important feature of the DIG systems was their capability to detect faces with narrow projection. For example, the contrast of white runway stripes with the grey runway color could be reduced as the face projection width became narrower than the Pixel width. Refer to my patent [105] on Face Resolvability Test.

### 6.2.1 DIG-1 with Analog Edge Smoothing (4x4 ABAA)

The edge smoothing in the DIG-1 was implemented by *Bob Lotz,* a talented analog design engineer.

While designing the DIG prototype at Link, there was no provision for edge smoothing, But, as the design took shape, a talented analog design engineer proposed an analog solution to edge smoothing. *Bob Lotz* was responsible for the digital to analog converter design (DAC, D/A, D2A, or D-to-A) in the last processing stage of the DIG. The D2As were driving the 3 image display monitors. He suggested to implement edge smoothing at the output of the D2A converter. It turned out that this analog implementation produced good results and was adopted for the DIG-1.

Refer to Figure 6-2.

Also refer to patent from *Robert W. Lotz*, Link Flight Simulation [108].

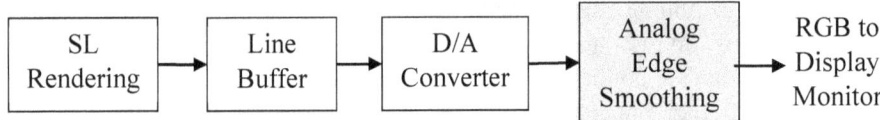

**Figure 6-2 DIG-1 with Analog Edge Smoothing**

*Delayed Transition for Vertical Edge Smoothing*

B. *Lotz* implemented the Vertical Edge (*VE*) Smoothing by providing 4 Subpixel starting times for edges within the Pixels. The starting time was determined by the 2 fractional bits of the *VE* edge intersection with the Pixel horizontal mid line. Refer to example in Figure 6-3.

In this figure, the edge transition is delayed by a fraction of a Pixel. There are in four possible delays of n*Pixel/4, ranging from n=0 to n=3.

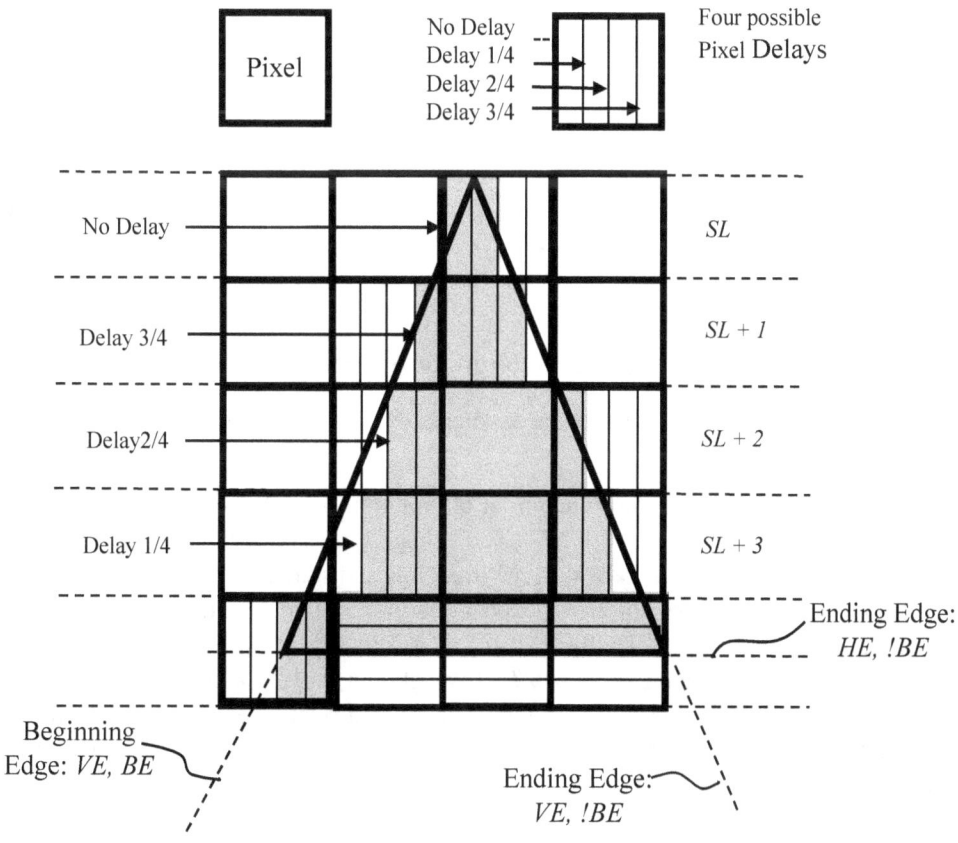

**Figure 6-3 Analog VE Edge Smoothing with 4 Subpixel Areas**

### *HE Smoothing with RC Circuit*

*B. Lotz* implemented Horizontal Edge (*HE*) Smoothing by producing an exponential function with RC circuits (Resistor Capacitor) to slow down the edge transitions along Scanlines

Refer to Figure 6-4, Exponential Function from RC Circuit.

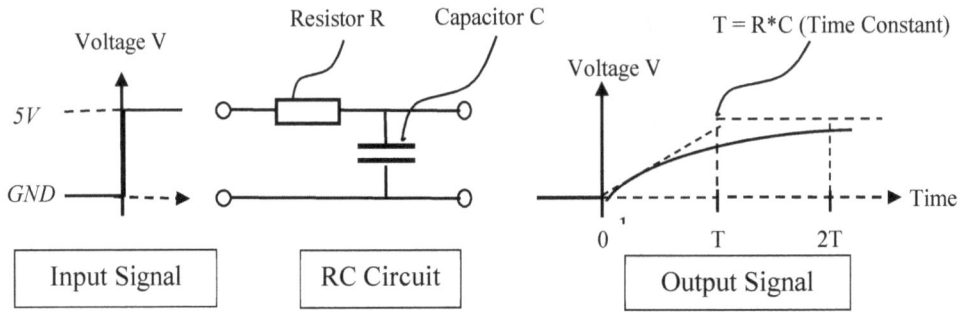

**Figure 6-4 Exponential Function from RC Circuit**

In this figure the horizontal transition uses the exponential function of an RC circuit. Typically, an RC circuit works as follows.

In this example, the voltage of a step function at the input at time 0 rises from *0* to *5V*. At the output, the voltage at time *0* is also *0V* (*GND*). The voltage across C is *0V*. The Voltage across R is *5 V*, which causes a current of *I=5V/R* to flow through R and start charging the capacitor C. Then, the voltage across the capacitor grows exponentially from *0* to *5* volt.
At time *T=RC*, the voltage reaches a value of *(1-1/e) * 5V*.
For edge smoothing, I guess that a value of *2T=2*RC* should provide a good approximation for horizontal edge smoothing. In order to cover a wide range of horizontal edge smoothing distances, several RC constants had to be selected. One approach would be to select different RC constant each time the smoothing distance doubles. The difference between linear and exponential transition was not noticeable.

In this approach there are also 4 Horizontal Subpixels.

### 6.2.2 DIG-2 with Digital Edge Smoothing (4x4 ABAA)

For the DIG-2, the analog edge smoothing was replaced with a digital implementation. In this implementation, the edge smoothing is done before the line buffer. Refer to Figure 6-5

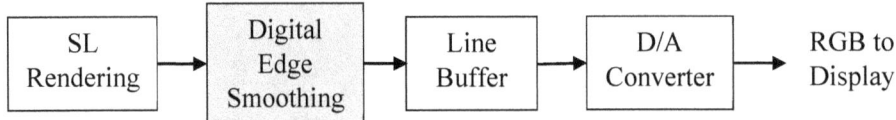

**Figure 6-5 DIG-2 with Digital Edge Smoothing**

In both of these approaches, analog or digital, edge smoothing is done according to the covered area at edge transition. So, these implementations can be referred to "Area-Based AA". But this approach has a limitation. Only 2 faces can be processed in each Pixel. It turns out that, in the majority of case, this limitation hardly affects the image quality.

# Evolution of ABAA

In this area-based AA implementation, the edges are categorized as vertical (*VE*) and horizontal (*HE*) edge types. The Pixels are subdivided into four *VE* or four *HE* Subpixel areas, according to the edge type of the front face. Refer to Figure 6-6.

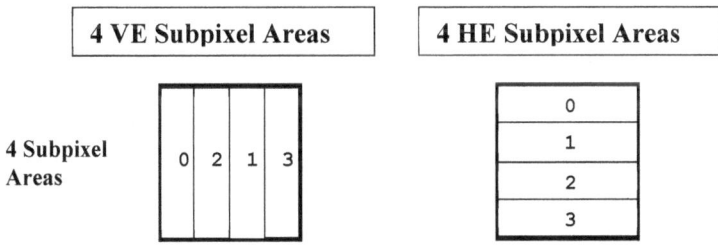

**Figure 6-6 VE and HE Subpixel Areas**

*Blended Color between left and right of VE Edge Transition*

For Vertical Edge Smoothing, the 2 colors are blended proportionally to the areas of the front and back faces.

*Horizontal Edge Smoothing According to the HE Slope*

For *HE* transitions, Digital ABAA for *HE* with 4 steps area increments. Refer to Figure 6-7.

For these cases, two color-components have to be mixed: these should be from the Top Face with an accuracy of ¼ Pixel, and the bottom face. At the corners of triangle faces, there could be 3 or more color components. By only keeping the top 2 faces, artifacts should be rare or negligible. Again, the number of small projected faces was reduced in the DIG systems. The DIGs had the capability of detecting faces with narrow projection. Refer to my patent [105] on Face Resolvability Test.

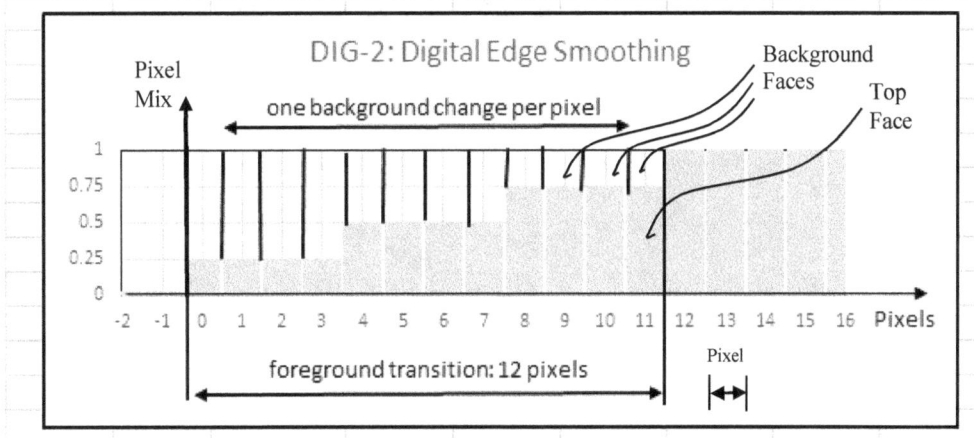

**Figure 6-7 *HE* with 4 Steps Area Increment: Mix Faces with Top 2 Priorities**

This approach works well when only 2 colors are blended in a Subpixel. In case there are a *VE* and a *HE* in the same Pixel, the last partial edge, *VE* or *HE* determine the Subpixel type. In the Link

Evolution of ABAA

DIG, this method produced good results. An important feature of the DIG systems was their capability to detect faces with narrow projection. For example, the contrast of white runway stripes with grey runway color could be reduced as the face projection width became narrower than the Pixel width. Refer to my patent [105] on Face Resolvability Test.

## 6.3 Edge Smoothing with Bed of Nail

In the early 1980s, the increase in semiconductor density made it feasible to designs RT CGI systems with frame buffers in real time. Several companies switched from the SL-to-SL approach in a Scanline Computer (SLC) to a Face Processor using a face buffer. They still relied on object priorities for occulting in front to back processing. For AA and edge smoothing, they used a Bed of Nail (BON) approach. Most system used 8 sample points as BON, arranged in a sparse nail distribution in Pixels. In the BON approach, the Subpixels are processed at once. By comparison, in the MSAA approach, several images are produced using Z-buffers with 1 sample point each and then averaged to produces the AA images.

Several RT CGI systems used Tiled architecture, where the image is divided into square Tiles and Spans of 8x8 Pixels. Each Pixel can contain 4 or 8 Subpixels as BON, Refer to Figure 6-8. For a BON example, also refer to *Rick Fadden's* Patent 6445392 [127].

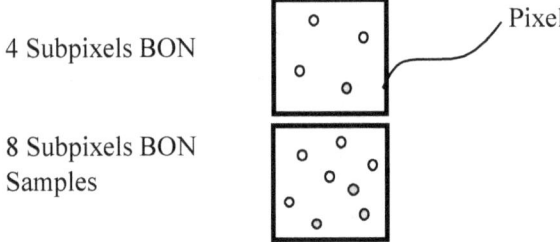

**Figure 6-8 Pixel with 4 or 8 Subpixel BON**

## 6.4 Optimized Edge Definition for Area Based Anti-Aliasing

Image rendering in CGI systems consists of many repetitive operations. Any improvement in the processing steps result in direct system performance. Processing edges requires many repetitive operations. In order to achieve optimum performances, I have defined an optimized edge definition that achieves this goal.

*Problem with Basic Edge Definition*

There are 2 disadvantages with the basic edge definition.

- The slope sizes are unlimited and would reach infinity when the component dy==0
- Beside the slope, 2 coordinate components $(x, y)$ are required to position an edge.

*Optimized Edge Definition*

The proposed edge definition requires only 2 components

- a slope with limited size *(|slope| <=1)*,
- only one other intersection component *(x or y)*.

By limiting the elope size, this reduces the number of bits for fixed point computations.

Two types of edges are defined to provide symmetry with respect to the $X$ and $Y$ screen coordinates: Vertical Edges (*VE*) and Horizontal Edges (*HE*).

This new edge definition optimizes the Tile-to-Tile and Pixel-to-Pixel traversing operations.

Note that this approach requires to define 2D square projection areas. The Pixel is the smallest Tile. In the general case these square areas can all be referred to as "Tiles".

*About Symmetric Edge Definition*

The problem of infinite slopes is solved by splitting edges into 2 edge types: *HE* and *VE*.

- *HE, HSlp = dx/dy*, when $|dy| > |dx|$
- *VE, VSlp = dy/dx*, when $|dy| < |dx|$
- *VE, VSlp = dy/dx*, when $|dy| == |dx|$

When $|dy| == |dx|$, the edge type is selected as *VE*, since edges are usually processed on images in top-down order.

The optimized edge definition provides many advantages over the basic edge definition, such as:

- Limit the slope size to no-greater than 1.0: *|ESlp|<=1*
- Provide symmetry in horizontal and vertical directions.
- Provide for efficient computation of Subpixel area computations
- Optimize the Tile-to-Tile and Pixel-to-Pixel traversing operations

Evolution of ABAA

*About Fraction Rounding*

The problem with fraction Rounding is that most of us never forget about it, as if it was the only solution for handling fractional numbers. We blindly apply rounding without thinking of the disastrous consequences. In my 1st book [6], I have described several cases with problems that would have been avoided early in 3D graphics by applying averaging instead of rounding. Averaging consists of replacing discarded fraction with 0.5. About this subject, I have come across patents that have been awarded for solving these ghost problems. Most of these problems deal with corner cases. By replacing rounding with averaging, there are no corner cases.

*Area Computation for Trapezoids*

On the other hand, most of us have forgotten about how to compute the area of triangles, parallelograms and trapezoids. It turned out that the area of trapezoids is key to my new AA solution with ABAA. The area of each trapezoid is equal to its Height multiplied by the average of its top and bottom Width [16].

## 6.4.1 Area of Trapezoid

ABAA relies on computing the Pixel areas that are covered by the 3 edges of a triangle. The areas defined by each edge is first determined, then the triangle area is obtained by doing an AND function of the areas defined by these 3 edges.

There are 2 cases to be considered.

*Edge Intersections with Pixel Boundaries Within 0.0 and 1.0*

In the first case, it is assumed that the range of extended edge (EE) intersections with 2 opposite boundaries of Pixels is within *0.0* and *1.0*. The EE intersections with opposite Pixel boundaries divide the Pixel into 2 trapezoidal areas. The area of each trapezoid is equal to its Height multiplied by the average of its top and bottom Width. For *VEs*, the average of the Widths can be obtained on the Midline at half distance between the top and bottom Pixel boundaries. The area of these 2 trapezoids is easily computed using the intersection of the Midlines (*MidLn*) with the triangle edges. Two types of Midlines have to be considered. Refer to Figure 6-9.

- For *VEs*, the Pixel height is 1.0. The Horizontal Midlines (*H MidLn*) are at half distance between top and bottom boundaries of Pixels. The distance to the *H MidLn* is d. The area of the trapezoid is *1.0 \*d = d*.
- For *HEs*, the Pixel width is 1.0. The Vertical Midlines (*V MidLn*) are at half distance between left and right boundaries of Pixels. The distance to the *V MidLn* is d. The area of the trapezoid is *1.0 \*d = d*.

Using the Midlines, the distance, *d*, from the left or top Pixel boundaries to the Midline intersection is obtained with only one measurement. From the distance on the Midlines, the covered area can be easily computed. In this example, the triangle edge is a beginning edge, with *BE=1*. The distance is obtained with only one measurement. In this case, with a resolution of *1/16*, the maximum error will be:

*error = 1/16*.

Evolution of ABAA

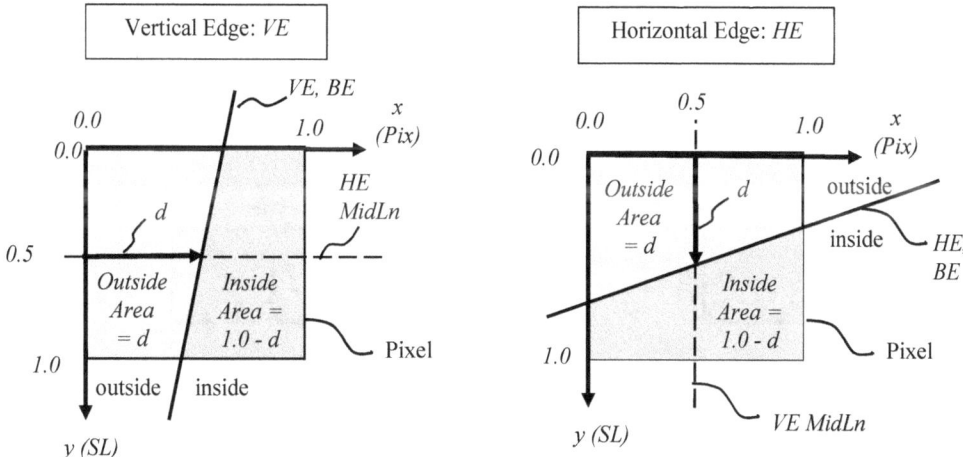

**Figure 6-9 Area Measurements when Intersection within *0.0* and *1.0***

*Edge Intersections with Pixel Boundaries Not within 0.0 and1.0*

In the 2$^{nd}$ case, the EE intersections with opposite boundaries of Pixels is not within *0.0* and *1.0*. The EE intersections with opposite Pixel boundaries divide the Pixel into 2 trapezoidal areas, that extend outside of the Pixels. The area of the extended trapezoid is also easily computed by measuring the distance on Midlines.

Two types of extended areas have to be considered. These two cases are similar for *VE* and *HE*.

For *VE*, refer to Figure 6-10.

For *HE*, refer to Figure 6-11.

For EE with slope size up to 1.0, the maximum area outside of the Pixel is 1/8. When 4 Subpixel areas are used, the error is < 1/2 Subpixel. So, it can be ignored.

When 8 Subpixels are used, 2 case have to be considered, identified with the *S* flag.

*S0* (*Flag S=0*), when the slope size is between *0.0* and *0.5*. The max extended area is <1/16. In this case, 15/16 of Pixel area is covered when the edge enters the Pixel.

*S1* (*Flag S=1*), when the slope size is between *0.5* and *1.0*. The max extended area is <1/8. In this case, 7/8 of Pixel area is covered when the edge enters the Pixel.

When the distance *d* is zero, the trapeze area outside of the Pixel is compensated by the area inside of the Pixel, so the area error is zero. Same thing when *d*==*1.0*, the inside area is *1.0*.

*Accuracy of Area computation with ABAA*

With ABAA, the distance is obtained with only one measurement. In this case, with a resolution of *1/16*, the maximum error will be:
 *error = 1/16*

New Area-Based Anti-Aliasing for CGI

Evolution of ABAA

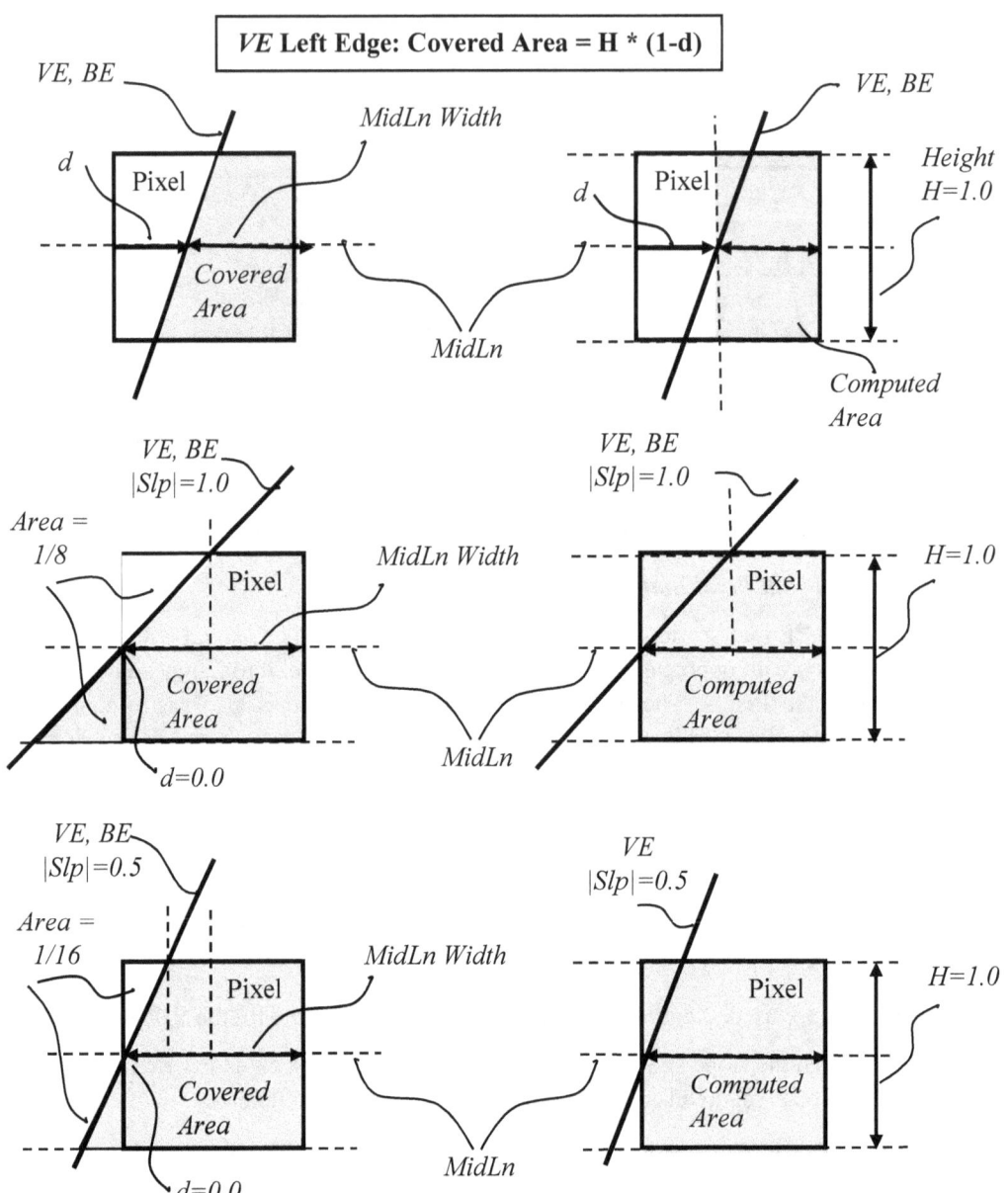

**Figure 6-10 Pixel Covered Area Computation for VE**

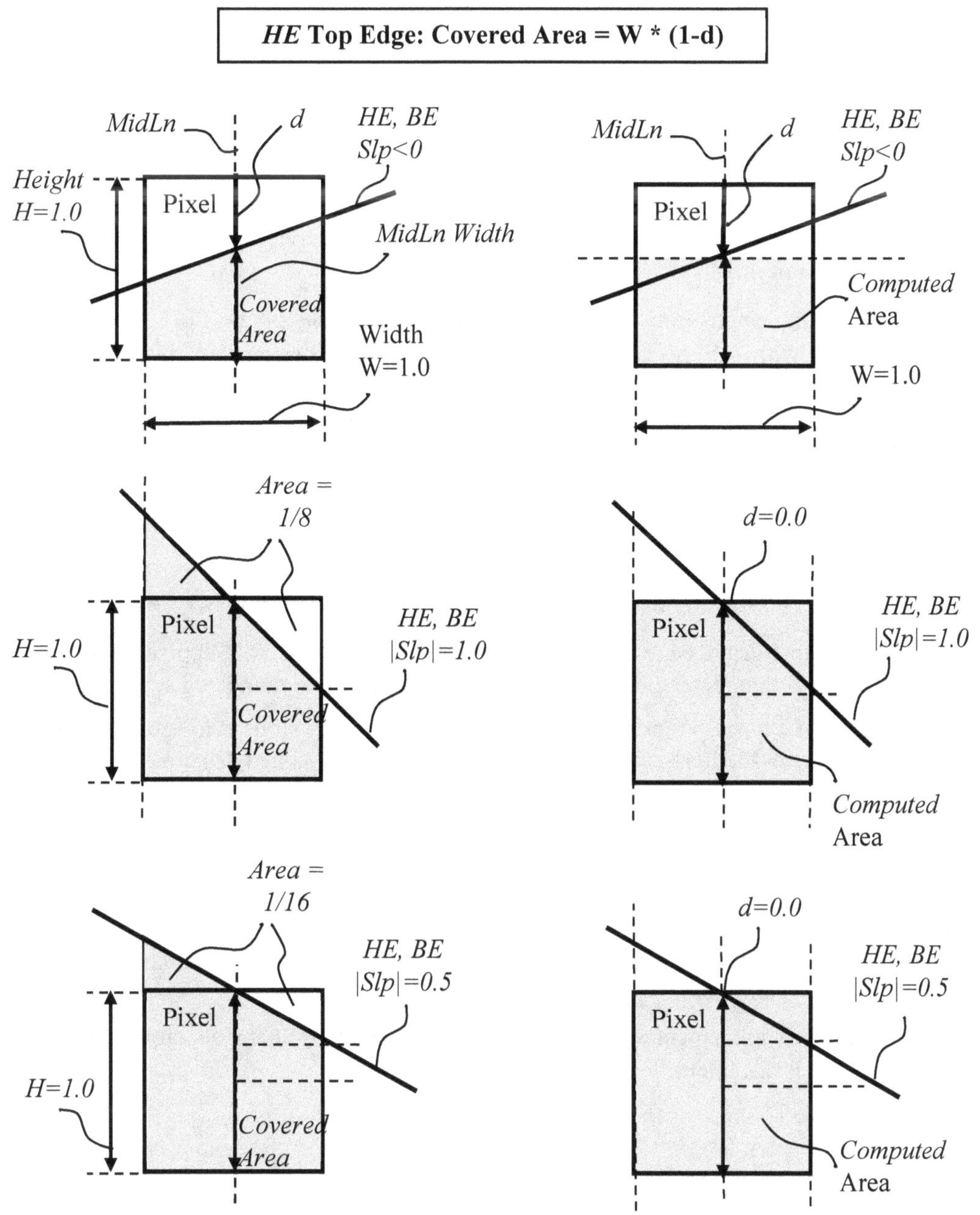

**Figure 6-11 Pixel Covered Area Computation for *HE***

### 6.4.2 Converting Trapezoidal Area into Subpixel Areas

When I was developing my implementation of a new algorithms for antialiasing, I wrote a simulation program in C++.

After describing how *VE* and *HE* edges traverse the Tiles on the screen, came time to simulate how to handle intersected Pixels. For *VEs*, I had the top and bottom intersections available. While making some sketches I realized that the *VE* divided the Pixels into trapezoidal area. I quickly remembered that by adding the top and bottom intersections and dividing by 2, I had the area of the covered portions of the Pixel.

At that time, most implementations of Subpixel sampling used 8 Subpixels. So, I was looking for an implementation with 8 Subpixel areas. I did not even consider an implementation with 4 Subpixels. I was trying to convert the 4x4 Subpixel area into 8 Subpixel area.

### 6.4.3 Implementation of ABAA with 4 Subpixel Areas

It was not until year 2021, when I started to write this book that I found out how simple the 4 Subpixels implementation is. So, here I introduce the solution with 4 Subpixel areas first, because it is so simple.

In this approach, the Pixel is divided into 4 Subpixel areas. Refer to Figure 6-12.

In order to accept more than 2 edges per Pixel, the Vertical and Horizontal Subpixel must have the same shape. So, the 4 thin rectangles are converted into 4 concentric numbered squares.

The edges consist of 2 types, *VE* and *BE*. Also, the sign of the edge slope is to decide the order of Subpixels. In Figure 6-13, there is a representation of a beginning edge (*BE*) crossing 4 Subpixel Areas for the 4 Edge cases. There are 4 edge cases:
- *HE* and *Slp>0*
- *HE* and *Slp<0*
- *VE* and *Slp>0*
- *VE* and *Slp<0*

For *VE* and *HE*, the cases transition from one case to another when the slopes reach zero. For zero slopes, the decision is arbitratry.

Using this 4 Subpixels implementation, I was able to improve my 8 Subpixels implementation, as shown later on in this document.

Evolution of ABAA

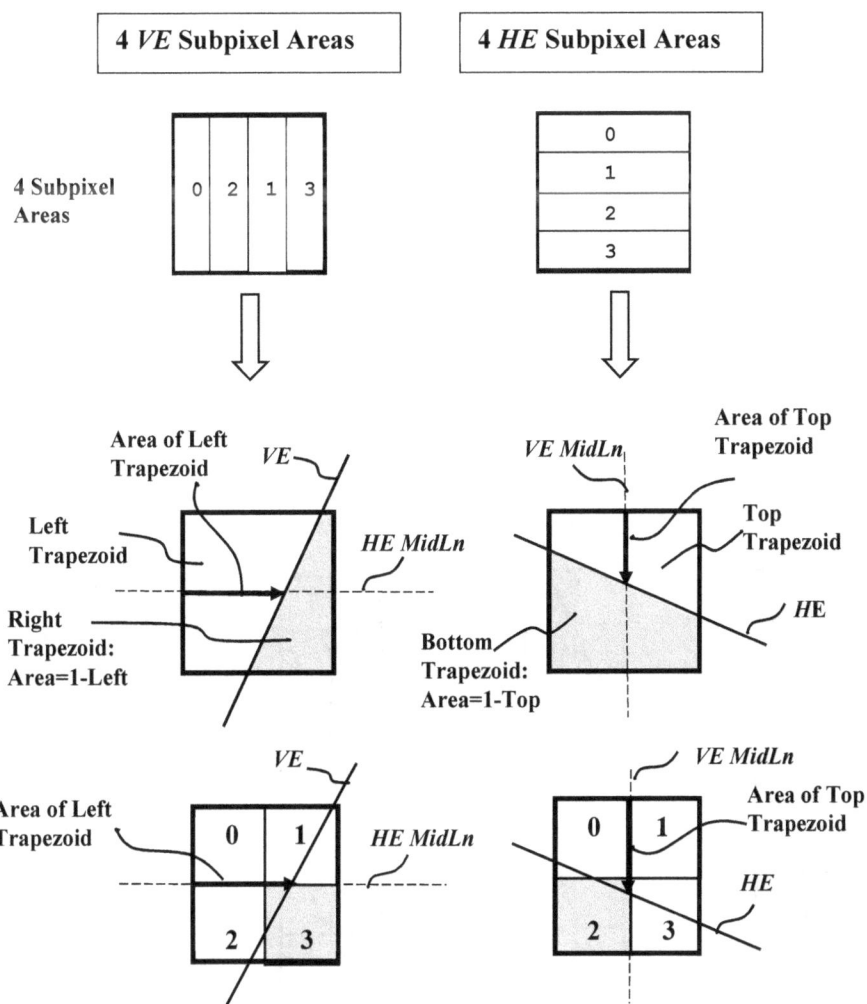

Figure 6-12 Four Subpixel Areas Intersected by *VE(BE)* and *HE(BE)*

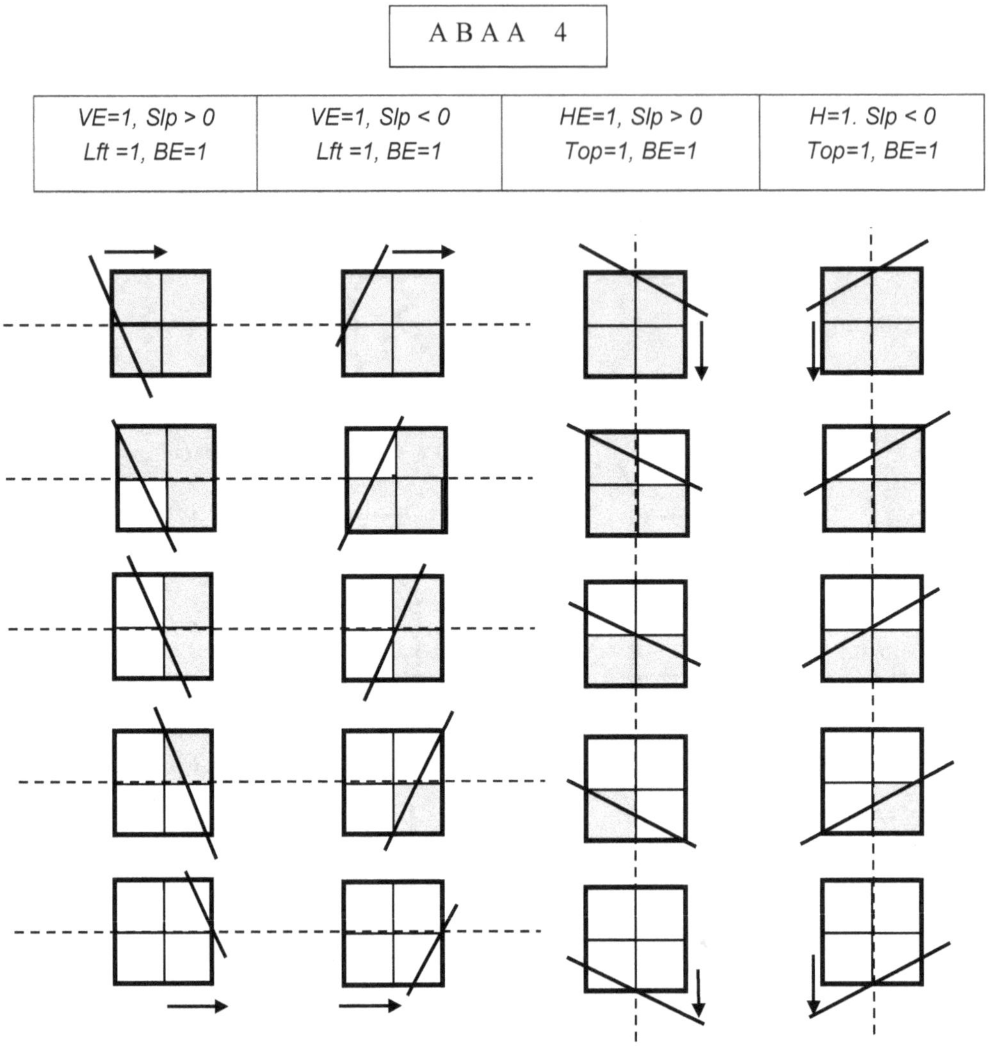

# Evolution of ABAA

| ABAA 4 | | | |
|---|---|---|---|
| VE=1, Slp > 0<br>Lft =1, BE=1 | VE=1, Slp < 0<br>Lft =1, BE=1 | HE=1, Slp > 0<br>Top=1, BE=1 | H=1. Slp < 0<br>Top=1, BE=1 |

**Figure 6-13 Four Cases of ABAA4 with Edge Crossing 4 Subpixel Areas**

## 6.4.4 Early Implementation of ABAA with 8 Subpixel Areas

The next step was to map the trapezoid into 8 equivalent rectangular Subpixel areas. Here is the implementation I adopted at first.

Staring with the 4x4 implementation in the DIGs, I divided the Subpixels by 2 to obtain the 8x8 implementation. Refer to Figure 6-14.

Although the Subpixel areas can be obtained by truncating or rounding the measured width, the best approach is obtained by adding the unused portion of the top half width to the bottom half width.

Evolution of ABAA

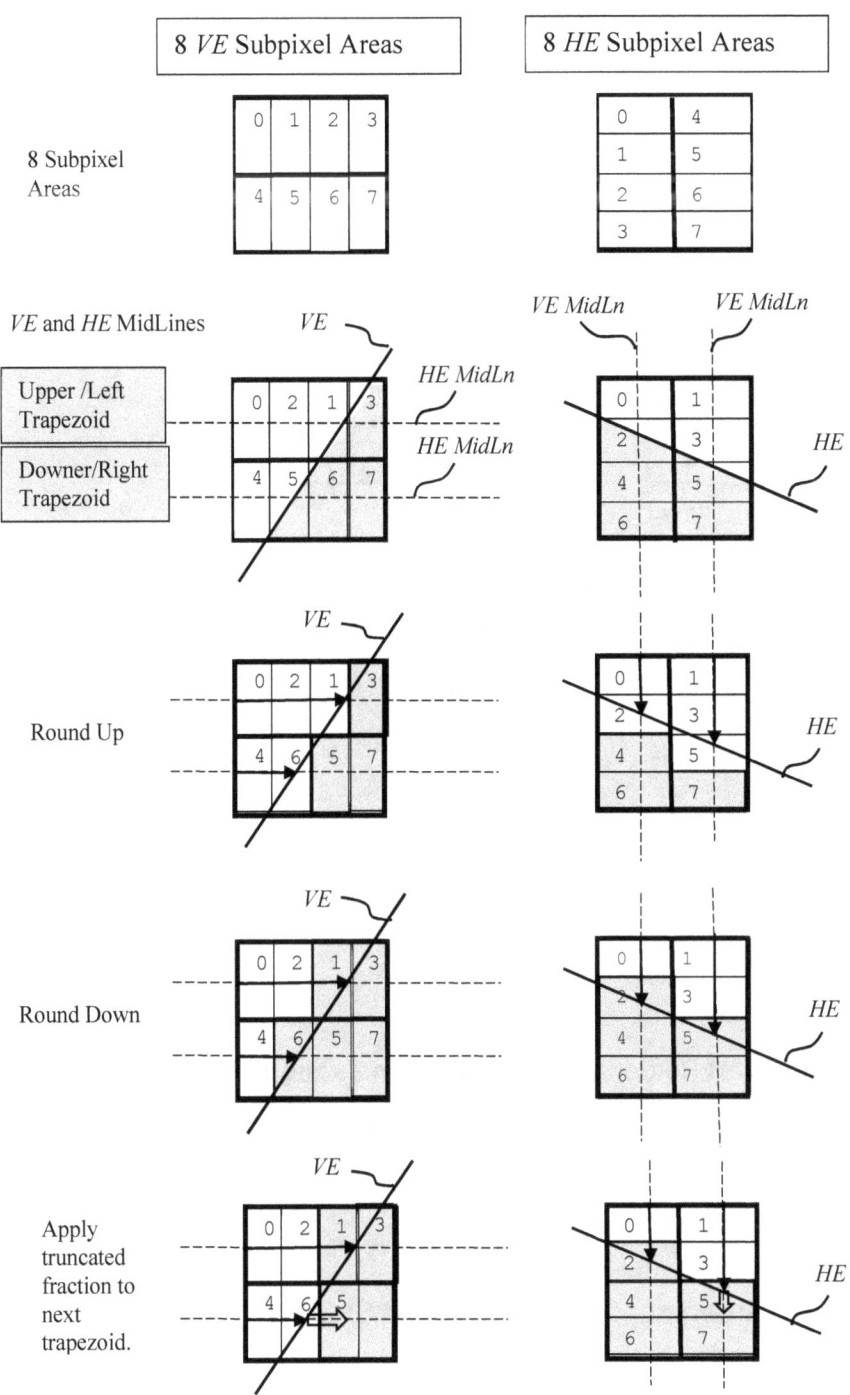

**Figure 6-14 Eight Subpixel Areas Intersected by *VE* and *HE***

Evolution of ABAA

*Convert Rectangular Subpixels into 8 Triangular Subpixel Areas*

Then, I replaced the rectangular Subpixels with triangular Subpixels and merged the VE and HE Subpixel areas. Refer to Figure 6-15.

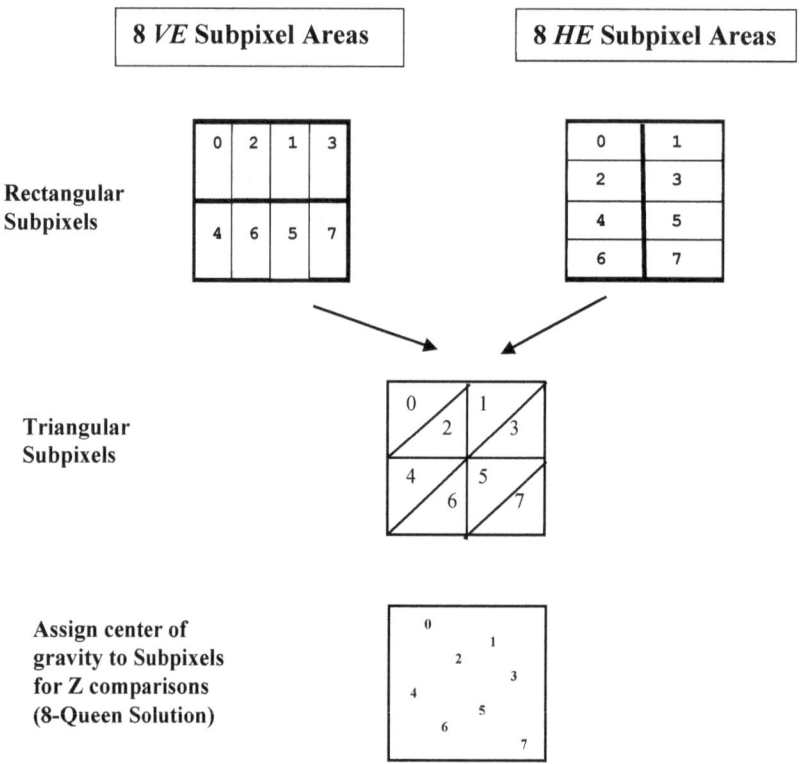

**Figure 6-15 Convert Rectangular Subpixels to Triangular Subpixels**

With this approach, I got good results, and I was able to demonstrate the improvements over point sampling with my C-simulation program.

For Z-Buffer comparisons, centers of gravity for each Subpixel can be assigned in a manner similar to the 8-Queen solutions.

## 6.4.5 Improved Implementation of ABAA with 8 Subpixel Areas

As I mentioned, when I started to write this book, I found out how simple the 4 Subpixels implementation is. I also found out that the 8 Subpixel implementation can be derived from the 4 Subpixel implementation by dividing the squares into 2 triangles. Also, this implementation should be symmetrical in $x$ & $y$. Refer to Figure 6-16.

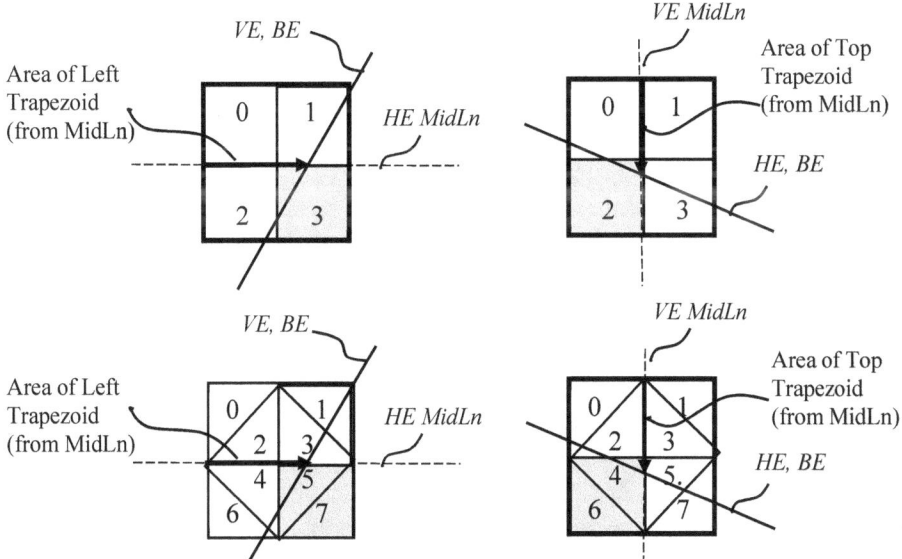

**Figure 6-16 Expanding from 4 Subpixels to 8 Subpixels**

In this figure, the area covered by a beginning edge (BE) is shown as:
- Area covered by *VE, BE* is: 1- (Area of Left Trapezoid)
- Area covered by *HE, BE* is: 1- (Area of Top Trapezoid)

For ending edges (*!BE*), the area would be:
- Area covered by *VE, !BE* is: Area of Left Trapezoid
- Area covered by *HE, !BE* is: Area of Top Trapezoid

Depending on the edge slope ($|Slp| < 0.5$, $|Slp| > 0.5$), the subpixel sequences will vary.

### *Example of ABAA with 8 Subpixel Areas*

Using this assignment of 8 subpixel areas, it can be shown that when an edge moves across a Pixel, it results in 8 equal steps.

In Figure 6-17, there are 4 examples of a *BE* with $|Slp| < 0.5$. Edges are moving across the Pixel in 9 steps. For *VEs*, they move from left to right and the covered area is determined on the horizontal midline of the right trapezoid. For *HEs*, they move from top to bottom and the covered area is determined on the vertical midline of the bottom trapezoid. That is:

*VE*: Covered_Area = 1- Area_of_Left_Trapezoid
*HE*: Covered_Area = 1- Area_of_Top_Trapezoid

For $|Slp| > 0.5$, the sequences will be slightly different.

# Evolution of ABAA

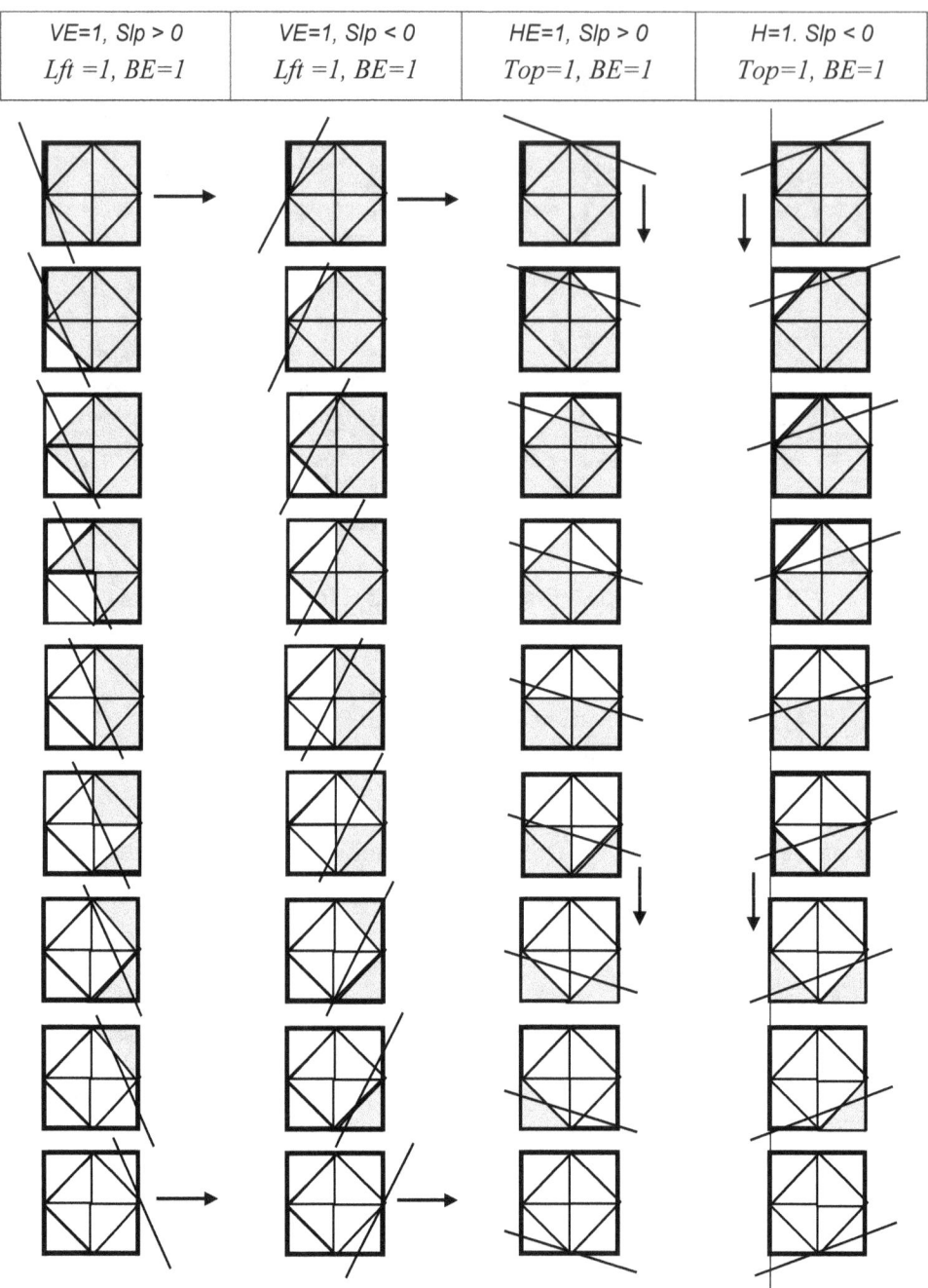

**Figure 6-17 ABAA8: 4 Cases with 4 *BE* Edges Moving Across Pixels (|*Slp*|<0.5)**

## 6.5 ABAA with N Subpixel Areas

In general, for N Subpixels the Decoding can be implemented with 2 levels of case statements, using the edge flags, *EFlg*, and the edge distance, *Dist*. N should be a power of 2.
Similar code can be implemented in either Verilog or C++. Refer to Figure 6-18.

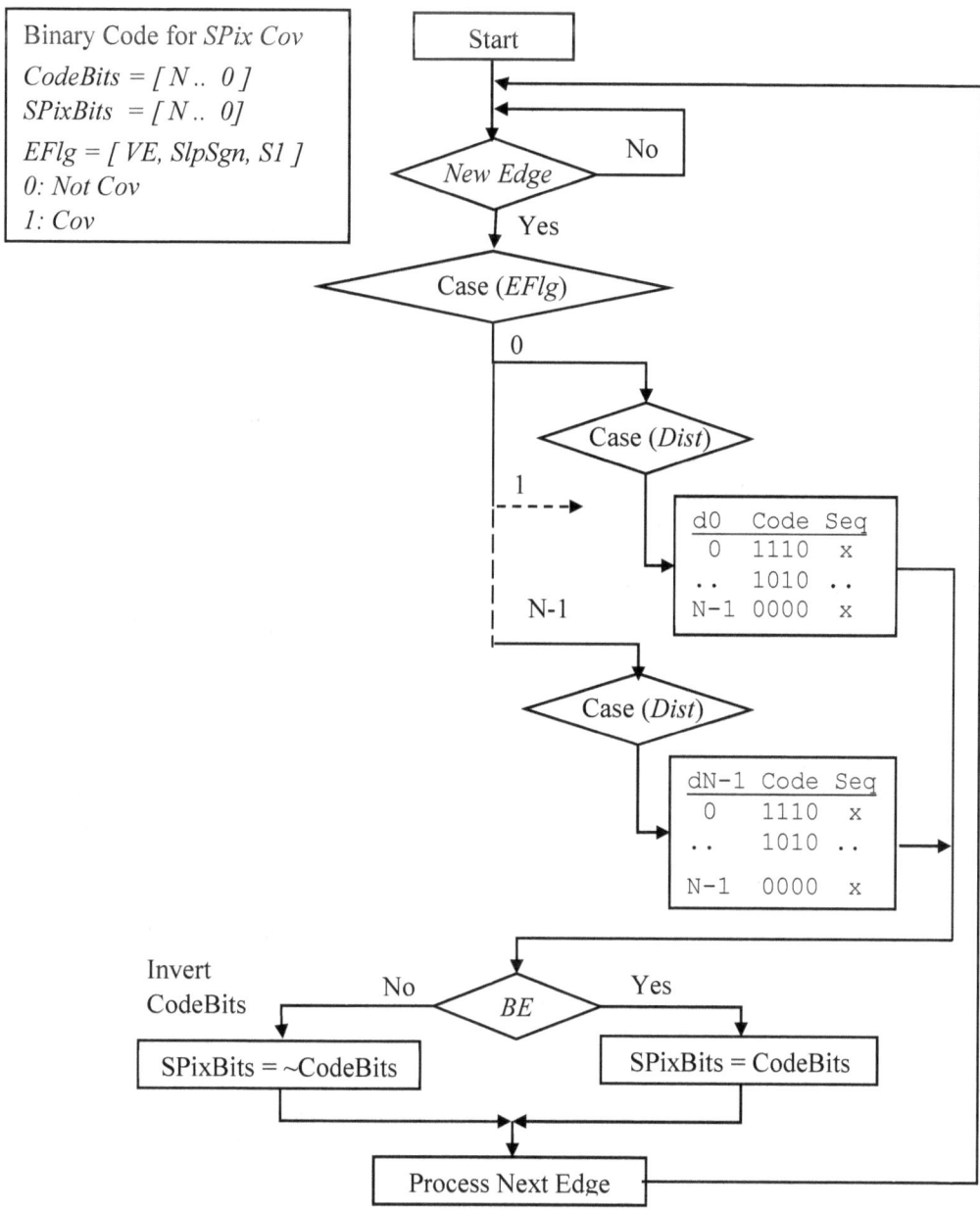

**Figure 6-18 Subpixel Coverage Decoder According *EFlg* and *Dist***

## 6.6 Delayed Implementation

Although this ABAA method was better than what was available in the industry at that time, I did not have the chance to completely implement this new design. Using my C++ simulation program, I was able to prove the feasibility of this approach.

Unfortunately, I was too early and there were several handicaps for my startup to succeed:
- the industry was not ready for antialiasing until they found out about the distracting effect caused by ugly jaggies in the PC add-on cards.
- this was before Microsoft introduced Direct3D.
- the Verilog design language for RTL (Register Transfer Logic) was not the standard yet.
- my team was too small and we lacked capital

After abandoning my project, I worked at 2 companies where I used some aspects of my AA invention to improved their products.

### *Saving Memory Chips*

As a consultant at KLA Instruments, I was writing a transaction accurate C simulation of their mask inspection system. The function of this system was similar to image rendering in CGI. As I remember, they were using an array of 8x8 sample points for Subpixel processing. They were struggling in bringing the product to market, I was responsible for the C model used for verification. By using the C-simulation, I was able to fix all the bugs during the design phase. We finished the project one week ahead of schedule. After that, I adapted my AA algorithm so that only 8 Subpixels instead of 64 were needed, with equal or better results. After demonstrating the results in my simulation, they were able to remove ~90% of the memory chips. This resulted in $40k saving per system. Considering that each of these systems cost a few $100k, this equaled to around 10% saving per system.

### *Designing the Warp5 at Oak Technology*

At that time, other engineers who used to work with me and other leading RT CGI companies had the same idea about designing a PC add-on 3D graphics card with AA. Among them were *Jonson Yan,* who used to be Director of R&D at Link, and *Rick Fadden,* who had simulated several RT CGI at GE. They started a 3D graphics group at Oak Technology. I was invited to join the team that was designing the Warp5. The Warp5 became the 1$^{st}$ PC add-on card with AA. As part of the verification team, I was writing C code for transaction accurate simulation. I also contributed to the system design. In particular, I did the implementation of non-uniform fog, for which I got a patent [106], 'Method and Apparatus for Generating Non-Homogenous Fog'.

I also implemented several of the math functions. I got another patent for Gradient clamping [107], 'Method and Apparatus for Clamping Image Gradients'.
This was needed to prevent functions gradients overflow. Very large gradients were caused by narrow projected polygons. In this implementation, I increased the size of polygons artificially to prevent gradient overflow.

I also started to work on the next generation as a follow up to the Warp5. The Warp5 was using a BON with 8 sample points. I was able to demonstrate in the simulation that by applying the dual edge types (*VE* and *HE*), I could significantly improve the quality of AA. Unfortunately, the project got cancelled.

### *From 3D Graphics to TV to Book Author*

I still worked for a few years at companies involved in 3D graphics. Then I was unable to get another job in 3D graphics and ended up designing chips for TV and HDTV. After that I was working on and off and started to write my $1^{st}$ book, combining my experience designing with fixed point math in 3D graphics and TV.

## 6.7 ABAA Implementation with 16 and 32 Subpixels

So far, a simple implementation for ABAA with 4 and 8 Subpixels has been presented. The solutions with 4 and 8 Subpixels are similar. Using the same measurement, the method with 4 Subpixels can be extended to 8 Subpixels using a Slope flag, *S1*. For 4 and 8 Subpixels, the area of the trapezoid that extends to adjacent Pixels is smaller than half a Subpixel. So, it can be ignored.

### *Symmetry between VE and HE Cases*

For 16 and 32 Subpixels, this area cannot be ignored. A finer resolution is required for the solutions. The approach is to divide the Pixel into 4 Quadrants.

Refer to figure 6-19.

For *VEs*, there are 2 rows of 2 Quadrants. For *HEs*, there are 2 columns of 2 Quadrants. The intersections with the Quadrants *MidLn* provide with 2 measurements.

There is complete symmetry between *VEs* and *HEs*. So, some of the details will be described for *VEs* only. For *HEs*, the figures are obtained by using the symmetry around the 45-degree axis (Sym Axis).

# Evolution of ABAA

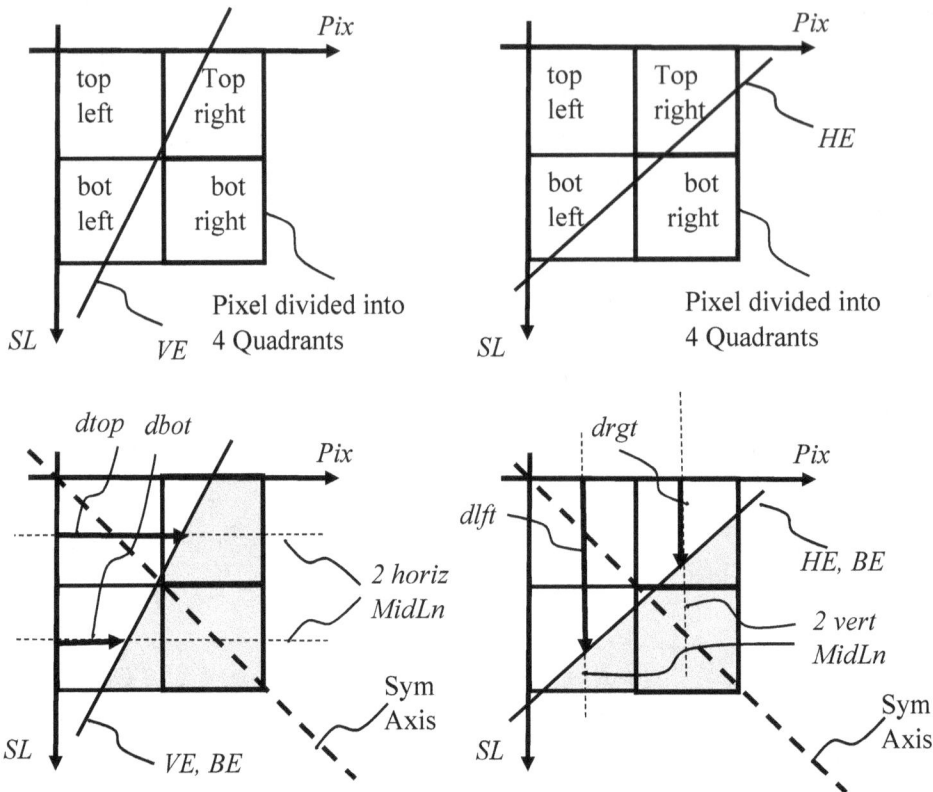

**Figure 6-19 Four Pixel Quadrants and VE and HE Symmetry**

For a beginning vertical edge (*VE, BE*) intersecting a *MidLn*, the Quadrant on the left side is not covered and the Quadrant on the right side is covered. For a beginning horizontal edge (*HE, BE*), the Quadrant on the top side is not covered and the Quadrant on the bottom side is covered.

When the *MidLn* in a Quadrant is intersected by an edge, the method for 4 or 8 Subpixels detection can be applied inside of that Quadrant to detect the covered Subpixels. The covered Subpixels inside a Quadrant need to be detected only when the *MidLn* is intersected.

With 4 Quadrants having each 4 Subpixels, the total is 16 Subpixels per Pixel.
With 4 Quadrants having each 8 Subpixels, the total is 32 Subpixels per Pixel.
Refer to Figure 6-20.

# Evolution of ABAA

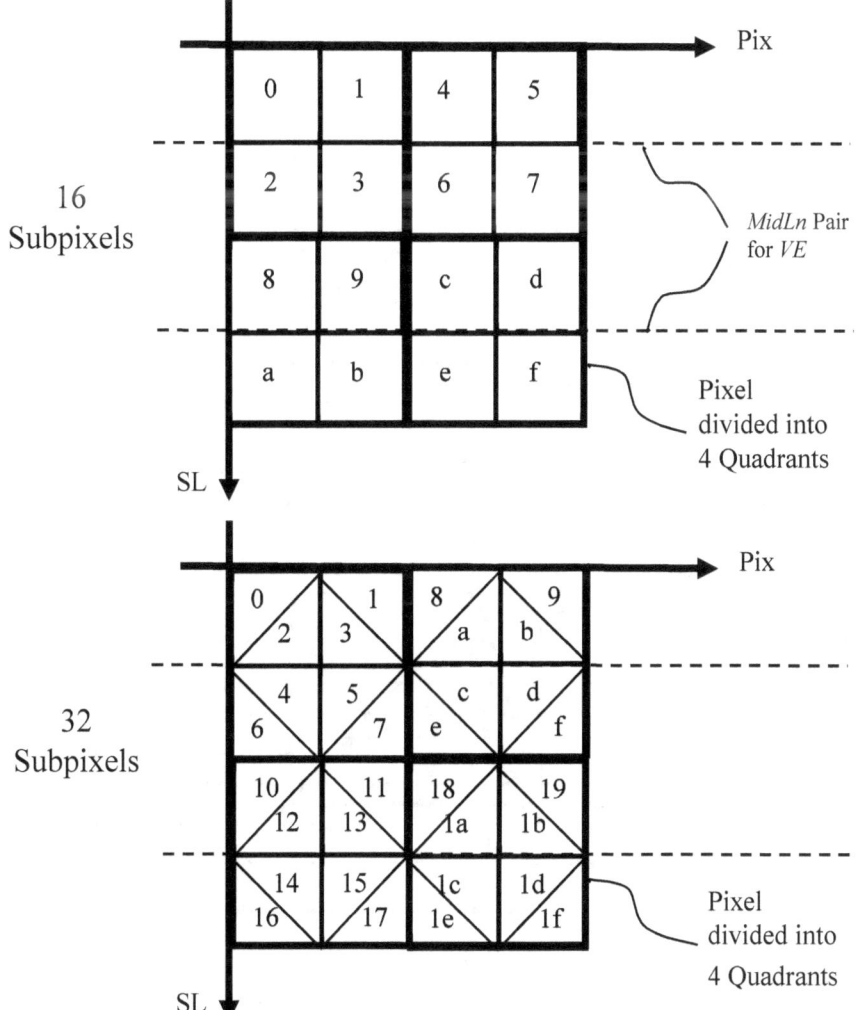

**Figure 6-20 Pixel Divided into 4 Quadrants of 4 or 8 Subpixels Each**

Note that the Subpixels are numbered with hexadecimal numbering. This is to emphasize that at this level, the implementation deals with binary numbers.
Also, for 32 Subpixels, the leading 1 indicates the second row of quadrants.

### Span intersected with Beginning Vertical Edge (VE, BE)

In Figure 6-21, 'Vertical Edge Intersection with 2 Pixel Midlines in a Span', there is an example of a *VE* traversing an 8x8 Span. Within each Span, the Subpixel Pixel covered areas are measured from the 2 intersections with Pixel Midlines.

New Area-Based Anti-Aliasing for CGI

Evolution of ABAA

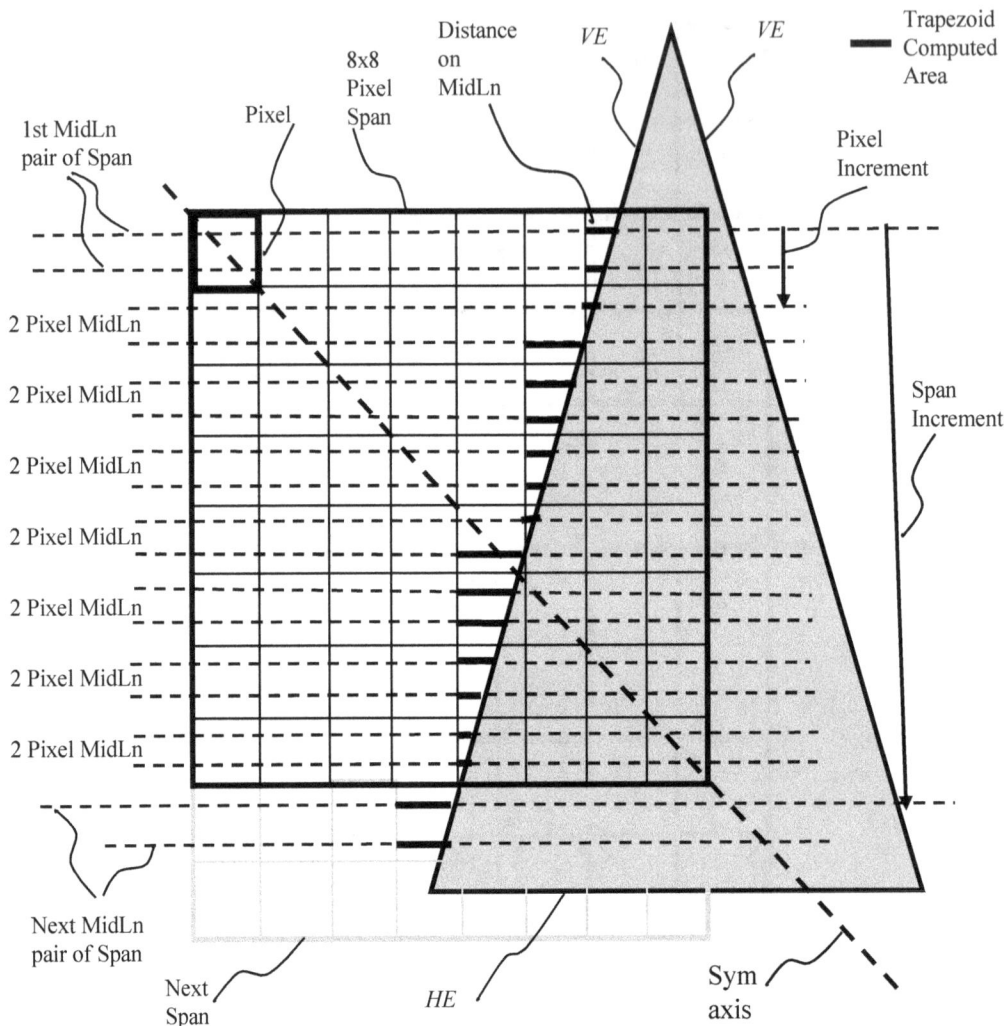

**Figure 6-21 Vertical Edge Intersection with Pixel Midlines in a Span**

The number of intersected Pixels per Span ranges between 8 and 16.
When the 2 intersected quadrants are within the same Pixel, it results into 1 intersected Pixel.
When the 2 intersected quadrants are on adjacent Pixels, it results into 2 intersected Pixels.

***Bit-Selection for Mid-Line Measurements***

In the 1st Chapter, there is an example for the format used for $x$, $y$ and edge intersections:

"For the *(xi, yi)* coordinates, a 16-bit fixed-point format is suitable for an image of *1k x1k Pixels* and an accuracy of *1/16Pixel*.
This 16-bit signed fixed-point format is:
 *sb.bbbbbbbbbb'bbbb*

where '*s*' represents the sign bit and '*b*' represent a bit. The last 4 characters '*bbbb*' represent a Pixel fraction with Subpixel resolution."

From this format, the 6 LSBs (Least Significant Bits) are used for edge intersection with the MidLn within a Span: '***bbb.bbbb***'. This provides a resolution of *1/16 Pixel*.

The 3 leading bits, '***bbb***,' indicates the number between 0 and 7 of the intersected Pixel'

The 4 fractional bits, '***.bbbb***' is the measurement inside Pixels to determine the covered area.

Refer to Table 6-1.

| Number of Subpixels | Quadrant Select | Measurement | # Measurements |
|---|---|---|---|
| 4 | No Quadrant | Use '*.bb00*' | 1 |
| 8 | No Quadrant | Use '*.bbb0*' | 1 |
| 16 | '*.b000*' | Use '*.0bb0*' | 2 |
| 21 | '*.b000*' | Use '*.0bbb*' | 2 |

### Table 6-1 Bits Selection for *MidLn* Measurements

*Span intersected with Beginning Horizontal Edge (HE, BE)*

The case of 'Horizontal Edge Intersection with 2 Pixel Midlines' is similar to that of the figure with Vertical Edge. It is the mirror image along the 45-degree axis of symmetry.

*Applications*

For most applications, especially for RT CGI, 4 and 8 Subpixel should provide good results

These solutions with 16 and 32 Subpixels are better suited for non-RT CGI applications. They most likely double the processing time. They should provide excellent results.

*Note about Intersected Pixels and Pixel Quadrant*

When computing the trapezoid covered area, the detection of intersected Pixels is determined by the intersection of edges with Pixel Midlines. A Pixel is intersected by an edge, only when the Midline is intersected within the Pixel boundaries. This limits the number of intersected Pixels.
For VE, the adjacent Pixels on the left and right sides are not intersected.
For HE, the adjacent Pixels on the top and bottom sides are not intersected.
This is not true for MSAA.

For Pixel Quadrant, the same apply. When detecting the Quadrants intersected by edges, first detect the intersected Pixels. There can be only 8 intersected Pixels in an 8x8 Pixel Span.
Then in each intersected Pixel, there can be only 1 or 2 intersected quadrants.
For VE, the adjacent Quadrants on the left and right sides are not intersected.
For HE, the adjacent Quadrants on the top and bottom sides are not intersected.
This limits the number of intersected Quadrants to 16 per 8x8 Pixel Span.

# Chapter 7 **Rendering Polygons and Triangles**

In the last stages of rendering in 3D graphics, processing deals mainly with triangles. Before rendering, polygons and bicubic patches are always converted into a group of triangles using tessellation. For this reason, triangles rendering is described in this section.

Several examples in this chapter require some knowledge of binary numbers, including octal and hexadecimal numbers. One of the last chapters in this book provides useful information about binary numbers vs decimal numbers.

A simple and effective method for rendering triangles is introduced. Several characteristics of triangle edges are identified and used to simplify the rendering operations. Edge slope and edge type help on determining the Pixel area covered by triangles. But first, the image coordinate system has to be introduced.

## 7.1 Image Coordinates

In 2D descriptive geometry, the *(X, Y)* orthogonal coordinate system is defined by 2 coordinate axes.

- X axis points toward the right side of the image.
- Y axis points toward the top of the image.

But in graphics display *(Xi, Yi)* coordinate system, the *Yi* axis points downward on the image. Refer to Figure 7-1.

- Xi axis points toward the right side of the image.
- Yi axis points toward the bottom of the image.

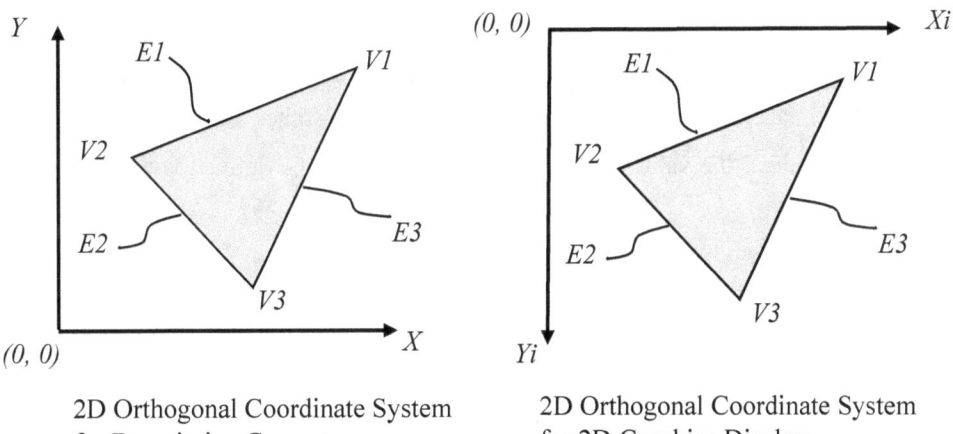

2D Orthogonal Coordinate System for Descriptive Geometry

2D Orthogonal Coordinate System for 2D Graphics Display

**Figure 7-1 2D Orthogonal Coordinate Systems**

I can guess why the 2D graphics displays use this coordinate system. This has to do with the evolution from text to 2D computer graphics. The earlier computer graphics were displaying text using the older CRT display monitors. Graphics images were developed later. Nowadays, the LCD and LED display monitors have been replacing CRT monitors. The earlier CRT display were displaying text before 2D images. And, since text (English for example) starts on the top left of the display, the top left of the screen is the origin of the coordinate system for displaying characters and images imbedded inside of text. If you want to scroll text, you scroll down, no up. I think that if the pioneers of computer graphics used languages other than English, where you read from right to left for example, the coordinate graphics system might be different from the current standard for TV.

When 3D graphics objects are projected into a 2D image plane, the projected *(Xi, Yi)* coordinates consist of fixed-point or floating-point values. The next step is to map that image onto an array of integer Pixels (*Pix*) and Scanlines (*SL*). Since the display area is described with binary numbers, a square area of size 2**N x 2**N is used as a drawing canvas.

## 7.1.1 Fixed-Point and Floating-Point Image Coordinates

The projected image is defined within a square area. The *Xi* and *Yi* limits of the image are described within a square canvas.

Refer to Figure 7-2.

The image coordinates are defined by two axes with *xi* and *yi* coordinates, as follows.

In the figure, the image is represented as a two-dimensional array of Pixels of integer size:
*PixMax * SLMax*

- As can be seen in these figures, there are 2 coordinates units on each axis:
  - integer (*Pix* or *SL*) coordinates and
  - fixed-point (*xi* or *yi*) coordinates
- In the Image Display system, the image is retrieved from the Frame Buffer using an 'integer' memory address specified by (*Pix, SL*) coordinates and converted from digital to analog. The image it then displayed on Video Monitors or other image display systems

Depending on the context, the values on the coordinate axes can be defined with fixed point or with integer numbers.

- Horizontal axis from left to right, using:
  - integer Pixel (*Pix*) coordinate (between *0* and *PixMax*) or
  - fixed-point *xi* coordinate (between *0.0* and *1.0*).
- Vertical axis from top to bottom, using:
  - integer Scanline (*SL*) coordinate (between 0 and *SLMax*) or
  - fixed-point *yi* coordinate (between *0.0* and *1.0*).

# Rendering Polygons and Triangles

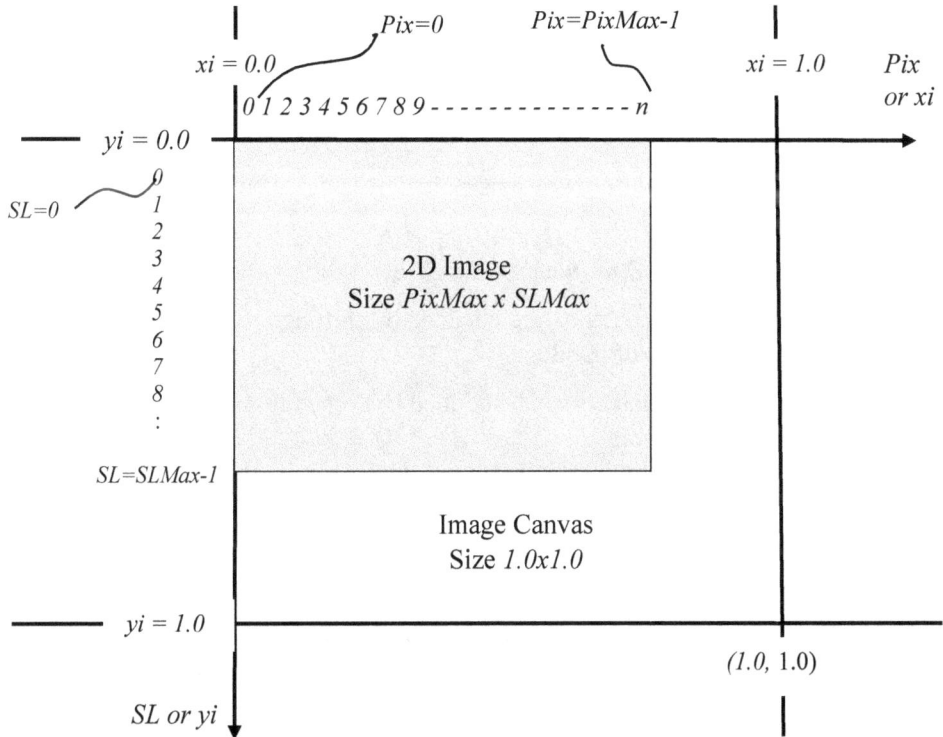

**Figure 7-2 (*Pix, SL*) and (*xi, yi*) Coordinates Inside Square Canvas**

*Integer (Pix or SL) coordinate*

*Pix* and *SL* are integer numbers that define Pixel positions in the 2D image.
The horizontal integer coordinate *Pix* ranges from *0* to *PixMax-1*.
The vertical integer coordinate *SL* ranges from *0* to *SLMax-1*.
*Pix* and *SL* Coordinates are used to store and retrieve the Pixel data to/from an image buffer memory. The Pixel data is defined inside of the *Pix* and *SL* boundaries. The integer Pixel Coordinates are also used to access the memory locations inside that image buffer.

The range of *Pix* and *SL* variables depends on the horizontal and vertical range.

- For ranges up to *511*, they are 9bit integers.
- For ranges up to *1023*, they are 10bit integers.
- For ranges up to *2047*, they are 11bit integers

*Fixed-point (xi or yi) coordinate*

The image coordinates *(xi, yi)* represent projection points in the image plane.
For example, for an *800x600* image, the fixed-point coordinates will fit within a *Pix* and *SL* range of *0* to *1024*. This corresponds to *1kx1k Pixels* and can be represented with 10bit *(Pix, SL)* coordinates. For each point in the image, the *(Pix, SL)* coordinates are obtained by multiplying the *(xi, yi)* coordinates by *1024* then converted to integer values.

*(Pix, SL) = (integer(1024\*xi), integer(1024\*yi)*

For the *(xi, yi)* coordinates, a 16-bit fixed-point format is suitable for an image of *1kx1k Pixels* and an accuracy of *1/16Pixel*.

This 16-bit signed fixed-point format is:

   *sb.bbbbbbbbbb'bbbb*

where '*s*' represents the sign bit and '*b*' represent a bit. The last 4 characters '*bbbb*' represent a Pixel fraction with Subpixel resolution.

### Conversion from Fixed Point (xi, yi) to Integer (Pix, SL)

The *(Pix, SL)* coordinates in binary notation are obtained by shifting the point position 10 places to the right and truncating the 4 bits of fraction.

The values of *x* and *y* fixed point numbers can be defined in a range from *-1.0* to *+2.0*.
This range covers a 3.0x3.0 image area.
The projected image has to fit within the 1.0x1.0 square Canvas area (that is *xi* and *yi* are within *0.0 to 1.0*). The extended area is used for intermediate computations.
The values outside of the image are used for interpolation. The portions of triangles that reside outside of the displayed image need to be clipped. Refer to Clipping patents [105][132].

## 7.2 Projected Triangles into Image Coordinates

In the 2D image, triangles can be defined by 3 vertices or 3 edges. Each triangle edge divides the image area into an inside area and an outside area. The triangle area is defined by an AND function of the 3 covered areas defined by the 3 triangle edges

### 7.2.1 Basic Triangle Edge Definition

The coordinate system for displaying computer generated images is aligned with the scan direction of TV and graphics display. That is:

- *Xi* coordinate is aligned with the Pixel display direction, that is from left to right.
- *Yi* coordinate is aligned with the Scanlines incremental direction, that is from top to bottom.

In Figure 7-3, there is a triangle defined within an *(Xi Yi)* coordinate system. It is defined by 3 vertices *V0, V1* and *V2*. The segments connecting the vertices define 3 edges *E0, E1*, and *E2*. So, the triangle can be defined in 2 ways:

- the triangle within the *(Xi, Yi)* coordinate system is defined by 3 vertices as:
   triangle *(V1, V2, V3)*.
- the triangle can also be defined by the 3 edges as:
   triangle *(E1, E2, E3)*.

# Rendering Polygons and Triangles

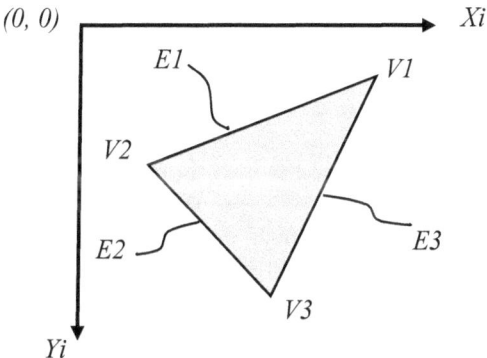

**Figure 7-3 Triangle Consisting of 3 Vertices or 3 Edges**

## 7.2.2 Edge Parameters Computation

An edge ($E$) can be represented by 2 vertices, or by a reference point (Vertex $V$) and a slope ($Slp$). This is the definition used when edges are first computed. The edge slope of a non-horizontal edge can be computed as:

$Slp = dx/dy$, when $dy \ne 0$.

In this definition, $yi$ is represented as the independent variable and $xi$ as the dependent variable. This is due to the fact that the image is processed in $SL$, or $Yi$, order.

According to this definition, a true vertical edge has a zero slope. But there is a problem with this definition. Edges near the horizontal axis have a very large slope approaching infinity. In the worst case, the edge slope is infinity for true horizontal edges.

In general, a Polygon Edge is defined by 2 entities, where $i=1, 2$ or $3$:

- Starting vertex: $Vi = (xi, yi))$
- Edge Slope: $Slpi = dxi/dyi$

With this definition, an edge is defined by 3 variables:

- $xi$
- $yi$
- $Slpi = dxi/dyi$, $dyi \ne 0$

The edge parameters are defined in Figure 7-4.

Rendering Polygons and Triangles

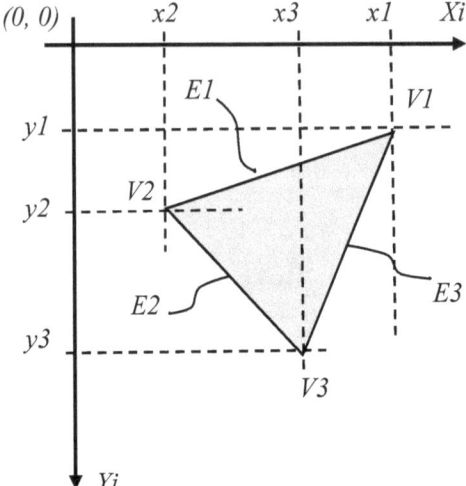

**Figure 7-4 Triangle in 2D Image Coordinates**

Note that this definition is suitable for a general description of the triangle. But, for computer graphics, millions of triangles need to be processed. There are several problems/limitations with this definition.

First, floating point computations use more hardware and memories and are slower than fixed point computations.

With floating point computations, the floating-point format could handle very large slope values. In the case of Horizontal Edges, a floating-point value near infinity could provide a good approximation. But, for fixed-point implementation, this poses a problem. For fixed-point computations a large number of digits are required for near horizontal edges. In the case of the DIGs that I worked on, the slopes had around 22 bits, while $xi$ and $yi$ were defined with only 14 bits. And with this limitation, the slope of horizontal edges could no represent the correct slope.

When polygons are rendered to generate a 2D image, the edge slope is iteratively used to compute edge intersections with Pixels and Scanlines. For Tile Traversing, the edge slope is iteratively used to jump from Tile to Tile. This type of operations is more efficiently accomplished with fixed point calculations.

*Optimized Edge Format*

In order to solve the problem of large slopes with fixed point representation, the edge format can be optimized to improve the efficiency of the traversing operation. One day, I realized that if there were two types of edges, vertical (*VE*) and horizontal (*HE* = !*VE*) edges, the maximum size of edge slopes could be limited to *1.0*. And also, there would be complete symmetry in *Xi* and *Yi* coordinates. The number of bits for edge slope *Slp* would be similar to the number of bits for *xi* and *yi*.

In this approach, edges use a format similar to the *(xi, yi)* coordinates. A 16-bit fixed-point format for edge slopes *Slp* is suitable for an image of *1k x1k Pixels* and an accuracy of 1/16Pixel. This 16-bit signed fixed-point edge format for *xi, yi* and *Slp* is:
    *sb.bbbbbbbbbb'bbbb*
where '*s*' represents the sign bit and '*b*' represent a bit. The last 4 characters '*bbbb*' represent a Pixel fraction with Subpixel resolution.

## 7.2.3 Edge Definition for Triangle Rendering

When rendering polygons or more specifically triangles, edges are tested to determine the area that they cover. Basically, each edge divides the rendering area into two sides: the *inside* and the *outside*. On the *outside* of the edge, the area is not covered by the triangle. On the *inside* of the edge, the area is partially covered by the triangle. But, until all the edges are tested, the whole *inside* area is potentially covered by the triangle.

In this ABAA algorithm, edges are used to detect the Subpixel area coverage in two directions:

- For *VE*, the direction is left to right
- For *HE*, the direction is top to bottom

Also, edges have to be defined as beginning and ending edges. The edges are processed in counter clockwise direction. Depending on edge slope size, they are organized into 2 main types: *VE* and *HE*. More precisely, depending on their direction they can be referred as beginning (*BE=1*) or ending (*BE=0*) edges.

- *VE Lft (left)*, *BE=1*, Direction down, with $dy>0$
- *VE Rgt (right)*, *BE=0*, Direction top, with $dy<0$
- *HE Top (top)*, *BE=1*, Direction left, with $dx<0$
- *HE Bot (bottom)*, *BE=0*, Direction right, with $dx>0$

Refer to Figure 7-5.

# Rendering Polygons and Triangles

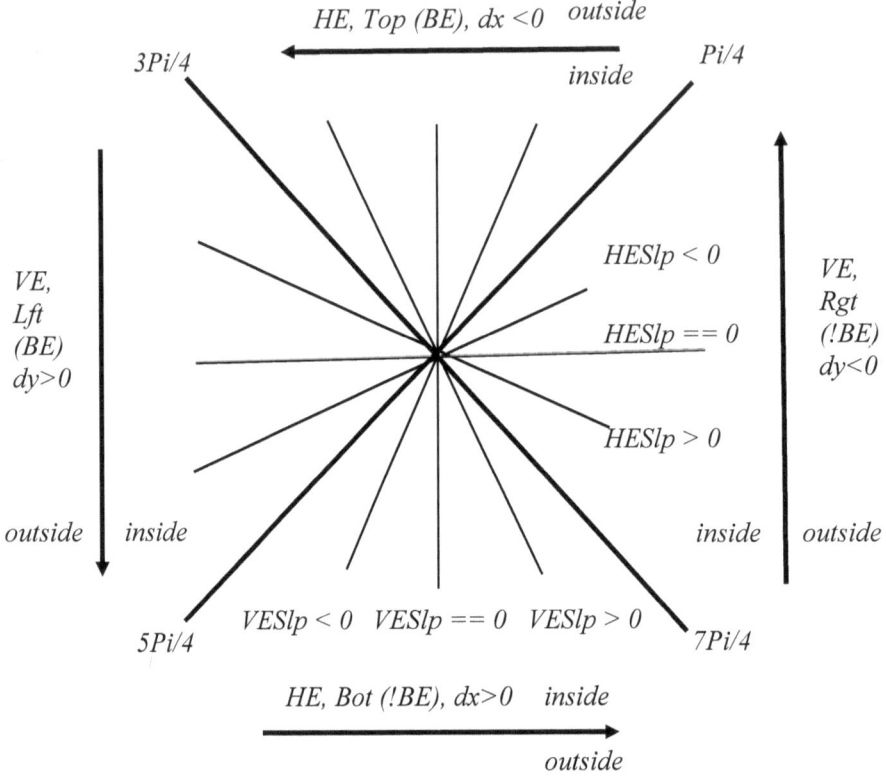

**Figure 7-5 Beginning and Ending Edge Types**

## 7.2.4 Definition of Edge Directions and Types

When a triangle is processed in the Geometric Processor, the order of triangle vertices has to be specified. The order can be clockwise like the movement of the hands on a clock, or counter-clockwise like the angle degrees in a circle.

In this document, the order of triangle vertices in 3D objects is counter-clockwise for the visible side of surfaces. For the back side of faces (not visible), the order is clockwise.

Edge Parameter Decoding is described in the flowchart of Figure 7-6.

The slope flags *S0* and *S1* are derived from the 3 most significant bits (*MSBs*) of the slope.

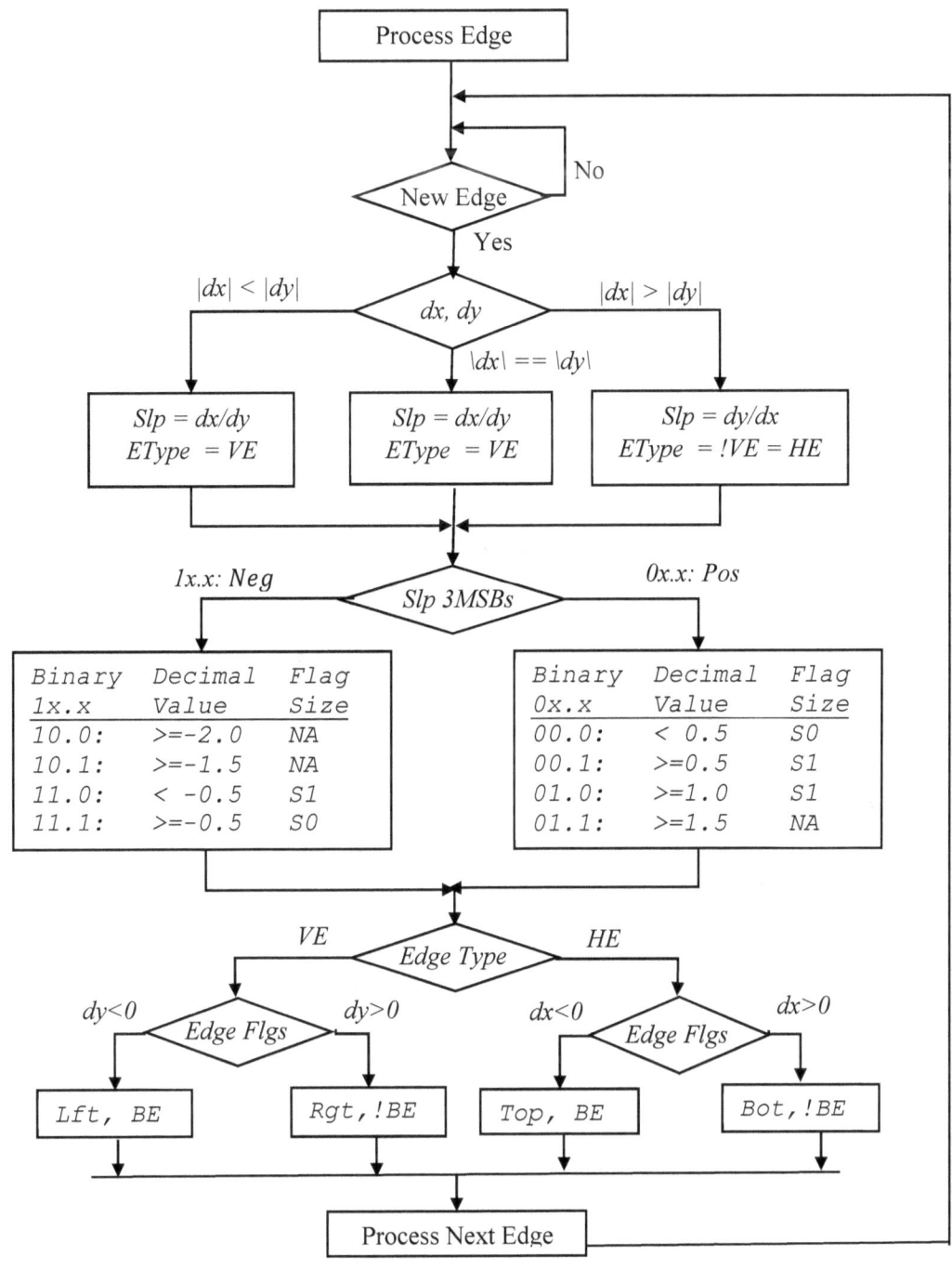

**Figure 7-6 Edge Parameter Decoding**

New Area-Based Anti-Aliasing for CGI

## Process Angles in Counter-Clockwise Order

In this document, the triangle vertices are processed in counter-clockwise order This definition is important for determining which side of the Pixel is covered when an Edge crosses a Pixel.

## 8 Main Edge Types

Also, depending on their direction, edges can be Beginning *(BE)* or Ending *(!BE)* Edges.

There can be 8 edge types, depending on edge-angle, edge-direction and slope sign.
Refer to Figure 7-7, "Eight Edge Types".
The 4 side types are: *VE Left/Right (Lft/Rgt)* and *HE Top/Bottom (Top/Bot)*
Then, each side type can have a positive or a negative slope.

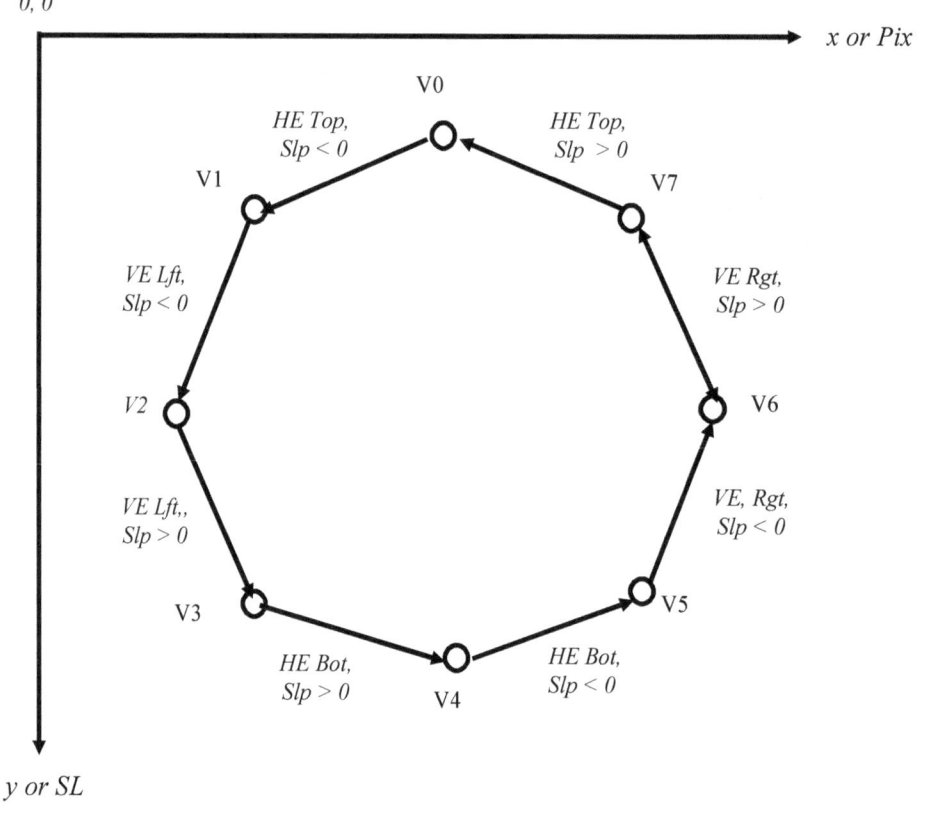

**Figure 7-7 Eight Edge Types**

## 7.2.5 Rendering a Triangle Inside of Spans

In Figure 7-8, a triangle inside of a Span is rendered according to info from the 3 edges

In this example, the Span area is defined by an array of 8x8 Pixels. Each Pixel area is divided into N Subpixels. So, the Span area consists of is 64*N Subpixels.
The Span area covered by the triangle is derived in 3 steps.

Step 1:
Identify the parameters of the 3 triangle edges.
In this example the 3 edges have the following flags: '*HE Top*', '*VE Lft*' and '*VE Rgt*'.

Step 2:
For each edge, evaluate the Span covered area. The state of covered Subpixel areas is set toto '*1*'. The state of the not-covered Subpixels is set to '*0*'. *Area0*, *Area1* and *Area2* are the covered areas for edges E0, E1, E2, respectively.

Step 3:
The area '*TriArea*' covered by the triangle is obtained by doing an *AND* function on the Subpixels of the 3 covered areas: *Area0*, *Area1* and *Area2*. This *AND* operation on the 3 covered areas is performed bitwise on all *64*N* Subpixels inside of the 8x8 Pixel span.

After Step 3, the triangle area '*TriArea*' inside of the Span consists of the covered Subpixels areas that are set to '*1*'.

Rendering Polygons and Triangles

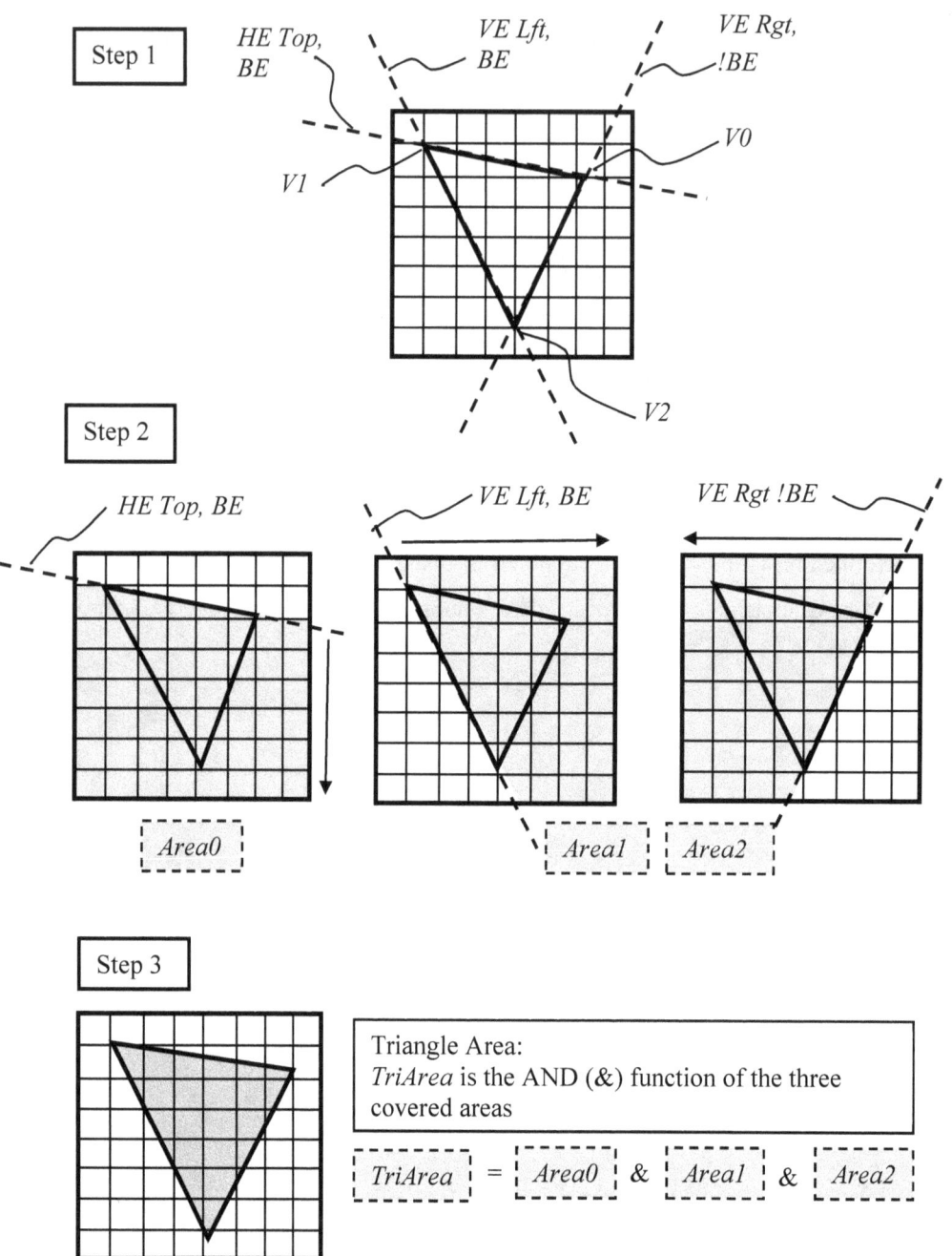

**Figure 7-8 Triangle Rendering According to Edge Info**

## 7.2.6 Edges Traversing Spans for Triangle Rendering

When the whole image is considered, the intersected Spans can be identified by rectangular area defined by *Min* and *Max* values of the 3 vertices of the triangle to render.

In order to render triangles, the triangle edges are used to traverse Spans. The covered area of Spans is limited by the *Min/Max* dimensions of the triangle such as:

- *PixMin* and *PixMax*
- *SLMin* and *SLMax*.

As example, a triangle is inside of an area of 4x3 Spans intersects 9 Spans. The Pixel covered areas are obtained by using the 3 edges to traverse these Span areas.
Refer to In Figure 7-9, "Span Traversing with 3 triangle Edges".

Note that in this example, the triangle bottom edge is an *HE* with slope<0. In this case, there are 2 solutions: The selected approach depends on the algorithm implementation.

- Traverse the Spans from top to bottom. In this case the starting intersection point will be on the right side of the Rendering Area. This is approach used in this example.
- Traverse the Spans from left to right. In this case the starting intersection point will be on the top side of the Rendering Area.

Rendering Polygons and Triangles

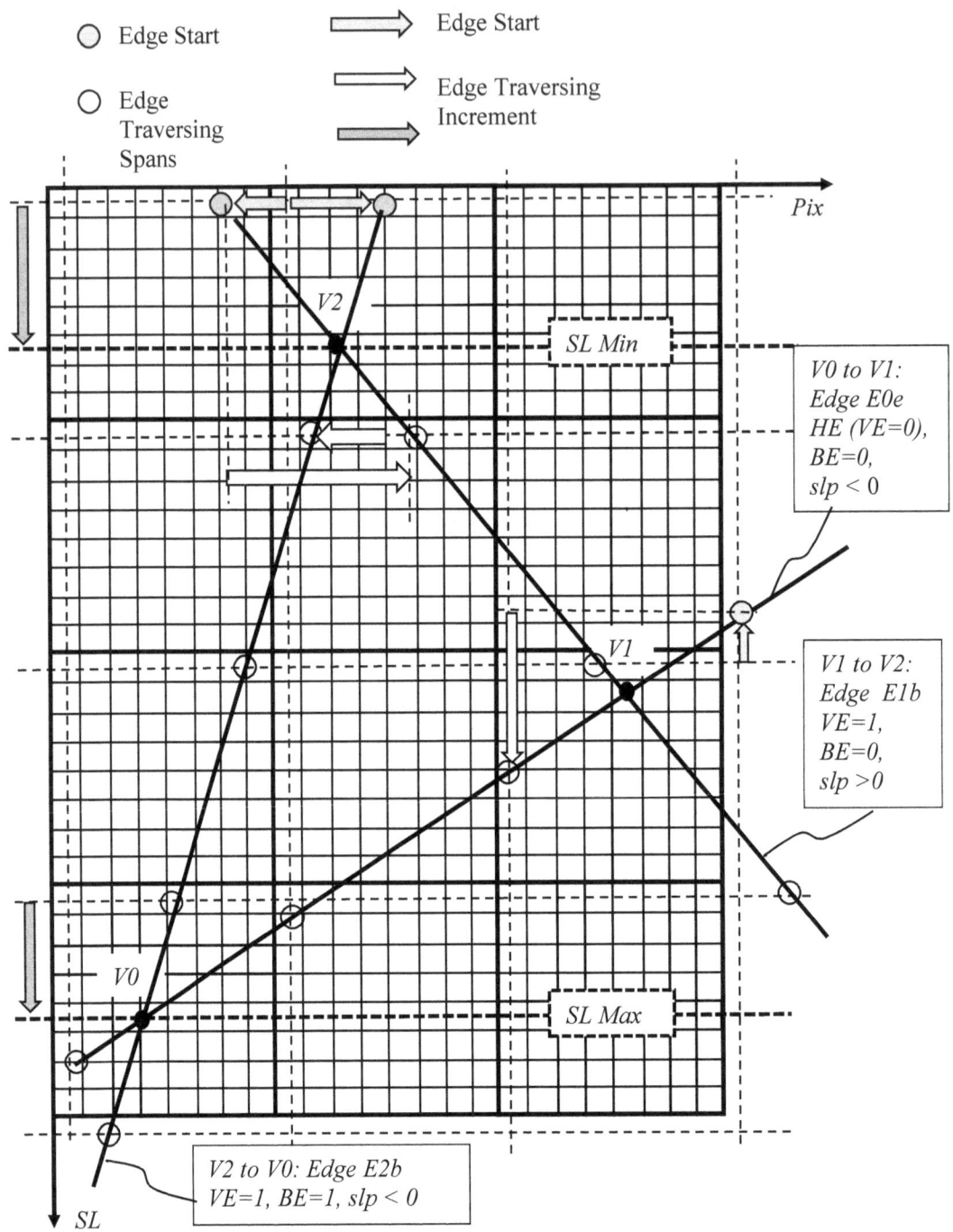

**Figure 7-9 Span Traversing with 3 Triangle Edges**

## 7.2.7 Span-to-Span Traversing with ABAA

While traversing spans, in each span, there are up to 8 intersected Pixels. With ABAA, there can be only 8 intersected Pixels, since there is only one measurement (computation) per Pixel. The measured distance is within 0/16 to 15/16 inside of each Pixel. When an HE Edge starts or ends inside of a Pixel, use the *PixMin* or *PixMax* to clip the edge. When a VE edge starts or ends inside of a Pixel, use the Edge starts or ends inside of a Pixel, use the *SLMin* or *SLMax1* to clip the edge.

In Figure 7-10, 'Edge Intersection with Pixel Midlines', there is an example of a VE traversing two 8x8 Spans. Within each Span, the Pixel covered areas are measured from the intersections with Pixel Midlines.

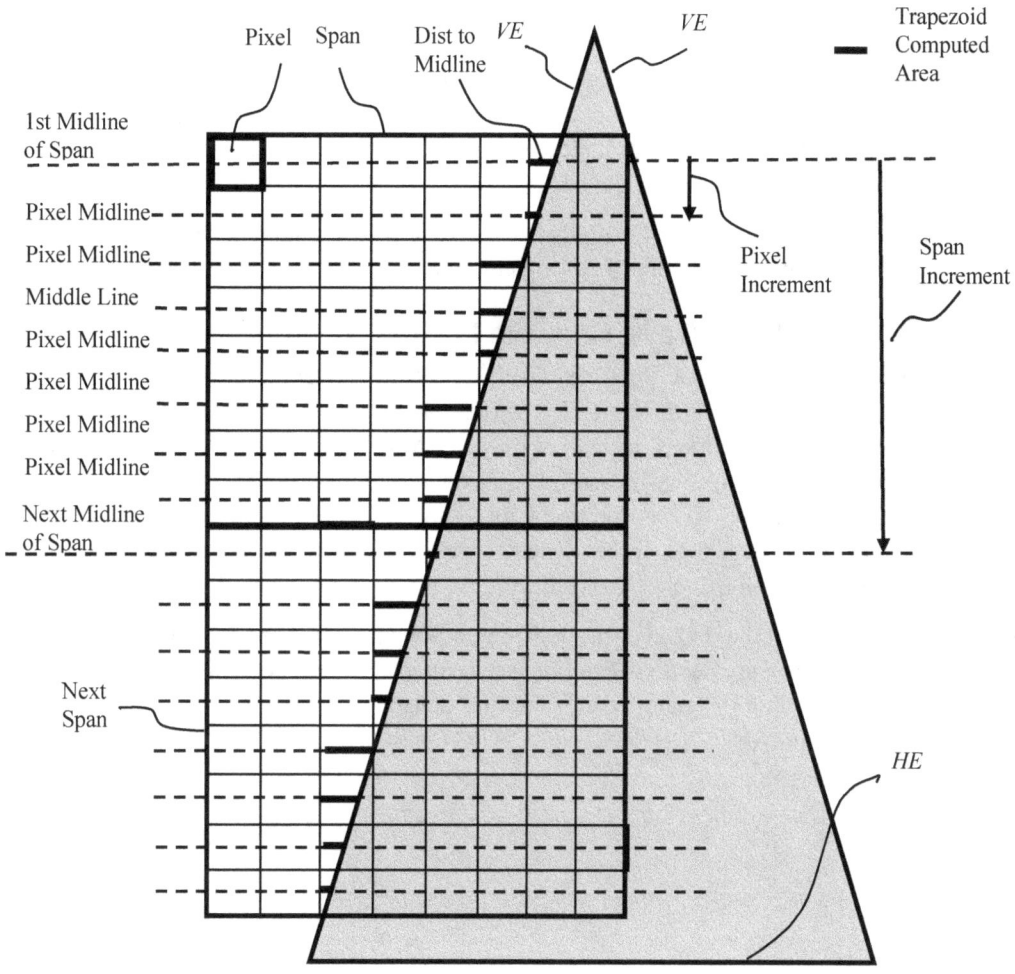

**Figure 7-10 Edge Intersection with Pixel Midlines**

Rendering Polygons and Triangles

### 7.2.8 Span-to-Span and Pixel-to-Pixel Traversing with ABAA

With MSAA, the determination of Subpixel coverage can be done using horizontal distance for VE and vertical distance for HE. This approach is similar to that of ABAA, using 2 types of edges: VE and HE.

This simplifies the problem considerably. This is the approach used in the simulation of MSAA4 and MSAA8 in the next chapters.

### 7.2.9 Span-to-Span Traversing with MSAA

While traversing Spans with MSAA, the Span-to-Span traversing is similar to ABAA, but it differs inside of Pixels, because there can be 4 or 8 Subpixels. 4 or 8 distances are measured for each Subpixel, compared to only one with ABAA. Refer to the previous figure.

There can be more than 8 intersected Pixels when edges cross Pixel boundaries. The maximum number of intersected Pixels within a Span is 16. The measured distance inside Pixels is within 0/16 to 15/16. When an *HE* Edge starts or ends inside of a Pixel, use the *PixMin* or *PixMax* to clip the edge. When a *VE* edge starts or ends inside of a Pixel, use the Edge starts or ends inside of a Pixel, use the *SLMin* or *SLMax1* to clip the edge.

Here, with the use of *VE* and *HE* types of edges, the distance computations are faster and more accurate than when the edge normal distances are computed.

### 7.2.10  Pixel-to-Pixel Traversing with MSAA

While traversing Pixels with MSAA, the Pixel-to-Pixel traversing operation is similar to the Span-to-Span traversing with ABAA, as described in the previous figure. But it differs inside of Pixels, because there can be 4 or 8 Subpixels, instead of only one Midline with ABAA. In each Pixel, the distance of up to 8 Subpixels has to be measured. Here the distance from edge to Subpixel (Queen) is computed. In Figure 7-11, 'Edge Intersection with Subpixel Midlines', there is an example of a *VE* traversing two Pixels with 8 Subpixels each (organized as Queens on a chessboard). The situation will be similar when using 4 Queens only.

With MSAA, in each Pixel the 8 Queens are located on Subpixel midlines. The distance between the edge and each Queen on the Subpixel Midline is measured. The measured distance inside Pixels is within 0/16 to 15/16. For *VE* edges, the horizontal distance is computed. For *HE* edges, the vertical distance is computed.

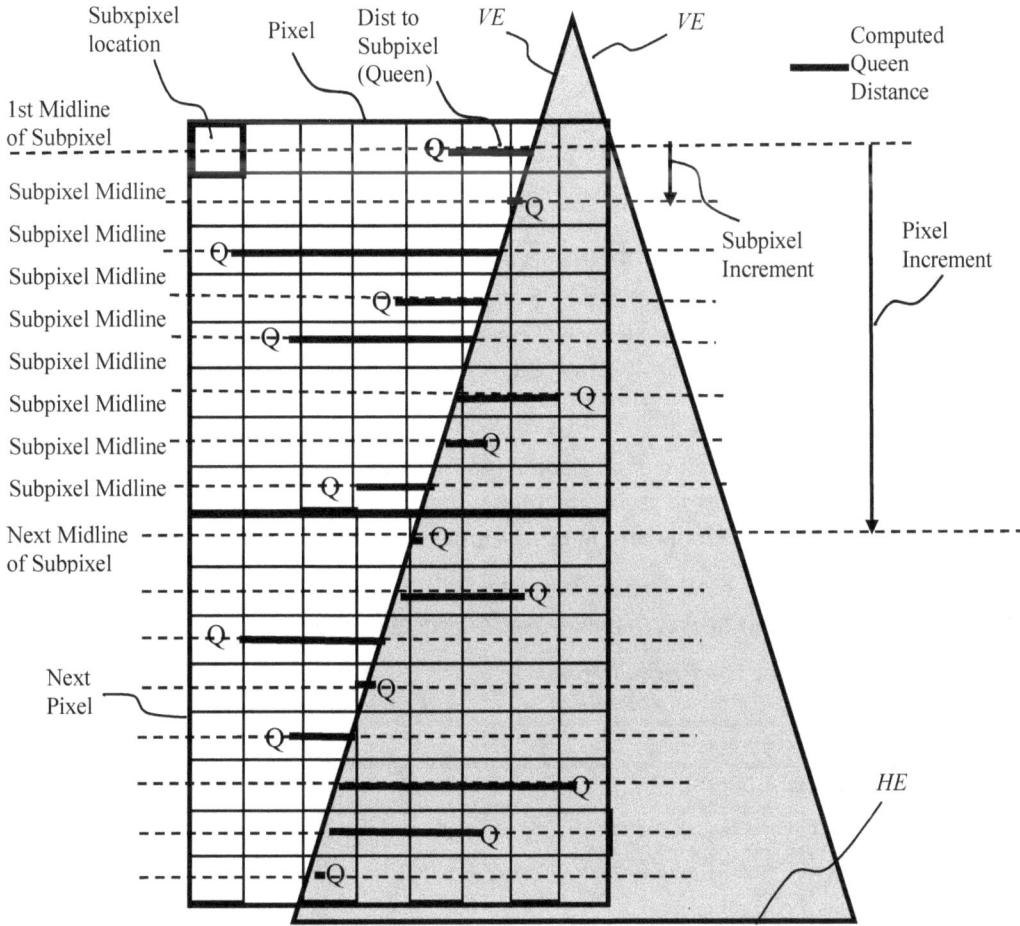

**Figure 7-11 Edge Intersection with Subpixel Midlines of the Queens**

## 7.3 ABAA Example of Triangle Processed with 4 Subpixels

The images in these examples have been generated by a C-program. Since there are 8x8 Pixels in a Span, and up to 8 Subpixels in a Pixel, there are advantages to use octal binary numbers in the simulation. The edge coordinates and slopes are defined with octal numbers. The program input consists of edges defined as 'octal-char' input using numbers in 'octal ASCII' format.

In this example, the triangle is defined by 3 edges within an 8x8 Pixel Span.

*No gray shade images*

It is not practical to show images with gray shades. When printed, the gray shade images can be easier to evaluate at first. But, because of the limitation of the printing process, it would be difficult to evaluate the number of covered Subpixels between 0 and 8 inside of each Pixel with gray shades. The results would be inconclusive.

## Show results with a character Printer

By showing the covered Subpixels with an '*' or an ID number, the covered Subpixel are easily identified. By showing the covered Subpixel count inside of Pixels instead gray shade, it is easier to evaluate and compare the ABAA vs MSAA approaches in the next Chapters. Also, by showing a number for the covered Subpixels, it helps identify the face to which the Subpixel belong. When there is only one face, the covered Subpixels are indicated with an '*'.

### 7.3.1 Definition of Data Structures in C for Simulation

In the first example, the triangle is defined by 3 edges using the following format.
The Edge starting point and Edge slope are entered in ASCII octal format (octal-char), then converted by an octal-char to binary function that produces 16-bit binary integer for processing.

### Data Structure for Edge Type

Two Edge data structures are defined in C language. There are declared in Listing 7-1. There is a data structure that defines edges in ascii octal format for entering edge data. There is another data structure for processing edges in binary (integer) format.

- Edge data defined in octal-char format (edgeascii_type)
- Edge data defined in integer16 binary Format (edgebin_type).

### Listing 7-1 C-Structure for Edge Type

```
// ================================================================
// Edges Type in ASCII and Binary
// ================================================================
typedef struct edgeascii_type{
// Ascii Octal string, format "aa.aa" (7 chars + NULL for endstring)
  char EStrt[8];   // Oct string in ASCII
  char EEnd[8];    // Oct string in ASCII
  char ESlp[8];    // Oct string in ASCII
  byte VE;         // VE, !HE
  byte BE;         // Beginning edge
} edgeasc_t;

typedef struct edgebin_type{
    int16 EStrt;   // Oct strings converted to 16 bits binary
    int16 EEnd;    // Oct strings converted to 16 bits binary
    int16 ESlp;    // Oct strings converted to 16 bits binary
    byte VE;       // Fkag for VELeft or HETop
    byte BE;       // Flag for Beginning edge
    byte SlpSgn;   // Flag for Slope Sign
    byte SlpGtr;   // Flag for |Slope| >= 0.5
} edgebin_t;
// ================================================================
```

## Convert Edges from ASCII octal to binary format

Two functions are used to convert Edges from ASCII octal to 16-bit binary format. The two C functions to convert from 'char octal' to 'integer16' are shown in Listing 7-2. Note that for ascii integer, or 16-bit integer, the point position is "implied".

- int OctAsc2Bin ( ); // Conversion for Edge Start
- int EdgeAsc2Bin ( ); // Conversion for Edge Slope

## Listing 7-2 Edge Conversion from ASCII to Binary

```
// ========================================================================
// Edge Conversion from ASCII to Binary
// ========================================================================
int OctAsc2Bin(byte& Sgn, int16& B16, char* A8) { // Conversion for Edge Start
// Input Char string: "aa.aa", Edge Start in octal format (0 to 7).
// Output 16-bit integer: 's bbb bbb bbb.bbb bbb'
// Note: For ascii or 16-bit integer, the point position is "implied"
// Edge example: Beginning VE Edge and Ending VE Edge
// char* EStart[8]= "00.00";}
// Convert first char (3 LSBs, on right side)
  B16 = (int16)A8[0] - (int16)'0'; // convert a char to int16
  if (B16 > 7)  B16 = 7; // Error, octal cannot be greater than 7
  // Detect negative when A8[0]=='7' (or >4)
  if (B16 >=4) {  // bit 11
    Sgn = 1;
    B16 = B16 | 0xff8; // insert 9 sigh bits before 9 left shifts
  } else
    Sgn = 0;
  // Convert and insert next 3 chars on the right side, one at a time.
  B16 = (B16 << 3) + (int16)A8[1] - (int16)'0';
  // A8[2] is the point position and is ignored
  B16 = (B16 << 3) + (int16)A8[3] - (int16)'0';
  B16 = (B16 << 3) + (int16)A8[4] - (int16)'0'; // negative when A8[0]=='7'
  return 0;
}

int EdgeAsc2Bin(edgebin_t &EdgB, edgeasc_t EdgA) { // Conversion for Edge Slope
// Input Char string: "aa.aa", Edge Slope in octal format (0 to 7).
// Output 16-bit integer: 's bbb bbb bbb.bbb bbb'
// Edge example: Beginning VE Edge
// edge_t EParam = {"00.00", "00.00", "00.00", 3, 0 };
  byte Sgn;
  OctAsc2Bin(Sgn, EdgB.EStrt, EdgA.EStrt);
  OctAsc2Bin(Sgn, EdgB.EEnd,  EdgA.EEnd);
  OctAsc2Bin(EdgB.SlpSgn, EdgB.ESlp,  EdgA.ESlp);
  EdgB.VE = (EdgA.VEBE >> 1) & 1;
  EdgB.BE = EdgA.VEBE & 1;
  // Detect Large Slopes (|slope|>0.5): FractMSB != SlpSgn
  if ( EdgB.SlpSgn == 0) {
    // Pos Examples: 01.00, 00.7x, 00.6x, 00.5x. 00.4x (Pos Slope > 00.37,
    // that is .0.49 dec)
    if ( EdgB.ESlp>>5 ) EdgB.SlpGtr = 1;
    else                EdgB.SlpGtr = 0;
  } else {
    // Neg Examples: 76.3x, 77.3x (should be smaller than 77.4x)
    if ( ((EdgB.ESlp>>5) & 3) < 3 ) EdgB.SlpGtr = 1;
    else                EdgB.SlpGtr = 0;
  }
  return 0;
}
// ========================================================================
```

# Rendering Polygons and Triangles

*Define 3 triangle edges*

The three triangle edges are defined in Listing 7-3.

## Listing 7-3 Definition of Three Triangle Edges

```
// =====================================================================
// Triangle Inside 8x8 Pixel Span
// =====================================================================
edgeasc_t SPANTRI[] = // 3 triangle edges
   //   Start      End       Slope<0   VE BE
   { {"03.60",  "01.60",   "77.60",   1, 1 },
   //   Start      End       Slope<0   HE !BE
     {"07.60",  "02.20",   "77.24",   0, 0 },
   //   Start      End       Slope>0   HE BE
     {"00.60",  "03.00",   "00.22",   0, 1 } };
// =====================================================================
```

*Simulation Printout*

For the simulation, an 8x8 Pixel Span is used to simulate the test cases and to show the output results. The 8x8 Pixel Span is generated by printing the vertical and horizontal Line characters.

For the Subpixels within a Pixel, the following format is used.
The covered Subpixels are indicated with an 'asterisk': *
The not-covered Subpixels are indicated with a 'dot': .

In order to make the Pixel output square, a 6x3 array of Subpixels is used for the printouts.
The Subpixels selection within the 6x3 is selected so that they represent their actual position as close to the 8x8 array. Listing 7-4 shows the printed format for a 'Not-Covered' and 'Covered' Pixel with 4 Subpixels. This consists of a 6x3 'char' array that prints each Pixel as a square. The C indicates that the Pixel is 'Completely Covered'.

## Listing 7-4 ABAA4 Subpixel Char Array for Printing

```
//==================================================
// C Listing
//==================================================
// ABAA4 Subpixel Printout
//==================================================
//#define SPix_ARRAY 16
//
// Pix Not-Covered
//==================================================
// 6x3 char Array for Pix Not-Covered
char SPA_NC[3][16] = { "|.     .",
                       "|       ",
                       "|.     ." };

// Pix Covered
//==================================================
// 6x3 char Array for Pix Completely Covered
char SPA_Cov[3][16]= { "|*     *",
                       "|   C   ",
                       "|*     *" };
//==================================================
```

*Printout Results of Simulation*

Figure 7-12 and 7-13 show the result from processing the 3 triangle edges and the final triangle, using ABAA 4. The final triangle is obtained by ANDing the results of the 3 triangle edges.

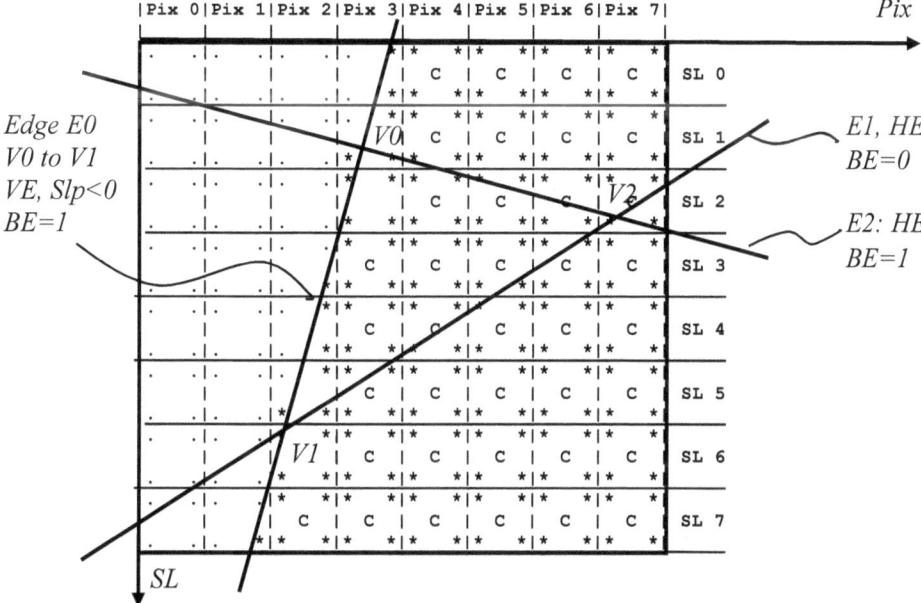
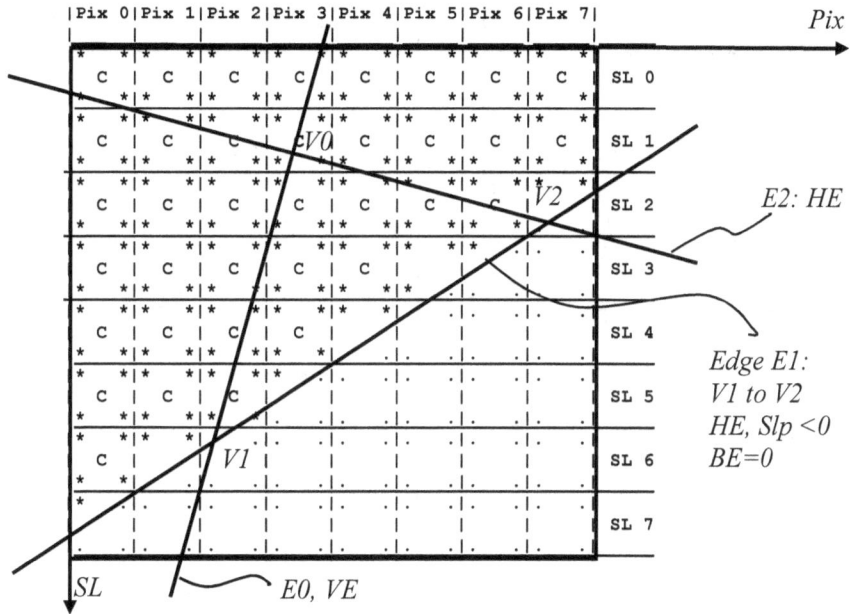

**Figure 7-12 Processing of Edges *E0* and *E1***

# Rendering Polygons and Triangles

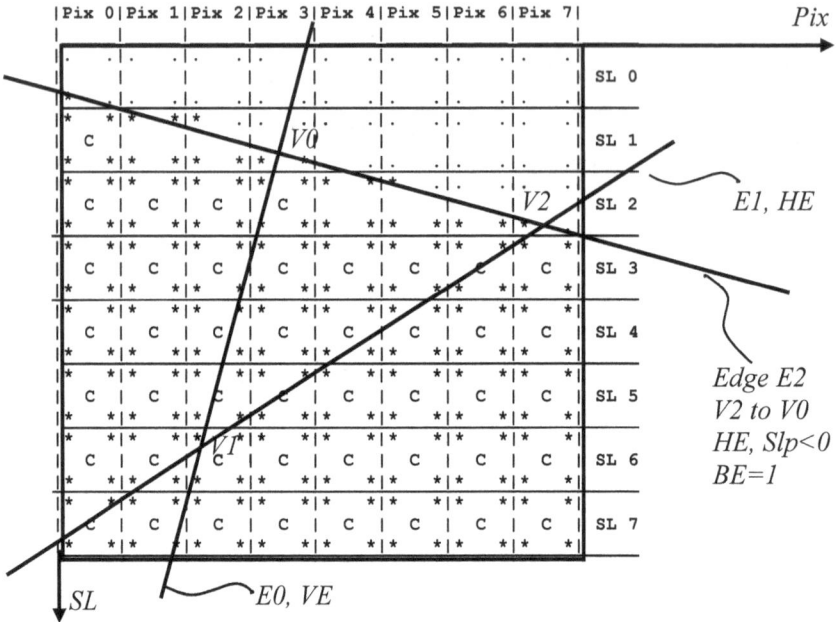

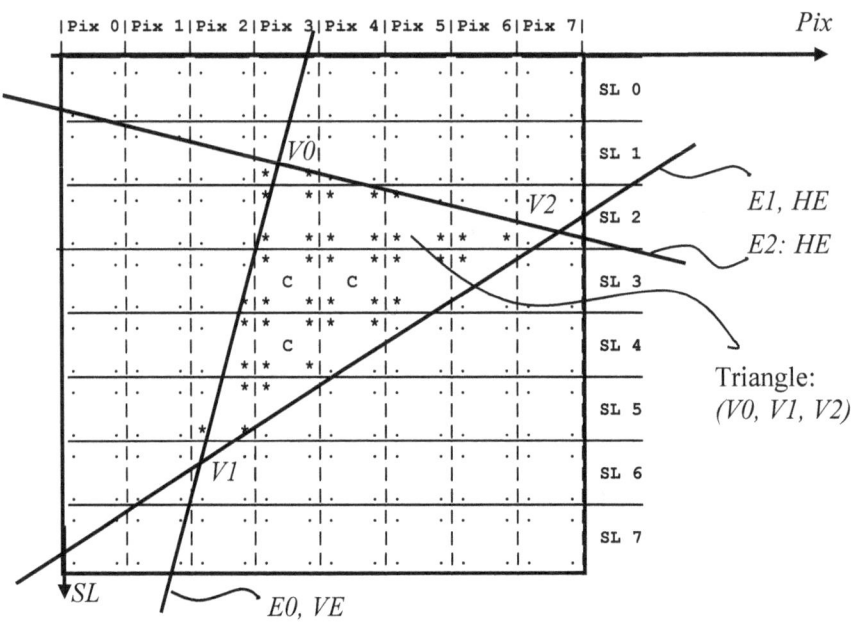

**Figure 7-13 Processing of Edge *E2* and Final Triangle**

# Chapter 8  ABAA with 4 Subpixel Areas

In this section, a solution for 4 subpixels assignment is presented, followed by a simulation comparing ABAA with MSAA.

## 8.1 Solution with 4 Square Subpixel Areas

The Pixel covered area is determined by the edge distance, $d$, on the Pixel MidLn. The distance is obtained with only one measurement. In this case, with a resolution of *1/16*, the maximum error will be:  $e = 1/16$

In Figure 8-1, there are 2 cases for a negative *VE*, according to distance: $d>0.0$ and $d==0.0$. In both cases, the Computed Area is equal to the Covered Area.

- In the first case, it is assumed that the range of extended edge (EE) intersections with 2 opposite boundaries of Pixels is within *0.0* and *1.0*. The EE intersections with opposite Pixel boundaries divide the Pixel into **2 trapezoidal areas**. Here the distance is $d>0.0$.
- In the 2$^{nd}$ case, the distance $d==0.0$, the slope is $|Slp|=|-1|=1.0$. This is the worst case. On the left boundary of the Pixel, the covered area on the left side is 1/8. It is equal to the uncovered are on the right side.

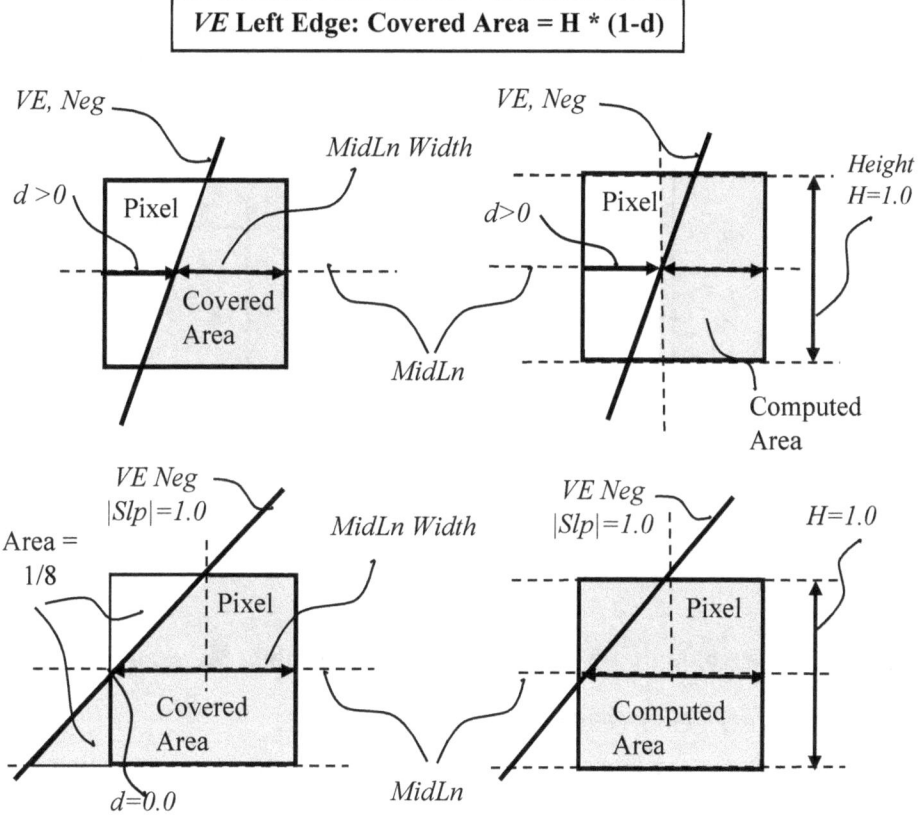

**Figure 8-1 Pixel Covered Area Computation for Negative VE**

## ABAA with 4 Subpixel Areas

The 4 Subpixel transitions are identified according to 3 edge Flags. Refer to Figure 8-2.
- Edge orientation Flag: *VE vs HE*
- Edge Polarity Flag: *Pos vs Neg*
- Edge beginning or ending flag: *BE* vs *!BE*.

### Pixel-Map for 4 Subpixels

In Figure `8-2, the 4 Subpixel solution is represented in a Pixel-Map. This Map describes the 4 edge cases with their corresponding Subpixel sequences.

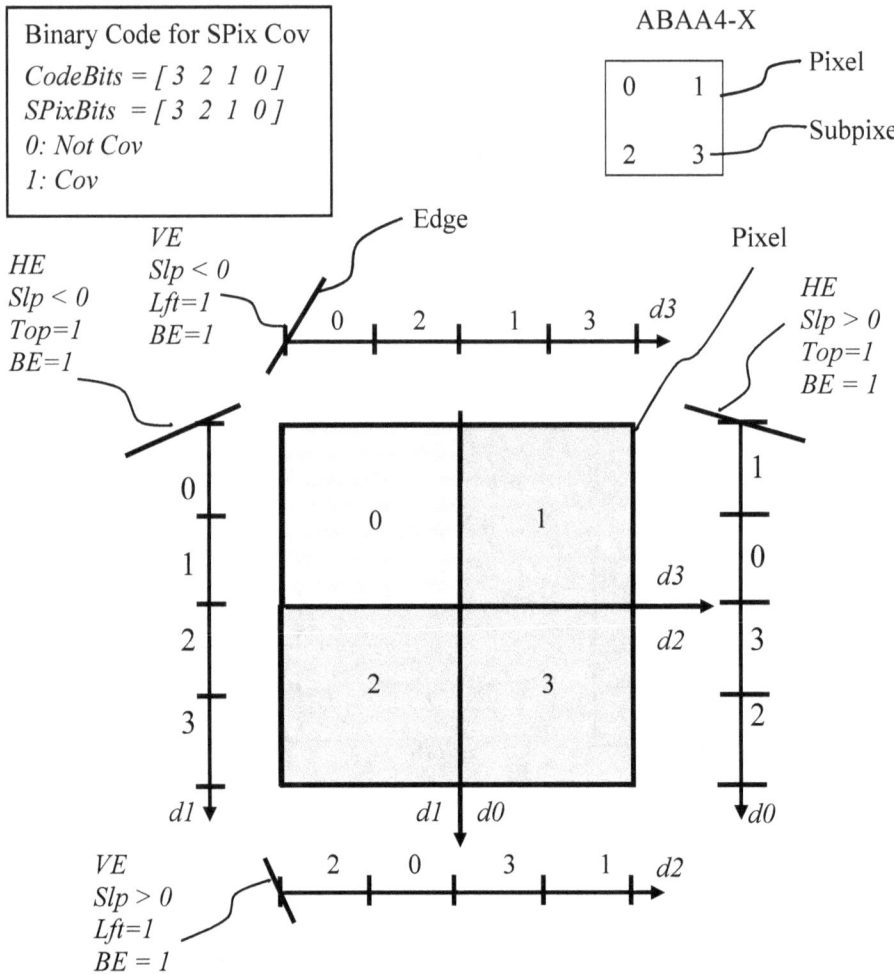

**Figure 8-2 Pixel Map Showing 4 Cases of Subpixel Mapping for ABAA4-X**

### Flowchart for 4 Subpixel Decoding

The same information can be represented in a flowchart. The decoding for the Subpixel sequence is described in the flowchart of Figure 8-3.

The Subpixel sequences can be stored in a local table in a local memory or other storage.
This figure shows the transitions when the Subpixels are turned on for beginning edges (*BE=1*).
For ending edges (*BE=0*) the sequence indicates when the Subpixels are turned off.

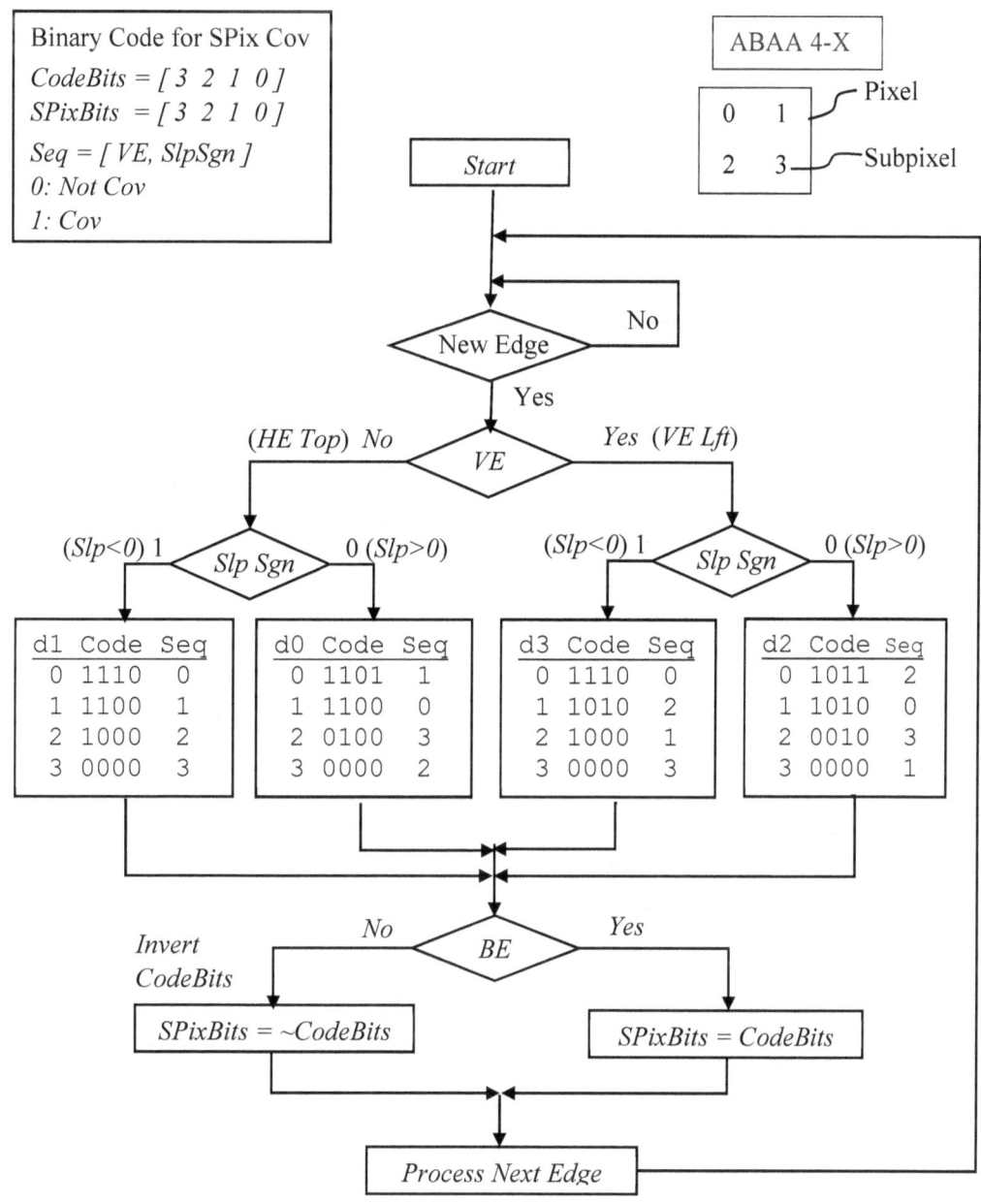

**Figure 8-3 Flowchart to Decode Subpixel Mapping for ABAA4-X**

# ABAA with 4 Subpixel Areas

## *Example with 4 Subpixels*

In Figure 8-4, there is a representation of an edge crossing 4 Subpixel Areas for the 4 Edge cases.

Each group of 4 edges that intersects the MidLn in the same quarter of distance *d* covers the same number of Subpixels.

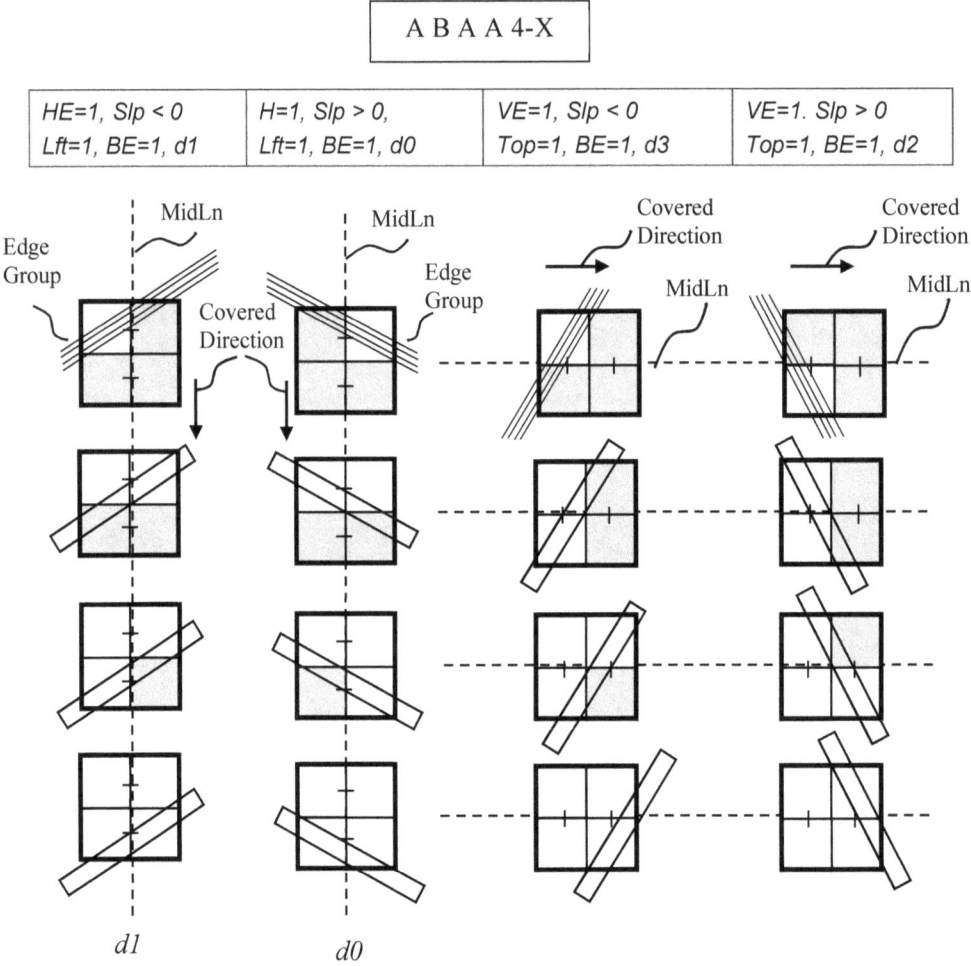

Figure 8-4 ABAA4-X: Four Cases of Edge Crossing 4 Subpixel Areas

## 8.1.1 ABAA vs MSAA Examples with 4 Subpixels

In Figure 8-5, there is a comparison of ABAA vs MSAA, for an edge movig across 4 Subpixels.

With ABAA, as the edge moves from left to right across the Pixel, there are 4 equal intensity transitions. With MSAA, when an edge crosses a pair of Subpixels that are aligned with that edge, there can be double intensity transitions.

# ABAA with 4 Subpixel Areas

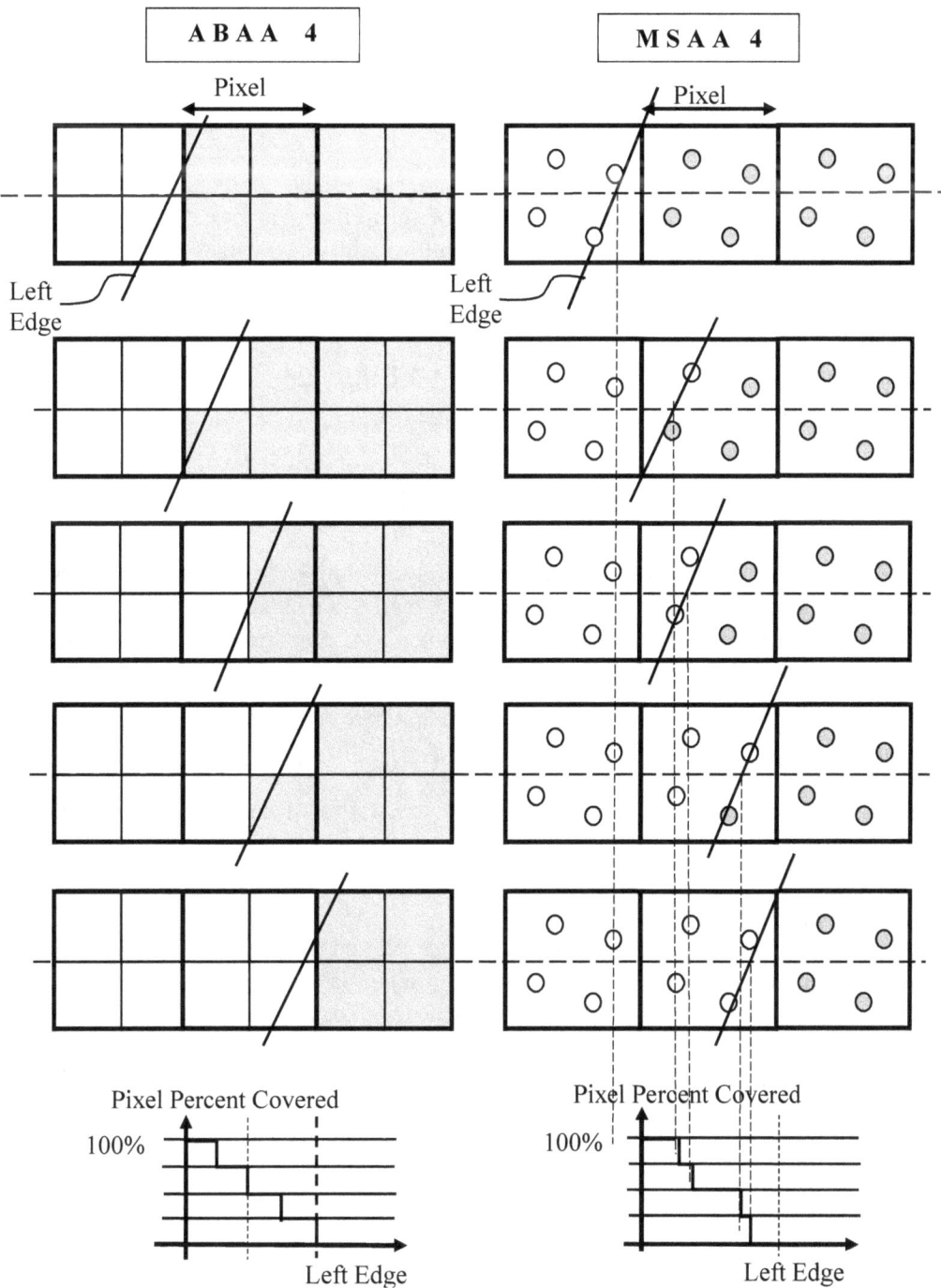

**Figure 8-5 ABAA vs MSAA: Moving edge across 4 Subpixels**

New Area-Based Anti-Aliasing for CGI

## 8.2 Example of ABAA4-X with Fans of Thin Triangles

These examples have been generated by a C-program.

In each figure there is a fan of 8 thin triangles. Each triangle is defined by 3 edges within an 8x8 Pixel Span.

It is not practical to show images with gray shades. When printed, the images can be easier to evaluate at first. But, because of the limitation of the printing process, the results can be inconclusive. Instead, the covered Subpixels are identified with a '*' character, or a face number, instead gray shades. This makes it is easier to evaluate and compare the ABAA vs MSAA approaches.

### 8.2.1 Comparison of ABAA vs MSAA with 4 Subpixels

*Test Results Displayed with Text instead of Graphical Images*

For the simulation results of Subpixels processing, the set of ASCII text characters have been selected to show square Pixels. The characters are displayed using the Courier text font, that there equal spacing between characters.

In order to make the Pixel output square, a 6x3 array of Subpixels is used for the printouts. The selection of Subpixels within the 6x3 is selected to represent their actual position as accurately as possible. The Subpixels within a Pixel are defined in a 6x4 'char' array, so that the Pixels look square.

For the simulation, the data structures used in the examples are described in the following listings.

For ABAA with 4 Subpixels, the 'Not-Covered and 'Covered' Pixels are defined as follows.

For ABAA 4, refer to Listing 8-1 for Subpixel Character Array for Printing with Courier fonts.

For MSAA 4, refer to Listing 8-2 for Subpixel Character Array for Printing with Courier fonts.

*Using Octal Format to Specify Test Cases*.

The size of Spans is 8x8 and the processed data for Pixel and Subpixels use fixed point binary numbers. For this reason, using a decimal format to input data was not convenient. Also, the subpixel count is 4 or 8, which can be easily represented with octal numbers.

It turned out to be easier and more convenient to specify the input for the test data using octal numbers, using a 12-bit format: 6 integer bits and 6 fractional bits.

The input data consist of ASCII text that is converted into octal using an interpreter.

## Listing 8-1 ABAA 4 Subpixel Character Array for Printing

```c
// ================================================================
// C Listing
// ================================================================
// ================================================================
// ABAA 4 Subpixels in 6x3 Char Array for Printing
//=================================================================
//#define SPix_ARRAY 16

// 6x3 char Array for Pix Not Covered
//=================================
char SPA_NC[3][16] = { "|.    .",
                       "|      ",
                       "|.    ." };

// 6x3 char Array for Pix Covered
char SPA_Cov[3][16]= { "|*    *",    // 0   1
                       "|  C   ",
                       "|*    *" }; // 2   3

// Position of 4 Subpixels in 4x4 array
//=====================================
int16 DistToVE[4] = { 0, 0, 3, 3 };   // S0, S1, S2, S3
int16 DistToHE[4] = { 0, 3, 0, 3 };   // S0, S1, S2, S3
```

## Listing 8-2 MSAA 4 Subpixel Character Array for Printing

```c
// ================================================================
// MSAA 4 Subpixel Sample Points in 4x4 array (Example for Nvidia)
// ================================================================
// |_0_1_2_3__| Horiz Dist to VE
// |   S0     | 1
// |       S1 | 3
// | S2       | 0
// |     S3   | 2
// |----------|
// | 2 0 3 1  | Vert Dist to HE
//
// 4x4 Array
int16 DistToVE[4] = { 1, 3, 0, 2 };   // S0, S1, S2, S3
int16 DisttoHE[4] = { 2, 0, 3, 1 };   // S0, S1, S2, S3


// ================================================================
// MSAA 4 Subpixels in 6x3 Char Array for Printing
// ================================================================
// 6x3 char Array for Pix Not Covered
char MS_NC[3][16] =
     { "| .    ",    // S0
       "|.    .",    // S2, S1
       "|    . " }; // S3

// 6x3 char Array for Pix Covered
char MS_Cov[3][16] =
     { "| *    ",    // S0
       "|* C *",    // S2, S1
       "|    * " }; // S3

// 4 SubPix Col and Row positions for VE and HE in 4x4 Subpixel Array
// 4 SubPix:        S0,S1,S2,S3
int16 DistToVE[4] = { 1, 3, 0, 2 };  // S0, S1, S2, S3
int16 DistToHE[4] = { 2, 0, 3, 1 };  // S0, S1, S2, S3

// ================================================================
```

## ABAA with 4 Subpixel Areas

### *Edge Definition for 8 Triangle-Fans*

In each of the 4 examples, the 8 thin triangles are organized in a fan-array.
The pairs of left and right edges are defined in Listing 8-3, 'Triangle Edges in Octal Format'.

## Listing 8-3 Triangle Edges in Octal Format for 8 Triangle-Fans

```
// Edge Oct Char Format: { EStrt[8], EEnd[8], ESlp[8], VE, BE }
// VE and HE Edges in Octal Format
// Edges are defined with 12 bits of Resolution:
// 6 bits for Pixel and 6 bits for Subpixels separated with Point Position.
// ======================================================================
// Fan Left A
// ==========
edgeasc_t FANLEFT0[] = // Fan starts on left side at 00.00
    //   Start      End      Slope>0 VE BE (Lft)  Start      End      Slope>0  VE !BE Rgt)
    { {"00.00", "00.00", "00.00", 1, 1 }, {"00.00", "01.00", "00.10", 1, 0 },  // VE Lft Down
      {"00.00", "02.00", "00.20", 1, 1 }, {"00.00", "03.00", "00.30", 1, 0 },  //  |\
      {"00.00", "04.00", "00.40", 1, 1 }, {"00.00", "05.00", "00.50", 1, 0 },
      {"00.00", "06.00", "00.60", 1, 1 }, {"00.00", "07.00", "00.70", 1, 0 },
    //   Start      End      Slope>0 HE BE(Top)  Start      End      Slope>0 HE !BE(Bot)
      {"00.00", "06.00", "00.60", 0, 1 }, {"00.00", "07.00", "00.70", 0, 0 },  // HE Lft to Rgt
      {"00.00", "04.00", "00.40", 0, 1 }, {"00.00", "05.00", "00.50", 0, 0 },  // =<
      {"00.00", "02.00", "00.20", 0, 1 }, {"00.00", "03.00", "00.30", 0, 0 },
      {"00.00", "00.00", "00.00", 0, 1 }, {"00.00", "01.00", "00.10", 0, 0 } };

// Fan Left B
// ==========
edgeasc_t FANLEFT1[] = // Fan starts on left side at 00.00
    //   Start      End      Slope>0 VE BE (Lft)  Start      End      Slope>0  VE !BE Rgt)
    { {"00.00", "01.00", "00.10", 1, 1 }, {"00.00", "02.00", "00.20", 1, 0 },  // VE Lft Down
      {"00.00", "03.00", "00.30", 1, 1 }, {"00.00", "04.00", "00.40", 1, 0 },  //  |\
      {"00.00", "05.00", "00.50", 1, 1 }, {"00.00", "06.00", "00.60", 1, 0 },
      {"00.00", "07.00", "00.70", 1, 1 }, {"00.00", "07.70", "00.77", 1, 0 },
    //   Start      End      Slope>0 HE BE(Top)  Start      End      Slope>0 HE !BE(Bot)
      {"00.00", "07.00", "00.70", 0, 1 }, {"00.00", "10.00", "01.00", 0, 0 },  // Start 00.00,00.00
      {"00.00", "05.00", "00.50", 0, 1 }, {"00.00", "06.00", "00.60", 0, 0 },  // -<
      {"00.00", "03.00", "00.30", 0, 1 }, {"00.00", "04.00", "00.40", 0, 0 },  // HE Left to Right
      {"00.00", "01.00", "00.10", 0, 1 }, {"00.00", "02.00", "00.20", 0, 0 } };

// Fan Right A
// ===========
edgeasc_t FANRIGHT0[] = // Fan starts on right side at 10.00
    //   Start      End      Slope<0 VE BE (Lft)  Start      End      Slope<=0 VE !BE Rgt)
    { {"10.00", "07.00", "77.70", 1, 1 }, {"10.00", "10.00", "00.00", 1, 0 },  // VE Rgt to Down
      {"10.00", "05.00", "77.50", 1, 1 }, {"10.00", "06.00", "77.60", 1, 0 },  //  |/
      {"10.00", "03.00", "77.30", 1, 1 }, {"10.00", "04.00", "77.40", 1, 0 },
      {"10.00", "01.00", "77.10", 1, 1 }, {"10.00", "02.00", "77.20", 1, 0 },
    //   Start      End      Slope<0 HE BE(Top) Start      End      Slope<0  HE !BE(Bot)
      {"06.00", "00.00", "77.20", 0, 1 }, {"07.00", "00.00", "77.10", 0, 0 },  // Lft 6 to Rgt 0
      {"04.00", "00.00", "77.40", 0, 1 }, {"05.00", "00.00", "77.30", 0, 0 },  // >-
      {"02.00", "00.00", "77.60", 0, 1 }, {"03.00", "00.00", "77.50", 0, 0 },  //
      {"00.00", "00.00", "00.00", 0, 1 }, {"01.00", "00.00", "77.70", 0, 0 } };// HE horizontal

// Fan Right B
// ===========
edgeasc_t FANRIGHT1[] = // Fan starts on right side at 10.00
    //   Start      End      Slope<0 VE BE (Lft)  Start      End      Slope<0  VE !BE Rgt)
    { {"10.00", "06.00", "77.60", 1, 1 }, {"10.00", "07.00", "77.70", 1, 0 },  // Start Rgt to Down
      {"10.00", "04.00", "77.40", 1, 1 }, {"10.00", "05.00", "77.50", 1, 0 },  //  |/
      {"10.00", "02.00", "77.20", 1, 1 }, {"10.00", "03.00", "77.30", 1, 0 },  //
      {"10.00", "00.00", "77.00", 1, 1 }, {"10.00", "01.00", "77.10", 1, 0 },
    //   Start      End      Slope<0 HE BE(Top) Start      End      Slope<0  HE !BE(Bot)
      {"07.00", "00.00", "77.10", 0, 1 }, {"07.70", "00.00", "77.01", 0, 0 },  // Lft 7 to Rgt 0
      {"05.00", "00.00", "77.30", 0, 1 }, {"06.00", "00.00", "77.20", 0, 0 },  // >-
      {"03.00", "00.00", "77.50", 0, 1 }, {"04.00", "00.00", "77.40", 0, 0 },  //
      {"01.00", "00.00", "77.70", 0, 1 }, {"02.00", "00.00", "77.60", 0, 0 } };// HE horizontal
// ======================================================================
```

## 8.2.2 Comparison of ABAA vs MSAA with 4 Subpixels

The algorithms used for Subpixel processing can be evaluated by using thin triangles, of size approximately 8 Pixels long and 1 Pixel wide at the base. The test uses groups of 8 such triangles organize into fans spreading over an angle of Pi/2 (90 degrees).

*Test Cases Consisting of 8 Narrow Triangle Fans*

For the comparison of ABAA with MSAA, the test cases consist of 8 thin triangles organized as a fan displayed across a Span of size 8x8 Pixels. In each fan, there are four triangles (a, b, c & d) with vertical edges eight SL long (*VE*) and four triangles (e, f, g & h) with horizontal edges eight Pixel long (*HE*). The triangle bases are roughly 1 Pixel wide.

Since the triangle tops are 0 Pixel wide and the bottoms are 1 Pixel wide, the number of Subpixel increments per Pixel from top to bottom of triangle is expected to be 1/8 Pixels. In the case of 4 Subpixels, there should be 8 increments of ½ Subpixel. There are only 4 incremental steps of size 1/4 within a Pixel. Each number of Subpixels is repeated so that the triangle width is near 0 at the top and near 4 Subpixels at the base, after 7 half Subpixel increments.

*Four Test Cases with 8 Narrow Triangle Fans*

Four cases of 8 thin triangle fans have been selected. They cover a wide range of cases: Even (A) and Odd (B) triangles. The cases are also mirrored into Pos and Neg edges.

Since there are gaps between the 8 triangles, the tests are organized into 2 sets A and B. In set A, there are 8 thin triangles with edges ranging from 0 to 90 degrees. In set B, there are also 8 thin triangles consisting of the gaps between the triangles of set A. Also, there are cases for Pos and Neg Edges. In all, there are 4 test cases.

The Four Fan examples are shown in 4 figures as follows:

Figure 8-6, ABAA 4 vs MSAA 4 for Pos Edges A

Figure 8-7, ABAA 4 vs MSAA 4 for Pos Edges B

Figure 8-8, ABAA 4 vs MSAA 4 for Neg Edges A

Figure 8-9, ABAA 4 vs MSAA 4 for Neg Edges B

ABAA with 4 Subpixel Areas

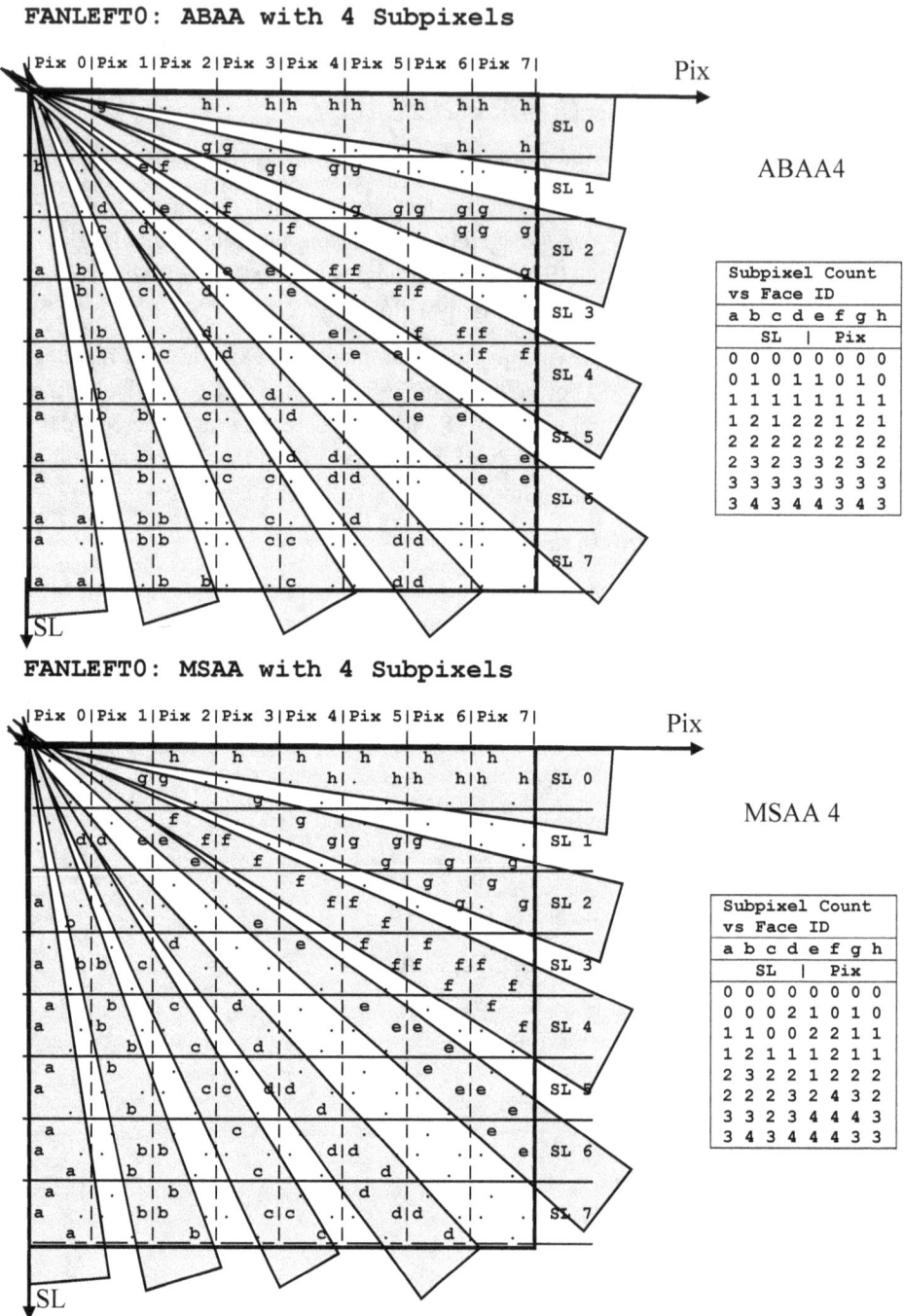

Figure 8-6 ABAA 4 vs MSAA 4 for Pos Edges A

# ABAA with 4 Subpixel Areas

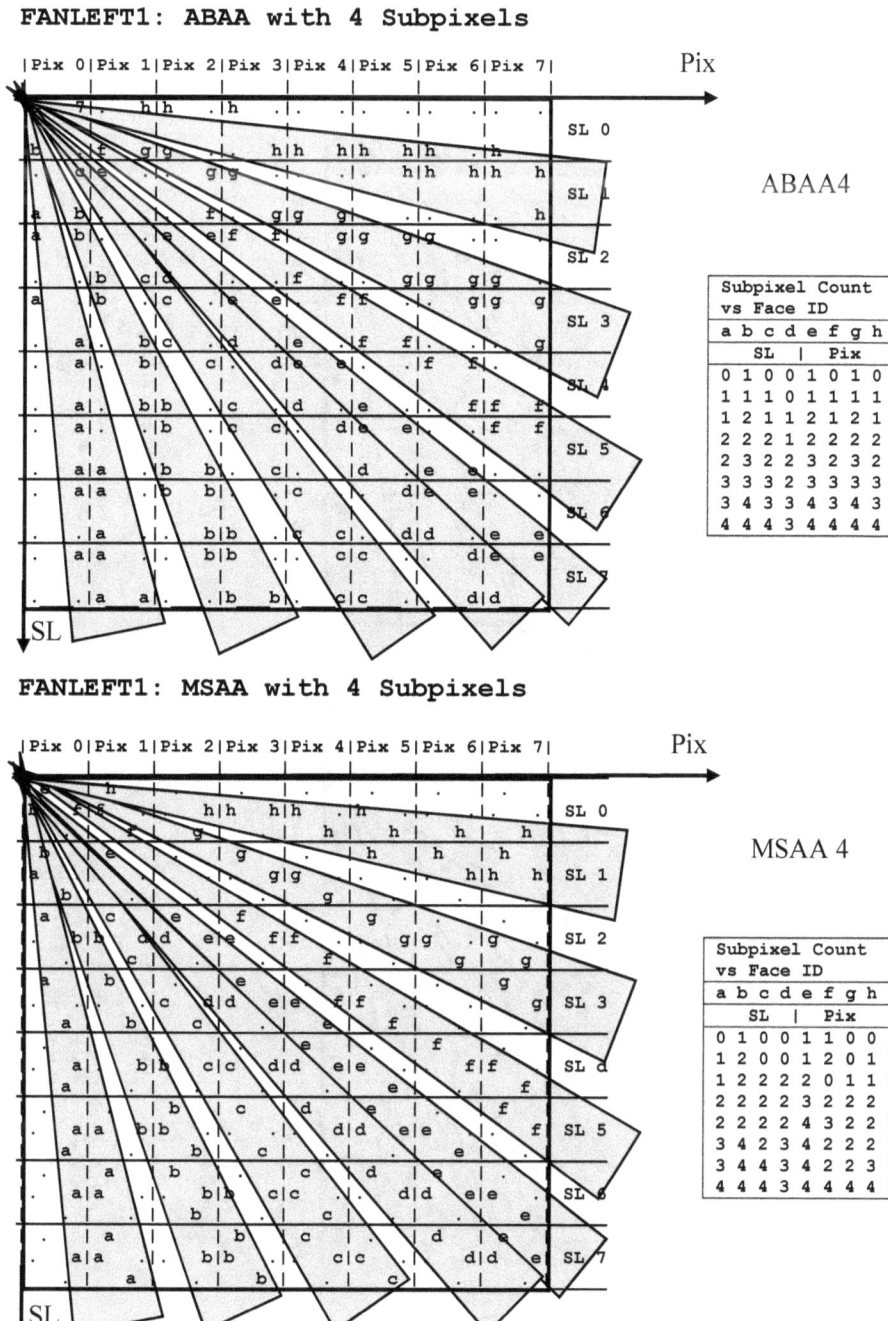

**Figure 8-7 ABAA 4 vs MSAA 4 for Pos Edges B**

## ABAA with 4 Subpixel Areas

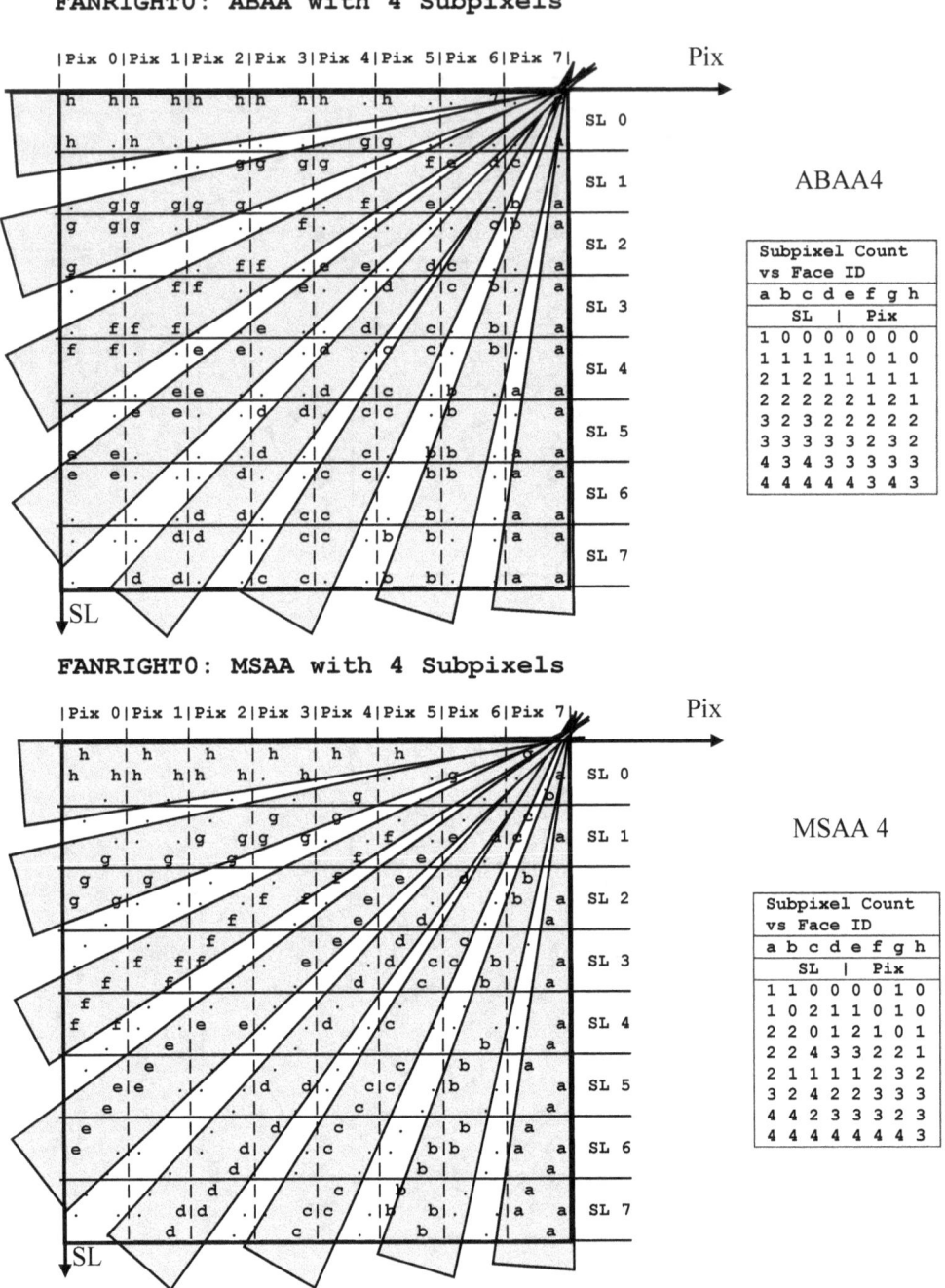

**Figure 8-8 ABAA 4 vs MSAA 4 for Neg Edges A**

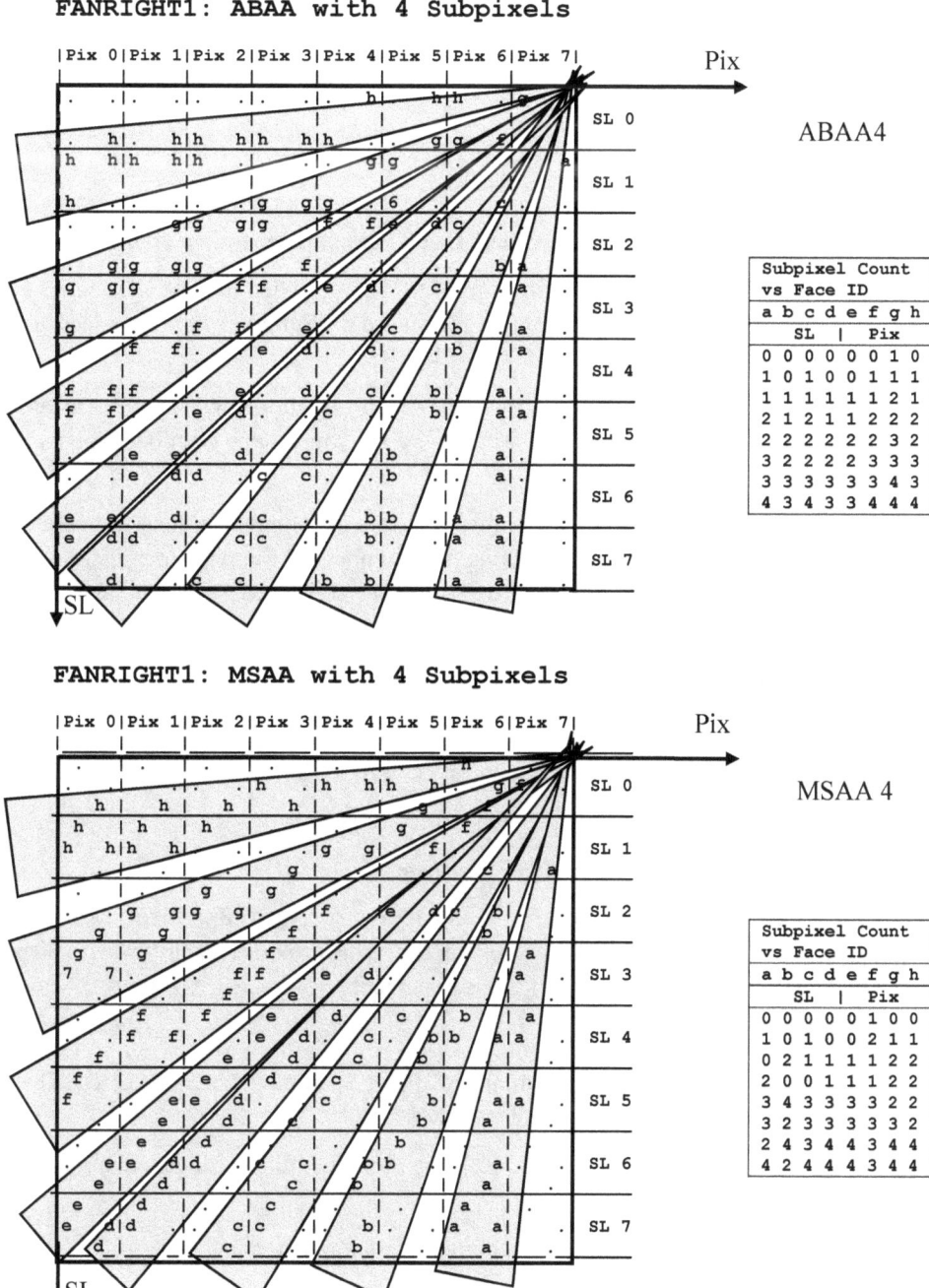

**Figure 8-9 ABAA 4 vs MSAA 4 for Neg Edges B**

### Results for ABAA

In most cases, with ABAA, the increments are:
0, 0, 1, 1, 2, 2, 3, 3, or
0, 1, 1, 2, 2, 3, 3, 4, or
1, 1, 2, 2, 3, 3, 4, 4

### Results for MSAA

For MSAA, some triangles are smoothly rendered, other are not, depending on the orientation.

Some Good: For MSAA, the increments are similar to ABAA, when the triangles edges are near Vertical (face a) or near Horizontal (face h). This is because the Subpixels are positioned according to the 4 Queen algorithm.

Some Bad: For other edge orientations, the increments are not constants. There are many increments of 2. There is also 'hesitation', when there are some steps with decrements (reverse count).

The results of Subpixel count per Pixel are shown in 4 sets of figures, for the 4 test cases. Beside the fan figures there are small tables showing the number of Subpixel per increments. The simulation results for ABAA and MSAA are shown and compared. The summary tables are explained in Figure 8-10.

### Counting the Subpixels

When estimating the number of Subpixels per Pixel, there are 2cases:

For *VE* (faces a to d), the Subpixels are counted for each SL.

For *HE* (faces e to h), the Subpixels are counted for each Pix.

### Results of Simulation Displayed with ASCII Characters

In order to make the computer output easy to read and to display, the 8x8 Pixels Span-Grids and the Subpixels are displayed using ASCII text characters. This provides an easy way to display the results and include valuable information into this document.

### Summary of Results

Four Cases of Thin Triangle Fans' inside of an 8x8 Pixel Span have been presented. The results are summarized in 8 tables, 4 for ABAA and 4 for MSAA.

The results from the 4 test cases with 4 Subpixels are combined into a single figure, as shown in Figure 8-11.

By comparing the ABAA 4 and MSAA 4 columns, is should be clear that ABAA 4 is vastly superior to MSAA 4.

ABAA with 4 Subpixel Areas

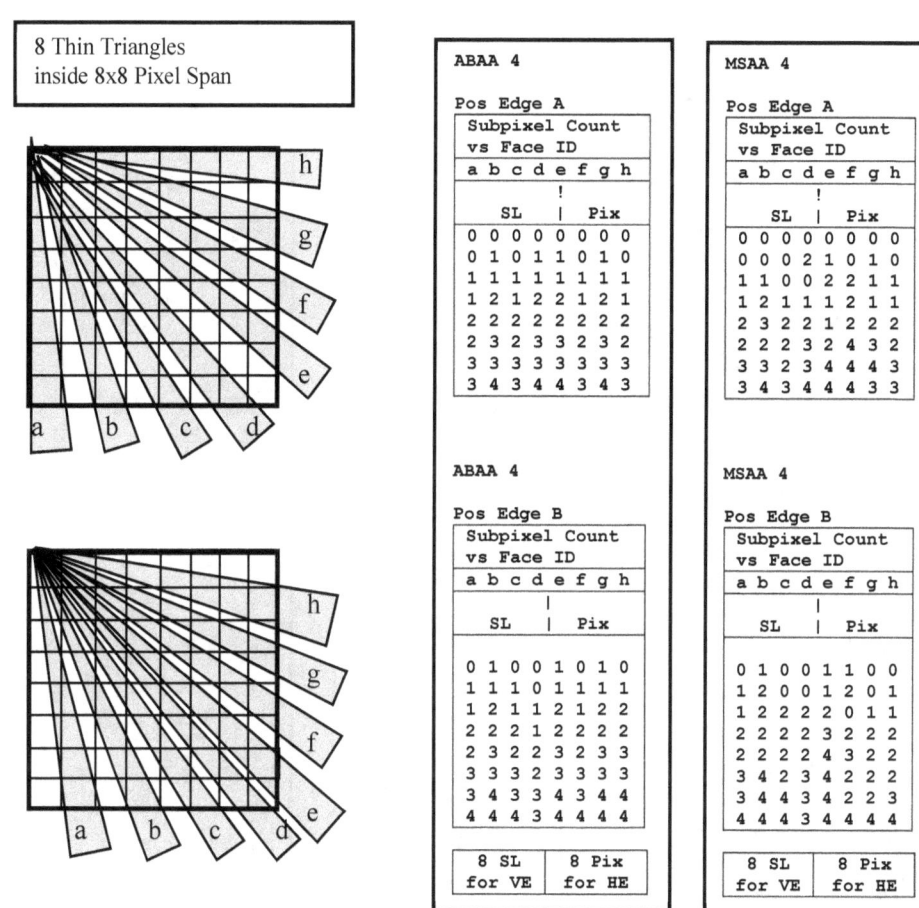

Figure 8-10 Description of the Summary Tables

ABAA with 4 Subpixel Areas

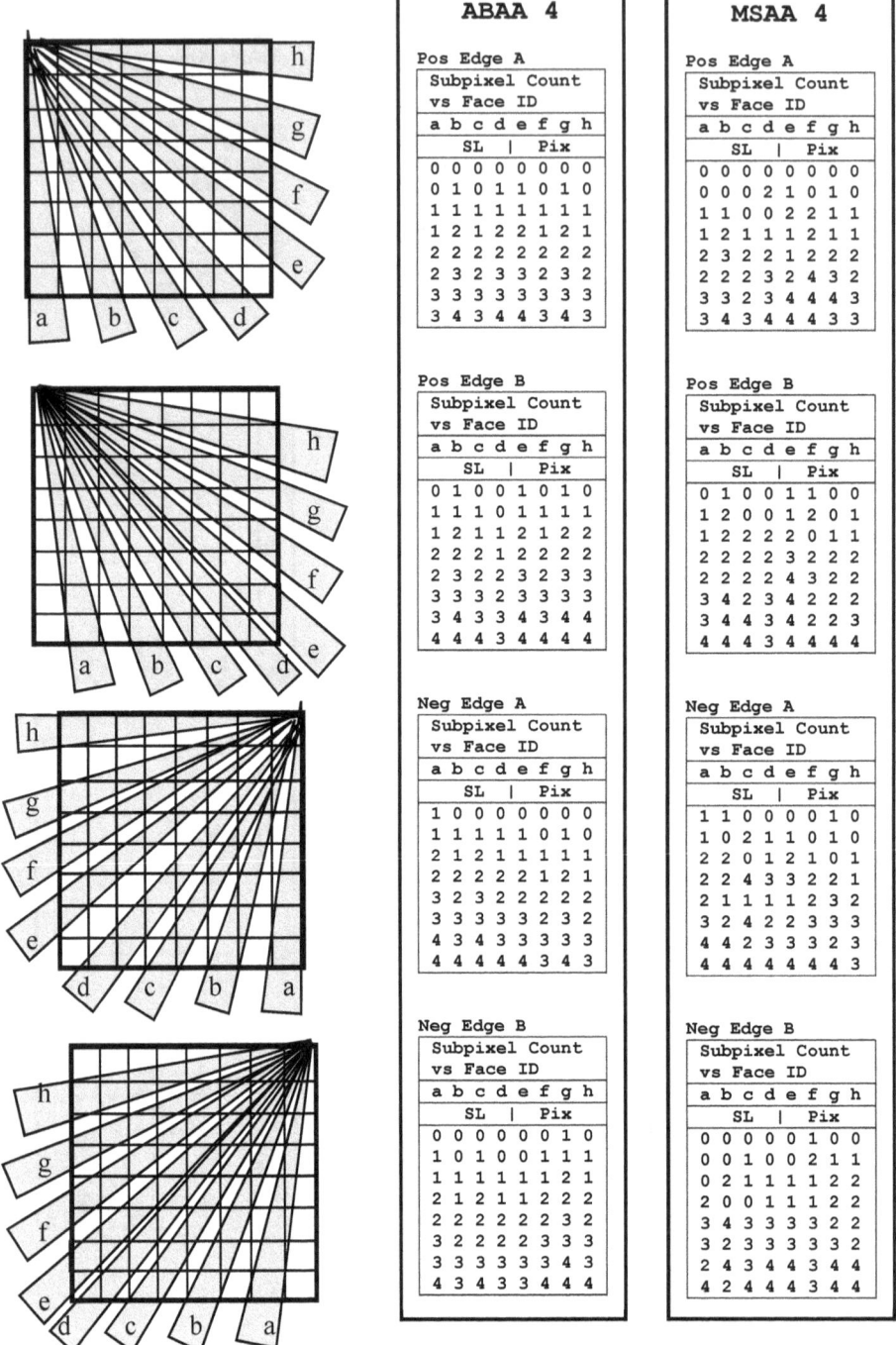

**Figure 8-11 Summary of Results for 4 Examples with 4 Subpixels**

## 8.3 Combined Examples of ABAA4 vs MSAA4

All the examples presented in this Chapter, consist of static images. It would be nice, if the ABAA vs ABAA implementation could be compared dynamically with moving images. In this book, the best I could provide is several sequences of narrow triangles organized as fans. This provides a wide range of cases. In the previous sections, there were 4 examples of narrow triangles sequences organized as fans within an 8x8 Pixel span.

For the fans that start on top left of span (Examples 1 & 2 with positive slopes), the 2 sets of 8 triangles can be combined into a single table using even and odd triangle sequences.

For the fans that start on top right of span (Examples 3 & 4 with negative slopes), the 2 sets of 8 triangles can be combined into a single table using even and odd triangle sequences.

When each pair of examples is considered, there are 16 adjacent triangles covering an angular range of Pi/2, that is Pi/32 (or 3 degrees) per triangle.

### *Static Images with 4 Subpixels*

Examples 1 & 2 (fan starts on top left) consists of 8 pairs of complementary triangles with positive edge slopes. The results can be combined as shown in Figure 8-12.

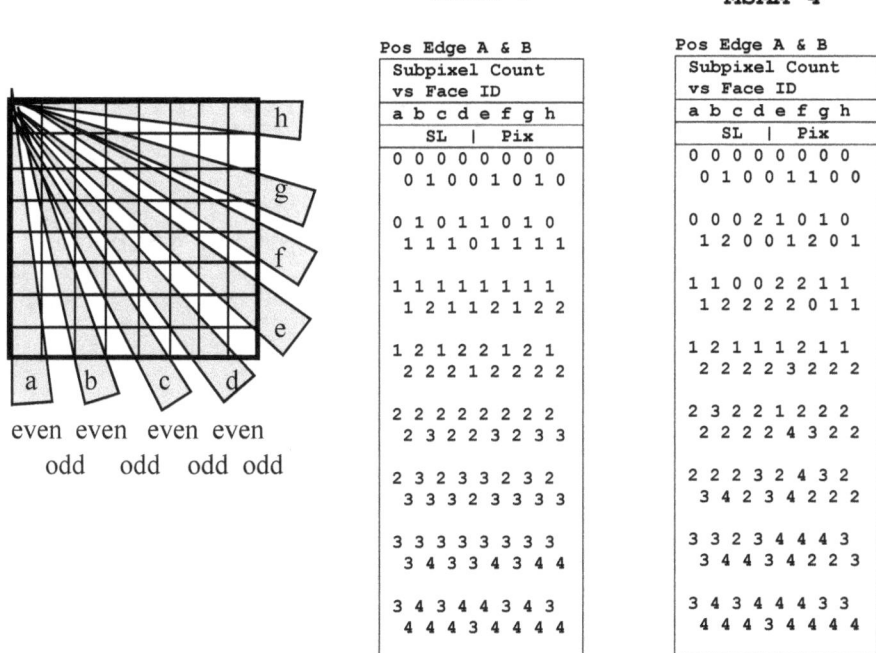

Figure 8-12 Fan of 16 Triangles with Pos Edge Slopes and 4 Subpixels

## ABAA with 4 Subpixel Areas

Examples 3 & 4 (fan starts on top right) consists of 8 pairs of complementary triangles with negative edge slopes. The results can be combined as shown in Figure 8-13.

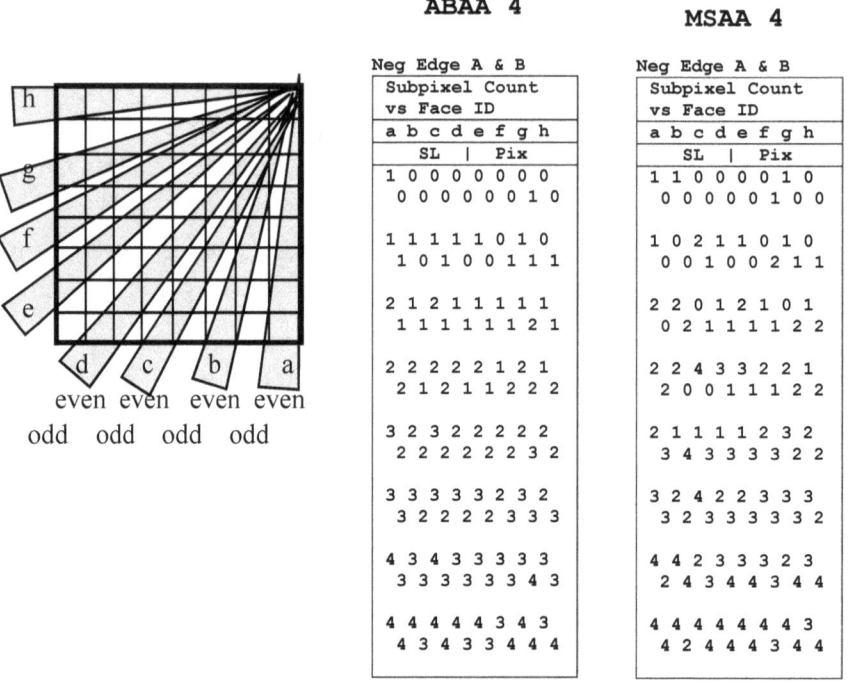

Figure 8-13 Fan of 16 Triangles with Neg Edge Slopes and 4 Subpixels

# Chapter 9 **ABAA with 8 Subpixel Areas**

The implementation of ABAA with 8 Subpixel Areas is a little more involved than the 4 Subpixel solution. It is derived from the 4 Subpixel solution by dividing the subpixels square areas by 2 along the 2 Pixel diagonals. In order to handle the additional cases, the slope size is used to create 2 Subpixel sequences. A slope flag, $S1$ (and $S0 = !S1$), is introduced to indicate when the slope size is greater than 0.5.

Note, that it is not necessary to indicate greater or equal (>=), since the slopes are truncated fixed point numbers, where the truncated portion is unknown. For this reason, the '>' symbol will be used to indicate '>='.

The binary format for the slope inside of a Pixel is: $Slp = (s)s.bbbb$.
$Slp$ can be expressed in decimal or binary notation.
Decimal notation:   $-1.0 < S1 < -0.5 < S0 < 0.0 < S0 < 0.5 < S1 < 1.0$
Binary notation:   $(1)1.0000 < S1 < 1.1000 < S0 < 0.0000 < S0 < 0.1000 < S1 < (0)1.0000$

## 9.1 ABAA8-X Solution with 8 Half-Square Subpixel Areas

The Pixel covered area is determined by the edge distance, $d$, on the Pixel $MidLn$. The distance is obtained with only one measurement. Using 4 fractional bits resolution, the maximum error will be:   $e = 1/16$

Refer to Example in Figure 9-1, for a Negative $VE$.

The 8 Subpixel transitions are identified according to 3 edge Flags.
- Edge Slope Flag:      $S0$, when $|Slp| < 0.5$; $S1$, when $|Slp| > 0.5$
- Edge orientation Flag: $VE$ vs $HE$
- Edge Polarity Flag:    $Pos$ vs $Neg$
- Edge beginning/ending flag: $BE$ vs $!BE$

The $BE$ flag is used to invert the Subpixel active flags when $BE==0$..

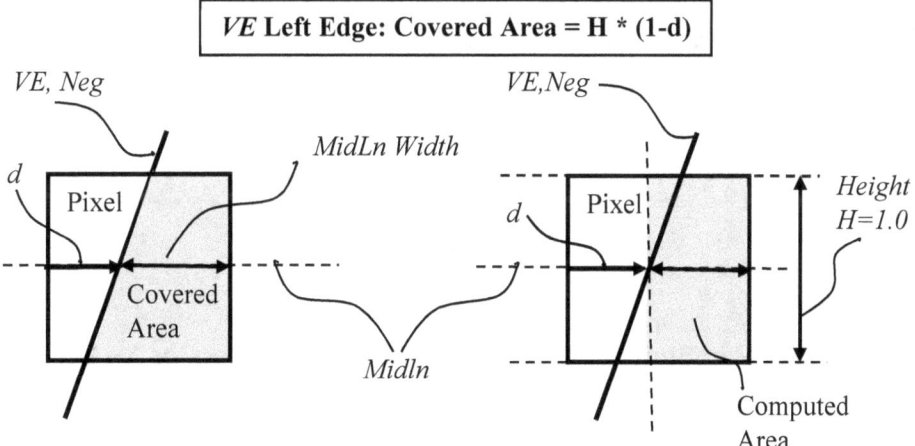

**Figure 9-1 Example of Pixel Covered Area Computation for Negative *VE***

# ABAA with 8 Subpixel Areas

## Pixel Map for 8 Subpixels

In Figure 9-2, the 8 Subpixel solution is represented in a Pixel-Map. This Map describes the 8 edge cases with their corresponding Subpixel sequences.

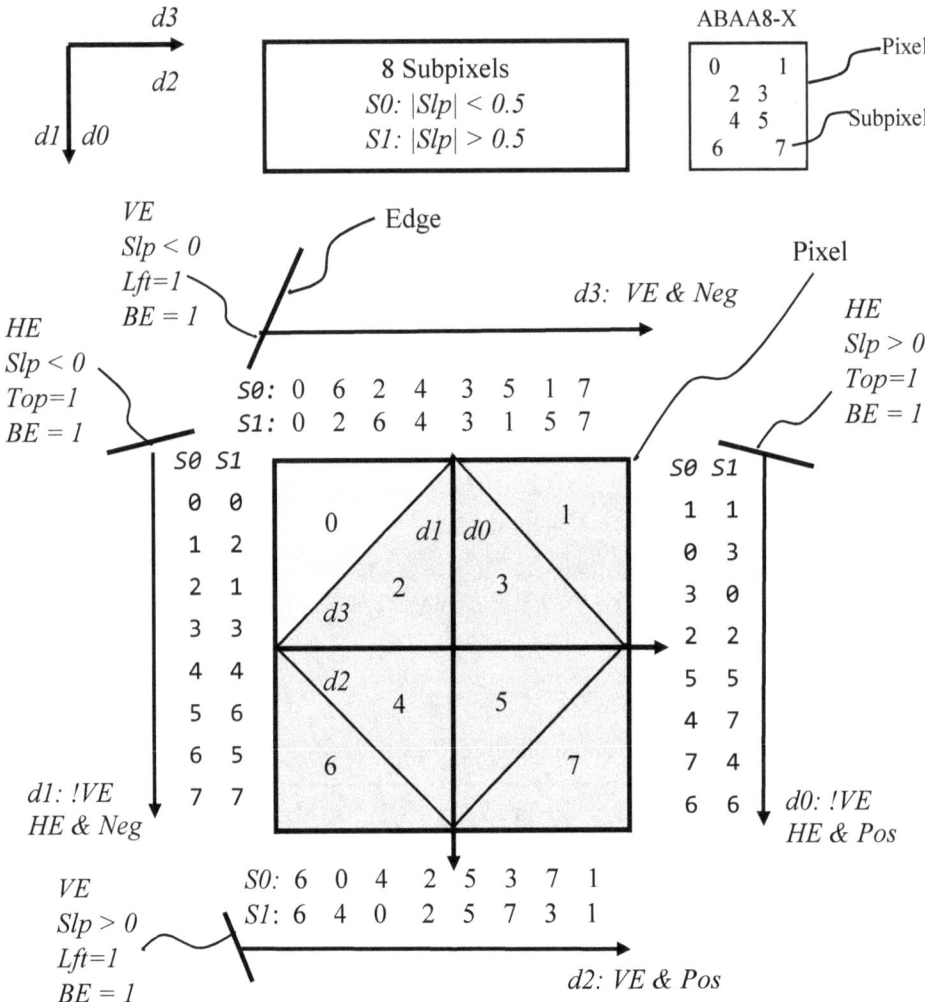

**Figure 9-2 Pixel Map Showing 8 Cases of Subpixel Mapping for ABAA8-X**

## Flowchart for 8 Subpixel Decoding

The decoding for the Subpixel sequences is described in the flowchart in Figure 9-3. The Subpixel sequences can be stored in a table located in local memory or other storage.

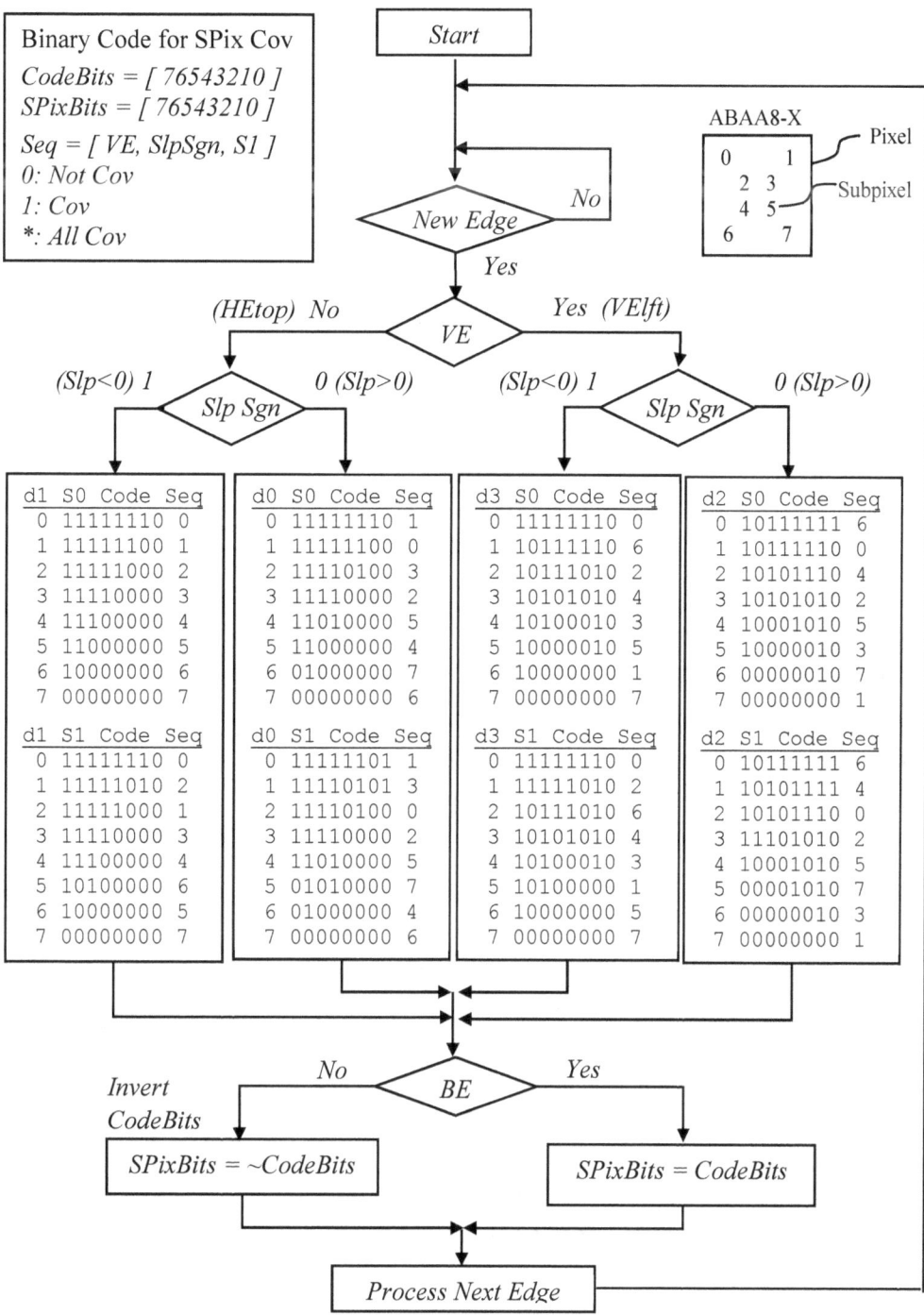

**Figure 9-3 Flowchart to Decode Subpixel Mapping for ABAA8-X**

# ABAA with 8 Subpixel Areas

This flowchart describes the processing of triangle edges for ABAA8-X. For each edge, the Subpixel sequence of active Subpixels is detected according to 3 Edge Flags. The 8 Subpixel sequences indicate which Subpixel areas are turned on according to these flags.

The first tested flag is *VE* vs *HE*.

The next tested Flag is the edge polarity according to the slope sign (Slp Sgn): $Slp<0$ vs $Slp > 0$.

The 3$^{rd}$ flag is the slope size flag, *S1* vs *S0*. One Subpixel sequence is selected according to the slope size flag (*S0* or *S1*) and the edge distances (*d0, d1, d2* and *d3*) inside the Pixel boundaries along the *MidLn*. The edge distances are selected according to 2 flags: *VE, Slp Sgn*.

The Subpixel sequences are presented for beginning edges, that is $BE == 1$.

The fourth tested flag is the beginning edge flag *(BE* vs *!BE)*. For ending edges, the Subpixel active flags (*CodeBits*) in the table have to be inverted.

## Esge Slope Size S1 vs S0

The 2 cases of Slope Size flags, *S0* vs *S1*, are illustrated in 2 examples. This Slope Size flag is needed to compensate for the 1/8 Pixel area portion outside of the left/top side of the trapezoid, when $|Slp|>0.5$.

In Figure 9-4 there are 2 examples of Slope transition at $|Slp|=0.5$ and $|Slp|=1.0$, with $d=0.0$.

The case of $|Slp|==1.0$ is the transition case when edges transition between *VE* and *HE* types.

## ABAA Examples with 8 Subpixels

There are 2 similar figures that illustrate the 8 steps of *BE* edges moving across 8 Subpixels within a Pixel: one with $|Slp|<0.5$ *(Flag S0)*, one with $|Slp|>0.5$ *(Flag S1)*.

In Figure 9-5 ABAA: 4 Cases of Edge Moving Across 8 Subpixels (*S0:* $|Slp|<0.5$)

In Figure 9-6 ABAA: 4 Cases of Edge Moving Across 8 Subpixels (*S1:* $|Slp|>0.5$)

In these examples, the edges are shown with a rectangle. For each edge case, the rectangle represents the range of edge positions that define the same Subpixel area.

## Detect "Inside" and 'Outside" Areas Defined by Edges

In the flowchart used for determining Subpixel areas sequences, the *BE* flag is tested to detect if the processed edge is a starting or an ending edge.

When $BE==1$, it is a starting edge and the Subpixel bit sequence indicates which Subpixels are turned on.

When $BE==0$, it is an ending edge and the Subpixel bit sequence indicates which Subpixels are turned off. The Subpixel sequence has to be inverted.

## Example of BE and !BE Edges According to VE and HE Flags

In Figure 9-7, 'Tile Intersected by Vertical Edge (*VE*)', Shows the decoding of the BE flag, and examples of "Inside" and 'Outside" areas defined by *VE* edges

In Figure 9-8, 'Tile Intersected by Horizontal Edge (*HE*)', shows the decoding of the BE flag, and examples of "Inside" and 'Outside" areas defined by *HE* edges.

## Comparison of ABAA vs MSAA for 8 Subpixels

As examples for ABAA vs MSAA comparison, an edge moving across a pixel is shown for a beginning edge (VE, *BE*) moving across a Pixel.

In Figure 9-9 ABAA vs MSAA: Compare Moving Edge Across 8 Subpixels.

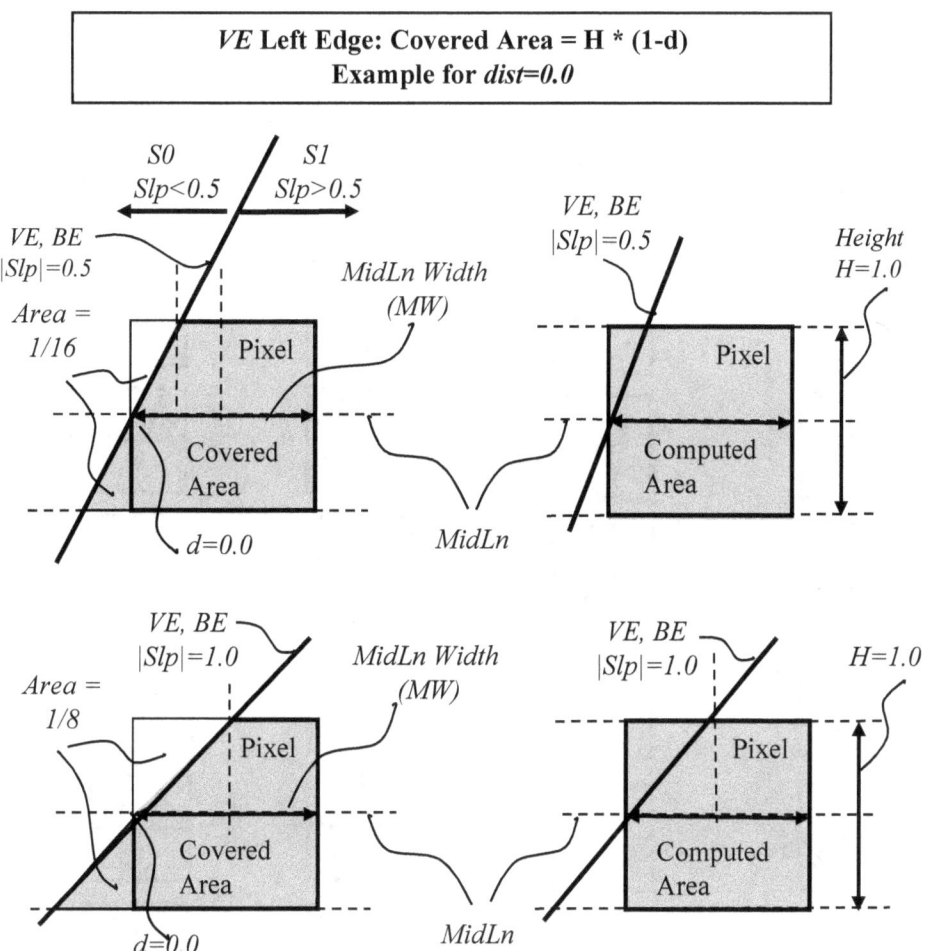

**Figure 9-4 Example of Slope Transition from *S0* to *S1* for *dist=0.0***

ABAA with 8 Subpixel Areas

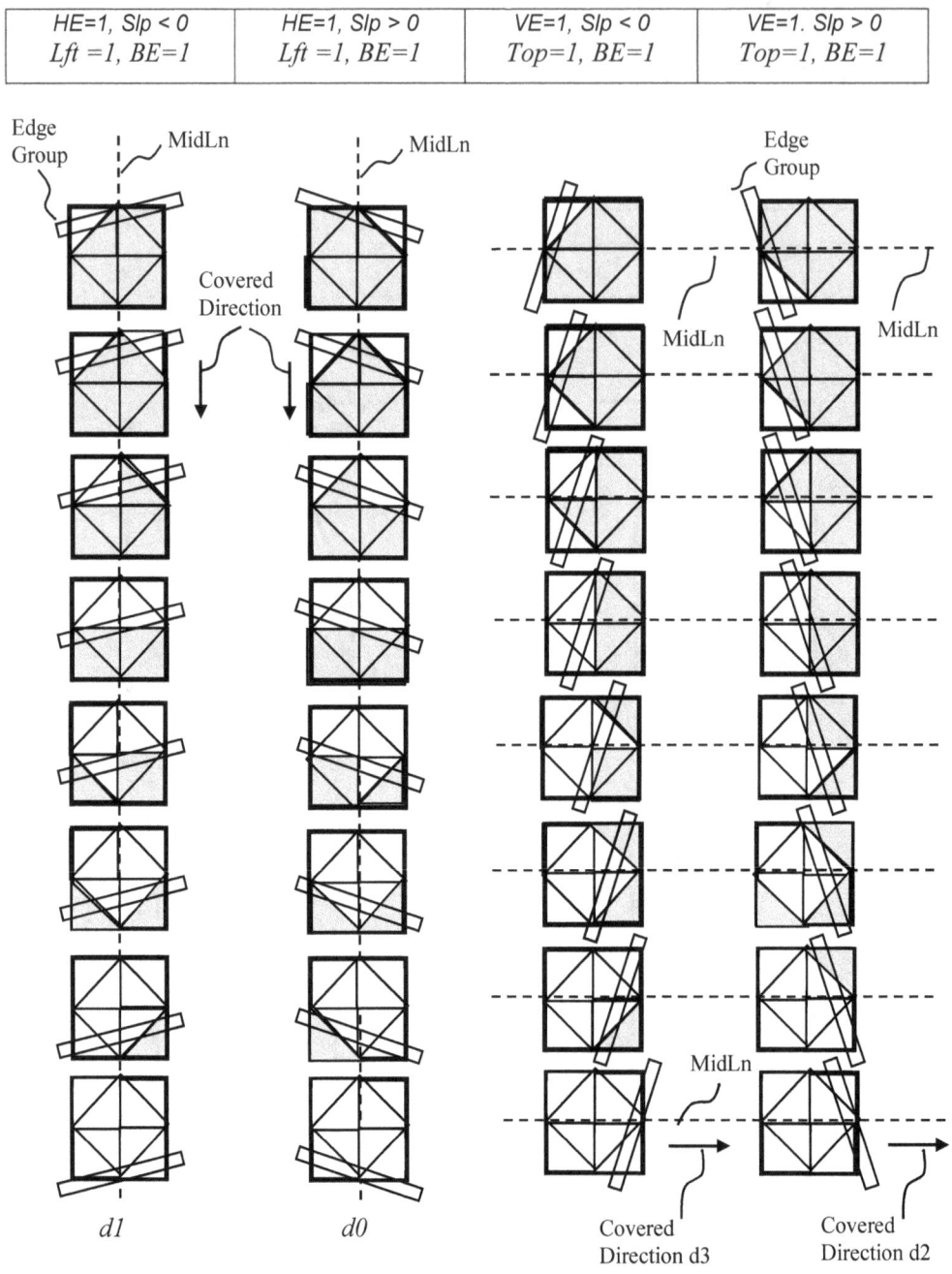

**Figure 9-5 ABAA8-X: 4 Cases of Edge Moving Across 8 Subpixels ($S0: |Slp|<0.5$)**

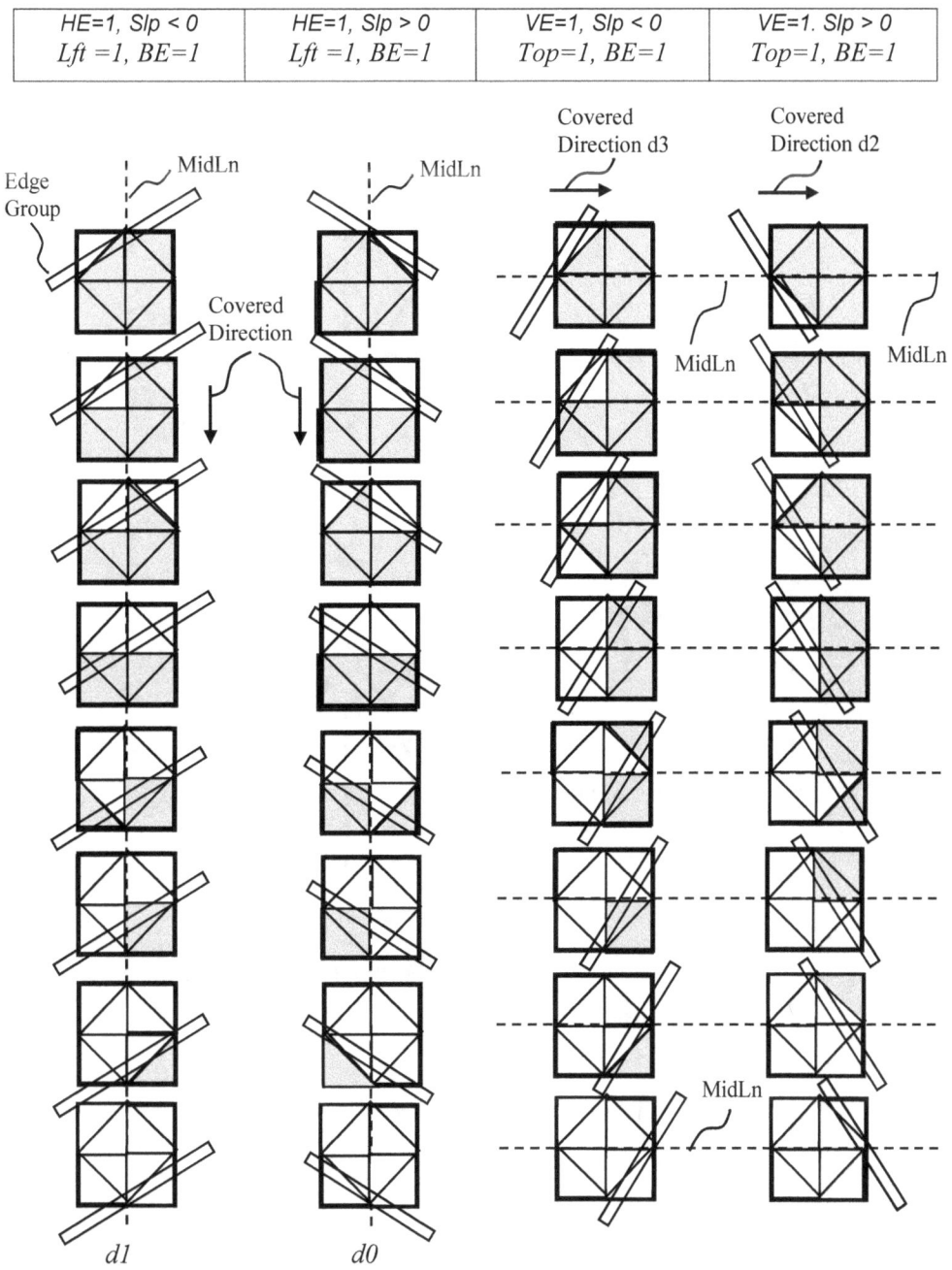

**Figure 9-6 ABAA8-X: 4 Cases of Edge Moving Across 8 Subpixels (*S1:* |*Slp*|>0.5)**

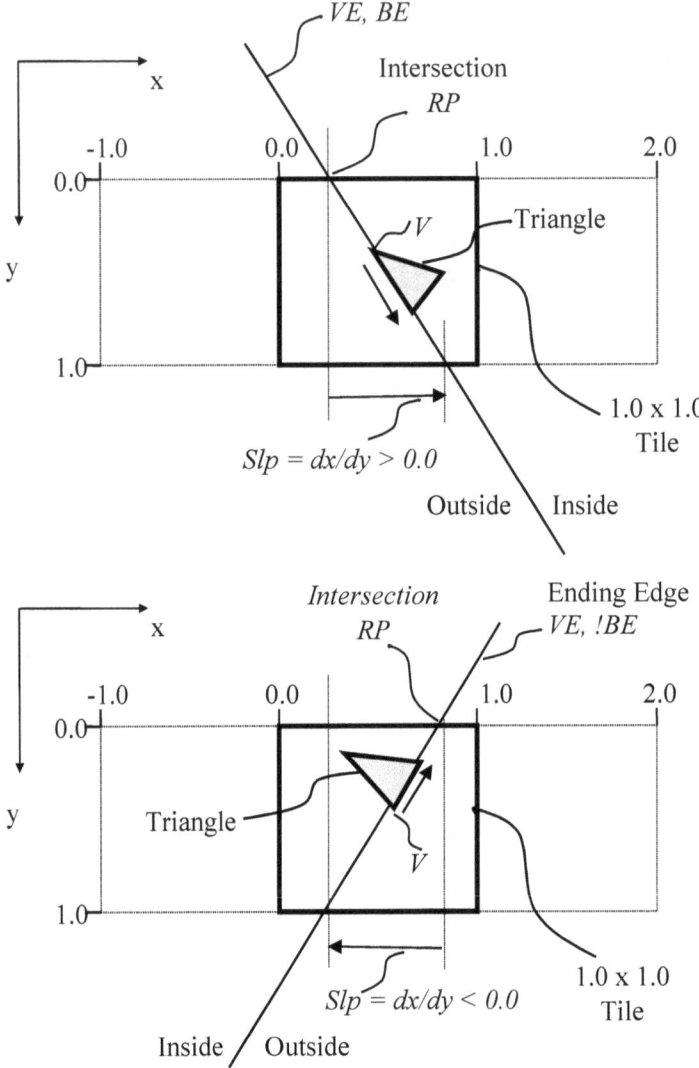

**Figure 9-7 Tile Intersected by Vertical Edge (VE)**

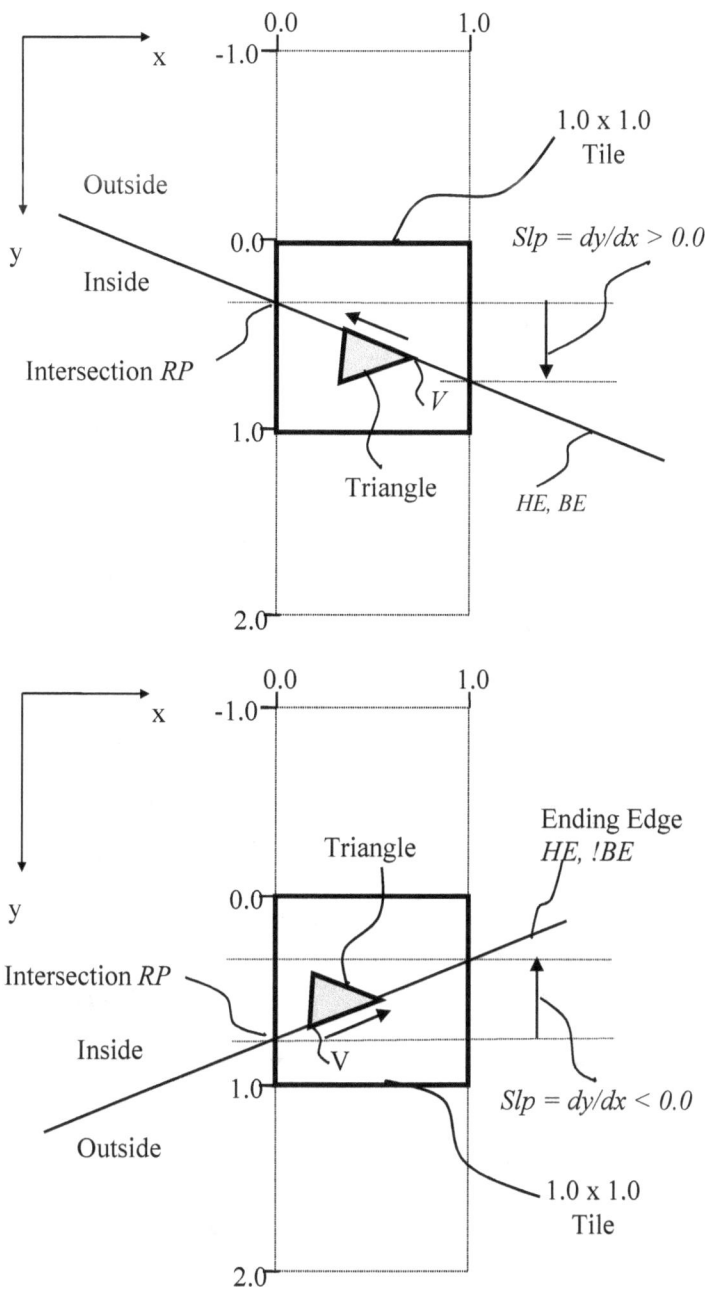

**Figure 9-8 Tile Intersected by Horizontal Edge (*HE*)**

# ABAA with 8 Subpixel Areas

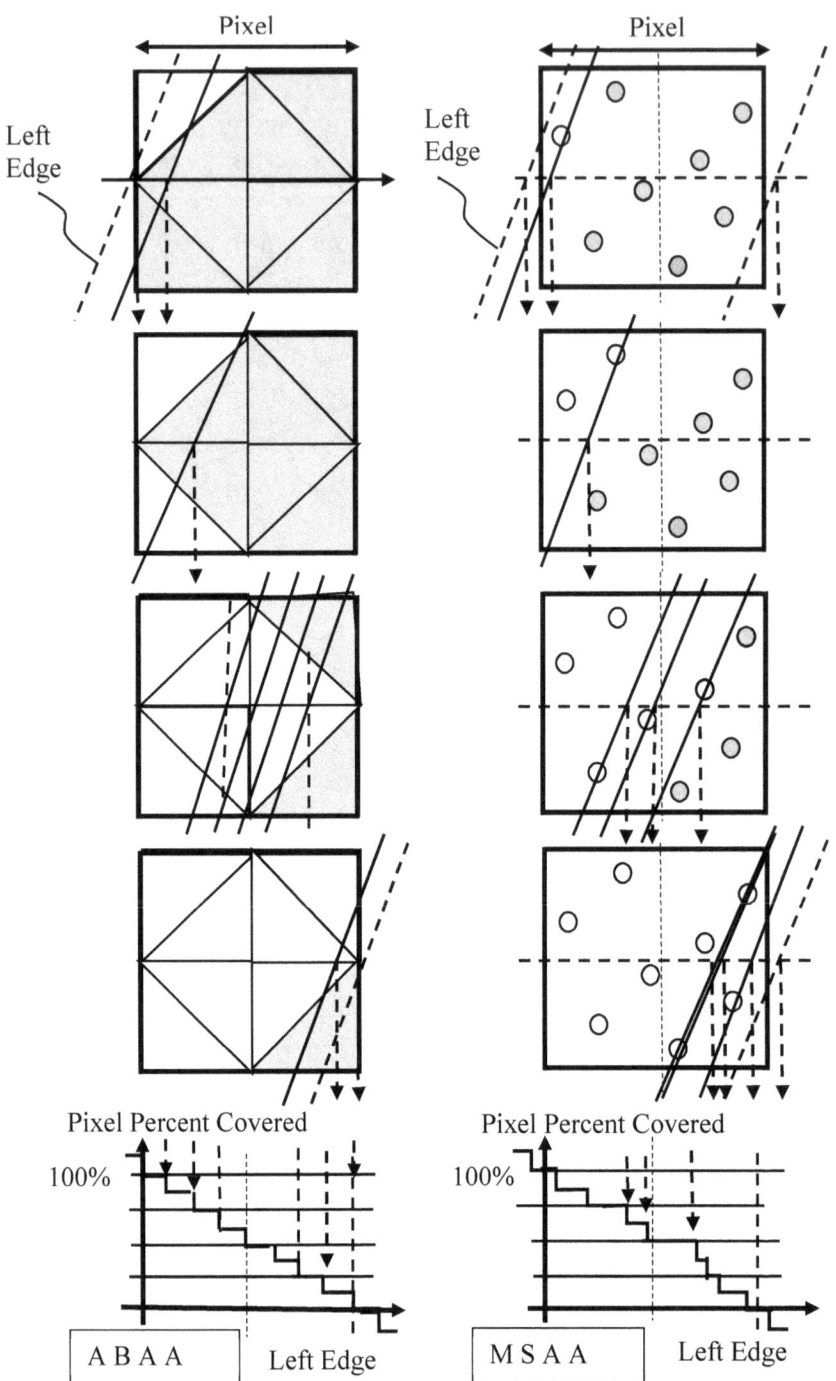

**Figure 9-9 ABAA vs MSAA: Edge Moving Across 8 Subpixels**

## 9.2 Comparison of ABAA8 vs MSAA8

For the comparison of ABAA with MSAA, using 8 Subpixels, the same approach as was used for 4 Subpixels is used here. The examples consist of the same test case with 4 fans with 8 thin triangles each.

### 9.2.1 Thin Triangles Processed with 8 Subpixels

These examples have been generated by a C-program.

In each figure there is a fan of 8 thin triangles. Each triangle is defined by 3 edges within an 8x8 Pixel Span.

It is not practical to show images with gray shades. When printed, the images can be easier to evaluate at first. But, because of the limitation of the printing process, the results can be inconclusive. Instead, the covered Subpixels are identified with a '*' character, or a face number, instead gray shades. This makes it is easier to evaluate and compare the ABAA vs MSAA approaches.

### 9.2.2 Four Examples of ABAA8 vs MSAA8 with Tri-Fans

For each of the 4 examples, 8 thin triangles are organized in a fan-array. The pairs of left and right edges are the same as in the example with 4 Subpixels. In each fan, four triangles have vertical edges (a, b, c & d with VE) and four triangles have horizontal edges (e, f, g & h with *HE*).

The 4 Fan examples are shown in 4 figures as follows:
Figure 9-10, ABAA8 vs MSAA8 for Pos Edges A
Figure 9-11, ABAA8 vs MSAA8 for Pos Edges B
Figure 9-12, ABAA8 vs MSAA8 for Neg Edges A
Figure 9-13, ABAA8 vs MSAA8 for Neg Edges B

ABAA with 8 Subpixel Areas

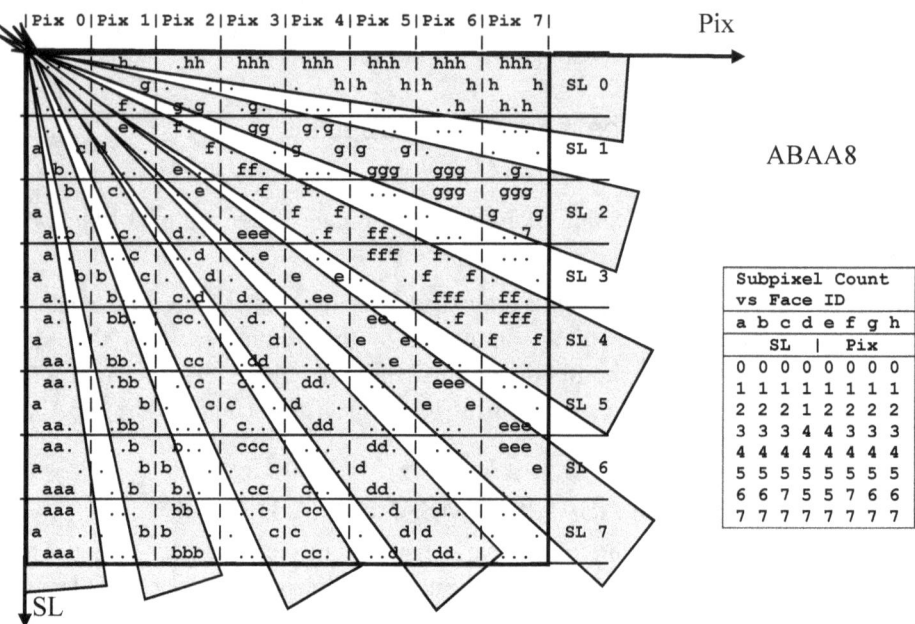

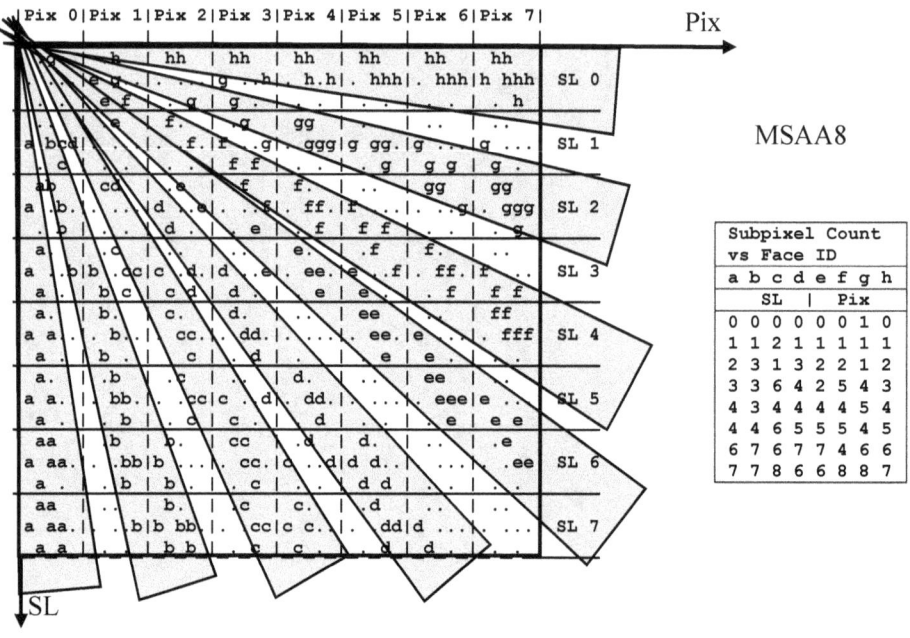

**Figure 9-10 ABAA8 vs MSAA8 for Pos Edges A**

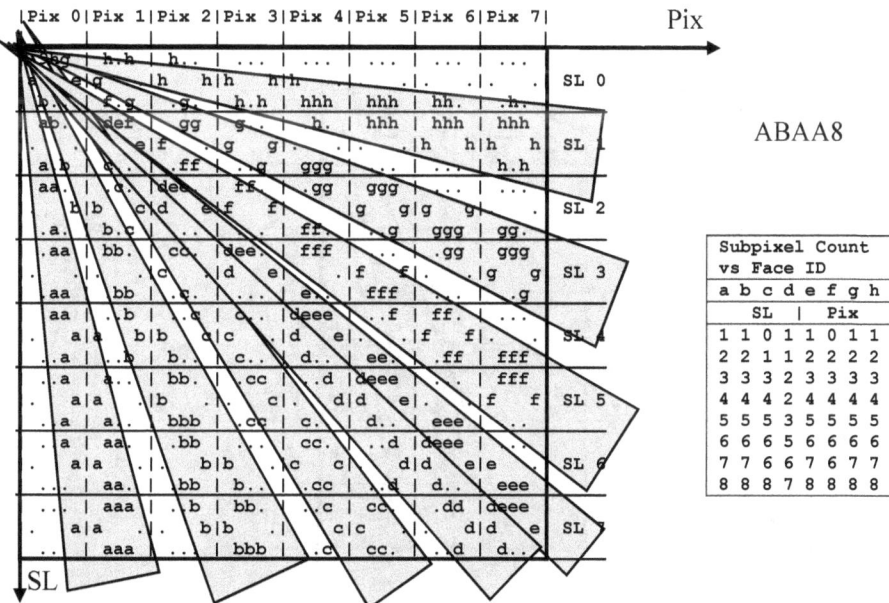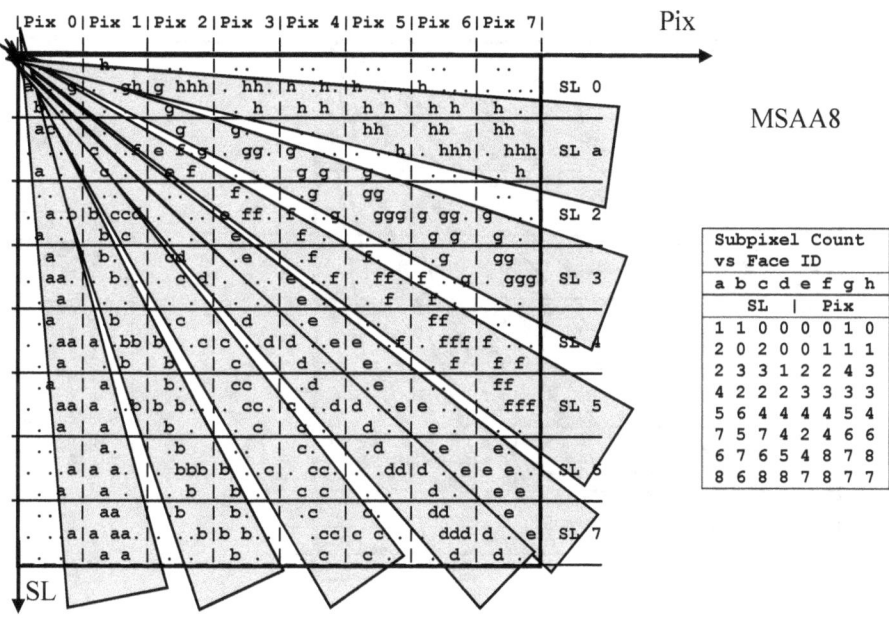

Figure 9-11 ABAA8 vs MSAA8 for Pos Edges B

ABAA with 8 Subpixel Areas

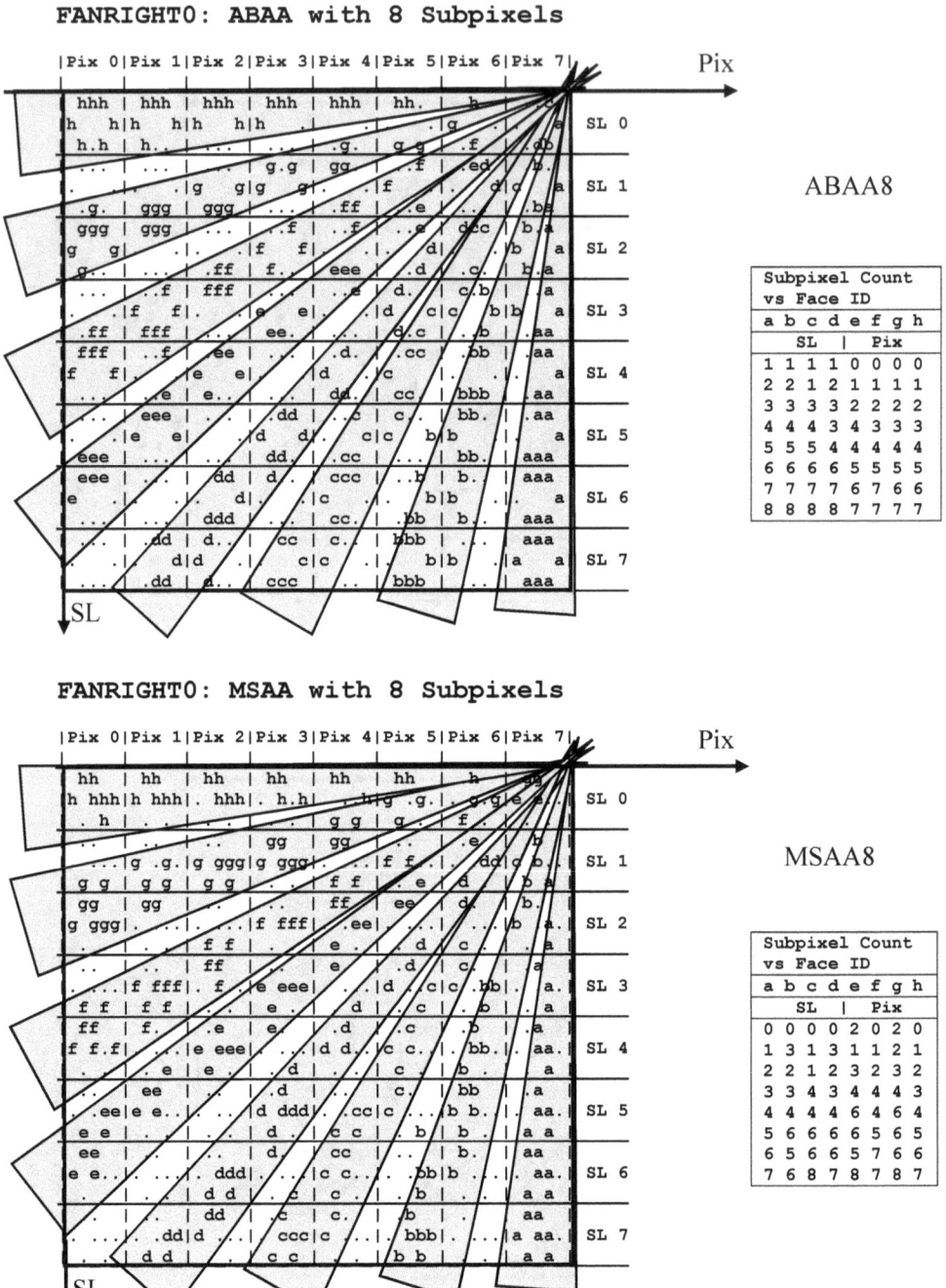

Figure 9-12 ABAA8 vs MSAA8 for Neg Edges A

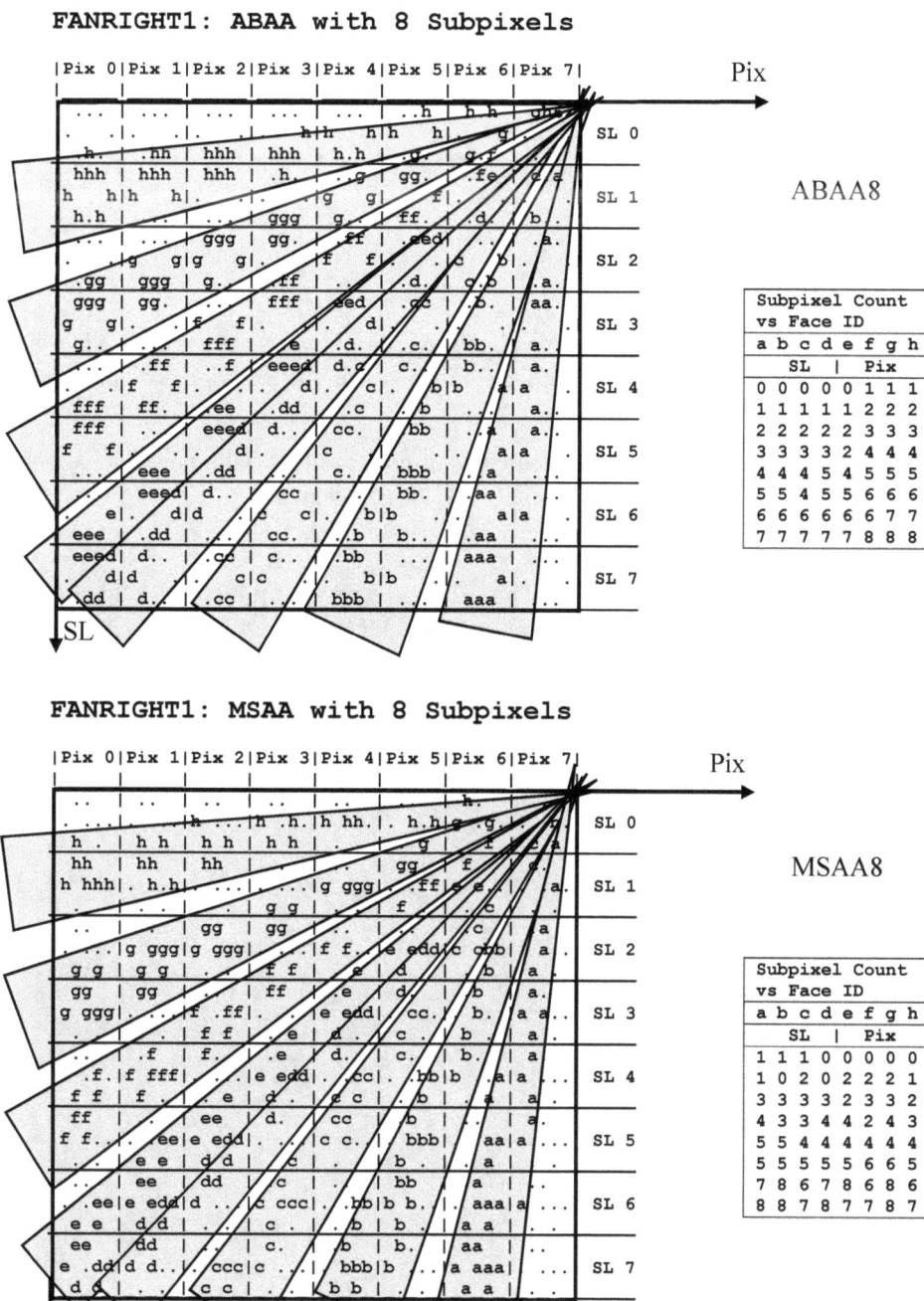

**Figure 9-13 ABAA8 vs MSAA8 for Neg Edges B**

# ABAA with 8 Subpixel Areas

For 8 Subpixels, the incremental steps should be half the size, when compared with 4 Subpixels. The 8 steps should be 1/8 Pixel each. The results here are similar to the results in examples with 4 Subpixels.

## *Results for ABAA8*

For ABAA, in most cases, the increments are:
0, 1, 2, 3, 4, 5, 6, 7, or
1, 2, 3, 4, 5, 6, 7, 8

## *Results for MSAA8*

Some Good: For MSAA, the increments are similar to ABAA when the triangles edges are near Vertical (face a) or near Horizontal (face h). This is because the Subpixels are positioned according to the 4 Queen algorithm.

Some Bad: For other orientations, the increments are not constants with many increments of 2. There is also 'hesitation', when there are some steps with decrements.

## *Summary of Results*

Using 8 Subpixels for AA, four Cases of Thin Triangles within an 8x8 pixel Span have been presented. The results are summarized in 8 tables, 4 for ABAA8 and 4 for MSAA8. The 8 tables are summarized in Figure 9-14.

ABAA with 8 Subpixel Areas

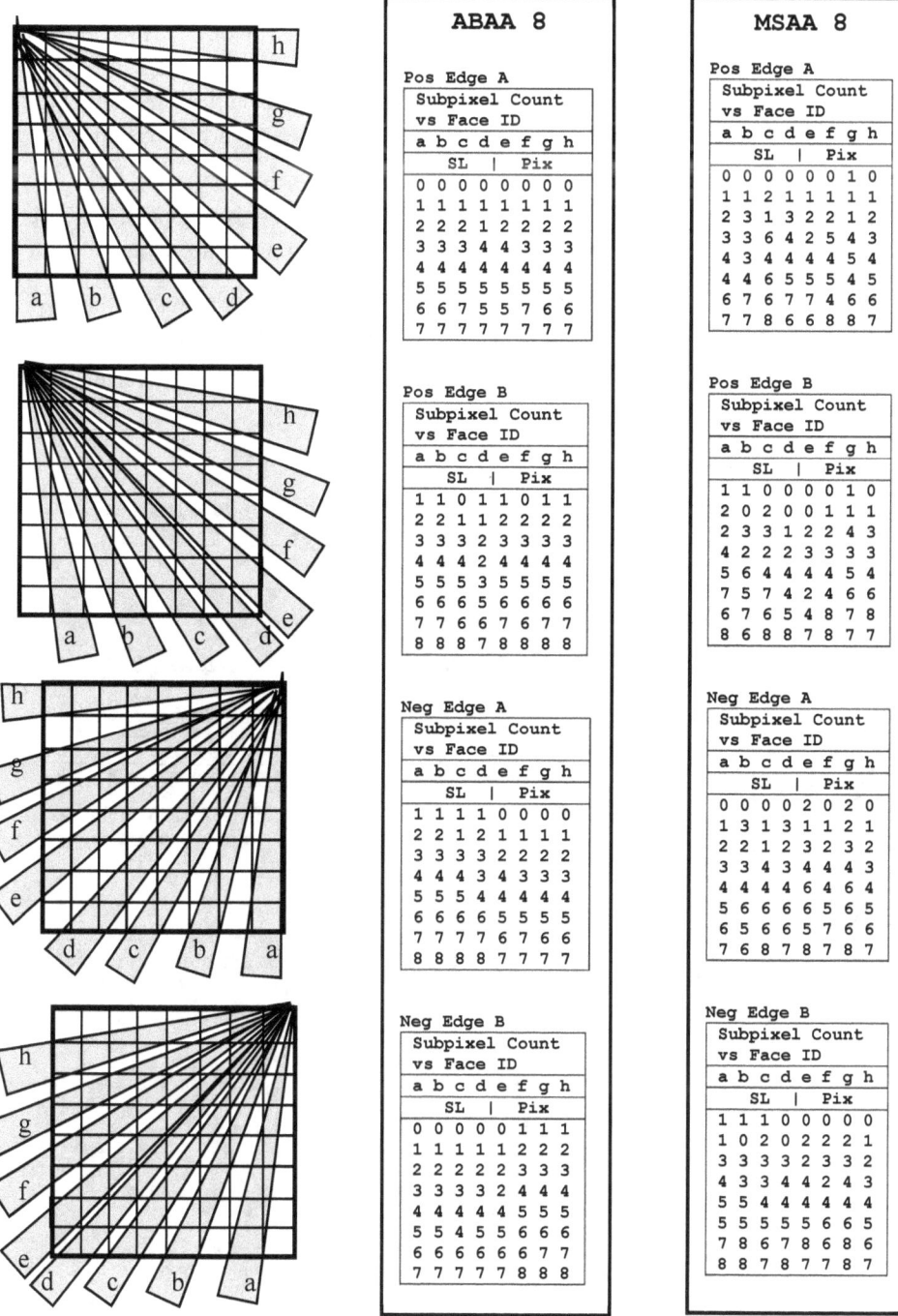

Figure 9-14 Four Cases of Thin Triangles with ABAA8 vs MSAA8

ABAA with 8 Subpixel Areas

## 9.3 Combined Examples of ABAA8 vs MSAA8

All the examples presented in this Chapter, consist of static images. It would be nice, if the ABAA vs ABAA implementation could be compared dynamically with moving images. In this book, the best I could provide is several sequences of narrow triangles organized as fans. This provides a wide range of cases. In the previous sections, there were 4 examples of narrow triangles sequences organized as fans within an 8x8 Pixel span.

For the fans that start on top left of span (Examples 1 & 2 with positive slopes), the 2 sets of 8 triangles can be combined into a single table using even and odd triangle sequences.

For the fans that start on top right of span (Examples 3 & 4 with negative slopes), the 2 sets of 8 triangles can be combined into a single table using even and odd triangle sequences.

When each pair of examples is considered, there are 16 adjacent triangles covering an angular range of Pi/2, that is Pi/32 (or 3 degrees) per triangle.

***Static Images with 8 Subpixels***

Examples 1 & 2 (fan starts on top left) consists of 8 pairs of complementary triangles with positive edge slopes. The results can be combined as shown in Figure 9-15.

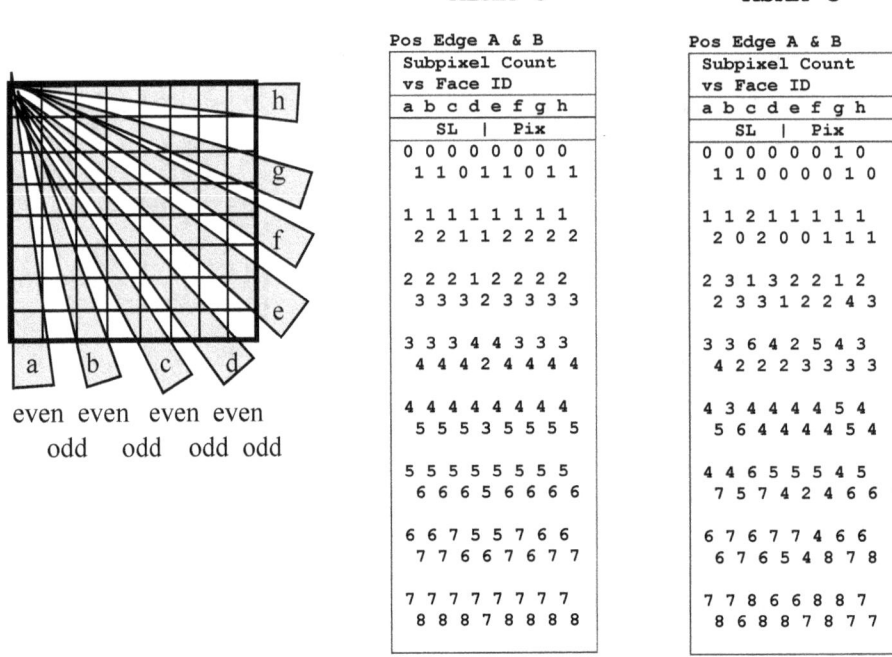

Figure 9-15 Fan of 16 Triangles with Pos Edge Slopes and 8 Subpixels

Examples 3 & 4 (fan starts on top right) consists of 8 pairs of complementary triangles with negative edge slopes. The results can be combined as shown in Figure 9-16.

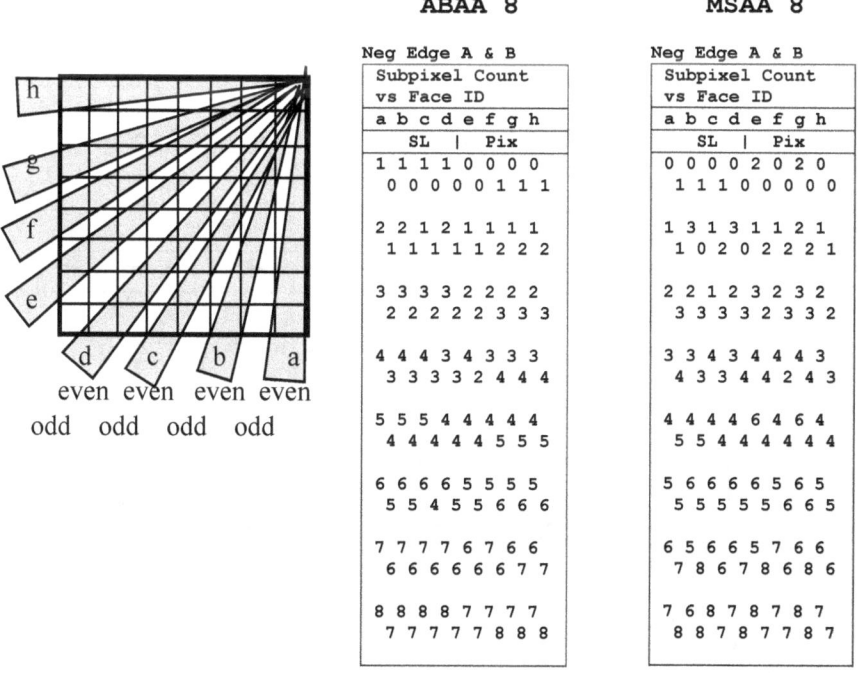

**Figure 9-16 Fan of 16 Triangles with Neg Edge Slopes and 8 Subpixels**

*Dynamic Images*

I have the intention to write a program in a Windows environment so that I can more easily demonstrate the improvement provided by ABAA over MSAA. With a dynamic demonstration, the movements can be demonstrated at varying speed.

Using the same examples, the single triangle presented at the beginning can be rotated over 4 quadrants (2Pi range, or 360 degrees) at varying rates. The triangle fans can be combined to form 4 quadrants of narrow triangles, that can be rotated around 360 degrees.

*Anti-Aliased Triangle Fans*

As was done in the Chapter about one-dimensional sampling, the dynamic behavior of triangle fans can be evaluated. In the following 2 examples, triangle fans are evaluated.

In Figure 9-17, there is a fan of 7 triangles equally spaced: 4 even (grey) triangles and 3 odd (white) triangles in between. The fan resides within an array of 16x16 Pixels (2x2 spans). As the width of the triangles increases from top to bottom, the rendering can be divided into 4 stages. Refer to Table 9-1. There is a problem for evaluating the grey shade of the Pixels in the SL range from 0 to 7. In several pixels, 2 grey or 2 white triangles cover the same Pixel.

ABAA with 8 Subpixel Areas

| Scanlines | Pixel Colors | Comment |
|---|---|---|
| 0 - 3 | Almost Uniform Grey | >2 Triangles per Pixel |
| 4 - 7 | Grey Moiré Patterns | 2 Triangles Can Overlap |
| 8 -11 | Grey, Light Grey or White | No Triangles Overlap |
| 12-15 | Grey, Light Grey and White | No Triangles Overlap |

Table 9-1 Four Rendering Stages with Triangle Fan

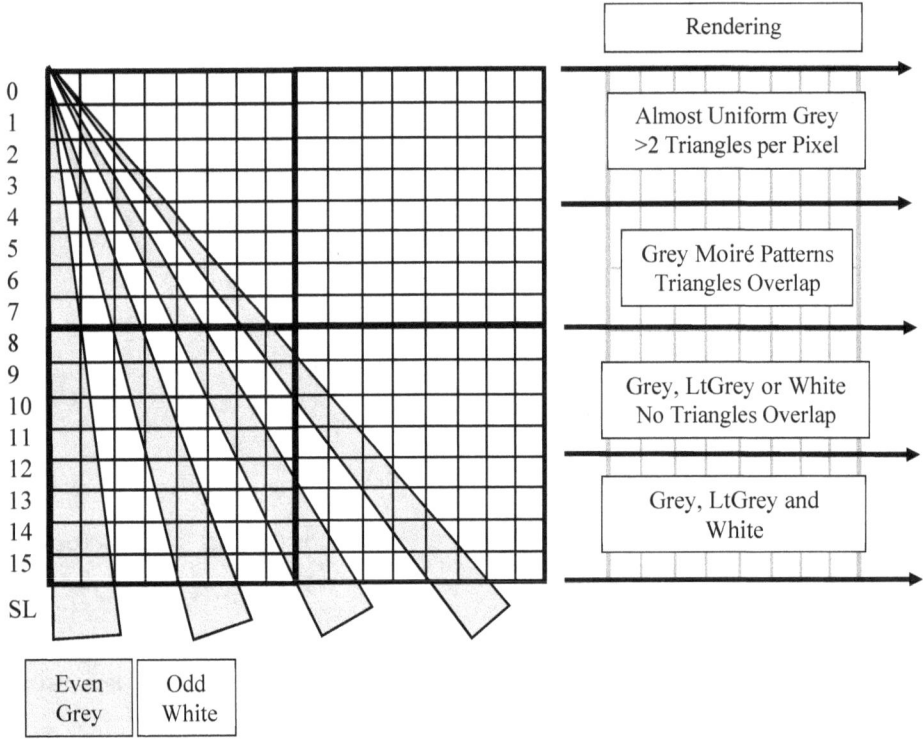

Figure 9-17 Four Stages when Rendering Triangle Fan

In Figure 9-18, there is a fan of 3 dark grey triangles and 3 white triangles in between. The triangles are not equally spaced. The white (odd) triangles are 3 times wider: 3 even (black) and 2 odd (white) triangles. The fan resides within an array of 16x16 Pixels (2x2 spans). As the width of the triangles increases from top to bottom, the rendering can be divided into Three stages. Refer to Table 9-2.

| Scanlines | Pixel Colors | Comment |
|---|---|---|
| 0 - 3 | Almost Uniform Grey | Some Triangles Overlap |
| 4 - 7 | Grey or White | No Triangles Overlap |
| 8 -15 | Grey, LtGrey and White | No Triangles Overlap |

**Table 9-2 Three Rendering Stages with Not Equally Spaced Triangle Fan**

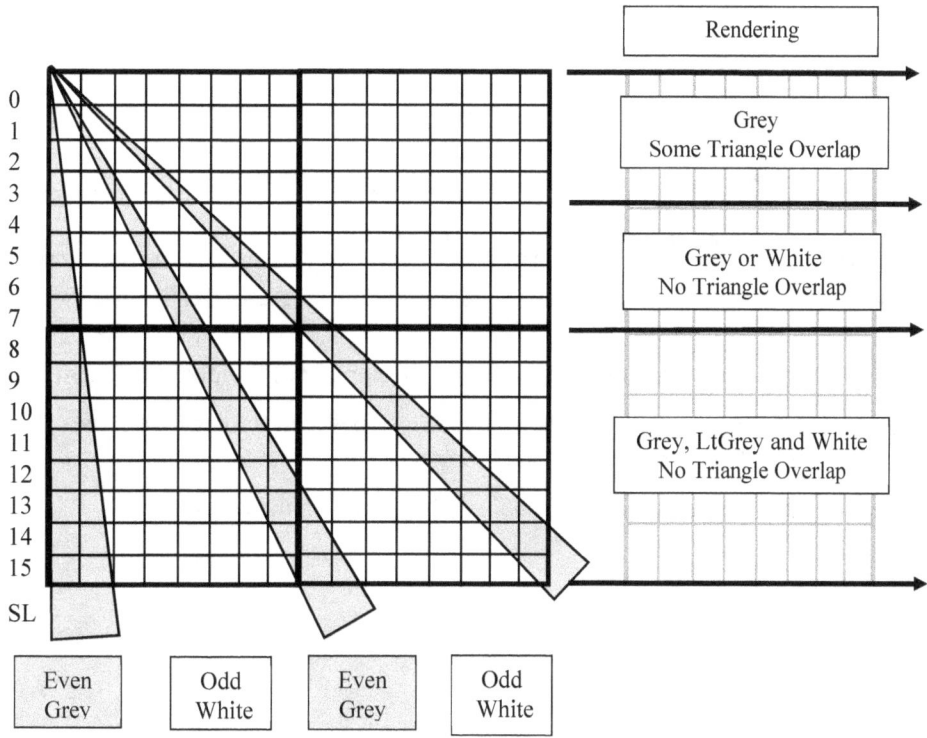

**Figure 9-18 Rendering of Not Equally Spaced Triangle Fan**

Isolated triangles are more suitable for the evaluation of narrow triangle rendering with Subpixels. In this example, because the space between the black triangle is wider, it should be a better test for Subpixel Rendering.

### 9.3.1 Other Example of Thin Faces

In this example there are 2 faces at angle +/- Pi/4. This is at the transition of VE vs HE. So, each face is defined by 2 parallel edges, one VE and one HE. The 2 thin faces are specified in Listing 9-1.

The result is shown in Figure 9-19.

**Listing 9-1 Two Thin Faces at +/- 45-degrees (Pi/4)**

```
// =========================================================================
// =========================================================================
// Edges at +/- 45 degrees (Pi/4)
// ==============================
// VE and HE edges cannot overlap
// VE Edge Slopes range from 77.00 to 00.77. VE Edges can have a slope of -1.0, but not 1.0
// HE Edge Slopes range from 77.01 to 01.00. HE Edges can have a slope of 1.0, but not -1.0
edgeasc_t EDG45[] =
  // Pos Slopes, Face a
  // Start    End       Slope>0  VE BE     Start    End      Slope>0  HE BE
  { {"77.70", "07.70",  "01.00", 1, 1},   {"00.00", "10.00", "01.00", 0, 1}, // VELft 45, HETop 45
  // Neg Slopes, Face b
  // Start    End       Slope<0  HE BE     Start    End      Slope<0  VE !BE
    {"07.70", "77.70",  "77.00", 0, 1},   {"10.00", "00.00", "77.00", 1, 0} };//HEBot-45, VERgt-45

// =========================================================================
```

As expected ABAA performs better at Pi/4 and -Pi/4. The number of Subpixels is 2 per Pixel.

For MSAA, there are 4 time more Subpixels for positive slopes than for negative slopes. That are 4 Subpixels for positive slopes and one Subpixel for negative slopes.

This can be explained when observing the Subpixel distribution in the MSAA Pixel.

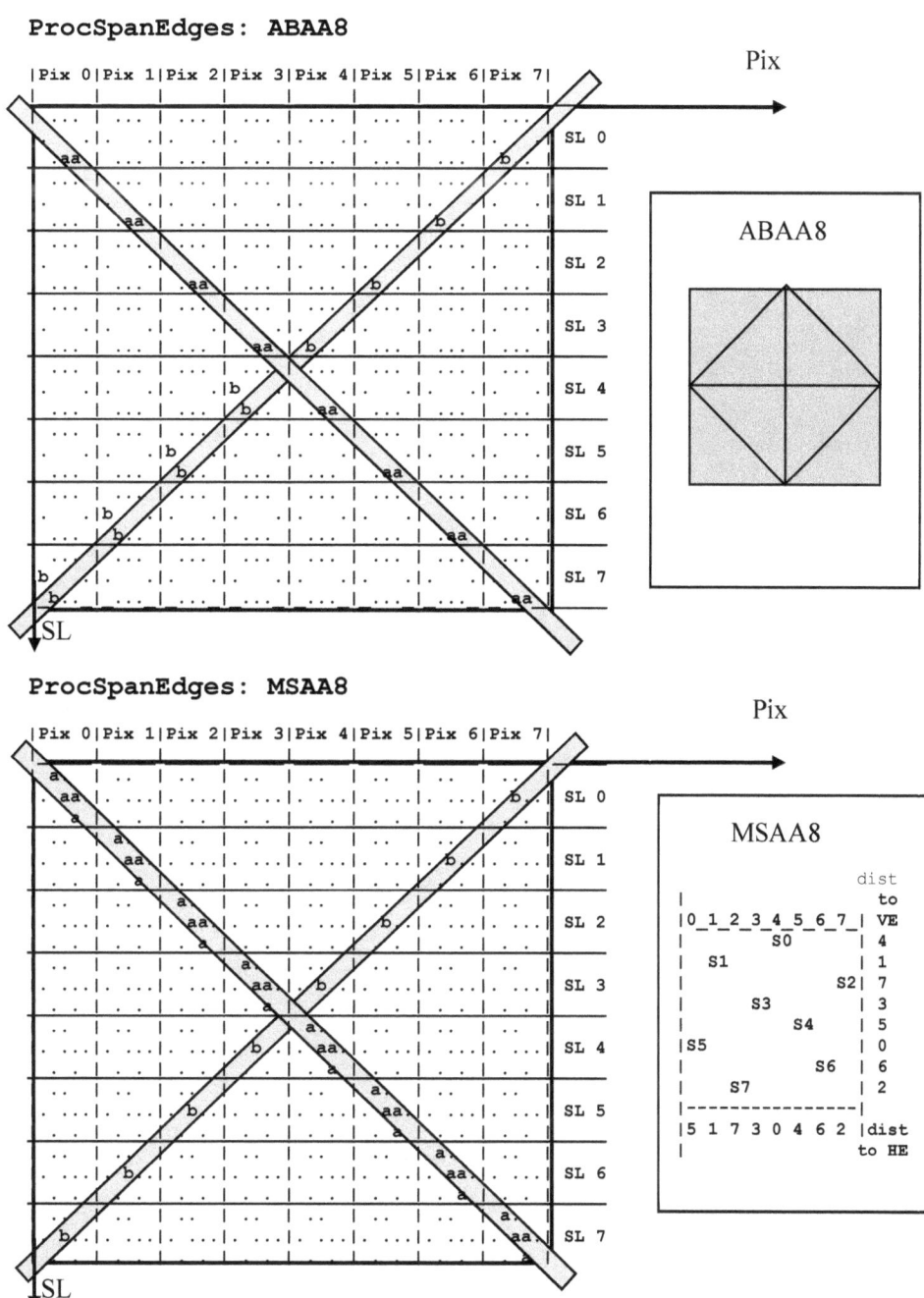

**Figure 9-19 ABAA8 vs MSAA8: Two Thin Rectangles at +/- 45-Degrees**

# Chapter 10  Flight Simulation and RT CGI

In this chapter, several aspects of RT CGI are presented.

- Early Flight Simulators
- Requirement for RT CGI Systems to 'Have Anti-Aliasing'
- Increase in Chip and Memory density
- Memory Requirement for Frame Buffer Implementation
- RT CGI and the Personal Computer
- The Warp5 from Oak Technology

The interest in CGI stared in the late 1960s. Many algorithms were developed for generating more and more complex images using CGI. The push for AA came first from the movie and advertising industry with non-real time implementations. In the 1970s and 1980s, the implementations of AA solution required general purpose super computers like the Cray1 or, later on with arrays of workstations from Silicon Graphics or Sun Microsystems.

In the early 1970s came requirements from NASA and the US military for RT CGI with AA to be used for training in their flight simulators. There was a strong requirement for no distracting artifacts, that is edge smoothing and no in-and-out popping faces. There were a very limited number of companies who could design and deliver such high-speed special purpose computer costing above $1M.

## 10.1 Visualization for Flight simulation

At first, I could not find any references about these early 3D RT CGI systems on the Internet. Then, I came across a few articles. Among them, an interesting slide presentation about the major steps in Flight Simulation and CGI. This slide presentation, 'GPU-Based Visualization for Flight Simulation', was presented by '*Tim Woodward*' from 'Diamond Viewsonic', at 'GPU Tech 2014' [85]. In his presentation, *Tim Woodward* presents the evolution of CGI, starting with Flight Simulation and evolving into the PC market. In this section, I use similar steps plus some additional information to present a quick history of CGI in flight simulation.

Following this presentation, I will share my own experience from the 30 years I have spent designing several 3D RT CGI systems.

### 10.1.1   Flight Simulation Takes off

*Ed Link* is the inventor of the Link Trainer [91], a flight simulator and trainer that was used to train around half a million pilots during WW II. The Link Company has been the leader in flight and space simulation for at least 50 years, starting with the Blue Box in 1940 [98].

***Link's Blue Box 1940s***

Using his experiences from flying and working in his father's piano and organ company, *Ed Link* put together a flight trainer. A patent application filed March 12, 1930, was granted September 29, 1931.

# Flight Simulation and RT CGI

The first significant interest for use of the trainer for instrument flight training occurred in 1934, for mail delivery. The Army became interested in the Link Trainer and ordered six trainers to improve the mail pilots' skills. The Link Trainer came into widespread use during World War II when over 10,000 "Blue Box" trainers were used to improve safety and shorten training time for over 500,000 pilots. Pilots of many nations were trained to fly by instruments. Besides the US: Australia, Canada, Germany, New Zealand, United Kingdom, Israel, Japan, Pakistan, and the USSR (Now Soviet Union).

Refer to Video Demo [98]: Blue Box, The First Flight Simulator
https://www.youtube.com/watch?v=PYTrjch_G64

Other Link References: [92]

### Terrain model-board and film, 1950s and 1960s

The legacy of the Link Trainer is visible today, with flight simulators being an integral part of pilot training. In recent years, Link simulators have been used in many historic applications including the training of the Apollo astronauts for the moon landing in the 1960s [94] and the training of Space Shuttle pilots with CGI systems (Link DIGs) in the 1970s [95][96].

## 10.1.2   "Image Generators", 1970s to Present

### 1970s: The Big Irons

In the 1970s, only a few companies were delivering 3D RT CGI systems for Flight Simulation.

They are referred to as "Big Iron" because they were big systems. Their hardware was contained in several steel cabinets the size of refrigerators, with a cost above $1M.

- General Electric Company
- Evans and Sutherland/Redifon:
- McDonnell Douglas Electronics Company
- Singer Company - Link Division

### 1980s: New Entrants in 3D RT CGI

In the 1980s, a few companies entered the 3D RT CGI market with lower cost systems:

- Silicon Graphics Inc (SGI): Iris workstations and Onyx
- Computervision Corp in Raleigh, NC

### 1990s: Rise of the PC

In the mid 1990s 3D graphics adapters for the PC appeared in the market [77]:

- S3 Inc: Virge, Savage4
- 3DFx; Voodoo and Banshee
- Rendition
- Nvidia: Riva and TNT
- Advanced Technology International - ATI

- Oak Technology: Warp 5 (first chip and PC graphics adapter with AA) [78]
- Even Intel entered that market

By 1999, only a few companies remained in the 3D PC adapter market;

- 1999, NVIDIA: GeForce 256
- ATI: 3D Rage
- Intel

*2000s: GPU and the Rise (and fall?) of the PC*

A GPU (Graphics Processing Unit) [84] is a specialized processor originally designed to accelerate graphics rendering.

GPUs can process many pieces of data simultaneously, making them useful for machine learning, video editing, and gaming applications. GPUs first appeared in video graphics adapter. Nowadays they may be integrated into computer's CPU or offered as a discrete hardware unit.

Moving to the PC-based GPU brought huge cost savings.
But meant giving up a lot of capability and control

- Real-time determinism
- Anti-aliasing
- Gen-lock
- Unified memory
- Computational power

## 10.1.3 Flight Simulation vs. Gaming

- Instructor-controlled conditions (time, weather, etc.)
- Subjective tuning
- Fidelity Requirements: No aliasing No Z-fighting, No LOD popping
- Performance
- *Never* drop frames
- 20+ channels

Data Source:

- Large gaming areas – "database" (e.g. continental, even planetary)
- Legacy database standards (Government-defined)
- Typical gaming approaches do not scale to massive datasets... (nor do traditional simulation approaches)

## 10.1.4 Throw Hardware at It!

More and more hardware dedicated to CGI

- Moore's Law continues…
- Via parallelism, not speed (for nearly 10 years now)
- First with CPU, now with GPU [84][85]

Flight Simulation and RT CGI

### 10.1.5    More powerful CGI systems with GPU
- Parallel THREAD
- Create Data Bases
- Compute all LODs
- Under-utilize GPU
- Large, fast memory buffers

## 10.2 Big Irons as 3D RT CGI Systems

For the readers interested in the evolution of CGI systems from the early flight simulators to the present 3D real time CGI systems, this Section provides a selection of links to Video and PDF in the References section.

In the following sections, I present my own experience with Big Irons as 3D RT CGI systems. Several topics in the evolution of RT CGI systems are presented.

- First Big Iron 3D RT CGI Systems
- Early RT CGI: From Analog ABAA to Digital ABAA
- Link DIG Special-Purpose Processing Hardware
- RT CGI with Full Frame Buffer
- Increase in memory density
- Texture Maps and Coplanar Detail Faces
- RT CGI and the Personal Computer

### 10.2.1    The Purpose of Flight simulators is to "Save Lives"

From the beginning, the intent of flight simulators was to save lives caused by human errors. Although, there is not much glory at working on flight simulators that look like toys, one of the main goals is always "saving lives". When aircraft or space fight accidents occur, there is intense coverage on the news. Although the intent of flight simulators is to save lives, there is little coverage of the many hours of training that the future pilots spend in flight simulators.

On the other hand, although I don't have a pilot license, I have enjoyed flying in high end flight simulator. During system testing I was privileged to fly in several flight simulators: Space Shuttle, F-111 fighter, B-52 bomber and the Black-Hawk & Apache Helicopters. The plane cockpit is true replica of the real thing. With RT CGI scenes from 3 windows, 6 degrees of freedom motion system and the noise, it is very close to the real thing.

I remember a presentation from a government representative, where the main subject of the talk was about pilot training and the simulator industry. The presenter told us that our mission is to save lives. He repeated that we "should be extremely proud" of our job, because in the military we are saving many lives!

"You are saving lives"

## 10.2.2  Early RT CGI Systems

When 3D CGI became available in early 1970s, there was a need for high-speed 3D RT CGI systems that could produce images in real-time for training [95]. These RT CGI systems had to produce 3D CGI with smooth interlaced images at 60 fields per second.

When I started to work on the RT CGI prototype at Link, in Sunnyvale, CA, only a few computer companies were able to produce such RT CGI systems. At first, 3 companies had produced CGI systems that could produce 1000 to 2000 edges per frame.

- Evans and Sutherland (E&S) in Salt Lake City, Utah
  NovoView (for dusk and night only)
- General Electric Ground System Division (GE GSD) in Daytona Beach, Florida
- McDonnell Douglas Electronics Company
  Vertical Image Takeoff and Landing (VITAL) II

At first, these companies had also been producing calligraphic CGI systems for **night only**. These calligraphic RT CGI systems were used train aircraft pilots to fly at **night and dusk only**, including take-off and landing. They were displaying runways and surrounding cities with point lights only, but no polygons.

## 10.2.3  Big Iron RT CGI Systems had AA

For the Air Force and NASA, the RT CGI systems system had to be full day-and-night with polygon processing.

These RT CGI systems had to produce 'Out the Window' (OTW) scenes in real-time to train pilots for aircraft take-off, landing, special missions and emergency situations. They consisted of three window-images (for left, front and right windows) for most simulators, or 4 window-images for plane-to-plane dogfights (2 window per plane, at NASA Ames). For the RT CGI systems used in these simulators, an important requirement was that they had AA, or Edge Smoothing. Jaggies, Edge crawling and polygons popping in-and-out of scenes were not acceptable. In mission simulations, distracting image artifacts would result in negative training. This means that in order to produce smooth edges, the RT CGI systems had to do some kind of Subpixel processing to avoid edge crawling and polygon popping.

The purpose of these highspeed RT CGI systems was to generate OTW scenes used in aircraft and spaceship trainers/simulators. While pilots in flight simulators were flying through a terrain data base, the image information had to be retrieved from the data base and processed in a fraction of second at the rate of 30 (frame rate) or 60 images (field rate) per second. This task was accomplished by proprietary RT CGI systems from a few companies.

Since there were no such systems available in the market, the companies in this market had to develop and build their own proprietary special purpose RT CGI computers, from scratch. Each company had to develop their own HW and also the SW for data base development and real-time operating system. These systems were quite large. Typically, the special purpose hardware occupied 6 cabinets, each cabinet being the size of a refrigerator. They were driven by a 16 or 32-bit minicomputer. For example, these minicomputers were designed by from Digital Equipment

Flight Simulation and RT CGI

Corp (DEC) or InterData from Perkin Elmer. The size of the hard disks was 300Mbyte. The size of these minicomputer was also similar to the size of refrigerator.

By the mid 1970s, only a few companies could deliver RT CGI systems for Flight Simulation. They are referred to as "Big Iron" because they were big systems. Their hardware was contained in several steel cabinets the size of refrigerators, and costed above $2M.

- Evans and Sutherland (E&S) in Salt Lake City, Utah
  CT-1 to CT-4(Continuous Tone) CGI systems, ESIG systems
- General Electric Ground System Division (GE GSD) in Daytona Beach, Florida
  CompuScene CGI systems
- McDonnell Douglas Electronics Company
- A fourth company, the Advanced Product Operation (APO) of Link Flight Simulation in Sunnyvale CA, was a late entrant.

There is a good description of these systems in two sources:

- A Report from US Army Material Development and Readiness Command:
  'Computer Generated Imagery (CGI) Current Technology', 1980 [82]
- Book from Bruce J. Schachter 'Computer Image Generation', 1983 [83]

---

From the US Army Report:
'Computer Generated Imagery (CGI) Current Technology', 1980 [82]

Identifying a vanguard of technology in almost any field requires the determination of a basis for the selection of a vanguard. For the purposes of this study, the vanguard is deemed to be those vendors with a capability of meeting current PMTRADE needs for real-time and CGI visual systems, as demonstrated by having delivered such systems for use in a military simulator. Based on this criterium, the current CGI vanguard is deemed to be:

General Electric Company

Evans and Sutherland/Redifon:

McDonnell Douglas Electronics Company

Singer Company - Link Division


(cont'd)

---

(cont'd)

*General Electric Company*: Compu-scene
Although GE is not the oldest company involved in flight simulators, it was the first company to produce a simulator utilizing CGI technology (1958).

*Evans and Sutherland/Redifon*: CT-1 to CT-5 and ESIG
Evans and Sutherland Company (E&S) and Redifon Simulation, Ltd., must be discussed as one (E&S/Redifon) because, in a sense they are one. While E&S does market a line of interactive graphics systems, their CGI visual systems are generally sold to Redifon for integration into total simulators.

The NOVOVIEW line represents a low cost, real-time CGI visual capability (for dusk and night only). The Continuous Tone systems have higher capacity and better scene quality as compared to the NOVOVIEW series. The first system (CT-1) was delivered in 1973. In 1975, a CT-2 system was provided to the National Maritime Research Center for use in ocean navigation, harbor operations and docking. A CT-3 system was delivered to Johnson Space Center in 1976 and offered higher performance capability.
(My Note: The CT-5 appeared in 1980.)

*McDonnell Douglas Electronics Company*: VITAL

McDonnell Douglas has been offering relatively low cost, simple design CGI systems since 1971 when the first Vertical Image Takeoff and Landing (VITAL) II system was delivered. VITAL III offered a much higher resolution than VITAL II with respect to front window runway approach and landing scenes. VITAL IV systems represent McDonnell Douglas' current color, day/dusk/night CGI system.

*Singer Company-Link Division*: DIG

Although Singer-Link has been in the flight trainer business for 50 years, they followed GE, E&S and McDonnell-Douglas in entering the CGI visual system market. After introducing their CGI visual systems in the mid-seventies, however, they have been strong in the market. Singer-Link has, or will, deliver systems for the NASA Space Shuttle Simulator, F-Ill, Black Hawk and the B-52. Singer-Link has also supplied a system to NASA Ames.

Flight Simulation and RT CGI

## 10.2.4 The Link DIG and the E&S CT-5

*The Link DIG*

What is not commonly known, is that the 1$^{st}$ RT CGI system with higher performances and AA was the Link DIG built by the APO Link Division of Singer in Sunnyvale, CA.

By 1975, Link has built an R&D DIG (Digital Image Generator) prototype that could output around 1500 edges/field (1/60 sec). Then, in 1977 the DIG production unit could produce 12,000 edges/field. This corresponds to 240,000 triangles per sec. I was one of the key architects and a main designer of the Link DIGs. The first DIG was delivered to NASA in Houston in late 1977. A total of 4 DIGs have been used to train all the Space Shuttle Astronauts in Houston before their missions in space [96]. A 5$^{th}$ DIG was also delivered to NASA Ames in Mountain View, CA, for their Vertical Motion Simulator [97]. Few people have heard about the Link DIGs, because they were designed under NASA or US military contracts and required security clearances to work on the projects.

Note: Although, the references from [82] and [83] rated the DIG performance at 12k images per frame (1/30 sec), it was actually 12k images per field (1/60 sec). This was probably due to a confusion in the marketing department at Singer Link. As the principal designer, I can attest for sure that the correct number is 12,000 edges/field (1/60 sec).

During the years I spent designing the first and fastest RT CGI systems at Link Flight Simulation, I was always faced with the requirements of high image quality and AA. When the DIG was designed, the 1kx1 Static Random-Access Memory chips (SRAM) was the densest semiconductor memory modules available. Even though, the DIG-1 had edge smoothing using analog circuits. The DIG-1 was also the first RT CGI system with Area-Based Anti-Aliasing.

There were 2 versions of the DIG: DIG-1 and DIG-2. For AA, the DIG-1 had analog edge smoothing. The DIG-2 had digital edge smoothing.

Because of its superior performances, the Link DIG was responsible to win important contract against the competition: Space Shuttle Motion Simulator (4 DIG-1), F-111 Fighter Bomber (10 DIG-1), NASA the Vertical Motion Simulator t NASA Ames (1 DIG-1 with 4 windows, also used for Dog Fight), and 1 DIG-1 to All Nippon Airways (ANA) to train for take-off and landing in the Hong Kong airport. With gradual improvements, the DIG -2 continued to win contracts for several simulator/trainer programs for the Air Force (12 DIGs for B-52 Bomber, and F-117 Fighter-Bomber) and 40 DIG-2 for Army helicopters training program (AH-64 Apache, AH-1 Cobra, CH-47 Chinook and UH-60 Black Hawk). During a period of 12 years, a total of 70 DIGs were sold.

*DIG Video Demo*:

In the DIG, the problem of face popping was solved with 'Coplanar Detail Faces' (CDF). The CDFs could be graciously introduced and fade from the scene by controlling their contrast when smaller than a Pixel. This algorithm could accurately compute the projection size of polygons early in the geometric processor. There is a great YouTube Video demo of the DIG-2 at:

[99] Link Flight Simulation Demo, Video, DIG-2 Demo, 1984:
    https://www.youtube.com/watch?v=uy8sJ9AxvYI

There are also several references about the DIG delivered to NASA with 4 OTW scenes to simulate fighter-plane dogfights.

[97] NASA Ames Vertical Motion Simulator
   https://www.youtube.com/watch?v=0WaiAyU-3mU
   https://www.nasa.gov/simlabs/vms/technical-details
 DIG-1: Simulator Facility for Helicopter Air-to-Air Combat at NASA Ames
   https://apps.dtic.mil/sti/citations/ADA160693
   https://apps.dtic.mil/sti/pdfs/ADA160693.pdf
   NASA Ames Research Center (ARC):
     https://en.wikipedia.org/wiki/Ames_Research_Center

### *E&S CT-5 Demos with Texture*

A few years later, the CT-5 from E&S was announced in 1981. The CT-5 and the DIG-1 had similar performances, although the DIG-1 was produced 5 years earlier. The DIGs used the SL-to-SL processing approach. The CT-5 and the GE Systems used a Face Buffer approach.

The CT-5 (Continuous Tone 5) was designed around 5 years after the DIG. At that time, face buffer and texture mapping became feasible [32].

By comparison, there are similar scenes in the CT-5 demos from E&S.
Refer to 'YouTube' videos about *Evans & Sutherland CT 5 Flight Simulator (1981)* [86] [87]

In this video there are examples of contrast decreasing with distance, simulated with translucency. In these cases, the decrease in contrast depends on distance only and is less natural than in the examples of details implemented with CDF in the DIG scenes.

[86] Evans & Sutherland (E&S) Wikipedia
   https://en.wikipedia.org/wiki/Evans_%26_Sutherland
 E&S History 2005:
   https://www.youtube.com/watch?v=FHhYAUgY3S0
   https://forum.beyond3d.com/threads/ct5-evans-sutherland-simulator-how-did-it-work.57664/
 Utah inventions: The birth of computer graphics
   https://www.ksl.com/article/36039333/utah-inventions-the-birth-of-computer-graphics

[87] E&S CT-5 Videos
 CT-5 Flight Simulator, 1981
   https://archive.org/details/CT5FlightSimulator
   https://www.youtube.com/watch?v=6W-qb_jHRhA
 Evans & Sutherland 'The Tactical Edge'
   Part 1: https://www.youtube.com/watch?v=06mbwNg1Vw4
   Part 2: https://www.youtube.com/watch?v=7e7_GiCc-HA

### *GE CompuScene*
 [89] The Simulator Revolution
   https://www.airforcemag.com/article/1289simulator/

Flight Simulation and RT CGI

*Color-Buffer and Z-Buffer*

Because of the lower memory density at that time, the color and Z-Buffer approach was not feasible wen the first DIGs were designed. The RT CGI systems used Priority ordering instead of Z-Buffer. Because of the limited memory density at that time, the DIGs used a SL Computer as Image Renderer. There was no Image buffer. The SL computer was building the image in SL order since only a few SLs could be processed and stored at a time.

Ten years later, in the 1980s, the density of memory had increased by a factor of 32x ($2^5$x for 10yrs, according to Moor's Law). The use of frame buffer became feasible for RT CGI systems and opened the door for 2 types of architecture:

- Z-buffer with 1 sample per Pixel
- Tiled architecture with anti-aliasing (E&S, GE and Link)

By the mid 1990s, increase in chip density made it possible to implement RT CGI systems inside PCs. After leaving Link, I had tried to apply new technologies at a startup, 'GrafiCube'.
In 1993, I developed an earlier version of the ABAA algorithm described in this book
At Oak Technology, I was developing a variation of this ABAA technology for a follow-on chip to the Warp5.

### 10.2.5 First 3D RT CGI with Edge Smoothing

The Link DIG (Digital Image Generator) was the 1$^{st}$ RT CGI system built by the APO Link Division of Singer in Sunnyvale, CA.

This system was a real milestone in the development of RT CGI and AA. This system had several innovative features for AA implementation.

- The problem with jaggies was solved with an analog implementation of edge smoothing.
- The problem with image jerking and double images was eliminated by updating images at field rate, that is 60 times per sec.
- For the distracting effects caused by narrow face breakup and small faces popping in-and-out of the scenes, I implemented an algorithm for estimating the projection size of polygons. I got a patent for the 'Resolvability Test and Projection Size of Polygons' [105]. The narrow face breakup was solved by replacing polygons with lines when the width of polygons became narrower than 1 or 2 Pixels. The problem of face popping was solved with 'Coplanar Detail Faces' (CDF). The CDF could be graciously introduced and fade from the scene by controlling their contrast when smaller than a Pixel. This algorithm could accurately compute the projection size of polygons early in the geometric processor.

The first DIG was delivered to NASA in Houston in 1977 [96]. Few people have heard about the Link DIGs, because they were designed under US military and NASA contracts. They were not publicized, because they required Government issued Security Clearance.

I was one of the architects and a main designer of the Link DIGs. I worked with many talented Engineers, programmers and test people. For me, they were unsung heroes.

*Judy Florence* did the research and the ground work. She is the inventor of the DIG R&D prototype. I was one of the HW design engineers for the DIG prototype. After working on the prototype, I made significant improvements and contributions for the production unit to be delivered to NASA. As a reward, I got 6 patents [100] related to 3D RT CGI. I was responsible for the speed and quality improvements. This 3D RT DIG was the fastest in the world when delivered. It could display 240,000 anti-aliased triangles per second. It used a 4x4 ABAA (Area-Based AA) analog solution, invented by *Robert (Bob) Lotz* [108].

*Bob Lotz* was a very talented analog circuits designer. When the DIG was designed, there was no digital to analog converters (DAC) to drive the display monitors for digitally generated image. He implemented the DACs for the DIG output circuitry. He also implemented the Edge Smoothing solution using analog circuitry.

This was the first version of the DIG, or DIG-1. A total of 4 DIG-1 have been delivered to NASA in Houston, to train all the Space Shuttle Astronauts before their missions in space [96]. A $5^{th}$ DIG-1 was also delivered to NASA Ames for their Vertical Motion Simulator [97]. Another lot of 10 more DIG-1 were delivers to the Air Force for the F-111 program. Another DIG-1 was delivered for evaluation to the Army Black Hawk helicopter. A DIG-1 was also delivered to ANA (All Nippon Airways), to train pilots for take-off and landing in the Hong-Kong Airport.

For occulting and hidden surface removal, the DIGs did not use a Z-buffer. Instead, a priority number was assigned to each object. Objects with lower priority numbers were in front of objects with higher priority numbers.

## 10.2.6   Shading, Fog and Texture with Multi-Sample

*CGI with Texture Maps*

In earlier images generated with CGI, the memory size of the computer was limited. For this reason, the early images with AA did not include texture mapping [32]. With texture mapping, color of sample points are selected on texture maps and projected onto Pixels.

There is a difference between computing a color inside a Pixel or sampling a Texel (texture element) color inside of a texture map. For texture sampling, only one Texel needs to be sampled per Pixel, preferably at the center of the Pixel. In a texture map, AA is resolved by providing different level of details (LODs) so that there is no aliasing when sampling a Texel at the center of Pixels.

When doing MSAA or BON sampling on a group of Subpixels, the same result can be achieved by sampling only one Texel at the center of the Pixel, and applying the same texture sample to all Subpixels.
In Fig. 10-1, there are examples of how samples are selected for ABAA. For color, the sample is taken at the Pixel center. For Z-Buffer, the samples are taken at the Subpixels center of gravity.

The same comment can be applied with smooth shading and Fog effect. In this case the same color sample can be applied to all Subpixels within the Pixel. When the Pixel color depends on the contribution of several intersecting triangles, all samples belonging to the same triangle will share the same color.

# Flight Simulation and RT CGI

For very narrow faces, the color gradients should be clamped, in order to avoid overflow outside of narrow faces. Refer to my patent [107], 'Method and apparatus for clamping image gradients'.

## Z-Buffer

With ABAA, for detecting which Subpixel is in front of another, a Center of Gravity is assigned to each Subpixel to compare the Z-Distances. The Z-Distance can be computed at the Centers of Gravity. For very narrow faces, the gradients (for shading, texture and Z-Distance) have to be clamped to avoid problems when Center of gravity is outside of the triangle area. In the Warp 5, this problem was solved by limiting the gradient for narrow faces. Refer to my patent [107], 'Method and apparatus for clamping image gradients'.

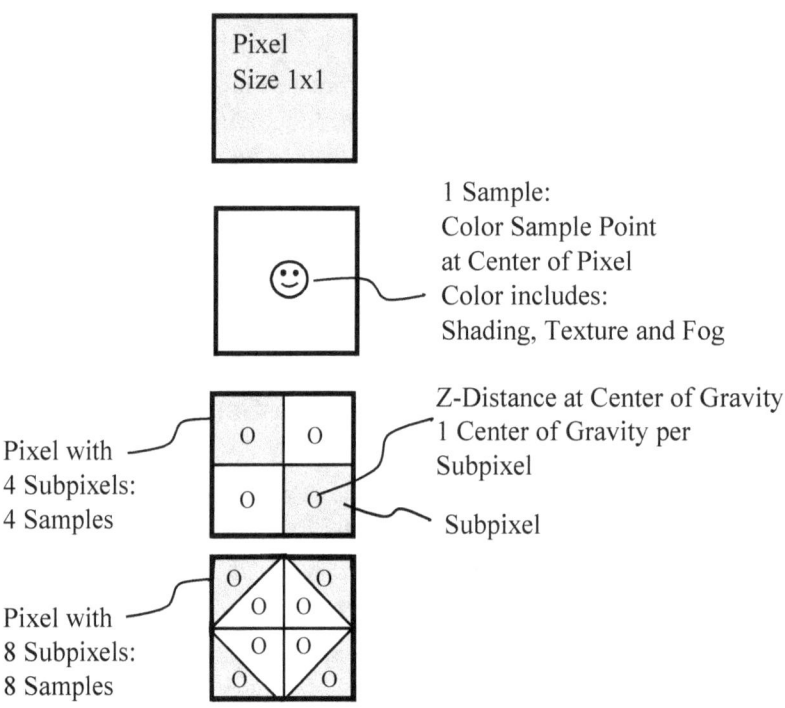

**Figure 10-1 Color at Pixel Center and Z-Dist at Subpixel Center of Gravity**

## *CDF ('Coplanar Detail Faces') and Texture Demos*

At first, I could not find much info about the Link DIG and the E&S CT-5 CGI systems on the Internet. Luckily, I came across several demos on 'youtube.com' about these 2 competitive systems.

# Flight Simulation and RT CGI

## *Back to the DIG Demo with CDFs*

There is a great demo comparing image details implemented with texture mapping [32] vs details implemented with CDFs in the following 'YouTube' video:

Link Flight Simulation Demo, Video [99]
  DIG-2 Demo, 1984:
  https://www.youtube.com/watch?v=uy8sJ9AxvYI

This demo was made by the Link R&D department using scenes of the DIG-2 (1978) and the ModDIG (1984). While I was busy implementing new features in the DIG product line, *Dave Hinkle* a talented SW and HW engineer, helped producing this video. *Dave* was also involved in the design of the Link ModDIG.

## *This DIG demo can be divided into 4 sequences*

- Time 0 to 1 min: The scenes demonstrate the texture mapping capabilities of the ModDIG. There are several examples of texture mapping on the ground, terrain and buildings. There are also examples of texture used to display leaves on tree branches using translucency. But, as can be observed, the image details represented with texture maps don't have sharp edges.
- Time 1 min to 4 min: These scenes have been generated by the DIG-2, with digital edge smoothing. There are several examples of detail faces where the contrast is reduced with distance. The polygon edges of CDFs are sharp and edge smoothed.
  - on the hills, square patches are displayed inside of displayed green triangles. These patches improve the 3-dimensional effects and orientations of the hills. They are implemented with CDF that fade away with distance.
  - the terrain patches on the ground are implemented with CDF. As can be observed, their contrasts gradually (and gracefully) decrease with distance.
  - the symbols and writing on the plane are implemented with CDF. This eliminates the aliasing when the markings get close to a Pixel.
  - there are also several examples of runways with polygons implemented with CDF.
- Time 4 min to 5 min: These scenes show several examples of take-off and landing. As can be seen, the CDFs on the runways are introduced and removed smoothly in the scenes.
- Last 10 sec, starting at 4min and 50sec:
  **You have to see this!** This is a view of the runway from an aircraft taking off. The effect of the approaching white runway stripes and black tire marks implemented with CDFs are introduced gradually into the scene. They provide the sensation of speed, without looking cartoonish. There is no aliasing. I have heard several observers saying 'whoah' the first time they observed this take-off scene.

## *CT-5 Demos with Texture*

The CT-5 (Continuous Tone 5) was designed around 5 years after the DIG. At that time, face buffer and texture mapping became feasible.
By comparison, there are similar scenes in the CT-5 demos from E&S.
Refer to 'YouTube' videos about *Evans & Sutherland* CT 5 Flight Simulator (1981) [86] [87]

## Flight Simulation and RT CGI

In this video there are examples of contrast decreasing with distance, simulated with translucency. In these cases, the decrease in contrast depends on distance only and is less natural than in the examples of details implemented with CDF in the DIG scenes.

In one example showing runway stripes during landing, the contrast of the runway stripes is reduced with distance, but is does not take into account the viewing angle. For this reason, although their contrast is reduced, the stripe contrasts remain too large with distance. They look bunched up as if they have increased size. For proper rendering, the contrast should decrease as the plane gets closer to the ground. This cannot be simulated with the distance only. In the DIG, the estimated projection size of CDF takes into account the distance and the viewing aspect angle.

The CT-5 had texture mapping and some translucency effects. The DIG-1 had no texture. The DIG-2 delivered for the Apache Helicopter had a texture implementation invented by *Johnson Yan* [112]. As another advantage of the DIGs, the implementation of CDF reduced aliasing artifacts by providing smooth transition of narrow faces in the scene.

### *RT CGI Systems Not Advertised*

Although the Link DIG was ahead of the competition when first delivered, it was not widely advertised. We needed to have security clearance when working on these systems. But the DIG success in winning important contracts with the Air Force did not remain unnoticed: F-111 for 9 systems and B-52 for 12 systems. It pushed the competition to design better RT CGI systems to remain competitive. Five years later, both E&S and General Electric (GE) started to produce RT CGI systems with better performances in the early 1980s.

The CT-5 had much better performances than the previous CGI systems from E&S, such as the CT-1 to CT-4.

GE was also a great contributor with its line of CompuScene CGI systems [89].

## 10.3 Memories and Memories of Memories

In digital computers, the processing elements consist mainly of 2 types of semiconductors chips, or modules, consisting of: combinational logic circuits and memory. The combinational logic modules consist of gates, multiplexers (muxr), registers (reg) and adders. There are also few analog elements such a s resistors, capacitors and inductors (coils). The semiconductor memories consist of array of flip-flops where the bit can be accessed with memory addresses.

The implementation of memory chips uses a process similar to logic circuits, but it is optimized for large memory density. For this reason, memory chips use a semiconductor process that is slightly different from the logic circuits chips. For large memory density, memory chips include only memory.

Both memory and logic circuit densities increased at a similar pace. Since the density of memory can be measured by the number bits contained in memory chips, it is easier to evaluate the circuit density using the memory density representation. The computer memory is referred to as Random Access Memory (RAM). The memory size is usually measured in bytes (B), where 8bits = 1byte = 1B.

## 10.3.1 Increase in Chip and Memory Density

According to Moore's law (from *Gordon Moore* at Intel), the chip density doubles every 2 years. During the 40 years following the DIG-1 introduction, the chip density has increased considerably.

As an example, in the mid 1970s, the DIG-1 used static memory (SRAM) chips from Intel with a density of only 1k bits. At that time there were dynamic memory chips (DRAM) from Mostek with 4k bit density. Four years later, there were 4 kbit (or 0.5 KB) SRAM and 16 kbit (or 2kB) DRAM.

Starting with 4kbit DRAM in 1976, 2 years later the density had increased to 8kbit = 1kB in 1978. Twenty years later, the chip density had increases by a factor of $2^{10}=1024$. So, in 1998, the chip density was around 8Mbits (=1MB) DRAM, in a larger package, a 1024x increase. This allowed to build RT CGI systems that fit insides of a single chip.

During the following 20 years until 2018, there was another 1024x increase in chip density. The memory density is now 1Gbyte. The 3D processing logic for CGI can now fit insides of a cell phone. In Figure 10-2, using Moore's law, the chart shows an estimate of the increase memory density as a function of time.

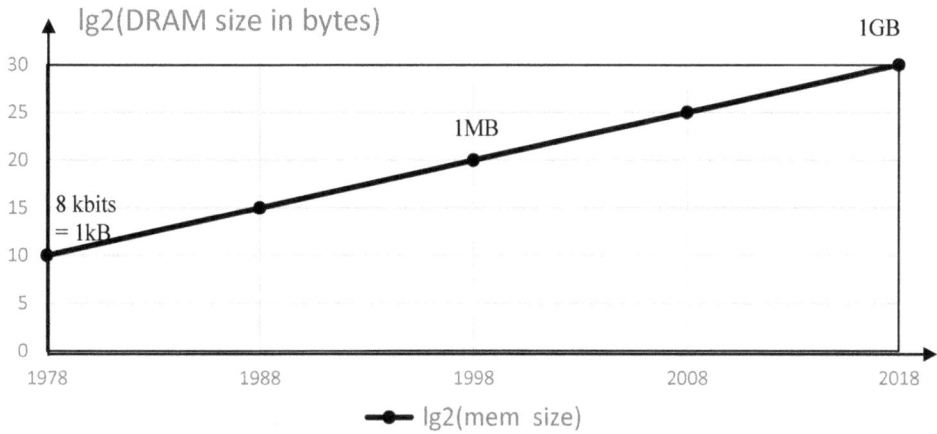

**Figure 10-2 Estimated Density of Memory Chip**

During these years, the 3D real-time computing units have evolved from very large systems designed with off the shelf MSI circuits, to compact ASIC designs fitting in Micro Computers such as the high-end PCs. In 1998, the chip density was around 8Mbits (=1MB) DRAM, in a larger package, a 1024 time increase from 1978. This allowed to build RT CGI systems that fit insides of a single chip.

## 10.3.2 Memory Requirement for Frame Buffers

The technology used to build RT CGI systems has been driven by the available chip density.

In order to build a Frame Buffer, or Z-buffer, the number of memory chips can be evaluated.

Flight Simulation and RT CGI

*Edge List and Face List*

Number of Bytes for Edge List: 2 * 16k edges * 32B/edge= 1MB
Number of Bytes for Face List: 2 * 16k edges * 32B/edge= 1MB (rough estimate)

*Color Buffer*

Number of bytes/address per Sample Point for R, G, B, alpha:  4 bytes
Number of Pixel addresses (*2 for double buffered):   2 *1024 Pix * 512 SL* 4 = 4M

*Z Buffer*

Number of bytes/address per Sample Point for Z:   2 to 4 bytes
Number of Pixel addresses Non-double buffered):   1 *1024 Pix * 512 SL * 4 = 2M

*Pixel Memory*

Total memory size for Color and Z-Buffer: 6MB

In Table 10-1, the number of memory chips requires for different implementation is shown for a 20year period ranging from 1978 to 1998. In the DIG, the size of the Active Data Base (ADB) is similar to the Edge List (EL).

|  | Size of Mem Chip | Chip count: 2*16k Edge List or 2*16k Face List | RGBA Double Buffer: 4MB | E-List + F-List: 2MB RGBA & Z Buffers Double Buffer: 6MB |
|---|---|---|---|---|
| 1978 | 1 kB | EL: 1MB/1k = 8k |  |  |
| 1982 | 4kB | FL: 1MB/4k = 2k | 4MB/4k = 1k chips |  |
| 1986 | 16kB |  | 4MB/16k = 256 chips | 6MB/16k = 512 chips |
| 1990 | 64 kB |  | 4MB/256k = 64 chips | 6MB/64k = 128 chips |
| 1994 | 256 kB |  |  | 6MB/256k = 32 chips |
| 1998 | 1MB |  |  | 6MB/1M = 8 chips |

**Table 10-1 Size of Memory Chips During a 20 Years Period**

## 10.3.3  RT CGI and the Personal Computer

After 1985, several computer companies entered the RT CGI business for simulators, including Silicon Graphics Inc (SGI) in Mountain Silicon View, CA, and Computervision Corp in Raleigh, NC. I am not sure about the details of their implementations. Most of them used the traditional Z-buffer approach.

Table 10-2 shows how large RT CGI systems have evolved from 1970 to 2000 and beyond.

| Year | Product | Occulting | Front End | Setup | Rendering |
|---|---|---|---|---|---|
| 1970 | RT CGI System | Priority Ordering | Mini Computer (Mini C) | Special Purpose Hardware | Special Purpose Hardware |
| 1976 1981 | Link DIG-1 Link DIG-2 | DIG-1: Mini C DIG-2: PSP | Mini C + PSP in DIG-2 | Frame Calculator | 1 SLC for 4 windows + 1 VG/window display |
| 1982 | E&S CT-5 | Mini C | Mini C | Geometric Processor | 1 SP/window display |
| 1982 | Link ModDig | Mini C | Mini C | Geometric Processor | 1 SP/window display |
| 1986 | SGI and Computer Vision | Z-Buffer? | Workstation | Workstation | ASIC Chips |
| 1996 | PC Add-on Card | Z-Buffer | Personal Computer (PC) | Setup: Geometric Transformations | Rendering: 1 ASIC Chip/window |
| 1998 | Warp5 Chip | ASIC | PC | Setup in PC | SP in ASIC Chip |
| 2008 | Game Cards | ASIC | PC | 1 ASIC Chip/window display | |
|  | CPU+GPU | Z-Buffer | Single Chip: PC processor (Front End) + Arrays of GPUs | | |
| 2018 | CPU+GPU | ASIC, GPU | Single Chip: PC processor (Front End) + Arrays of GPUs | | |

**Table 10-2 Evolution of Real-Time 3D Graphics Processing**

During these years, the 3D real-time computing units have evolved from very large systems designed with off the shelf MSI circuits, to compact ASIC designs fitting in Micro Computers such as the high-end PCs.

By the mid 1990s several companies were developing 3D graphics adapter for the gaming market. All of these companies produced 3D PC graphics adapters that were fast, but with jaggies and no AA. By 2000s, some of these companies started do AA using MSAA, but with greatly reduced performances.

In 1998, the chip density was around 8Mbits (=1MB) DRAM, in a larger package, a 1024 time increase from 1978. This allowed to build RT CGI systems that fit insides of a single chip. The first video cards for Personal Computers with 3D graphics chips appeared between 1996 and 1998 [77]. During that time, several companies like S3 Inc (Virge), 3DFx, Oak Technology (Warp 5), Rendition, Nvidia (Riva), and even Intel entered that market.

Among these designs, the Warp5 from Oak Technology [78] was the only chip that had Subpixel anti-aliasing. The other chips used the Z-buffer approach with only one Sample Point.

Flight Simulation and RT CGI

## 10.3.4 The Warp5 from Oak Technology

Oak Technology who had developed 2D graphics adapters in Sunnyvale, was looking for a team to develop a 3D graphics adapter. Oak Technology in Sunnyvale, was able to produce a 3D PC graphic with AA as standard feature.

*Jonson Yan* who had developed the Texture used in the DIG systems and who was Director of R&D at Link and *Rick Faden* who used to work at GE GSD, also had the same idea about developing a 3D PC graphics adapter with RT CGI and AA.

*Johnson* became Director of the 3D graphics department that included *Rick* an myself. We successfully produced the Warp5, the first 3D graphics chip with AA. The Warp 5 was warmly accepted in 1997 at the E3 show in Las Vegas.

In 1996 at Oak Technology in Sunnyvale [78], I joined a group of engineers including *Johnson Yan*, *Dan Weaver*, *Gary Daniel*, *Pankaj Patel* and *Doug Allen* (real-time SW) who used to work with me at Link Flight Simulation in Sunnyvale, CA. The 3D team at Oak Technology consisted several former employees of leading companies in RT CGI systems that were used for simulation and training. Under the direction of *Johnson Yan*, Oak Technology was developing a 3D graphics chip, the Warp5, for the Personal Computer market. *Johnson* was sharing my idea of creating a chip with high image quality and no jaggies, just like the real-time CGI systems designed at Link and also at General Electric. We wanted to be the first to share RT CGI technology with anti-aliasing with the general public. Included in our team was *Rick Fadden* (architect), *Chris Owen* (verification) and *Charles Lee* (Architect), who had decided to join us. *Rick* was a colorful 3D architect from General Electric Ground System Division (GSD), our previous competitor. He brought many important algorithms from his experience designing RT CGI systems at GE, including anti-aliasing with Subpixel processing and Tile (2D Span) traversing algorithm with polygon edges.

There is a twenty years difference between when the DIG-1 was delivered and when the Warp 5 was delivered. In 1977, the DIG-1 was the fastest RT CGI system with antialiasing. When introduced in 1997, among all the PC add-on graphics cards, the Warp 5 was the First and only PC 3D graphics adapter with anti-aliasing.

The Warp5 was introduced by Oak Technology [78] at the E3 trade show in June 1997, where it received the best of show award.

> Subject: interesting comment found on the net
> Author: TomW at Oak1po
> Date: 6/27/97 4:19 PM
>
>   From          "DARREN" <blade@ihug.co.nz>
>   Organization  The Internet Group Ltd
>   Date          25 Jun 1997 04:09:45 GMT
>   Newsgroups    comp.sys.ibm.pc.games.flight-sim
>   Message-ID    01bc811d$ca7aa040$b4f031ca@legacy.ihug.co.nz
>
> E3 Best of Show - WARP 5 wins Gold medal
> WARP 5 has been featured in the latest issue of an online gaming magazine. The editor had visited us at E3. They have awarded WARP 5 a gold medal in their technology review. This is what they had to say about WARP 5:
>                 Gold Medal, Technology
> Warp 5 Video Accelerator; Oak Technologies. After I saw their demonstration board running side-by-side with 3Dfx, I spent a good hour wandering around E3, talking to video card manufacturers telling them they'd better get their butts over to Oak's booth, and after they asked why watching their jaws drop when I explained. The Warp 5, a 2D/3D accelerator chipset that hit silicon just two weeks ago, is head and shoulders above any other accelerator for the consumer PC. It puts the Power-VR to shame not only in speed, but in technology as well.
> It features real-time anti-aliasing, a RAM-less on-chip 24-bit floating-point Z-Buffer, order-independent translucency rendering, true trilinear mipmap filtering with perspective correction, non-linear fogging, object morphing, multiple hardware windows with bilinear video scaling, and over 50 million pixels per second with all features active. Incredibly, the OEM price for the chip will be just $35, comparable to units that only two weeks ago were the best in the world. (Late summer '97)

Although the Warp5 was well received and a won best of show award at E3 trade show, Oak Technology decided to abandon the 3D graphics card market.

But it was the PC graphics adapters with the fastest 2D performances that won the race, because they were primarily used in business applications. After a couple of years, while I was working on the next generation of Warp5 using an early version of my ABAA approach, Oak Technology cancelled the 3D graphics project.

A few years later, other PC graphics adapter companies started to implement AA with Super Sampling, or MSAA. They were using brute force by computing several images followed by averaging. This was a trade-off between image quality vs processing speed.

## 10.3.5   RT CGI and the PC after 2000

After 2000, the 3D Graphics processing has evolved from a dedicated pipeline of subsystems into programmable array of Graphics Processing Units (GPU) [84][85].

# Chapter 11  Inside the Binary World

Some of the concepts described in this chapter might seem simple and obvious to some readers. If the reader has a good understanding of designs with binary logic, this should be helpful. On the other hand, other readers might need some time to understand. For this reason, I have provided several references to Wikipedia, the free encyclopedia on the Web. These references should provide the necessary information to bring the reader up to date.

In this chapter, I provide several examples with binary numbers and also the related 'octal' and 'hexadecimal' notations.

## 11.1 Programmer and Computer Interaction

Most of the modern computers are based on PCs, with Intel processors, the Apple Mac, or families of ARM processors [74]. Data and operations are entered in high level language using *decimal* numbers. Then, the compiler converts the decimal numbers into *binary* numbers and all the operation are executed in *binary* arithmetic.

### 11.1.1   Fixed Point vs Floating Point

One nice thing about Floating Point (FloatPt) over Fixed Point (FixedPt) is that they have an almost infinite range of number values. In most applications, there is no need to worry about overflow during computations. The binary FloatPt format is described by the IEEE 754 Standard [18]. Another nice thing about FloatPt numbers is that they are implemented with *signed magnitude binary* numbers. This means that FloatPt numbers are symmetrical with respect to the *integer zero*. They have a *positive zero* that is slightly larger than the *integer zero*. They have a *negative zero* that is slightly smaller than the *integer zero*.

But, FloatPt numbers cannot accurately represent the values of integer 0. This is because the FloatPt numbers have a limited number of fraction bits. After the limited number of fraction bits, the truncated fraction of FloatPt numbers is *unknown*. For this reason, "*integer zero* cannot be represented with a FloatPt *zero*". The smallest FloatPt number has an *exponent 0* minus an offset of *-126,* corresponding to $2^{-126}$. It has a fraction made of *23 zero bits*. But who knows what comes after these *23 zero bits*? There are an infinity number of bits, that have been truncated and ignored on the right side of these *23 zero bits*.

When implementing AA in Real-Time, the image processing has to be really fast, since the computations are performed on image Pixels. The number of Pixels on displayed images is roughly 1 million Pixels, or 1 Mega Pixel. AA computations have to be performed on all the Pixels that are intersected by triangle edges. The best approach is to implement the computation hardware and also programs with FixedPt integers or binary numbers. FixedPt integers in the computers and also digital integrated circuits consist of integer binary numbers, where a point position is "assumed" by the context and the programmer.

For simulation purpose, computations could be performed with FloatPt, although FloatPt numbers are not well suited for the AA implementations. FloatPt HW is efficient for multiplications. But for addition and subtraction FloatPt HW is inefficient and requires more circuitry. Also, AA computations require logic and math operations that can be easily implemented with integer numbers.

## 11.1.2 Inside each Computer there is a Binary World

From the outside, a computer is programmed by writing code using decimal numbers and decimal arithmetic. Then the compiler converts these decimal numbers into binary numbers for the program execution. When the results need to be printed on paper or displayed on a terminal, the printer driver converts these binary numbers into decimal numbers.

Most SW programmers are not aware of what's happening inside of the computer HW. The interaction between programmers and computers HW is hidden by the operating system. Inside of the computer, "Binary is the Law". There are millions of bits inside of the computer fighting for computing time and memory space. So, unless you are involved with the operations inside computers, you are not aware that 'Inside each Computer there is a Binary World'.

Refer to Figure 11-1, "Interaction between Programmer and Computer".

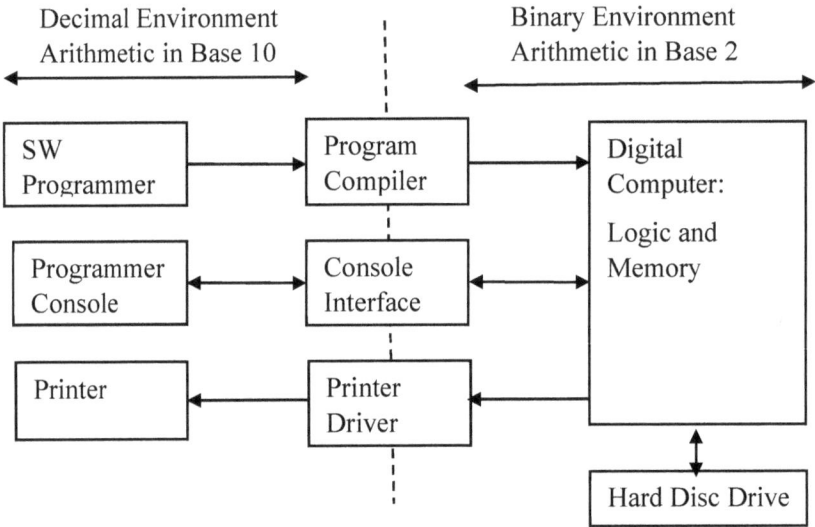

**Figure 11-1 Interaction between Programmer and Computer**

While the math functions can be described with *decimal* integers, FixedPt or FloatPt numbers, the operations inside of the computer are always performed with *binary* numbers. For *binary* integer numbers in computer hardware, the notion of FixedPt and Point Position does not exist. It exists in our "head" as we keep track of the point position during the operations. This similar to doing operation on paper and pencil with fractions of decimal numbers. Regardless of the point position, the operations with FixedPt *binary* numbers remain the same.

## 11.1.3   Pixel Colors and ARGB Color Components

The output of CGI systems consists of rectangular images made of arrays of *PixMax* x *SLMax* color Pixels, displayed at 30 or 60 fields per sec. The image size is on average 1k x 1k Pixels.

Because the color output can be defined by a number of bits such as 16, 24 or 32 bits, the Pixel color is computed with binary number calculations.

Since the purpose of designing a CGI system is to produce color images, the reader should be familiar of the CGI system output format.

Each Pixel if of size 1x1 and has a uniform color defined by 3 or 4 components (*Alpha, Red, Green, Blue*). The (*A, R, G, B*) components can be defined with:

- 32 bits with (*A[8], R[8], G[8], B[8]*), where *A* is the alpha transparency.
- 24 bits (*R[8], G[8], B[8]*)
- 16 bits (*R[5], G[6], B[5]*)

For 32-bit color, the components are defined by 8-bit integer values ranging from *0* to *255*.

```
31      28      24      20      16      12      8       4       0
+-------+-------+-------+-------+-------+-------+-------+-------+
|      A[8]     |      R[8]     |      G[8]     |      B[8]     |
+-------+-------+-------+-------+-------+-------+-------+-------+
```

For the 16-bit format, *R[5]* and *B[5]* range from 0 to 31. *G[6]* ranges from 0 to 63.

```
15      12      8       4       0
+-------+-+-----+-----+-+-------+
|  R[5] |   G[6]  |  B[5] |
+-------+-+-----+-----+-+-------+
```

## 11.2 Decimal vs Binary Number

Since I am trying to be clear in presenting my ideas, I have to be cautious and may over explain some of the concepts. Some readers might not agree with my selections for describing the AA operations with a mix of Decimal and Binary numbers. I will use the number base that make the most sense. They might react in many different ways. Our World is not limited to Decimal and Binary numbers.

I have several examples where we all use bases other than base 10. To begin, we count in base 10 because the early men used to count with their 10 fingers. They also used other numbering base, derived from our interaction with the Sun, Moon and Earth.

For example, when we want to date the first day of Summer, we usually say:
 "June 21$^{st}$ of year 2021", which means "Century 20$^{th}$, Year 21$^{st}$, Month 6th, Day 21$^{st}$.
We usually don't say the "145th day of the 21$^{st}$ Year in 21$^{th}$ Century", which is in decimal notation. Instead, we rely on the interaction between the Sun, Moon and Earth.

The Moon rotates around the earth in 28 days (i.e. base 28), which is close to a month. It takes 4 weeks at 7 days per week (i.e. base 7). In base 7, the count goes from 0 to 6 and the 8$^{th}$ day is represented by 10 (base 7). So, using count in base 7, the Moon rotates around the Earth in 40 days (in base 7).

Inside the Binary World

There is something special about the number 7. Experiments have shown that when you are given a sequence of numbers or names, humans can easily remember up to a count of 7, but usually cannot remember past 7.

The Earth rotates around the Sun in around 365.25 days (i.e. base 365). So, for the early man, the number of months was obtained by dividing 365/28= ~13. But 13 is not practical. I can imagine why a year with 12 months was selected, instead 13 months, which is a primary number greater than 7. The number 12 is more manageable because it can be divided into 4 seasons of 3 months each. Then the sizes of the 12 months have been adjusted to a number of days between 28 and 31 to fit within a year. So, using a notation in base 12, a year has 10 (in base 12) months.

When looking at numbers base other than 10, there many events in life that use base 2 or other bases. Refer to Table 11-1, "Example of Number Bases".

Since most readers already use base 7 for week days and base 12 for month numbering (and buying dozen of eggs). It should be easy to adapt to binary numbers in base 2.

| Event | Number of States | Off | On or Count | base |
|---|---|---|---|---|
| Electrical switch | 2 | 0 | 1 | 2 |
| Computer Bits | 2 | 0 | 1 | 2 |
| Boolean Algebra | 2 | 0 (false) | 1 (true) | 2 |
| Car Engine | 2 | 0 | 1 (running) | 2 |
| Human life | 2 | 0 (dead) | 1 (alive) | 2 |
| Cat | 10 | 0 (dead) | 9, 8, 7, 6, 5, 4, 3, 2 ,1 (alive) | 10 |
| Days of Week | 7 |  | 1, 2, 3, 4, 5, 6, 7 (count) | 7 |
| Moon cycles | 4*7 |  | 1 to 7 (count) | 7 |
| Month, Eggs | 12 |  | 1 to 12 (count) | 12 |
| Hours of day | 2*12 |  | 0 to 11 (count) | 12 |
| Minutes & Sec | 60 |  | 0 to 59 (count) | 60 |

**Table 11-1 Example of Number Bases**

## 11.2.1 What's Funny about HW Designers?

There are situations in life that you will always visually remember.

As a HW designer for the Link RT CGI systems, I had several memorable moments, and I often think about it.

I was an early designer of the Link CGI prototype at Link Flight Simulation in Sunnyvale, CA. At that time NASA was requesting bids for a visual system to be used in its Shuttle Mission Simulator (SMS) program. Link was designing its own CGI prototype to be used in the bid for the SMS program. It happened that the Link Division in Binghamton, NY, had previously delivered a Flight

Simulator to NASA using and array of 25 minicomputers to produce CGI scenes. Besides programming the images, the SW engineers in Binghamton Simulation were also responsible for programming the Flight Computer and the simulators motion systems. The images produced by this early system were quite crude for simulation. NASA needed a better and more realistic system using "Virtual Reality". In order to have higher quality CGI for the Space Shuttle Mission simulation, special purpose computers for generating CGI in real-time were required. The task of developing the computer hardware (HW) for the CGIs was assigned to the Advanced Product Operation (APO) of the Link Division in Sunnyvale, CA. Link APO had previous experience designing high speed HW simulators for DRLMS (Digital Radar Landmass Simulators) and also for a Nuclear Power Plant simulator.

So, it was decided that the HW for the CGI prototype would be developed in a Sunnyvale "bubble", and the SW team in a Binghamton "bubble" would develop the Real-Time code to drive the CGI HW. This was before C-programming was available. The Real-Time computer programs were written in assembly language. At that time, beside the low-level assembly language, the high-level programming of choice was Fortran [71]. In Fortran and assembly, the low-level internal operations were hidden from the programmer to facilitate programming. The programmer did not have access the memory addresses and logic operations on integer variables. In the 1980s, C-programming was introduced [72]. In C, the introduction of 'pointers' and 'logic operations' ('&': AND, '|': OR, '<<': left shift, '>>': right shift) provided a bridge between low-level and high-level programming.

The CGI HW in Sunnyvale was initially tested with a simple flight simulation program and a flight panel. The window image was displayed on large high-resolution CRT (Cathode Ray Tube) provided by the Binghampton team from one of their existing motion simulator systems. Then, came the time to integrate the CGI HW from Sunnyvale with the RT SW in assembly language from the Binghamton SW team. Among these SW engineers were a Sr SW lead and 2 programmers. After the SW team was introduced, one of the junior programmers made the following comment:

"There is something funny about you, HW designers.
Why do you always have to select memory sizes in a power of 2?"

I was surprised at first, but since then, I often think about it. I had already spent a few years as a design HW engineer designing digital computer components. I was very familiar with HW implementations with binary logic circuits. After this comment, I became aware of the interaction between programmers and computers. The HW computations are hidden by the operating system. So, unless you are involved with the operations inside computers, you are not aware that 'Inside each Computer there is a Binary World'.

Since the SW RT programmers had developed their code in a Binghamton bubble, they were surprised by the memory sizes selected by the HW engineers in their CGI design. I understand that many readers will be surprised and may be annoyed by my insistence on using binary arithmetic for my AA implementation. For a while, they will wonder: "Why using arithmetic base 2? Programmers are doing fine doing their programs in base 10".

## Inside the Binary World

As mentioned by the Binghamton programmer, the use of powers of 2 for memory sizes is not obvious at first. But it is dictated by the memory address lines that consist of binary numbers made of 0's and 1's. Memory locations are accessed from the logic circuits address lines with binary numbers. With 10 bits of address, 1024 memory locations can be accessed. This is often referred to 1k memory locations. With 20 bits of address, 1'048'576 memory locations (or 1M) can be accessed. Since memories are part of the HW, they are located on memory boards (in case of semiconductor memories). In memory boards, because of the binary addressing, the memory size is a power of 2.

In computer memories, the memory addressing is organized in memory blocks. For practical reasons, the memory blocks are also organized in power of 2. This way, the base or starting addresses of memory block use incremental blocks sizes with lower bits being *0*. For example, for incremental block addresses of 1kB, the lower bits will consist of 10 zero bits. For incremental block addresses of 1MB, the lower bits will consist of 20 zero bits.

When writing a computer program, the SW programmer has the freedom to assign large memory blocks of any size. For example, a memory block of size 1 Million (decimal 1 M) locations can be specified. This makes sense.

But, when a HW designer has to allocate a large memory block for its local data base, he has no other choice than selecting a power of 2, such as binary 1M=1'048'576=0x100000 (in hexadecimal) locations. This makes sense.

The AA computation are performed near the end of the 3D image computations. They consist of simple and quick operations with binary numbers of size between 8 and 16 bits.

### 11.2.2 Decimal Digit vs Binary Digit

While most of the computations in every day's life deal with decimal numbers, in modern computers all operations are done with binary numbers.

Decimal numbers are defined as numbers base 10. They are made up of 10 decimal digits. Each digit can have one of the following values:
*0, 1, 2, 3, 4, 5, 6, 7, 8, 9*.

Logic Design [19] deals with defining circuit using Boolean expressions and binary arithmetic.

Binary numbers are defined as numbers base 2. They are expressed with bits binary digits, or that have only 2 states. Each "binary digit" can have one of the following values:
*0* and *1*.
A "binary digit" is referenced to as a "bit".

Just like digital numbers, the binary numbers are defined by a sequence of binary digits. They can be signed and unsigned. For signed numbers, the most significant bit (*MSB*) is *0* for positive numbers and *1* for negative numbers.

Binary numbers use 3 to 4 times more digits than decimal numbers to represent the same value. Refer to example in table 11-2

| Integer Number | Decimal: 3 decimal digits | Binary: 9 or 10 bits | Hexadecimal: 2 or 3 hex digits |
|---|---|---|---|
| unsigned | 255 | 0 1111 1111 | 0x0ff |
| unsigned | 255 | 1 0000 0000 | 0x100 |
| signed | +256 | 01 0000 0000 | 0x 100 |
| signed | -256 | 11 0000 0000 | 0x f00 = - 0x100 |

**Table 11-2 Comparison between Decimal and Binary Numbers**

The space between digits is used to facilitate reading.

A special case of binary number is the Boolean variable, which is a single digit with 2 values: *True (==1)* and *False (==0)*.

When comparing numbers or comparing alpha-numeric expressions (i.e. sentences), the result is expressed as "*True*" or "*False*".
Note that the symbol "==" (double =) indicates "equal" when expressions are "compared".

In order to make the binary numbers more readable, the bits in binary numbers can be organized in group of 3 to form "*octal*" numbers or in group of 4 to form "*hexadecimal*" numbers.

Octal numbers are defined as numbers base 8. They are made up of 8 octal digits. Each octal digit can have the following values:
*octal (0, 1, 2, 3, 4, 5, 6, 7)* corresponding to *binary (000, 001, 010, 011, 100, 101, 110, 111)*.

Hexadecimal numbers, or simply "hex numbers", are defined as numbers base 16. They are made up of 16 hexadecimal digits, or simply "hex digit". Each hex digit can have the following values:
*0, 1, 2, 3, 4, 5, 6, 7, 8, 9. a, b, c, d, e, f.*
Or:
*0, 1, 2, 3, 4, 5, 6, 7, 8, 9. A, B, C, D, E, F.*

Each hexadecimal digit, from 0 to f, corresponds to a group of 4 bits, as follows:
*0000, 0001, 0010, 0011, 0100, 0101, 0110, 0111, 1000, 1001, 1010, 1011, 1100, 1101, 1110, 1111*

A summary of numbers and Bases is shown in Table 11-3.
As example, the integer number 321 is used.

## Inside the Binary World

| Digits | Base | Single Digits | Zero | Number Example |
|---|---|---|---|---|
| decimal | 10 | 0, 1, 2, 3, 4, 5, 6, 7, 8, 9 | 0 | 321 |
| Boolean (single bit) | 2 | False, True | False | True (non-zero) |
| Binary (bit or bits) | 2 | 0, 1 | 0 | 1 0100 0001 (decimal 321 = 256 + 64 +1) |
| octal (group of 3 bits) | 8 | 0, 1, 2, 3, 4, 5, 6, 7 | o0 | o501 (binary 101 000 001 = decimal 320+0+1) |
| hexadecimal or hex (group of 4 bits) | 16 | 0, 1, 2, 3, 4, 5, 6, 7, 8, 9. a, b, c, d, e, f | 0x0 | 0x141 (binary 1 0100 0001 = decimal 256+64+1) |

**Table 11-3 Numbers and Bases**

### *Decimal 1k vs Binary 1k*

What is not commonly known is that there is a difference between Decimal 1k and Binary 1k.

When we buy 1kg of bread, we get 1000 grams of bread.

When we buy 1 kbit of memory, we get 1024 bits.

When we buy a 100 Megabyte of Hard Disk Drive, it can be either 100'000 bytes of HDD, or 102,400 bytes of HDD

In Table 11-4, "Decimal 1k vs Binary 1k", some decimal and binary numbers are selected to show the difference between the definition of Decimal 1k and Binary 1k.

| Decimal | Binary (3bits) | Octal | Binary (4bits) | Hexadecimal |
|---|---|---|---|---|
| 1 | 1 | o1 | 1 | 0x1 |
| 2 | 10 | o2 | 10 | 0x 2 |
| 4 | 100 | o4 | 100 | 0x 4 |
| 8 | 1'000 | o10 | 1000 | 0x 8 |
| 10 | 1'010 | o12 | 1010 | 0x a |
| 16 | 10'000 | o20 | 1'0000 | 0x10 |
| 32 | 100'000 | o40 | 10'0000 | 0x20 |
| 64 | 1'000'000 | o100 | 100'0000 | 0x40 |
| 100 | 1'100'100 | o144 | 110'0100 | 0x64 |
| 128 | 10'000'000 | o200 | 1000'0000 | 0x 80 |
| 256 | 100'000'000 | o400 | 1'0000'0000 | 0x100 |
| 512 | 1'000'000'000 | o1000 | 10'0000'0000 | 0x200 |
| 1000 = dec 1k | 1'111'101'000 | o1750 | 11'1110'1000 | 0x3e8 |
| 1024 = dec 2**10 | 10'000'000'000 = bin 1k (kilo) | o2000 | 100'0000'0000 = bin 1k | 0x400 |
| 1'000'000 = dec 1M (Mega) = dec 1k*1k | | | | 0x0f4240 = dec 1M |
| 1'048'576 = dec 2**20 | bin 1M (Mega) = bin 1k*1k | o4000000 | bin 1M = bin 1k*1k | 0x100000 |

**Table 11-4 Decimal 1k vs Binary 1k**

## 11.3 Binary Numbers

There are several references about binary numbers, logic design, integrated circuits, register transfer logic (RTL) and Verilog [19].

### 11.3.1 Operations with Binary numbers

The arithmetic computations with binary and decimal numbers consist mainly of 4 basic operations: addition *(+)*, subtraction *(-)*, multiplication *(\*)* and division *(/)*. The exponent operation is represented here by *(\*\*)* in C programs, or by *(^)* in Excel spreadsheets. For example, "*x to the power 4*" is represented by "*x\*\*4*", or "*x^4*".

Beside these four basic operations, the binary numbers can also be combined with Boolean operations.

Refer to Table 11-5 for Operations with Decimal and Binary Numbers.

In the case of Expression comparisons, the expression
$z = (x == y);$

## Inside the Binary World

Can be rewritten in Verilog language as:

*if (x == y)*
  *z = TRUE;   // or z = 1'b1;*
*else*
  *z = FALSE;   // or z = 1'b0;*

The symbol // is used to insert comments in Verilog and C program code.

There are 2 types of symbols for the operators *AND, OR, Invert* and *EXOR*.

The bitwise operators *(&, |, ~, ^))* apply to operations on bits of same weight in a group of binary numbers with same number of bits.

The single bit operators *(&&, ||, !, ⊕))* apply to a binary variables with value *True* or *False*.

| Type | Operations | Symbol | Examples | Result |
|---|---|---|---|---|
| Arithmetic (any base) | Addition subtraction multiplication division exponent | + <br> - <br> * <br> / <br> ** | z = x + y <br> z = x - y <br> z = x * y <br> z = x / y <br> z = x**4 <br>   = x * x * x * x | any base: (binary or decimal) |
| binary: bitwise operator | AND <br> OR <br> Invert <br> EXOR | & <br> \| <br> ~ <br> ^ | C = A & B <br> C = A \| B <br> B = ~A <br> C = A^B <br>   = (A & ~B) \| (~A & B) | binary |
| bit shift or binary exponent | left shift <br><br> right shift | << <br><br> >> | // 4 left shifts <br> B = A << 4  = A * 2**4 <br> // 4 right shifts <br> B = A >> A  = A * 2**(-4) | binary |
| Boolean: single bit operator | AND <br> OR <br> Invert <br> EXOR | && <br> \|\| <br> ! <br> ⊕ | C = A && B <br> C = A \|\| B <br> B = !A <br> C = A ⊕ B <br>   = (A && !B) \|\| (!A && B) | Boolean |
| Boolean Comparison (x and y can be of any base; z is Boolean) | equal <br> not equal <br> greater <br> greater or equal <br> smaller <br> smaller or equal | == <br> != <br> > <br> >= <br> < <br> <= | C = (x == y) <br> C = (x != y) <br> C = (x > y) <br> C = (x >= y) <br> C = (x < y) <br> C = (x <= y) | Compare x and y (Integer or Floats) <br> Result is Boolean C |

**Table 11-5 Operations with Decimal and Binary Numbers5**

## 11.3.2 Boolean Single-Bit Operator

In Figure 11-2, the four binary operations AND, NAND, OR and NOR are represented with their "Truth Tables" and "Gate" symbols. In these tables, the *1's* and *0's* could also be represented with their *True* and *False* states.

Note that in these examples, there are only 2 bits at the input of each symbol. In fact, each input can have more than 2 bits.

For example, for an AND gate with 3 inputs *A*, *B* and *C*, the output is $D = A \ \&\& \ B \ \&\& \ C$.

| 2 Input | AND Gate |
|---|---|
| Input A B | Output C = A && B |
| 0  0 | 0 |
| 0  1 | 0 |
| 1  0 | 0 |
| 1  1 | 1 |

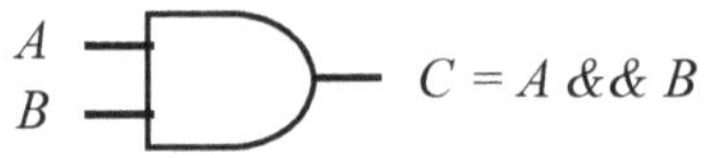

$A$, $B$ → $C = A \,\&\&\, B$

| 2 Input | NAND Gate |
|---|---|
| Input A B | Output C = ! (A && B) |
| 0  0 | 1 |
| 0  1 | 1 |
| 1  0 | 1 |
| 1  1 | 0 |

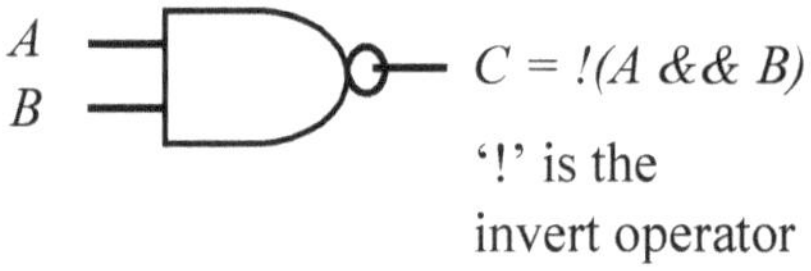

$A$, $B$ → $C = !(A \,\&\&\, B)$

'!' is the invert operator

| 2 Input | OR Gate |
|---|---|
| Input A B | Output C = A \|\| B |
| 0  0 | 0 |
| 0  1 | 1 |
| 1  0 | 1 |
| 1  1 | 1 |

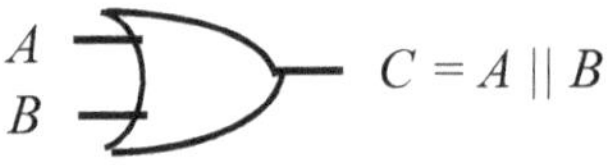

$A$, $B$ → $C = A \,\|\|\, B$

| 2 Input | NOR Gate |
|---|---|
| Input A B | Output C = ! (A \|\| B) |
| 0  0 | 1 |
| 0  1 | 0 |
| 1  0 | 0 |
| 1  1 | 0 |

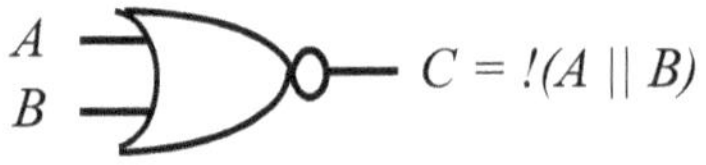

$A$, $B$ → $C = !(A \,\|\|\, B)$

**Figure 11-2 AND, NAND, OR and NOR Truth Tables and Gate Symbols**

The single bit operators *(&&, ||, !, ⊕))* apply to a pair of binary numbers with values:

*0 (= False) or 1 (= True)*

In Figure 11-3, the two binary operations exclusive OR (or EX-OR) and Exclusive NOR (or EX-NOR) are represented with their "Truth Tables" and "Gate" symbols.

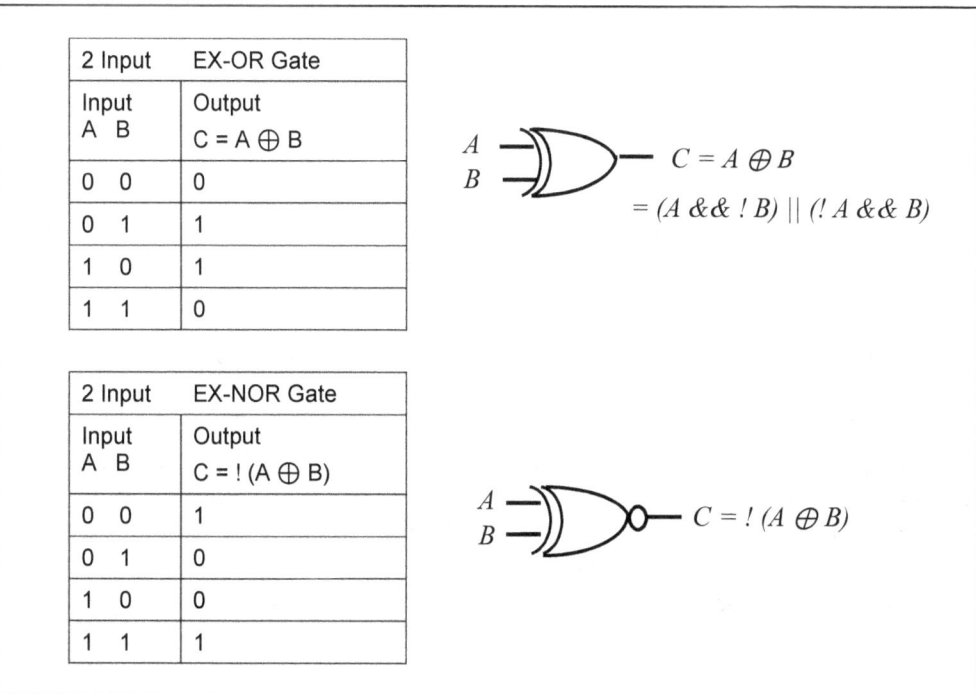

**Figure 11-3 Exclusive OR and NOR Truth Tables and Gate Symbols**

*De Morgan's Theorem*

The De Morgan's Theorem is a particularly powerful tool in digital design [19].
The theorem states that the complement *(boolean invert: !)* of ANDed *(&&)* terms Is Equal To the ORed *(||)* complemented *(inverted: !)* terms.
For example:
  *! (A && B) = !A || !B*

Likewise, the complement *(!)* of ORed *(||)* terms Is Equal to the ANDed *(&&)* complemented *(!)* terms.
For example:
  *! (A || B) = !A && !B*

### 11.3.3 Integer Multiple-Bits Bitwise Operator

The bitwise operators *(&, |, ~, ^))* apply to operations on bits of same weight applied to groups of binary numbers with same number of bits. Refer to examples in Table 11-6

Examples of Bitwise Operations:

| Bitwise AND | Bitwise OR | Bitwise EX-OR | Invert Bits |
|---|---|---|---|
| 1010 & 0101 = 0000; | 1010 \| 0101 = 1111; | 1010 ^ 0101 = 1111; | ~0101 = 1010; |
| 1010 & 0010 = 0010; | 1010 \| 0010 = 1110; | 1010 ^ 0010 = 1000; | ~1010 = 0101; |
| 0000 & 1111 = 0000; | 0000 \| 1111 = 1111; | 0000 ^ 1111 = 1111; | ~0000 = 1111; |
| 1111 & 1111 = 1111; | 1111 \| 1111 = 1111; | 1111 ^ 1111 = 0000; | ~1111 = 0000; |

**Table 11-6 Examples of Bitwise AND, OR, EX-OR and Invert**

### 11.3.4 Binary Coded Decimal Integers

For finance computations, the earlier computers used *base 10* binary numbers, instead of the more familiar *binary* numbers of *base 2*. The *number 10* is the product of two primary numbers: *2 and 5*. The computations were implemented with logic base ten using a *Binary Coded Decimal* numbering system (refer to IBM EBCDIC). The *Binary Coded Decimal* numbers in *base 10* consists of groups of *4 bits* that are a subset of the *binary* numbers *base 2*.

For *BCD* numbers, the maximum digit is *(decimal) 9*, or *(binary) 1001*. The next *BCD* increment is *(decimal) 10*, that is expressed as *BCD binary 10000*. The *binary* values of *decimal 10 to 19,* as represented in EBCDIC by *binary 10000 to 11001 (or hex 0x10 to 0x19)*.

Binary values *1010 to 1111 (or hex 0x0a to 0x0f)* are skipped. Refer to Table 11-7.

| Decimal 0 to 9:<br>0, 1, 2, 3, 4,<br>5, 6, 7, 8, 9 | Binary code in EBCDIC for decimal 0 to 9:<br>0 0000, 0 0001, 0 0010, 0 0011, 0 0100,<br>0 0101, 0 0110, 0 0111, 0 1000, 0 1001 |
|---|---|
| | Binary values<br>01010, 0 1011, 0 1100, 0 1101, 0 1110, 0 1111<br>are skipped. |
| Decimal 10 to 19<br>10, 11, 12,1 3, 14,<br>15, 16, 17, 18, 19 | Binary code in EBCDIC for decimal 10 to 19:<br>01 0000, 01 0001, 01 0010, 01 0011,0 1 '0100,<br>01 0101, 01 0110, 01 0111, 01 1000, 01 1001 |

**Table 11-7 Decimal Numbers vs EBCDIC**

While divisions in *base 2* will complete only if the divisor is a multiple of *2*, divisions in *base 10* will complete only if the divisor is either multiple of *2* and/or *5*.

### *Binary Hex vs BCD Integers*

In Table 11-8, there are examples of Binary, Binary Hex and BCD Integers.

---

Binary Integers:
*Decimal* numbers from *0 to 15* correspond to 16 *binary* values:

0'0000, 0'0001, 0'0010, 0'0011, 0'0100, 0'0101, 0'0110, 0'0111,   // octal o00 to o07
0'1000, 0'1001, 0'1010, 0'1011, 0'1100, 0'1101, 0'1110, 0'1111,   // octal o10 to o17

*Decimal* numbers from *16 to 32* correspond to 16 *binary* values:

1'0000, 1'0001, 1'0010, 1'0011, 1'0100, 1'0101, 1'0110, 1'0111,   // octal o20 to o27
1'1000, 1'1001, 1'1010, 1'1011, 1'1100, 1'1101, 1'1110, 1'1111,   // octal o30 to o37
1'0000     // hex 0x10 = decimal 16

Binary Hex Integers:
Decimal numbers from 0 to 16 correspond to 17 Binary Hex values as follows.
0x0, 0x1, 0x2, 0x3, 0x4, 0x5, 0x6, 0x7, 0x8, 0x9, 0xa, 0xb, 0xc, 0xd, 0xe, 0xf, 0x10

BCD Integers:
Binary Coded Decimal Numbers from 0 to 10 correspond to 11 binary values:
0'0000, 0'0001, 0'0010, 0'0011, 0'0100,
0'0101, 0'0110, 0'0111, 0'1000, 0'1001, 1'0000

---

**Table 11-8 Examples of Binary, Binary Hex and BCD Integers**

For most math operations, *Binary integers* and *BCD integers* produce identical results. But they behave differently when doing divisions.

When dividing a *Binary* number by a power of *2*, like $k/2^n$, the division will be accurate. For all other prime numbers, the division will have a remainder.

When dividing a *BCD* number by a power of *2* or *5*, like $k/(2^m * 5^n)$ the division will be accurate. For all other prime numbers, the division will have a remainder

In both cases, divisions by *3, 7* and larger primary numbers always produce a remainder.

## 11.4 Comparison of Different Integer Types

I have many years working with logic and binary numbers. But, for many readers, this can be a new experience. For this reason, in this section there are tables of different integer types. These tables are provided here so that the reader can get familiar of the different formats provided for integer numbers like: decimal integer, binary integer, octal, hexadecimal and binary coded decimal (BCD).

### 11.4.1    Integer Tables

A comparison of different types of Integers is shown in the following tables. For positive integers, refer to Table 11-9. For negative integers, refer to Table 11-10.

## Inside the Binary World

| Decimal Count | Binary Coded Decimal | Binary Count | Octal Count | Binary Octal Count | Hex Count | Binary Hex Count |
|---|---|---|---|---|---|---|
| 0  | 0000 0000 | 00000 0 | 0 0 0 | 000 000 000 | 0x0000 | 0000 0000 |
| 1  | 0000 0001 | 00000 1 | 0 0 1 | 000 000 001 | 0x0001 | 0000 0001 |
| 2  | 0000 0010 | 00001 0 | 0 0 2 | 000 000 010 | 0x0002 | 0000 0010 |
| 3  | 0000 0011 | 00001 1 | 0 0 3 | 000 000 011 | 0x0003 | 0000 0011 |
| 4  | 0000 0100 | 00010 0 | 0 0 4 | 000 000 100 | 0x0004 | 0000 0100 |
| 5  | 0000 0101 | 00010 1 | 0 0 5 | 000 000 101 | 0x0005 | 0000 0101 |
| 6  | 0000 0110 | 00011 0 | 0 0 6 | 000 000 110 | 0x0006 | 0000 0110 |
| 7  | 0000 0111 | 00011 1 | 0 0 7 | 000 000 111 | 0x0007 | 0000 0111 |
| 8  | 0000 1000 | 00100 0 | 0 1 0 | 000 001 000 | 0x0008 | 0000 1000 |
| 9  | 0000 1001 | 00100 1 | 0 1 1 | 000 001 001 | 0x0009 | 0000 1001 |
| 10 | 0001 0000 | 00101 0 | 0 1 2 | 000 001 010 | 0x000a | 0000 1010 |
| 11 | 0001 0001 | 00101 1 | 0 1 3 | 000 001 011 | 0x000b | 0000 1011 |
| 12 | 0001 0010 | 00110 0 | 0 1 4 | 000 001 100 | 0x000c | 0000 1100 |
| 13 | 0001 0011 | 00110 1 | 0 1 5 | 000 001 101 | 0x000d | 0000 1101 |
| 14 | 0001 0100 | 00111 0 | 0 1 6 | 000 001 110 | 0x000e | 0000 1110 |
| 15 | 0001 0101 | 00111 1 | 0 1 7 | 000 001 111 | 0x000f | 0000 1111 |
| 16 | 0001 0110 | 01000 0 | 0 2 0 | 000 010 000 | 0x0010 | 0001 0000 |
| 17 | 0001 0111 | 01000 1 | 0 2 1 | 000 010 001 | 0x0011 | 0001 0001 |
| 18 | 0001 1000 | 01001 0 | 0 2 2 | 000 010 010 | 0x0012 | 0001 0010 |
| 19 | 0001 1001 | 01001 1 | 0 2 3 | 000 010 011 | 0x0013 | 0001 0011 |
| 20 | 0010 0000 | 01010 0 | 0 2 4 | 000 010 100 | 0x0014 | 0001 0100 |
| 21 | 0010 0001 | 01010 1 | 0 2 5 | 000 010 101 | 0x0015 | 0001 0101 |
| 22 | 0010 0010 | 01011 0 | 0 2 6 | 000 010 110 | 0x0016 | 0001 0110 |
| 23 | 0010 0011 | 01011 1 | 0 2 7 | 000 010 111 | 0x0017 | 0001 0111 |
| 24 | 0010 0100 | 01100 0 | 0 3 0 | 000 011 000 | 0x0018 | 0001 1000 |
| 25 | 0010 0101 | 01100 1 | 0 3 1 | 000 011 101 | 0x0019 | 0001 1001 |
| 26 | 0010 0110 | 01101 0 | 0 3 2 | 000 011 010 | 0x001a | 0001 1010 |
| 27 | 0010 0111 | 01101 1 | 0 3 3 | 000 011 011 | 0x001b | 0001 1011 |
| 28 | 0010 1000 | 01110 0 | 0 3 4 | 000 011 100 | 0x001c | 0001 1100 |
| 29 | 0010 1001 | 01110 1 | 0 3 5 | 000 011 101 | 0x001d | 0001 1101 |
| 30 | 0011 0000 | 01111 0 | 0 3 6 | 000 011 110 | 0x001e | 0001 1110 |
| 31 | 0011 0001 | 01111 1 | 0 3 7 | 000 011 111 | 0x001f | 0001 1111 |
| 32 | 0011 0010 | 01000 0 | 0 4 0 | 000 100 000 | 0x0020 | 0010 0000 |

**Table 11-9 Decimal vs Binary Positive Integer Numbers**

# Inside the Binary World

| Decimal Count | Binary Coded Decimal | Binary Count | Octal Count | Binary Octal Count | Hex Count | Binary Hex Count |
|---|---|---|---|---|---|---|
| -1 | 1 10011001 | 11111 1 | 1 777 | 111 111 111 | 0xffff | 1111 1111 |
| -2 | 1 10011000 | 11111 0 | 1 776 | 111 111 110 | 0xfffe | 1111 1110 |
| -3 | 1 1001 0111 | 11110 1 | 1 775 | 111 111 101 | 0xfffd | 1111 1101 |
| -4 | 1 1001 0110 | 11110 0 | 1 774 | 111 111 100 | 0xfffc | 1111 1100 |
| -5 | 1 1001 0101 | 11101 1 | 1 773 | 111 111 011 | 0xfffb | 1111 1011 |
| -6 | 1 1001 0100 | 11101 0 | 1 772 | 111 111 010 | 0xfffa | 1111 1010 |
| -7 | 1 1001 0011 | 11100 1 | 1 771 | 111 111 001 | 0xfff9 | 1111 1001 |
| -8 | 1 1001 0010 | 11100 0 | 1 770 | 111 111 000 | 0xfff8 | 1111 1000 |
| -9 | 1 1001 0001 | 11011 1 | 1 767 | 111 110 111 | 0xfff7 | 1111 0111 |
| -10 | 1 1001 0000 | 11011 0 | 1 766 | 111 110 110 | 0xfff6 | 1111 0110 |
| -11 | 1 1000 1001 | 11010 1 | 1 765 | 111 110 101 | 0xfff5 | 1111 0101 |
| -12 | 1 1000 1000 | 11010 0 | 1 764 | 111 110 100 | 0xfff4 | 1111 0100 |
| -13 | 1 1000 0111 | 11001 1 | 1 763 | 111 110 011 | 0xfff3 | 1111 0011 |
| -14 | 1 1000 0110 | 11001 0 | 1 762 | 111 110 010 | 0xfff2 | 1111 0010 |
| -15 | 1 1000 0101 | 11000 1 | 1 761 | 111 110 001 | 0xfff1 | 1111 0001 |
| -16 | 1 1000 0100 | 11000 0 | 1 760 | 111 110 000 | 0xfff0 | 1111 0000 |
| -17 | 1 1000 0011 | 10111 1 | 1 757 | 111 101 111 | 0xffef | 1110 1111 |
| -18 | 1 1000 0010 | 10111 0 | 1 756 | 111 101 110 | 0xffee | 1110 1110 |
| -19 | 1 1000 0001 | 10110 1 | 1 755 | 111 101 101 | 0xffed | 1110 1101 |
| -20 | 1 1000 0000 | 10110 0 | 1 754 | 111 101 100 | 0xffec | 1110 1100 |
| -21 | 1 0111 1001 | 10101 1 | 1 753 | 111 101 011 | 0xffeb | 1110 1011 |
| -22 | 1 0111 1000 | 10101 0 | 1 752 | 111 101 010 | 0xffea | 1110 1010 |
| -23 | 1 0111 0111 | 10100 1 | 1 751 | 111 101 001 | 0xffe9 | 1110 1001 |
| -24 | 1 0111 0110 | 10100 0 | 1 750 | 111 101 000 | 0xffe8 | 1110 1000 |
| -25 | 1 0111 0101 | 10011 1 | 1 747 | 111 100 111 | 0xffe7 | 1110 0111 |
| -26 | 1 0111 0100 | 10011 0 | 1 746 | 111 100 110 | 0xffe6 | 1110 0110 |
| -27 | 1 0111 0011 | 10010 1 | 1 745 | 111 100 101 | 0xffe5 | 1110 0101 |
| -28 | 1 0111 0010 | 10010 0 | 1 744 | 111 100 100 | 0xffe4 | 1110 0100 |
| -29 | 10111 0001 | 10001 1 | 1 743 | 111 100 011 | 0xffe3 | 1110 0011 |
| -30 | 1 0111 0000 | 10001 0 | 1 742 | 111 100 010 | 0xffe2 | 1110 0010 |
| -31 | 1 0110 1001 | 10000 1 | 1 741 | 111 100 001 | 0xffe1 | 1110 0001 |
| -32 | 1 0110 1000 | 10000 0 | 1 740 | 111 100 000 | 0xffe0 | 1110 0000 |

**Table 11-10 Decimal vs Binary Negative Integer Numbers**

## 11.5 Examples: Detecting Bits within a Word

In some applications, there is a need to evaluate the bits within a word. The following examples are interesting, because they show how to evaluate binary numbers. These are good examples of problems that could come up during a job interview.

### Bit-Fields in Registers

When specifying a computation block in HW, the functions that the block performs are usually specified by a set of registers with 'bit-fields'. These 'bit-fields' specify the functions to be performed by the block. Depending on the design, the word width of the registers can be 16, 32 or 64-bit wide. In this section, there are several coding examples to show how to detect if some bits are set (1 if TRUE) or not set (0 if FALSE). In most examples the register width is w=32 bits (size of int in C), although it could be 16, 64 or other.

### 11.5.1  General Solution

*Counting the number of set-bits in a word*

Note: This is also known as the 'Hamming Weight', 'popcount' or 'sideways addition' [79].

The most obvious solution is to shift all the bits by one place at a time and count the bits. This is the general and obvious solution. The coding is simple and brute force. The computing time increases linearly with the register width. It is an 'Ugly' solution compared to other solutions in specific applications. For specific requirements, there are more efficient solutions. Refer to Listing 11-1.

**Listing 11-1 Ugly General Solution for Counting Set-Bits**

```c
// ====================================================================
// Ugly Solution:
// ====================================================================
// Count the 'number of bits set' by inspecting the word, 1 bit at a time.
// C Progr:
// This C-function counts the number of bits set in a word 'a' of width 'w'
// The function type is 'int'. It returns the int value of count.
int SetBitCount (int a, int w) {
  int count = 0;            // Start count
  for (int i=0; i<w; ++i) { // For 'int', word width is w=32.
    if (a & 1)              // Detect LSB '1' with bitwise '&' (AND).
      count++;              // Increment count if LSB of 'a' is '1'.
    a >> 1;                 // Shift 'a' 1 position right.
  )
  return count;
}
// ====================================================================
```

### 11.5.2  Specific Good Solutions

*Divide and Conquer*

A GOOD solution is to apply a divide and conquer approach.

Refer to C-code In Listing 11-2

**Example with w=16:** Counting the number of set-bits in a word.
When counting the number of bits in a word, the operation can be done by selecting groups of bits within a word, starting with 2 bits, then 4 bits, 8 bits and finally 16 bits.
**8 groups of 2 bits**: | b b | b b | b b | b b | b b | b b | b b | b b |
There are w/2=8 groups of 2 bits within a word. Each group can be identified by a 2-bit variable 'b2' having a value of 0, 1, 2 or 3.
The value of right-hand bit is 'b2 & 1'.
The value of left-hand bit '(b2 >> 1) & 1' (select left-hand bit shifted 1 place right).
The sum of the 2 bits, 's2', can be obtained by adding the 2 bits: s2 = b2 & 1 + (b2 >> 1) & 1;
The sum 's2' of the 2 bits ranges from 0 to 2.

**4 groups of 4 bits**: | b b b b | b b b b | b b b b | b b b b |
There are w/4=4 groups of 4 bits within a word.
For groups of 4 bits, it is convenient to express their values as hex-digits such as:
0x0, 0x1, 0x2, 0x3, 0x4, 0x5, 0x6, 0x7, 0x8, 0x9, 0xa, 0xb, 0xc, 0xd, 0xe, 0xf. // in C
Or
'4h0, '4h1, '4h2, '4h3, '4h4, '4h5, '4h6, '4h7, '4h8, ..., '4hf. // in Verilog
For example: 0xc + 0x3 = 0xf; // binary: 1100 + 0011 = 1111
Each group of 4 bits can be identified by a variable 'b4'.
b4' is made of 2 groups of 2 bits, each having a count value of from 0 to 2.
The value of two right-hand bits is 'b4 & 0x3'.
The value of two left-hand bits is '(b4>> 2) & 0x3' (select 2 left-hand bit shifted 2 places right).
The sum of the 4 bits, 's4' is obtained by adding the right 2 bits to the left 2 bits:
s4 = b4 & 0x3 + (b4 >> 2) & 0x3;
The sum 's4' of the 4 bits can be from 0 to 4, and fits within 3 bits of s4 (i.e. '0 b b b').

**2 groups of 8 bits**: | 0 b b b 0 b b b | 0 b b b 0 b b b |
There are w/8=2 groups of 8 bits within a word. Each group can be identified with a variable 'b8'.
'b8' consist of 2 groups of 4 bits, each having a value from 0 to 4
The value of 4 right-hand bits is 'b8 & 0x0f'.
The value of 4 left-hand bits is '(b8>> 4) & 0x0f' (select 4 left-hand bit and shift 4 places right).
The sum of the 8 bits, 's8' is obtained by adding the right 4 bits to the left 4 bits:
s8 = b8 & 0x0f + (b8>> 4) & 0x0f;
The sum 's8' of the 8 bits can be from 0 to 8, and fits within 4 bits of s8 (i.e. '0 0 0 0 b b b b').
The sum 's16' for 16 bits in 'b16' is:
s16 = b16 & 0x00ff + (b16>> 8) & 0x00ff; // value 0 to 16
For larger words, the process can be expanded with larger groups.
Note that some C compilers might have a function to count bits:
*popcount(int n), _builtin_popcount(int n)*
There are more examples at reference [79]

## Listing 11-2 Good 'Divide and Conquer' Solution for Counting Set-Bits

```
// ====================================================================
// Good Solution: Detect how many bits are set in a word.
// ====================================================================
// This solution uses the Divide and Conquer Approach by dividing
// the word into groups of 2, 4, 8, and 16 bits.
// The processing time increases with the log(w).
// C-code (similar code in Verilog, using masks 32'h55555555)
int a;
int w = 32;
int SetBitCount (int a) {
  // Mask single bits with hex masks 0x55555555 and 0xaaaaaaaa
  int a1 =  a & 0x55555555 + (a>>1) & 0x55555555;    // Add 2 adjacent bits
  // Mask pairs of bits with hex masks 0x33333333 and 0xcccccccc
  int a2 = a1 & 0x33333333 + (a1>>2) & 0x33333333);  // Add bit pairs
  // Mask 4 bis with hex masks 0x0f0f0f0f and 0xf0f0f0f0
  int a4 = a2 & 0x0f0f0f0f + (a2>>4) & 0x0f0f0f0f;   // Add groups of 4 bits
  // Mask 8 bits with hex masks 0x00ff00ff and 0xff00ff00
  int a8 = a4 & 0x00ff00ff + (a8>>8) & 0x00ff00ff;   // Add groups of 16 bits
  int count = a16 & 0x0000ffff + a16>>16; //Add counts of groups of 16 bits
  return count.
}
```

### 11.5.3  Another Divide and Conquer approach

Another way to divide a word is to split it into 2 halves, using the Least Significant Bit (LSB) that is set to 1. By subtracting '1' from an integer variable, the word can be divided into 2 half portions:
- the bits on the right side of the LSB that is set to 1 are inverted, including that LSB.
- the bits on the left are unchanged.
Example: a = 'b00001000; -> a-1 = 'b00000111; ~(a-1) = 'b11111000;
Using this property, when 1 or more bits are set to 1, the LSB set to 1 can be cleared with:
  a1 = a & (a-1);  // in a1, the non-zero LSB is cleared
Refer to Listing 11-3

Using this property, when only one bit is set to '1', the LSB set to 1 can be detected with:
  a1 = a & ~(a-1); // a1 is non-zero if a single bit set, a1=0 otherwise.
Refer to Listing 11-4. Refer to examples in Listing 11-5 and Listing 11-6.

## Listing 11-3 Good Solutions for Clearing the LSB Set

```
// ====================================================================
// Good Solution:
// ====================================================================
// Detect "the LSB that is set to '1'" using a single expression.
// Using binary notation like in Verilog: wire [7:0] a, a1;
// Using integer notation like in C=prog: int a, a1;
//
// Solution for clearing the LSB set
// =================================
// Clear the least significant bit set in C: int a1 = a & a-1;
// Clear the least significant bit set in Verilog: assign a1 = a & a-1;
```

## Listing 11-4 Good Solutions for Detecting 1Bit Set

```
// ================================================================
// Good Solution:
// ================================================================
// Solution for single bit set
// ===========================
// Detect Single bit set
bool OneBitSet;
int a;   // 8, 16, 32 or 64  bits
OneBitSet = a & ~(a-1); // Boolean Var (TRUE or FALSE)
```

## Listing 11-5 Examples with w=8

```
// ================================================================
// Examples with w=8
// ================================================================
// wire [7:0] a; // Verilog
// int8 a;       // C-prog
//              No bit set     One bit set    One bit set    Two bits set
//              ----------------------------------------------------------
// a            = 00000000     00000001       00001000       00100100
// a-1          = 11111111     00000000       00000111       00100011
// ~a-1         = 00000000     11111111       11111000       11011100
// a & ~a-1     = 00000000     00000001       00001000       00000100
// OneBitSet =     0;             1;             1;             1;
//                                                           2nd bit ignored
```

## Listing 11-6 Other Good Solutions for Counting Set Bits

```
// ================================================================
// Good Solution: Detect iteratively each bit set.
// ================================================================
// Function to count the total number of set bits in `a`
// clear the least significant bit set: int a1 = a & a-1
int countSetBits(int a) {
    // `count` detects the bits set in `a`
    int count = 0;
    while (a){
        a = a & (a - 1); // clear the least significant bit (LSB) set
        count++;
    }
    return count;
}
// Examples:
//                  4bit set  ->   3bit set  ->   2bit set  ->   1bit set
//                  -------------------------------------------------------
// a              = 01101010       01101000       01100000       01000000
// a-1            = 01101001       01100111       01011111       00111111
// a1 = a&(a-1)   = 01101000       01100000       01000000       00000000
// count          =     1      ->      2      ->      3      ->      4
// End Listing
// ================================================================
```

## 11.5.4 Integer, Fixed-Point and Floating-Point Numbers

As an example, the decimal FixedPt number *321.75* is used to illustrate the difference between Integer, FixedPt and FloatPt numbers. Refer to Table 11-11.

An "integer" number can represent a "count" or a "rounded FixedPt" number. It has no fraction. For example, FixedPt *321.75* has a fraction of *0.75* and is rounded to integer *322*, by adding *0.5*, then truncate:

*321.75 + 0.5 = 322.25*, then truncate to *322*.

Inside of computers, FixedPt numbers are similar to integers, but they have an "implied" point position.

| Number Base | Integer | Fixed-Point | Floating-Point |
|---|---|---|---|
| 10: decimal | 322 | 321.75 = 32175 / 100 (implied *1/100) | 3.2175 exp 2 = 3.2175 * 10**2 (x exp 2 = x * 10**2 = x*100) |
| 2: binary | binary 1 0100 0010 (= decimal 322 = 256 + 64 + 2) | 1 0100 0001.11 | 1. 0100 0001 1100 exp 01000 (x exp 8 = x * 2**8 = x*256) |
| 16: hexadecimal | hex 0x142 | 0x141.c | 0x1.41c exp 0x2 = 0x1.41c * 0x10**0x2 (x exp 2 = x * 16**2 = x*256) |

**Table 11-11 Example of Integer, Fixed-Point and Floating-Point Number**

*Fixed-Point vs Floating Point-Numbers*

One nice thing about FloatPt over FixedPt is that they have an almost infinite range of number values. In most applications, there is no need to worry about overflow during computations. The binary FloatPt format is described by the IEEE 754 Standard [18]. Another nice thing about FloatPt numbers is that they are implemented with *signed magnitude binary* numbers. This means that FloatPt numbers are symmetrical with respect to the *integer zero*. They have a *positive zero* that is slightly larger than the *integer zero*. They have a *negative zero* that is slightly smaller than the *integer zero*.

But FloatPt numbers cannot accurately represent the values of integer 0. This is because the FloatPt numbers have a limited number of fraction bits. Beyond that limited number of fraction bits, the truncated fraction of FloatPt numbers is *unknown*. For this reason, "*integer zero* cannot be exactly represented with a FloatPt *zero*". The smallest FloatPt number has an *exponent 0* minus an offset of *-126,* corresponding to $2^{-126}$. It has a fraction made of *23 zero bits*. But who knows what comes after these *23 zero bits*? There are an infinity number of bits, that have been truncated and ignored on the right side of these *23 zero bits*.

# References

## Books

[1] Schottky and Low-Power Schottky Data Book, from AMD Inc. 1977.

[2] Blinn, James F.: *Jim Blinn's Corner: A Trip Down The Graphics Pipeline*,
Morgan Kaufmann Publishers, Inc., 1996, ISBN 1-55860-387-5
Websites: http://www.jimblinn.com/
Wikipedia: https://en.wikipedia.org/wiki/Jim_Blinn

[3] Blinn, James F.: *Jim Blinn's Corner: Dirty Pixels*,
Morgan Kaufmann Publishers, Inc., 1998, ISBN 1-55860-455-3
Chapter 2: 'What We Need Around Here is More Aliasing'
Chapter 8: 'The Wonderful World of Video'
Chapter 3: 'Return of the Jaggy'
Chapter 13: ' NTSC: Nice Technology, Super Color'

[4] Blinn, James F.: *Jim Blinn's Corner: Notation, Notation, Notation*,
Morgan Kaufmann Publishers, Inc., 2003, ISBN 1-55860-860-5

[5] Franklin C. Crow:
'The Aliasing Problem in Computer-Generated Shaded Images,'
Comm. ACM, Vol. 20, No. 11, Nov. 1977, pp. 799-805.
Franklin C. Crow: 'A Comparison of Antialiasing Techniques', IEEE CG&A, 1981

[6] 'New Fixed-Point Math for Logic Design', Michel Rohner
Lulu.com, 2020.

[7] Video Demystified, Paperback, 5th Edition by Keith Jack

## Websites URL

[8] Author's Website: Michel A Rohner
https://www.michelrohner.net
https://www.michelarohner.com
https://www.anti-aliasing.com

[9] Website of Michael A. Rohner Jr:
https://www.rohnerart.com
https://www.instagram.com/rohnerart

## [10] Computer Graphics, Geometry and Other

[11] Computer Graphics Tutorial
https://www.tutorialspoint.com/computer_graphics/index.htm

[12] Bresenham's Line Drawing Algorithm
Wikipedia: https://en.wikipedia.org/wiki/Bresenham's_line_algorithm

[13] 'Bézier curves', 'Bicubic Patches' and 'B-Spline'
Bézier surfaces: https://en.wikipedia.org/wiki/B%C3%A9zier_surface
Bicubic Patches: http://www.inf.ed.ac.uk/teaching/courses/cg/d3/bezierPatch.html
B-Spline: https://www.sciencedirect.com/science/article/pii/S0010448520300488

# References

   Paul de Casteljau: https://en.wikipedia.org/wiki/Paul_de_Casteljau
   De Casteljau's algorithm: https://en.wikipedia.org/wiki/De_Casteljau%27s_algorithm
[14] Wikipedia: Triangle, Strip and Fan
   Triangle: https://en.wikipedia.org/wiki/ Triangle
   Strip: https://en.wikipedia.org/wiki/Triangle_strip
   Fan: https://en.wikipedia.org/wiki/Triangle_fan
[15] Examples of 3D Representation with Polygons Mesh
   Polygon Mesh: https://en.wikipedia.org/wiki/Polygon_mesh
   https://graphicsjourney.wordpress.com/2015/12/09/3d-representation/
   https://www.blender.org/support/tutorials/
   https://conceptartempire.com/polygon-mesh/
   https://en.wikipedia.org/wiki/File:Mesh_we2.jpg
   https://en.wikipedia.org/wiki/File:Vertex-Vertex_Meshes_(VV).png
[16] Wikipedia: Area of Trapezoid and Parallelogram
   https://en.wikipedia.org/wiki/Trapezoid
   https://en.wikipedia.org/wiki/Parallelogram
[17] Engineering Notes – Home, by D. Rose: Coordinate, Interpolation & Quaternions
     http://danceswithcode.net/engineeringnotes/index.html
     http://danceswithcode.net/engineeringnotes/rotations_in_3d/rotations_in_3d_part2.html
[18] IEEE 754, Floating-point arithmetic, from Wikipedia, the free encyclopedia
   https://en.wikipedia.org/wiki/IEEE_754
   https://en.wikipedia.org/wiki/Floating-point_arithmetic#Addition_and_subtraction
[19] Logic Design, Digital Circuit Design, Register-Transfer Level (RTL) and Verilog
  Integrated Digital Circuit Design
     https://en.wikipedia.org/wiki/Integrated_circuit_design#Digital_design
  RTL Design and Verilog
     https://en.wikipedia.org/wiki/Register-transfer_level
     https://en.wikipedia.org/wiki/Verilog
  Logic and De Morgan Theorem
     https://www.sciencedirect.com/topics/computer-science/de-morgans-theorem
*[20] Wikipedia: Coordinate System and Linear Algebra*
   https://en.wikipedia.org/wiki/Coordinate_system
   https://en.wikipedia.org/wiki/Linear_algebra
[21] Wikipedia: Dot Product or Scalar Product (Result is a Scalar number)
   https://en.wikipedia.org/wiki/Dot_product
[22] Wikipedia: Cross Product or Vector Product (Result is a Perpendicular Vector)
   https://en.wikipedia.org/wiki/Cross_product
   https://en.wikipedia.org/wiki/Perpendicular
*[23] Rotations in Three-Dimensions, Rotation Matrix*
[24] Wikipedia: Rotation Matrix
   https://en.wikipedia.org/wiki/Rotation_matrix
[25] Wikipedia: Matrix Multiplication
   https://en.wikipedia.org/wiki/Matrix_multiplication_algorithm

[26] Wikipedia: Aircraft Principal axes Roll, Pitch and Yaw
   https://en.wikipedia.org/wiki/Aircraft_principal_axes
[27] Wikipedia: Euler Angles and 'Roll, Pitch and Yaw'
   https://en.wikipedia.org/wiki/Euler_angles#Tait%E2%80%93Bryan_angles
[28] Yaw, pitch, and roll rotations
   https://hallaweb.jlab.org/experiment/g2p/survey/Yaw_Pitch_Roll_Rotations.pdf
[29] Swedish pop group ABBA,1974 to 1983
   https://en.wikipedia.org/wiki/ABBA

*[30] Coordinates, Texture Mapping and Occulting*

[31] Wikipedia: Bari Centric Coordinates.
   https://en.wikipedia.org/wiki/Barycentric_coordinate_system
[32] Wikipedia: Texture Mapping
   https://en.wikipedia.org/wiki/Texture_mapping
   Wikipedia: Texture Mipmap
   https://en.wikipedia.org/wiki/Mipmap
   Wikipedia: Texture Anisotropic Filtering
   https://en.wikipedia.org/wiki/Anisotropic_filtering
[33] Occulting and Hidden Surface Removal
   Wikipedia Hidden-Surface Determination
   https://en.wikipedia.org/wiki/Hidden-surface_determination
[34] Warnock algorithm
   Wikipedia: Hidden Surface Algorithm using Divide and Conquer
   https://en.wikipedia.org/wiki/Warnock_algorithm
[35] Z-Buffer and Rasterization
   https://en.wikipedia.org/wiki/Z-buffering
[36] A Characterization of Ten Hidden-Surface Algorithms
   I. Sutherland, R. Sproull, R. Schumacker. Published 1974, ACM Computer Survey
   https://dl.acm.org/doi/10.1145/356625.356626   or
   https://web.archive.org/web/20160103063614/http://design.osu.edu/carlson/history/PDFs/ten-hidden-surface.pdf
[37] E. C. Catmull, 'A Hidden-Surface Algorithm with Anti-Aliasing',
   Computer Graphics, Vol. 12, No.3, Aug. 1978, pp. 6-11.  (From Siggraph '78 proceedings.)
[38] J. F. Blinn, 'Computer Display of Curved Surfaces',
   Univ. of Utah PhD dissertation, Dec. 1978.

*[40] TV Standards*

[41] Standard-Definition Television
   https://en.wikipedia.org/wiki/Standard-definition_television
[42] Graphics Displays
   Graphics Display Resolution
   https://en.wikipedia.org/wiki/Graphics_display_resolution
   Refresh Rate
   https://en.wikipedia.org/wiki/Refresh_rate
   Interlaced Video
   https://en.wikipedia.org/wiki/Interlaced_video

# References

[43] Standard TV: STV
  ITU (International Telecommunication Union)
    https://en.wikipedia.org/wiki/International_Telecommunication_Union
  Comité Consultatif International pour la Radio, a forerunner of the ITU-R
    https://en.wikipedia.org/wiki/CCIR
  Recommendation BT.601 for TV digital encoding
    https://en.wikipedia.org/wiki/Rec._601
    https://www.itu.int/rec/R-REC-BT.601-6-200701-S/en
  Recommendation BT.656 for TV digital encoding
    https://en.wikipedia.org/wiki/ITU-R_BT.656
    https://www.itu.int/rec/R-REC-BT.656-5-200712-I/en
  Television ChannelFrequencies
    https://en.wikipedia.org/wiki/Television_channel_frequencies
[44] Video Compression and HDTV
  H.264, Advanced Video Coding (AVC):
    https://en.wikipedia.org/wiki/Advanced_Video_Coding
  H.265, High Efficiency Video Coding (HEVC):
    https://en.wikipedia.org/wiki/High_Efficiency_Video_Coding
  DCT Discrete Cosine Transform
    https://en.wikipedia.org/wiki/Discrete_cosine_transform
  Motion compensation:
    https://en.wikipedia.org/wiki/Motion_compensation
[45] Color Space and Color Conversion
  Color Space: https://en.wikipedia.org/wiki/Color_space
  Color Conversion: https://docs.opencv.org/4.5.0/de/d25/imgproc_color_conversions.html
  YCbCr: https://en.wikipedia.org/wiki/YCbCr
[46] sine and cosine function:
    https://en.wikipedia.org/wiki/Sine_and_cosine
[47] Wikipedia: Integrated Circuit (IC)
    https://en.wikipedia.org/wiki/Integrated_circuit
    https://en.wikipedia.org/wiki/Planar_process
    https://en.wikipedia.org/wiki/Jean_Hoerni
    https://en.wikipedia.org/wiki/Robert_Noyce
    https://en.wikipedia.org/wiki/Gordon_Moore

*[50] Computer Generated Imagery (CGI)*

[51] Wikipedia: Computer graphics 1950s, 60s, 70s, 80s, 90s, 2000s, 2010s
    https://en.wikipedia.org/wiki/Computer_graphics
[52] Wikipedia: Computer-generated imagery (CGI)
    https://en.wikipedia.org/wiki/Computer-generated_imagery
[53] David C. Evans and Ivan Sutherland (E&S)
    https://en.wikipedia.org/wiki/Evans_&_Sutherland
[54] Wikipedia: Real-time 3D computer graphics
    https://en.wikipedia.org/wiki/Real-time_computer_graphics

[55] TV and Graphics Display Resolution. Refresh Rate
   Wikipedia: https://en.wikipedia.org/wiki/Standard-definition_television
   Wikipedia: https://en.wikipedia.org/wiki/Broadcast_television_systems
   Wikipedia: https://en.wikipedia.org/wiki/High-definition_television
   Wikipedia: https://en.wikipedia.org/wiki/Graphics_display_resolution
   Wikipedia: https://en.wikipedia.org/wiki/Refresh_rate (TV or CGI Refresh Rate)
   Wikipedia: https://en.wikipedia.org/wiki/Interlaced_video

*[60] Aliasing and Anti-Aliasing*
   Definition of Aliasing According to Mariam Webster Dictionary
     https://www.merriam-webster.com/dictionary/aliasing
[61] Wikipedia: Aliasing, Jaggies, Moiré Pattern, Spatial Anti-Aliasing, Multi-Sample
   Aliasing:       https://en.wikipedia.org/wiki/Aliasing
   Jaggies:        https://en.wikipedia.org/wiki/Jaggies
   Moiré Pattern:  https://en.wikipedia.org/wiki/Moir%C3%A9_pattern
   Spatial AA:     https://en.wikipedia.org/wiki/Spatial_anti-aliasing
   MSAA:           https://en.wikipedia.org/wiki/Multisample_anti-aliasing
   Solutions to 8 Queens Puzzle: https://en.wikipedia.org/wiki/Eight_queens_puzzle
[62] Wikipedia: Nyquist and sinc() function
   Nyquist frequency: https://en.wikipedia.org/wiki/Nyquist_frequency
   Nyquist Rate: https://en.wikipedia.org/wiki/Nyquist_rate
   Nyquist–Shannon sampling theorem:
     https://en.wikipedia.org/wiki/Nyquist%e2%80%93Shannon_sampling_theorem
   Sampling Function sinc(): https://en.wikipedia.org/wiki/Sinc_function
   Triangular, tent or Bartlett window: https://en.wikipedia.org/wiki/Triangular_function
[63] Wikipedia: Convolution Theorem and Fourier Window
   Convolution Theorem: https://en.wikipedia.org/wiki/Convolution_theorem
   Window Function: https://en.wikipedia.org/wiki/Window_function
[64] Subpixel Rendering and MSAA
   https://www.gpumag.com/anti-aliasing/
[65] A Quick Overview of MSAA, Written by MJP, Oct 24 2012
   https://mynameismjp.wordpress.com/2012/10/24/msaa-overview/
[66] Tutorial Multisampling Anti-Aliasing, A Closeup View (8 Pages)
   May 22, 2003 / by aths / page 1 of 8 / translated by 3DCenter Translation Team
   http://alt.3dcenter.org/artikel/multisampling_anti-aliasing/index_e.php
[67] Anti-Aliasing Analysis from Toms Hardware
  Part 1: Settings and Surprises (8 pages), by Don Woligroski April 13, 2011
     https://www.tomshardware.com/reviews/anti-aliasing-nvidia-geforce-amd-radeon,2868.html
     https://www.tomshardware.com/author/don-woligroski
  Part 2: Performance (19 Pages), by Don Woligroski, November 21, 2011
     https://www.tomshardware.com/reviews/anti-aliasing-performance,3065.html
[68] Nvidia Presents Adaptive Temporal Anti-Aliasing Technology, by Zhiye Liu July 31, 2018
     https://www.tomshardware.com/author/zhiye-liu
     https://www.tomshardware.com/news/nvidia-adaptive-temporal-antialiasing,37534.html

References

[69] MSAA Example at flickr.com for 2x2, 3x3 and 4x4 Subpixel array:
https://www.flickr.com/photos/dominicspics/3991177364/in/photostream/

*[70] Computers Programming and 3D Graphics*

[71] Assembly and High-Level Languages
https://en.wikipedia.org/wiki/High-level_programming_language

[72] C-Programming Language
https://en.wikipedia.org/wiki/C_%28programming_language%29

[73] Cray-1 Super Computer, 1976-77
The first Cray-1 system was installed at Los Alamos National Laboratory in 1976
https://en.wikipedia.org/wiki/Cray-1
http://ed-thelen.org/comp-hist/CRAY-1-HardRefMan/CRAY-1-HRM.html
https://www.cray.com/company/history

[74] Wikipedia: Apple II (1977) and IBM Personal Computer (1982)
https://en.wikipedia.org/wiki/Apple_II
https://en.wikipedia.org/wiki/IBM_Personal_Computer
ARM processors:
https://www.arm.com/products/silicon-ip-cpu

[75] Wikipedia: Microsoft Flight Simulator
In 1982, Artwick's company licensed a version of *Flight Simulator* for the IBM PC to Microsoft,
marketed as *Microsoft Flight Simulator 1.00*.
https://en.wikipedia.org/wiki/Microsoft_Flight_Simulator

[76] Computer Graphics Interfaces: Wikipedia:
Direct3D: https://en.wikipedia.org/wiki/Direct3D
OpenGL: https://en.wikipedia.org/wiki/OpenGL

[77] Wikipedia; Video Cards
https://en.wikipedia.org/wiki/Video_card
Supported Hardware/Video Cards (OpenGL)
https://reactos.org/wiki/Supported_Hardware/Video_cards

[78] Oak Technology Warp5, Wikipedia
https://en.wikipedia.org/wiki/Oak_Technology
http://fireeye.tripod.com/warp5.html
http://fireeye.tripod.com/benchgr.html

[79] Counting Bits
Hamming Weight:
https://en.wikipedia.org/wiki/Hamming_weight
Brian Kernighan's algorithm
https://www.techiedelight.com/brian-kernighans-algorithm-count-set-bits-integer/
https://graphics.stanford.edu/~seander/bithacks.html#CountBitsSetKernighan

*[80] Flight Simulators and CGI*

[81] Wikipedia: Flight Simulator
https://en.wikipedia.org/wiki/Flight_simulator
https://en.wikipedia.org/wiki/Flight_simulator#Vertical_Motion_Simulator_(VMS)_at_NASA/Ames

Wikipedia: Joystick
https://en.wikipedia.org/wiki/Joystick

[82] Report: 'Computer Generated Imagery (CGI) Current Technology',
US Army Material Development and Readiness Command, Orlando Florida, Sep 26 1980
https://apps.dtic.mil/dtic/tr/fulltext/u2/a091636.pdf

[83] Bruce J. Schachter
Publication: B. Schachter 'Computer Image Generation for Flight Simulation',
IEEE Computer Graphics and Applications (IEEE CG&A), October 1981.
Schachter 'Computer Image Generation', Book Hardcover
John Wiley and Sons; 1st Edition (January 1, 1983)
ISBN-10: 0471872873, ISBN-13: 978-0471872870

[84] Wikipedia: GPU
https://en.wikipedia.org/wiki/Graphics_processing_unit

[85] GPU Technology Conference 2014
GPU-Based Visualization for Flight Simulation,
Tim Woodard Director of Research and Development Diamond Visionics www.dvcsim.com
https://on-demand.gputechconf.com/gtc/2014/presentations/S4440-gpu-based-visualization-flight-simulations.pdf

[86] Evans & Sutherland (E&S) Wikipedia
https://en.wikipedia.org/wiki/Evans_%26_Sutherland
E&S History 2005:
https://www.youtube.com/watch?v=FHhYAUgY3S0
https://forum.beyond3d.com/threads/ct5-evans-sutherland-simulator-how-did-it-work.57664/
Utah inventions: The birth of computer graphics
https://www.ksl.com/article/36039333/utah-inventions-the-birth-of-computer-graphics

[87] E&S CT-5 Videos
CT-5 Flight Simulator, 1981
https://archive.org/details/CT5FlightSimulator
https://www.youtube.com/watch?v=6W-qb_jHRhA
Evans & Sutherland 'The Tactical Edge'
Part 1: https://www.youtube.com/watch?v=06mbwNg1Vw4
Part 2: https://www.youtube.com/watch?v=7e7_GiCc-HA

[88] E&S CT-5 CGI, 1981
a) Was Evans & Sutherland CT5 really created in 1981?
https://computergraphics.stackexchange.com/questions/5693/was-evans-sutherland-ct5-really-created-in-1981
b) CT5 Evans Sutherland Simulator - How did it work?
https://forum.beyond3d.com/threads/ct5-evans-sutherland-simulator-how-did-it-work.57664/#post-1914013

[89] GE CompuScene
The Simulator Revolution
https://www.airforcemag.com/article/1289simulator/

*[90] Link Flight Simulators*

[91] The Link trainer is a mechanical engineering historical landmark
http://web.mit.edu/digitalapollo/Documents/Chapter2/linktrainer.pdf
Wikipedia: Link Trainer
https://en.wikipedia.org/wiki/Link_Trainer

References

[92] Link Aviation History
   http://www.susandoreydesigns.com/genealogy/clirehugh/LinkAviationHistory.pdf
[93] Life After Link
   http://lifeafterlink.org/index.shtml
   http://lifeafterlink.org/brochure.shtml
[94] Computers in Spaceflight: The NASA Experience (until 1975, before DIG-1):
   Making New Reality: Computers in Simulations and Image Processing:
     https://history.nasa.gov/computers/Ch9-1.html
   Crew-training simulators:
     https://history.nasa.gov/computers/Ch9-2.html
   NASA Contractor Report 182505, CONTRACT NASW-3714, March 1988.
     James E. Tomayko, Wichita State University, Wichita, Kansas)
       https://history.nasa.gov/computers/Compspace.html
   June 10, 2021, Space shuttle simulator returns to NASA to be restored for display
       https://history.nasa.gov/computers/contents.html
   Old SMS with Images from Camera Model and Mini Computers, before 1977
       https://www.facebook.com/pg/The.Shuttle.Mission.Simulator/posts/
[95] NASA *S*pace Shuttle Program, 1972–2011
   Wikipedia: Space Shuttle program
     https://en.wikipedia.org/wiki/Space_Shuttle_program
   Wikipedia: Space Shuttle retirement
     https://en.wikipedia.org/wiki/Space_Shuttle_retirement
   NASA's Space Shuttle Program Officially Ends After Final Celebration, 8/31/2011
     https://www.space.com/12804-nasa-space-shuttle-program-officially-ends.html
   Computers in Spaceflight: The NASA Experience
     https://history.nasa.gov/computers/Ch9-2.html
[96] NASA Houston, TX, SMS Visual systems from Link APO (1977):
   Selection and Training of Astronauts: 4 DIG-1 used in Shuttle Mission Simulator (SMS)
     https://science.ksc.nasa.gov/mirrors/msfc/crew/training.html
[97] NASA Ames Vertical Motion Simulator
   https://www.youtube.com/watch?v=0WaiAyU-3mU
   https://www.nasa.gov/simlabs/vms/technical-details
   DIG-1: Simulator Facility for Helicopter Air-to-Air Combat at NASA Ames
     https://apps.dtic.mil/sti/citations/ADA160693
     https://apps.dtic.mil/sti/pdfs/ADA160693.pdf
   NASA Ames Research Center (ARC):
     https://en.wikipedia.org/wiki/Ames_Research_Center
[98] Video Demo: Blue Box, The First Flight Simulator
     https://www.youtube.com/watch?v=PYTrjch_G64
[99] Link Flight Simulation Demo, Video
   DIG-2 Demo, 1984:
     https://www.youtube.com/watch?v=uy8sJ9AxvYI
***[100] Patents Related to 3D Graphics and CGI Hardware***

[101] Michel Rohner, all 6 Patents: 102 to 107
   https://patents.google.com/?inventor=Michel+Rohner
[102] High speed sorter
   US CA GB US4030077A Judit Katalin Florence, Michel Alexandre Rohner,
   The Singer Company
      https://patentimages.storage.googleapis.com/2b/61/eb/1fc2ba543dddb7/US4030077.pdf
[103] High speed sorter with concurrent access
   US CA GB US4031520A Michel Alexandre Rohner, The Singer Company
      https://patentimages.storage.googleapis.com/c4/a3/48/dbdecc345681b2/US4031520.pdf
[104] Clipping Polygon Faces through Polyhedron of Vision
   US US4208810A Michel A. Rohner, Judit Katalin Florence, The Singer Company
      https://patentimages.storage.googleapis.com/a0/f3/44/a90fdf19a95f4d/US4208810.pdf
[105] Resolvability Test and Projection Size Clipping of Polygon Face Display
   US US4291380A Michel Rohner, The Singer Company
      https://patentimages.storage.googleapis.com/05/4c/81/99f8b15eeb1883/US4291380.pdf
[106] Method and Apparatus for Generating Non-Homogenous Fog
   US US6064392A Michel A. Rohner, Oak Technology, Inc.
      https://patentimages.storage.googleapis.com/a8/3c/64/0e9ba707aeecd1/US6064392.pdf
[107] Method and apparatus for clamping image gradients
   US US6184887B1 Michel A. Rohner, Oak Technology, Inc.
   https://patentimages.storage.googleapis.com/fc/12/09/fa30d26af5f2ba/US6184887.pdf
[108] Patents from Robert W. Lotz, Link Flight Simulation
   Edge smoothing for real-time simulation of a polygon face object system as viewed by a moving observer
      https://patents.google.com/patent/US4208719A/en?inventor=Robert+W.+Lotz
[109] Video processor for real time operation without overload in a CGI system
      https://patents.google.com/patent/US4703439A/en?inventor=Robert+W.+Lotz
[110] Patents from Johnson K. Yan and Judit K. Florence, Link Flight Simulation
      https://patents.google.com/?inventor=Johnson+K.+Yan
[111] Modular digital image generator
   US US4570233A United States, Johnson K. Yan and Judit K. Florence
      https://patents.google.com/patent/US4570233A/en
[112] Method and apparatus for texture generation
   US US4615013A, Johnson K. Yan
      https://patents.google.com/patent/US4615013A/en?inventor=Johnson+K.+Yan
[113] Computer-generated image system to display translucent features with anti-aliasing
   US US4679040A, Johnson K. Yan
      https://patents.google.com/patent/US4679040A/en?inventor=Johnson+K.+Yan
[114] Method and apparatus for processing translucent objects
   US US4918625A, Johnson K. Yan
      https://patents.google.com/patent/US4918625A/en?inventor=Johnson+K.+Yan
**[120]** *Other Patents from Rick Fadden at GE and ATI*
      https://patents.google.com/?inventor=Richard+G+Fadden

# References

[121] US4727365 Advanced Video Generator, General Electric Company, Syracuse, N.Y.
   https://patentimages.storage.googleapis.com/f9/a9/77/d6709f4495dbac/US4727365.pdf

[122] US4811245 Edge Smoothing
  Method of Edge Smoothing for a Computer Image Generation System
  William M. Bunker; Donald M. Merz; Richard G. Fadden, all of Ormond Beach, Fla.
  Assignee: General Electric Company, Syracuse, N.Y.
   https://patentimages.storage.googleapis.com/31/87/82/2c1dc6295665ef/US4811245.pdf

[123] US4905164 Modulating Color Texture, General Electric Company, Syracuse, N.Y.
   https://patentimages.storage.googleapis.com/ca/2c/35/44905db7758019/US4905164.pdf

[124] US4965745 YIQ Color Cell Texture General Electric Company, Syracuse, N.Y.
   https://patentimages.storage.googleapis.com/d2/df/35/1eb09fb7d6bfb9/US4965745.pdf

[125] US4974176 Micro Texture, General Electric Company, Syracuse, N.Y.
   https://patentimages.storage.googleapis.com/8e/79/0e/cac053ad4bbf38/US4974176.pdf

[126] US6002407 Cache Memory for Texture, Oak Technology, Inc., Sunnyvale, Calif.
   https://patentimages.storage.googleapis.com/98/76/08/873fe6f4564380/US6002407.pdf

[127] US6445392 Simplified Anti-Aliasing (Subpixel Generation), Ati International SRL
   https://patentimages.storage.googleapis.com/7b/1d/73/7b9778c52ca1d6/US6445392.pdf

***[130] Clipping Patents from Evans and Sutherland:***

[131] Wikipedia: Sutherland–Hodgman algorithm
   https://en.wikipedia.org/wiki/Sutherland%E2%80%93Hodgman_algorithm

[132] Reentrant polygon clipping
  I. Sutherland, G. W. Hodgman, Published 1974, Computer Science, Communication. ACM
  Patent: Computer graphics clipping system for polygons
    https://patents.google.com/patent/US3816726A/en?inventor=Sutherland+Hodgman
    https://patentimages.storage.googleapis.com/27/18/f3/578861e7cf22cf/US3816726.pdf

[133] US 3889107A System of polygon sorting by dissection, I. Sutherland
   https://patents.google.com/patent/US3889107A/en?inventor=Sutherland+Ivan&page=2
   https://patentimages.storage.googleapis.com/c0/5b/89/1050911af8995e/US3889107.pdf

[134] US3639736A Display windowing by clipping, I. Sutherland
   https://patents.google.com/patent/US3639736A/en?inventor=Sutherland+Ivan&page=3
   https://patentimages.storage.googleapis.com/fd/86/89/1881686afa716b/US3639736.pdf

# *About the Author*

Michel Alexandre Rohner was born in Neuchatel, in the French part of Switzerland
He graduated with a Matura in Math & Science from the Scientific Gymnasium in Neuchatel, Switzerland (in France, the equivalent of a Swiss Gymnasium is called a Lycée).
He earned his Diploma in EE at the ETH in Zurich, Switzerland
 (Germ: Eidgenössische Technische Hochschule, Eng: Swiss Institute of Technology).
He earned his MSEE from Santa Clara University in CA.
He holds 6 important patents in the field of 3D computer graphics.
He is an ACM Member and IEEE Lifetime Member.
He is gifted at math, drawing and playing music instruments. He plays accordion, piano and electric bass. Before coming to the US, he played in rock band, "The Sunshines", with his brothers and sister: *Jen-Jacques* (guitar), *Michel* (bass-guitar), *Anne-Lise* (keyboard) and *Mario* (drum). This band was popular in his home town of Neuchatel, Switzerland.

Michel worked many years at Link Flight Simulation, designing the fastest special purpose computers for 3D Real-Time Computer-Generated Imagery (RT CGI). He was a key designer and architect of the first Digital Image Generator (DIG) at Link flight Simulation. The DIG was a special purpose computer generating 3D scenes in real-time to be used in aircraft simulators. Four Link DIG systems were delivered to NASA Houston Space Center for the Space Shuttle Mission Simulator (SMS) [95][96]. At the time of delivery, the Link DIG had edge smoothing (anti-aliasing) and was the fastest RT CGI system in the world. It could produce out of the windows images made of 3400 projected triangles at a rate of 60 times per sec. With a price tag of more the $2M dollars, the DIG systems were not available to the general public. Michel continued working at Link, making significant improvements to the DIG, helping Link to win many simulator contracts.

## *First Job in the US*

Soon after graduation from the ETH, Michel immigrated to the US and landed in the Bay Area in California. He was fortunate to get his first US job at the Advanced Product Operation (APO) of Link Flight Simulation in Sunnyvale, CA. Link had a long history designing simulator and trainers for the Army, Navy, Air Force and NASA [90].

As first assignment at Link APO, he designed a subsystem for the First Digital Radar Simulator in the DRLMS (Digital Radar Landmass Simulator) group at Link. This digital radar simulator was designed to train radar operators for the successful Air Force F4F Fighter and the E2C advanced warning plane (small AWAC). He designed the radar Equation Return Subsystem (ERS) of the DRLMS, that computed the signals returned from simulated radar electromagnetic pulses. This subsystem performed the many computations of the Radar Equation in log base 2 domain, using a rigid pipelined architecture.

## *From Radar Simulator to Real-Time Computer-Generated Imagery*

After completing the ERS design in the DRLMS system, Michel was fortunate again to be introduced to the team that was designing the first special purpose 3D RT CGI system from Link in Sunnyvale. The Link version of RT CGI systems was the 'Digital Image Generator' (DIG). The DIG was optimized for generating 3 or 4 Out The Window (OTW) 3D graphics scenes in real-time for training in aircraft flight simulators [90].

Michel designed several subsystems for the R&D DIG prototype. The R&D DIG prototype from Link had edge smoothing and a good image quality. It could produce images of around 500 triangles (1.5k triangle-edges) at the rate of 60 images per sec.

### *Designing the Fastest 3D RT CGI System*

While waiting for the Space Shuttle contract award from NASA, he continued doing system testing and made significant improvements to the speed and image quality for the production DIG. He became familiar with all the subsystem implementations, and realized that by modifying some of the key subsystem processors, a speed improvement in the order of 5 to 10 times could be achieved, still using a single pipeline stream. He did the first speed improvement by optimizing the matrix and vector computations. After rotating the triangle vertices, the DIG has to perform Clipping to remove the portion of triangles that are outside of the field of view (FOV). While working on Clipping improvements, he invented and patented a faster Clipping algorithm [104]. After the Clipping operation, the triangles vertices are projected onto the image plane. For the projection, he implemented the divisions using log base 2 tables, so that each division could be executed in one cycle.

With these design improvements, Michel was awarded 6 important patents in the field of 3D RT CGI [100] to [107]. He became one of the lead engineers for the production DIGs from Link that could generate 4000 triangles (12000 edges) at the rate of 60 images per sec.

In the late 1970s, four Link DIG-1 systems were delivered to NASA Houston Space Center for the Space Shuttle Mission Simulator (SMS). At that time, there were only two other companies producing RT CGI systems at a cost above $1M, with a capability of generating 60 images per second, with around 1000 edges per image.

- Evans and Sutherland (E&S) in Salt Lake City, Utah
- General Electric Ground System Division (GE GSD) in Daytona Beach, Florida

At the same time, two other computers were announced:

- The Cray-1 super-computer [73] was announced and became the favorite platform for 3D graphics development, at a cost of $8M. It was used for general purpose non-RT CGI applications and algorithm development,
- The Apple II became available to the general public and could be used for playing simple 2D games, at a cost of less than $2k [74].

### *NASA Requirement for Virtual Reality Virtual Reality Visual System*

Back in 1968, NASA requested proposals for a Virtual Reality visual system to be used in the Shuttle Mission Simulators (SMS). Singer Link (later known as Link Flight Simulation) in Binghamton, NY, was the only company that responded.

About the Author

## *Link Digital Image Generators Delivered to NASA for the SMS*

There were two generations of visual systems from Singer Link that were delivered to NASA for the Shuttle Mission Simulators in Houston Space Center.

First, in the early 1970s, Singer Link in Binghamton delivered a computer system made of parallel mini computers (around 20) for the SMS visual system.
At the same time, Singer Link Advanced Product Operation (APO) in Sunnyvale, CA, began developing its Digital Image Generator (DIG) in R&D. The DIG was a special purpose digital computer, consisting of a single pipeline of optimized and dedicated subsystems. Each DIG could drive 3 or 4 display windows. Singer Link APO demonstrated the R&D DIG to NASA on time and was awarded the production contract for 4 DIGs. In 1977, the first production DIG-1 was delivered on schedule to NASA for the SMS in Houston Space Center, TX [96].

With the improved speed and image quality and edge smoothing, the DIG-1 was the best solution for the SMS program. No other system was available to prepare the Space Shuttle astronauts just in time for their first scheduled flights with Columbia on April 12, 1981. The four DIG-1s have been used to train all the Space Shuttle astronauts in Shuttle Mission Simulators (SMS), before they flew the actual Space Shuttles Missions into Space. There is a good description of the SMS DIG-1 in Reference [96].

At the time of delivery, the Link DIG was the fastest RT CGI system in the world. It could produce out of the windows images made of 4000 projected triangles (12,000 edges) at a rate of 60 images per sec (field rate). Overnight the standard for RT CGI performance moved from 1.5k triangle edges per image to 12k triangle edges.

After demonstrating the 10k edges/field capability to the military, Link got orders for 10 DIG-1 for the F-111 fighter simulators and one DIG-1 for the UH-60 Blackhawk helicopter simulator.
The DIG was upgraded to DIG-2 in response to the Air-Force requirement of ¼ Subpixel resolution requirement. Also, the number of intersections per Scanline was increased from 256 to 512. The DIG-2 was used in the B-52 bomber simulator and in 4 helicopter simulators, including the AH-64 Apache and UH-60 Blackhawk helicopters. Refer to image on book back cover.

With a price tag of more the $2M dollars, the DIG systems were not available to the general public. Within a period of 12 years, Link sold around 70 flight simulators, each with 3 or 4 window displays driven by DIG systems.

Michel worked many years at Link, making continuous improvement to the DIGs. He achieved the highest technical level of Senior Staff Scientist.

## *Designing 3D RT CGI Systems with Anti-Aliasing after Link*

After leaving Link, Michel became a key contributor for the designs of two 3D graphics chips for the PC market and a line of Quad TV encoders and decoders chips.

He wanted to apply his knowledge of 3D RT CGI system to design the first PC graphics adapter for the PC Market. He got the opportunity while working in the 3D Graphics department at Oak Technology, in Sunnyvale. He was a key architect of the Warp5, the first PC graphics adapter with Non-Homogeneous Fog and Anti-Aliasing.

## About the Author

He also worked for few companies that were producing 3D graphics chips for the PC market. As a logic designer and system architect, he also spent several years doing real time logic designs [19] in FPGA and ASIC for TV circuits at MetaVideo, in Los Gatos, CA.

Currently, Michel has been working as a consultant for FPGA/ASIC/SOC design, verification and programming in C/C++, System Verilog and UVM.

### *Writing Books*

Using its intensive experience with logic design [19] in 3D RT CGI and TV, Michel decided to write books to share his inventive designs and his novel approach to fixed point math.

In his first book, 'New Fixed-Point Math for Logic Design' [6], he introduces a new math approach for CGI computations. This approach solves several problems caused by 'rounding' results when implementing Fixed-Point Math in CGI applications. It uses 'averaging' instead of 'rounding' and was key in developing the ABAA solution for anti-aliasing.

In this new book, Michel has introduced a novel approach to AA, the Subpixel Area-Based Anti-Aliasing (ABAA). Because of his involvement in designing the fastest RT CGI systems and many years of experience dealing with AA, he has developed the ultimate approach to AA. Instead of sampling N fixed Subpixel points inside of a Pixel, ABAA accurately computes the area that is partially covered by polygons within that Pixel. This area is then allocated to N Subpixel areas. This approach and its implementation might appear simple. But it is the result of many years of research and refinements using a deep understanding on how 3D RT CGI systems are implemented.

There are many advantages of ABAA.

- Better Image Quality, with less Subpixel samples when compared to MSAA.
- Proposed implementations can be scaled to 4 and 8 Subpixels, and even 16 and 32 subpixels.
- Simpler implementation and lower system cost.

Michel expects that this new approach will be widely accepted and result in improved quality and lower cost for future 3D graphics adapters and 3D RT CGI systems.

### *Michel's Son is a Popular Artist*

Like his father, *Michael A. Rohner Jr* has a similar tendency for extreme attention to details. On the other hand, Michael Jr was not in particular fond of music and math, but was extremely gifted for drawing. So, instead of becoming an engineer like his father, he decided to become an artist. He has selected a challenging profession. It is difficult to be an independent producer of art and make a living of it. Luckily, he is popular in art shows in the Bay Area, New Mexico and Texas. He has won several 'Best of Show' prizes. His attention to details is reflected in his drawings. He will spend hours adding details to his drawings until he is satisfied.
Several of his creations are available and can be seen at his web site, *rohnerart.com* [9].

www.ingramcontent.com/pod-product-compliance
Lightning Source LLC
LaVergne TN
LVHW081537070526
838199LV00056B/3693